F

Hohner harmonica boxes.

HARMONICAS, HARPS,

a n d

HEAVY BREATHERS

Kim Field

A Fireside Book
Published by Simon & Schuster
New York   London   Toronto   Sydney   Tokyo   Singapore

FIRESIDE
Rockefeller Center
1230 Avenue of the Americas
New York, New York 10020

Designed by Richard Oriolo

Manufactured in the United States of America

10 9 8 7 6 5 4 3 2 1

Library of Congress Cataloging-in-Publication Data

Field, Kim.
    Harmonicas, harps, and heavy breathers / Kim Field.
        p.   cm.
    "A Fireside book."
    Includes bibliographical references (p.   ).
    "Selected discography": p.
    1. Harmonica. 2. Harmonica players. I. Title.
ML1088.F53   1993
788.8'2—dc20   93–24115
                                                        CIP
                                                        MN

ISBN   0-671-79633-X

*For the players
and to my parents,
who filled the house with music*

C o n t e n t s

A c k n o w l e d g m e n t s

Many thanks to the following players for their time and their music: Jerry Adler, Larry Adler, DeFord Bailey, Richard Bain, Robert Bonfiglio, Don Brooks, James Cotton, Herman Crook, George Fields, Al Fiore, William Galison, Lonnie Glosson, Mark Graham, Stan Harper, Richard Hayman, Cham-Ber Huang, Leon LaFell, Charles Leighton, Don Les, Howard Levy, Magic Dick, Eddy Manson, Hugh McCaskey, Charlie McCoy, Tommy Morgan, Mildred Mulcay, Joe Mullendore, Jerry Murad, Charlie Musselwhite, Charles Newman, Lee Oskar, Pete Pedersen, Alan Pogson, Jerry Portnoy, Wayne Raney, Mickey Raphael, Alan "Blackie" Schackner, Sam Scheckter, John B. Sebastian, Greg "Fingers" Taylor, Jean "Toots" Thielemans, Mike Turk, Junior Wells, and Kim Wilson.

Charles Leighton's warmth and intelligence made my first halting attempt at an interview for this book seem like a success. The introductions he provided to his many colleagues in the harmonica world got this book off the ground, and he and his wife, Ro, helped convince me that I could see the project through. One of the most satisfying payoffs in producing this book is the chance to thank them both publicly for their many kindnesses.

A special acknowledgment must go to Earl Williams, a fine player and tireless harmonica enthusiast who believed in this effort, served as an invaluable liaison with his friends (seemingly the entire mouth organ fraternity), and supplied me with a great deal of material from his own collection. His advice and help, the fruits of which appear throughout this book, are deeply appreciated.

Sam Scheckter was a wealth of information on the harmonica bands of the vaudeville era, and he lugged his legendary—and hefty—harmonica scrapbook more than three thousand miles so I could pore over it. This book might never have been finished without his keeping tabs on its progress.

I am also grateful to Jack Kavoukian, Kit Gamble, and Rick Epping at the Hohner Company; Martin Häffner of the Harmonica Museum in Trossingen; Dave Zaval and John Bryan for the priceless photographs; David Morton for the materials on his friend DeFord Bailey; Frank Scott for his help with the discography; Elizabeth McCullough of the Smithsonian Institution for her invaluable help in photographing antique instruments; Frank Zachary for the divine intervention; John Brancati; Steve Baker; Kem and Pat Miller for their translation assistance; Jeff Fereday and Kay Hummel for advice, proofreading, and encouragement; Paul Kotz for his darkroom wizardry; Bob Pinson of the Country Music Foundation; Elizabeth Schlappi for the Jimmy Riddle tapes and articles; Peter Guralnick for proving to me that music writers could make a contribution and for his help with photo sources; Jim Kelton; Les Leverett; Tom and Catherine Stryker for the all-star brunch; Alexandra Marculewicz; Jack Cook for the articles, the tapes, and for Rhythm Willie; David Flack for the contagious enthusiasm; Jim McLaughlin for his help with the details; Al Smith for the copy of Albert Raisner's book; Dave Corning for the rock and roll guidance; Pierre Beauregard; Chet Williamson; Sigmund Groven; Wally Schirra; Rick Stafford; Grant Dermody; Steve Boldt for the kind words and the keen eyes; John Paul Jones; Jackie Seow; Ray Varner; Harry Feinberg; Winslow Yerxa; Todd Lewis; Gordon Mitchell; Danny Wilson; and Shirley Williams for the encouragement early on.

Some of those who helped make this book possible did not live to see its publication. Alex Fogel was the editor of the Society for the Preservation and Advancement of the Harmonica (SPAH) newsletter for nearly a quarter of a century; he was one of the first to give me assistance with this book, and the back issues of his publication unlocked many mysteries for me. Hugh McCaskey, DeFord Bailey, and Herman Crook were all marvelous players and three of the most remarkable human beings I've ever spent time with.

Although relatively little has been published about the harmonica's history, the writings of Paul Oliver, Charles Wolfe, Bengt Olsson, and

Acknowledgments

David Morton deserve special mention; they rank as both first-rate scholarship and solid detective work and were invaluable to me.

I want to express my profound gratitude to Robin Straus, my agent, who appeared out of nowhere to rescue the manuscript from its author and place it between two covers, and to my talented and sympathetic editor, David Dunton, who was tailor-made for this effort. He knows his music and his job and he got a better book out of me.

Although my wife, Christine, was spared the ordeal of sharing my life during the phase when I was playing the harmonica eight hours a day, she did have to live through the entire, uneven history of this project. Her unflagging enthusiasm boosted my own countless times; she also read the rough drafts and made many valuable contributions along the way. I've managed to put together a hundred thousand words to tell the mouth organ's story, but there is no language that I know that could describe the love and gratitude I feel toward her.

I'm regularly reminded that music is a bottomless reservoir of joy, but nothing has brought that fact home more viscerally than the sight of my two sons, Austin and Devin, dancing around the living room. The realization that in their own way they will always keep the beat inspires me every day.

Introduction

Among musical instruments, only the first—the human voice—is more universal than the harmonica. This is appropriate, given that the mouth organ is the most ventriloquial of musical devices. "I throw my voice," explains Lonnie Glosson, the seller of millions of "talking harmonicas." DeFord Bailey, harmonica star of the early Grand Ole Opry broadcasts, approached his first mouth organ as an impressionist would: "Oh, I would wear it out, trying to imitate everything I heard! Hens, foxes, hounds, turkeys . . . everything around me."

Ventriloquists fall short with every performance—the audience never really believes that it's the dummy talking. Good mouth organists pull off this feat regularly. "I had a guy give me four hundred dollars for my harmonica," James Cotton once confided to *Living Blues* magazine. "I told him, 'Hey, man, you can go down to the store and pay eight dollars and get you one, you know.' He said, 'No, I want this one. There's something special in there that makes it sound like that.'" Luther Tucker, who played guitar behind blues harmonica genius Little Walter Jacobs, remembers how "people would come up and open up his hand to see what he had in there to make that beautiful sound." Devoid of keys, valves, strings, mouthpiece, or any other visible clue to its mysteries, the harmonica confounds the uninitiated. As jug-band mouth organist Will Shade explained to Charlie Musselwhite, "The harp is a blind man's instrument, 'cause you can't see nothin'."

You can't *be* everywhere unless you can *go* everywhere, and the mouth organ's small size and sturdiness has made it the most portable musical device. Less than two hundred years after its debut, the harmonica has become transcendent, arguably the most popular instrument in history. It has been to both poles, down the Amazon, and to the summit of Mt. Everest. In its most spectacular field trip, it became the first instrument to serenade us from outer space. But if handiness were the sole criterion used by consumers when deciding which instrument to buy, the landscape would be crowded with jaw harp factories.

The harmonica is based on the principle of the free reed, but unlike its cousin, the concertina, it is brought to life not with mechanical bellows but by the player's breath. This gives mouth organists several advantages not available to players of other free-reed instruments: a full dynamic range, draw *and* blow notes (and thus the ability to make music and breathe simultaneously), a variety of vibratos and attacks, and the capacity to play notes not built into the instrument. These are crucial differences. The harmonica is an accordion with soul.

Of course, it all comes back to whose voice is doing the throwing. The mouth organ is supposedly the one instrument that anyone can play, yet the truth is that the only thing rarer than a person who has never owned a harmonica is a player who has done it justice. There is no clear-cut career path for the professional mouth organist, and the players celebrated in these pages have as much in common with Magellan or Lindbergh as they do with Mozart or Paganini. These are some of the most remarkable musicians in history, and whenever possible I've tried to let them speak for themselves. Talking with so many of my favorite harmonica players was so enjoyable that I put off the actual writing of the book for as long as I could.

The harmonica has enjoyed its greatest success in the United States, and the players profiled here—with the exception of Tommy Reilly, who is one of our Canadian brothers and too important to ignore—are Americans. Their careers are, however, testaments to both the international scope of the instrument and the cross-cultural wonder that is American music. The most famous player in mouth organ history is the son of a Baltimore plumber who has spent most of his adult life in England. The most celebrated classical player is a Canadian who mastered the harmonica during a stay in a German prison camp. The mastermind behind the harmonica ragamuffin band, a concept that entranced American vaudeville audiences for two decades, hailed from Kiev. The first full-time American classical harmonicist was an authority on the Italian Renaissance who lived out his last years in a villa in the south of France. The most famous jazz blower is a Belgian who learned his craft listening to bootleg American records and who now divides his time between Long Island and Brussels. Constantinople is the birthplace of the leader of the most popular harmonica recording group, and one of the most prominent classical harmonicists had his first taste of success as the leader of a three-hundred-piece harmonica band in his hometown of Shanghai.

The tales of how these players became wedded to their instrument are just as roundabout and full of mixed motives as any love story. For Don Les, it was sex—a boyhood crush on a winsome teacher. For Stan Harper and Wayne Raney, it was a chance encounter on the street. James Cotton fell for the voice-throwing trick—his mother's chicken imitation. The first harmonicas of Stevie Wonder, Charles Leighton, Cham-Ber Huang, and Doc Watson arrived gift-wrapped. Toots Thielemans and Al Fiore were mesmerized by the wiry form of Larry Adler magnified a hundred times up on the movie screen. For me, it was the roiling sixties, the lure of which caused me to place my seventeen-year-old self in the middle of an ecstatic crowd on the ballroom floor of Seattle's Eagles Auditorium one night in 1968 as James Cotton rolled by, microphone cord trailing behind him while he stomped his feet and blew into a Marine Band cupped in his hands. Even before he'd gone past me I knew that this was a sound I wanted to learn how to make.

I was sold, and from that night on I've single-mindedly pursued

The Sound. The result has been more than twenty years of harmonica playing, several boxes filled with tarnished pieces of brass and tin, many valued friendships—and now this book. There were the "lessons" in Paul Oscher's Brooklyn basement and Charles Leighton's guided tours of the world of the chromatic harmonica in his art-filled apartment around the corner from Carnegie Hall. The backstage visit with Herman Crook on one of his three-thousand-odd Saturday nights on the Grand Ole Opry. Kim Wilson reeling off one twelve-bar jewel after another from the stage at Antone's. Cham-Ber Huang trying to explain the intricacies of tongue-switching to me while rocketing us down the Long Island Expressway in his car, and a ten-galloned Don Brooks spurring on Waylon Jennings's great band at Max's Kansas City. Howard Levy confounding a crowd of harmonica players jammed into a piano bar at a Detroit Holiday Inn. The solemn lecture I got one afternoon from DeFord Bailey on the absolute supremacy of the Hohner Marine Band. Walter Horton's crooked finger summoning me to share a stage with him at the Fabulous Rainbow in Seattle.

If there is a message in this book, it is that there are no limits to our artistic wiliness, even when armed with a tool as seemingly straightforward and uncomplicated as the harmonica. The variations on The Sound are infinite, as the stories in these pages make clear. These are the maverick geniuses who shared a love for a unique instrument, blew by its theoretical boundaries, and ensured its future—who threw their voices and made the harmonica sing.

*Miao tribesman from Thailand playing
a mouth organ*

Todd Lewis

East Meets West

As musical instruments go, the harmonica is a new thing. Its bicentennial is still decades away. We have the Germans to thank for it (as for the bassoon, the flute, and the clarinet). Its animating principle is the free reed, a device whose lineage snakes back nearly five thousand years and implicates several of humankind's most venerable cultures.

In fixed-reed instruments such as the clarinet or the saxophone, the reed vibrates against the side of the mouthpiece, and the pitch achieved by these instruments depends on the length of the resonant tube to which the reed is attached. To sound different notes, players use their fingers to open and close holes bored into the shaft—in effect changing the length of the instrument. The "free" reed, by contrast, can produce a tone without the help of any other surface when air is blown over it. The pitch of the note is determined by the length and thickness of the reed.

The free reed is an Asian invention. Not surprisingly, given their cultural and political dominance throughout most of oriental history, the Chinese number the free reed among their many contributions to humanity's march toward progress. Some sinologists maintain that the Emperor Huang Tri—ruler of what was at the time the world's largest empire—deserves credit for the concept, which would place the free reed in China as early as 4500 B.C., but an impressive body of Chinese folklore contends that it is the Empress Nyu-kwa whom we have to thank for perfecting the Asian mouth organ, a royal breakthrough that occurred sometime around 3000 B.C.

The earliest relic of a demonstrable ancestor of the harmonica is a mouth organ called a *yu* that was unearthed in China in 1973 during the excavation of a two-thousand-year-old Han dynasty tomb. Bas-reliefs gracing the walls of other Han period burial chambers in northeastern China depict musicians playing an instrument called the *sheng*. The most common of the many Asian variations on the free reed, the sheng (its name means "sublime voice") has played a prominent role in Asian music for at least three thousand years.

In the earliest shengs, five pipes tipped with mouthpieces and outfitted with free reeds of bamboo projected vertically from a small, bowl-shaped gourd that served as a resonator, a configuration believed to have been inspired by the shape of the legendary phoenix. (Because of this association with rebirth, the sheng has been prominently featured in Chinese funerals from very early times; some believed that its music could raise the dead.) As the sheng was improved, the hollow gourd gave way to a resonator fashioned from lacquered wood, and the bamboo reeds were replaced by metal tongues. To play the sheng, the player clasps the resonator in both hands and blows or, more commonly, draws air through a mouthpiece attached to it. Players sound different notes by using their fingers to cover tone holes on the pipes' shafts.

The Asian mouth organ is an expressive and versatile instrument, capable of both quiet subtlety and a shrill, barking attack. In its higher registers, it is reminiscent of the oboe. The musicologist Curt Sachs has contended that "this is one of the most attractive musical styles in the Orient: pure, serene, and transparent." Some of the techniques used by sheng players would be familiar to any harmonicist: tongue trills and vibrato are common, and an overblow technique is sometimes used that results in an effect similar to the note "bending" of Western mouth organists. The free reed's talent for mimicry is appreciated in China, where you can still see puppet shows enlivened with uncanny imitations of human and animal sounds made on short, closed pipes with free reeds set in them.

Despite tales of the inventiveness of the Empress Nyu-kwa, it is likely that the home of the free reed was the region we now call Laos, where the greatest variety of Asian free-reed instruments is found. From Southeast Asia, the sheng spread north to China, Korea, and Japan, and as far south as Java, the Malay States, and Borneo. After the Chinese were conquered by their less insular Mongol neighbors and trading pathways were finally opened to the Mideast, shengs accompanied the spices westward. The Asian mouth organ was introduced first to Bengal, then to Turkestan. By the sixth century, the instrument was being mastered by the Persians. But the story of the European mouth organ begins more than a thousand years later.

The term *harmonica,* first used in Europe and North America in the late eighteenth century, was a conveniently generic label that has been freewheelingly applied to many instruments. This has confused some musical historians. Benjamin Franklin, for instance, is often credited with playing a singular role in the mouth organ's invention. In fact, Franklin took out patents on something quite different—a device called the "glass harmonica," a row of drinking glasses that produced an eerie music when their moistened rims were rubbed by a player's fingers. The glockenspiel was originally dubbed the "metal harmonica," and *harmonica de bois* is the French name for the xylophone. There was also a "nail harmonica," a soundbox with metal pins that vibrated when a bow was run across them.

The expression *mouth organ* was equally all-purpose. Any such European reference prior to 1800 is most likely an allusion to some kind of panpipe or jaw harp. Literate harmonica boosters are fond of quoting Prince Hamlet's advice to a minstrel, "There is much music, excellent voice in this little organ . . . give it breath with your mouth and it will discourse most eloquent music," but Shakespeare was almost certainly referring to a recorder. In 1619, Michael Praetorius wrote about a trumpet that seems to have used a free reed, but his description is too vague to rank as the first European mention of such an instrument. That honor goes to the French writer Marin Mersènne, who described an Asian mouth organ in 1636. Within a few decades the free reed had penetrated the highest strata of French society—a *mémoire* left by a member of Louis XIV's court describes an evening's entertainment at Versailles that featured Persian mouth organs.

Nearly 150 years later, another Frenchman was familiarizing himself with the sheng on its own turf. Père Amiot, a Jesuit missionary based in China and author of the first thoughtful treatise on Chinese musical instruments, shipped several trunks of oriental artifacts to the minister of arts in Paris in 1776. Packed away among this exotic baggage were several shengs.

Contemporary accounts note the unusual speed with which the free reed spread throughout Europe. About the time Amiot's Chinese mouth organs arrived in Paris, an Irishman named John Wilde acquired a sheng during a stay in the Russian capital of St. Petersburg and learned to play it after a fashion. Gottlieb Kratzenstein, a Danish physicist, heard Wilde's experiments on the instrument and became obsessed with the notion of using the free reed to mimic human speech. In 1780, Kratzenstein unveiled a free-reed "talking machine" that he claimed could articulate five vowel sounds and the words *mama* and *papa*. Concluding that the free reed could revolutionize the organ, Kratzenstein took his case to a celebrated keyboard designer in St. Petersburg named Kirschnik, who produced a full-scale organ register of free reeds that was used in the *orchestrion,* an organ designed in 1792 by George Joseph Vogler. Vogler seems to have traveled widely, and the workshops he held throughout Europe did a great deal to further the free reed's cause.

Pipe organ designers eventually gave up on the free reed, but the principle was used successfully in smaller keyboard instruments, including the *terpodion,* unveiled in 1816 by Johann Buschmann of Thuringia. Buschmann's concept was perfected thirty years later in the portable *harmonium,* which became a favorite of missionaries and street hawkers and the most popular devotional instrument in European households.

These experiments led to a European version of the free reed that was radically different from the cane tongues traditionally used in the sheng. This was a strip of metal, attached to a metal frame over a slightly larger aperture, that would vibrate when air was moved across it. (Europeans discovered early on that the reed's response was greatly improved if it was sprung up slightly from its frame.) Fashioning the reed from metal allowed it to be tuned within a semitone. (Filing the tip of the reed raised the pitch of the note; filing its base flattened it.) Given the precise pitch requirements of Western music, this was a crucial development.

Metal free reeds could be plucked as well as blown, and nineteenth-century Europeans were familiar with the African *sansa,* or thumb piano, which had inspired the music box. Complex *guimbards* (jaw harps) using up to six tuned reeds surfaced in Austria, and according to musicologist James Howarth "it thus remains something of an open question as to what extent the wind-sounded [free-reed] instruments were conceived as improved shengs or as blown guimbards."

The first European mouth organ to resemble today's instrument seems to have been the creation of Christian Friedrich Buschmann, Johann's son.[1] The Buschmann family were famous instrument makers, repairers, and tuners. Johann Buschmann amassed a large collection of instruments that included one of Vogler's orchestrions and a Sicilian jaw harp. Boyhood experiments with the free reed showed Christian Buschmann that its pitch remained constant regardless of the degree of air pressure that was applied to it, that it was impervious to temperature fluctuations, and that it had a surprising dynamic range. To earn extra pocket money, Christian began making free-reed pitch pipes for organ tuners. Sometime around 1820, he arranged several pitch pipes together and in effect created a new instrument—or, more precisely, a new toy, for that is how Buschmann viewed his contrivance. His pipe clusters enjoyed a brief but intense vogue in Vienna. Women wore them as neck pendants; male sophisticates fastened them to the ends of their canes.

Buschmann's success was widely imitated, and he was challenged to keep improving his pitch pipe clusters, which came to resemble panpipes. In 1821, the sixteen-year-old Buschmann registered the first European patents for a mouth organ. He wrote his brother Edward about his new invention, which he called the *aura:* "I have also invented at Barmen a new instrument that is truly remarkable. In its entirety it measures but four inches in diameter . . . but gives me

---

1. Martin Häffner, the director of the Harmonica Museum in Trossingen, Germany, contends that there is no hard evidence for this claim.

twenty-one notes, all the pianissimos and crescendos one could want without a keyboard, harmonies of six tones, and the ability to hold a note as long as one would wish to."

Buschmann's aura was a horizontal arrangement of fifteen steel reeds placed in small channels arranged side by side. It was awkward to play (it offered only blow notes arranged chromatically), and dozens of competitors emerged with alternatives to Buschmann's design. The *psallmelodikon* unveiled in 1828 by the German Weinrich had twenty-eight valves similar to those that had been introduced to brass instruments only ten years before. England's Charles Wheatstone, who was later knighted for his work on the electric telegraph, filed patents in 1829 for two free-reed instruments: the *symphonium,* a shallow, metal box with a single blowhole in its center, and the *aeola,* which had button keys and a mouthpiece similar to that of today's melodica.

After Buschmann's initial attempts, the most important advances in early mouth organ design were made by an instrument maker from Bohemia named Richter. Although some have claimed that the use of two reed plates—one for blow notes and the other for draw notes—was lifted from the accordion, which was patented in 1829, it may be that it was Richter who introduced this concept in 1825 or 1826. Richter's mouth organ was a ten-hole, twenty-reed instrument with reed plates mounted on either side of a cedar comb whose segments formed separate channels for each pair of reeds. Designed to play simple melodies, the notes of Richter's harmonica were roughly the same as those of the white keys on the piano. Richter placed a full diatonic scale in the center of his instrument with gapped scales on either side. (On an instrument tuned to C, for example, the lower gapped scale would be missing the F and the A, and the higher scale would lack the B.) The blow reeds produced the major tonic chord and the draw reeds sounded the dominant seventh, an arrangement that substantially reduced the chance that a player would sound a note that was out of key.

There were several variations on the Richter model. The Weiner, or "Viennese," harmonica used a tremolo effect originally developed for the harmonium in which each note was sounded by two reeds, one being tuned slightly sharp to give a slight pulsation to the sound. "Band tuning" was a similar arrangement in which the two reeds were closely tuned; it was designed to give the instrument greater volume.

The end result of all this multinational tinkering was that lung-pow-ered, free-reed instruments gradually lost their keys, valves, mouth-pieces, and buttons, and Richter's variation on Buschmann's theme became the standard configuration. By 1830 most Europeans knew the mouth organ as the *mundharmonika* ("mouth harmonica") or the *mundaeoline,* names that reflected the influence of German crafts-men in its evolution.

The European mouth organ was still a novelty, but it was an ex-tremely popular one. Demand increased; the first instruction books were published. But free-reed instruments were controversial from the outset, and there was a segment of the population that took no pleasure in their steadily escalating popularity. There are contem-porary accounts of raids on music stores by bands of vigilantes who seized concertinas and harmonicas and tossed them into huge bonfires.

Mass production of mouth organs began in Vienna in 1829; within a few years they were being made in Austria, Switzerland, and Sax-ony. W. Thei's harmonica factory in Vienna was the center of mouth organ manufacture until the 1880s, but the first harmonica factory may have been built by Friedrich Hotz in Knittlingen, a small town in Germany's Wuerttemberg province, a region on the edge of the Black Forest noted for its clockmakers. These craftsmen, whose mainstay was the cuckoo clock, would spend the fall and winter making their timepieces and then take to the road during the rest of the year to hawk their wares. When a depression struck the clockmaking indus-try in the early 1800s, many of these artisans looked about for a means to augment their livelihoods.

In 1827, a peddler from the Wuerttemberg village of Trossingen re-turned from a visit to Vienna and presented his daughter with one of Buschmann's auras. When the device broke, her fiancé, a clockmaker named Christian Messner, took it apart and repaired it. Soon he and a cousin, Christian Weiss, were making mouth organs as a sideline, hewing wooden combs by hand and beating metal reeds from lead, brass wire, and bell metal.

Over the next two decades, Messner and Weiss turned their moon-lighting into a profitable business. Messner seems to have been highly proprietary about his production techniques. During a visit to Weiss's workshop Messner interrupted an informal lesson in harmonica man-ufacture that his partner was giving another local clockmaker named Matthias Hohner. Messner summarily ejected the interloper from the shop, but Hohner seems to have learned enough from this brief session to begin crafting his own harmonicas. He showed talent in this new sideline and, with a ready market for his instruments, was soon dividing his time between building timepieces and constructing mouth organs. In 1857, the twenty-four-year-old Hohner took a leap of faith and began manufacturing harmonicas full time, turning out 650 instruments that year with the help of his family and a single hired workman.

Of the three Trossingen harmonica makers, Matthias Hohner proved to be the most solid businessman. He chafed under the limitations of assembling handmade parts with the help of a loose organization of local helpers (each of whom might be able to produce only a dozen instruments a day under ideal conditions) and began introducing mass-production techniques. Hohner reinvested heavily in his fledgling enterprise and began systematically buying out his competitors, including the Hotz operation in Knittlingen. He also showed a flair for marketing, sandwiching his instruments between distinctive, ornate cover plates—prominently featuring their maker's name—that helped them stand out from those of his rivals.

It was Hohner's decision in 1862 to become the first harmonica manufacturer to export his instruments to North America that made his company a global giant. The demand from this new market became so great that for nearly a decade the Hohner Company sold its products exclusively to Americans. The profits from this trade were used to build a new factory, hire hundreds of new workmen, and establish a virtual worldwide monopoly. In 1867, Hohner produced twenty-two thousand mouth organs; twenty years later, the firm's annual output exceeded one million instruments.

Matthias Hohner was a craftsman as well as a shrewd executive, and he understood that the key to constructing a quality mouth organ lay in perfecting the metal reed. In 1878 machinery developed by Julius Berthold made it possible for Hohner to cease hammering reeds by hand and instead to stamp them from sheets of a brass and bronze alloy, the recipe for which is still guarded as a secret formula. The typical Hohner harmonica reed is a strip of metal approximately one-half inch to an inch and a half in length, three-sixteenths of an inch wide, and only one two-hundredth of an inch thick. This fragile-looking metal tongue is in fact tenaciously durable; it must vibrate freely several hundred times a second throughout its lifetime while maintaining something approximating true pitch.

When the American depression of 1893 led to a sudden—but short-lived—cessation of Hohner exports to North America, the company responded by aggressively seeking out new markets, launching marketing campaigns in South Africa, Russia, and Great Britain. For the English, there was the Druids Harp; the Blackpool model; the Alliance Harp, which hailed the pact between England and Japan; the Tally-ho! model; and the King George Harp. The Scots were lured by the Robbie Burns, Rob Roy, and Wee Macgregor models, while the Irish were offered The Emerald Isle harmonica. There were the L'Épatant and La Marseillaise instruments for the French and a Swedish mouth organ honoring Princess Ingeborg. Mexican mouth organists could purchase Hohner's Linda Mexicanas and El Centenario, which came in a box displaying Benito Juárez's portrait. One Hohner harmonica came with a loop of chain so that pocketless Africans could carry it around their necks or dangle it from their ears. A mouth organ based on a five-note scale created originally for Asians eventually became a favorite with South American Indians; there was also a model commemorating the liberator San Martín. Hohner harmonica boxes bore inscriptions in Japanese, Greek, and Arabic.

Having made the harmonica a citizen of the world, Matthias Hohner handed over the stewardship of his company to his five sons in 1900. Never an adept harmonica player himself, his determination to create an inexpensive instrument of quality led to his being lionized as "the Stradivarius of the harmonica," an overblown title in which he took great pride. A hard-nosed tradesman, Hohner zealously guarded his patents. ("I am able to prosecute whoever makes or sells an imitation," he once warned American retailers.) While he earned a reputation for being strict with his employees, Matthias Hohner was extremely proud of his company's pioneering efforts in providing insurance and affordable housing for its workers. He served as Trossingen's mayor for six years and once turned down a nomination to the German senate. Hohner died on December 11, 1902, one day short of his sixty-ninth birthday. When his firm celebrated its golden jubilee five years later, workers in the 300,000-square-foot Hohner factory were producing 887,000 reeds from fifteen tons of brass each day and 7 million harmonicas annually.

Hohner's sons expanded the firm's global scope. Not even the First World War slowed the harmonica's inexorable march to universal popularity. Between 1914 and 1918, the Musician's Association of

Great Britain raised large sums of money for a campaign to provide every British soldier with a harmonica. Hohner instruments—their ranks now included a Kaiser Wilhelm model—were issued in great numbers to German troops. On the first Christmas of the war, each soldier from the Wuerttemberg province received a mouth organ.

The diatonic harmonica had become one of the most popular instruments in the world, but it had not been able to compete in musical genres that demanded a complete chromatic range. Hohner's first attempt to give harmonica players access to all the notes of the chromatic scale was a bulky, cumbersome instrument that was essentially several diatonic mouth organs joined on a common cylinder. In 1924, Hohner introduced a ten-hole, chromatic mouth organ based on the Richter note arrangement, but this design was soon supplanted by a twelve-hole, three-octave model that avoided gapped scales by repeating the tonic note at the beginning of each octave. It had two reed plates tuned a semitone apart—for example, C and C#—fitted onto a wooden comb. Players could achieve all the notes of the chromatic scale by pushing a spring-loaded button fixed to a slide to alternate between these reed plates. To make the instrument as airtight as possible, the reeds were covered with leather windsavers. In the mid-1930s, Hohner unveiled a sixteen-hole chromatic, the 64 Chromonica, that had an additional lower octave. Now armed with a fully chromatic instrument, players began applying it to the classical repertoire and to the new music of jazz.

Hohner was still expanding, adding branch factories in several cities. The firm achieved absolute supremacy in Trossingen by finally absorbing its oldest rivals, the firms of Messner and Weiss, in 1928. Two years later, Hohner's yearly sales topped 25 million. American vaudeville had spawned the professional harmonica group, and the musical demands of this concept led to the development of new mouth organ models, including the bass harmonica, which had a sixteen-note chromatic scale spanning from C to C# in the bass clef; the chord harmonica, on which a player could perform an accompanying role similar to that of a rhythm guitarist; and the polyphonia, which allowed the player to achieve glissandos and other special effects. Hohner's willingness to make custom instruments gained it a publicity coup in the 1930s, when the firm announced that it had produced the most expensive harmonica ever made. Crafted for Pope Pius XI, it was encrusted with ivory and precious gems and boasted a comb and faceplate cast in solid gold.

Political changes in Germany during the Depression were reflected in Hohner's SA Marches model, which celebrated Hitler's brownshirts. (The mouth organ narrowly escaped a notorious honor when the Nazis officially pronounced the accordion "the people's instrument.") World War II brought a halt to the flow of Hohner harmonicas to the United States and the other Allied nations, depriving the firm of its largest market. Wartime conscription drastically reduced Hohner's work force, and materials (especially brass) became scarce. Its factories were partially converted to munitions manufacture, an effort that was made possible, as at other German firms, by the use of prisoners of war and the importation of forced labor from Russia and Eastern Europe. Despite this upheaval, Hohner managed to make millions of its Greetings From Home harmonica, which was designed for the German troops.

For the Hohner Company, World War II ended when French troops occupied Trossingen in April of 1945. Hohner moved quickly and successfully to recover its worldwide market, a comeback that was not surprising, given its reputation and its supremacy in harmonica production techniques. Individual craftsmanship was still crucial, however; a typical postwar Hohner diatonic required fifty separate hand operations to assemble, and the hundreds of millions of Hohner reeds stamped each year were still individually checked and tuned by workers (often recruited from Trossingen families that had shown a genetic tendency toward perfect pitch) sitting in isolated booths and listening carefully as fans blew air over them. "No machine can put soul into the reed—only the human ear," explained a man who had spent more than half a century tuning reeds for Hohner.

By the end of the 1950s harmonica sales were sagging, and Hohner tried to interest the public in a new instrument called the harmonetta, a small, hexagonal harmonica on which players could achieve chords by pressing keys, but the ingenious model never caught on. (It was discontinued in the 1970s.) As Hohner celebrated its centennial, the company found itself having to further expand its product line to include keyboard instruments, guitars, and drums, but the "blues harp" phenomenon that exploded in America during the 1960s rejuvenated mouth organ sales.

Over the years the Hohner Company has offered over fifteen hundred different harmonicas, ranging from the Little Lady, a four-hole instrument only one and one-quarter inches long, to the twenty-three-inch chord harmonica, which offers ninety-six double holes, 384 reeds, and forty-eight chords. In 1986 the firm produced its one billionth mouth organ and helped establish a harmonica museum in Trossingen that houses a collection of over twenty-five thousand mouth organs. Today, Hohner's annual harmonica sales top 2 million.

Although still formidably dominant, Hohner is facing competition from several quarters, the most radical being the Millioniser 2000, a harmonicalike synthesizer introduced in 1986 by Walt Müller, a Swiss mouth organist, and the most serious being the inroads made into the company's traditional markets in the last fifteen years by the Asian harmonicas exported by two American firms, Huang and Lee Oskar, founded by well-known players. Hohner is currently making plans for a transition from manual assembly to robotics, a potentially risky gamble that has led to the redesign of such time-honored favorites as the Marine Band, the company's most popular harmonica and an instrument that had been essentially untouched since its debut in 1896. Hohner has continued to introduce new models in recent years, including the high-priced Meisterklasse and Amadeus models and two new chromatic harmonicas featuring jazz master Toots Thiele-mans's imprint. It is likely that the recent challenges from the mouth organ's ancestral home in the Orient will be answered with other new advances from the harmonica's German champion.

First in space: Astronaut Wally Schirra plays the Little Lady he took with him on the Gemini VI flight, 1965.

c h a p t e r   t w o

America

Nowhere has the mouth organ been more popular than in the United States. The supremacy of the common people is the favorite theme of American folklore, and our instrument—the harmonica—has become enshrined in myth along with us. As we tame the frontier, the mouth organ is along for the ride: Jesse James's brother Frank is saved from a bullet by a shirt-pocket harmonica, Wyatt Earp and Billy the Kid are mouth organ fanciers. As we perfect our republic, our leaders embrace the instrument: "Douglas has a brass band with him in Peoria but this will do me," says Carl Sandburg's Abraham Lincoln, waving a harmonica during his 1856 Senate campaign against Stephen A. Douglas. The tale is spurious—Lincoln's eldest son, Robert, could not recall his father ever expressing an interest in anything musical—but it serves our collective, subconscious notion that such a universal and unassuming device is a fitting symbol for humankind's boldest democratic experiment.

We know that the harmonica had reached North America by 1830; there are surviving copies of an instruction manual published in New York that year. Visitors to the Ford Museum in Dearborn, Michigan, can view a handmade harmonica with the date 1837 crudely carved on its comb. Several regions settled largely by German immigrants— notably Texas, Illinois, and the Carolinas—became known for the high caliber of their harmonicists. By the middle of the nineteenth century, mouth organs were commonly displayed on the shelves of general stores throughout the United States. They usually sold for ten cents, but models that went for half that price were available until the turn of the century. The imported novelties were popular gift items, and they may even have been used as peace offerings during the western expansion; according to musicologist Michael Licht, the mouth organ "seems to have replaced the Jew's harp in the Indian trade by midcentury." Harmonica reed plates have been uncovered by archaeologists at the sites of nineteenth-century Native American settlements.

The first Hohner instruments to reach the United States may have been sent to some relatives of Matthias Hohner who had immigrated to Chicago. Hohner signed its first export agreements with buyers in the United States in 1862, and the firm began introducing harmonicas named after popular American musical heroes, including the Marine Band (a bow to John Philip Sousa's celebrated aggregation) and the Caruso. Some mouth organs bore the legend *French harp,* a lyrical allusion that may account for a pseudonym that is still common in the Southern United States. By 1880, 70 percent of Hohner's annual production was being shipped to North America. In 1901 the company established an office in New York City under the stewardship of Matthias's son Hans.

In true Yankee fashion, American mouth organists were quick to put their own stamp on the European gadget. The harmonica's uncanny capacity for impersonation became a fetish for rural players, who perfected a genre of "talking" harmonica pieces in which they duplicated words like *mama, papa,* and *water* (shades of Kratzenstein). "Harp" players came to be judged by how realistically they could duplicate the feral chaos of fox-and-hounds chases and the aural magnificence of the steam locomotive, themes that had long been staples in fiddlers' repertoires. (W. C. Handy recalled hearing these specialties as a child in the late 1870s.)

The highlight of these harmonica train pieces, an eerie approximation of the lonesome whine of the steam whistle, was usually achieved by inhaling clusters of notes. Michael Licht has argued persuasively that the train song led to the development of the "cross harp" style. Before the advent of this approach, a player who wanted to play a tune in the key of C would use a C harmonica. Because a C harmonica is so designated because its blow notes make up the C major chord, the player would end up playing mostly blow notes. As they perfected their train whistles, American mouth organists came to realize that draw notes not only offered a wider range of tonal effects than blow notes but could also be "bent" (that is, flattened to sound a lower note) by making slight changes in the shape of the mouth and the direction of the airstream. Many came to prefer the draw scale, an approach they dubbed "cross harp" or "second position." (The traditional method became known as "straight harp" or "first position.") Because the draw notes on a C harmonica make up the G_7 chord, cross-harp players use a C harmonica to play in the key of G instead of a G instrument. "Several country harp players have told me that they were able to figure out the 'cross harp' style for themselves after older musicians showed them the elements of their train pieces," Licht has written.

Americans elected a bona fide harmonica player as president in 1912. Visitors to Woodrow Wilson's White House were often summoned to the portico to hear the chief executive render "Swanee River," "The Star-Spangled Banner," and other popular airs on his mouth organ. One of Wilson's successors was similarly afflicted. Calvin Coolidge practiced the harmonica regularly; an associate claimed he could find his way around on the instrument "with more than ordinary ability." During the ultranormal reign of "Silent Cal," the first stirrings were felt of a vogue that would help make the period between 1918 and 1940 the golden age of the mouth organ in America: the harmonica band movement.

The instigator of this craze was a wealthy Philadelphia brahmin named Albert Hoxie. In the spring of 1923, Hoxie helped organize a harmonica contest during the Boy Council of Philadelphia's "Boy Week" celebration. The competition was hugely successful, and the

Hohner Company fed this newfound enthusiasm by sending harmonica experts into the Philadelphia schools. Several harmonica youth bands sprung up, the largest led by Hoxie himself. When the city harmonica championship was reprised the following year, more than ten thousand schoolchildren queued up to vie for the honors. One of them was a fifteen-year-old named Leon LaFell.

"It wasn't a little thing to become a harmonica champion," recalls LaFell. "Different stores supplied spectacular prizes. One of the finest stores in Philadelphia supplied a complete wardrobe for the winner. You got a college scholarship and quite a bit of cash. Hoxie was a millionaire and philanthropist who liked to help young people. He didn't play the harmonica, but he knew music and conducted all the rehearsals. He was very, very strict. Sometimes, if he wasn't getting what he wanted, he'd take that baton, aim it at someone, and throw it like a javelin.

"The Hoxie band traveled quite a bit—mostly in the summer so it wouldn't affect our schoolwork. I remember playing for President Hoover at the White House, which was quite a thrill. I'll never forget one mummers' parade we marched in. It was New Year's Day, and it was so cold that we had to keep those harmonicas up to our mouths because if we took them away, they would stick to our lips." Hoxie's group appeared in concert with such baton-wielding luminaries as Leopold Stokowski and John Philip Sousa. They played for Lindbergh when he visited Philadelphia after his historic transatlantic flight, provided the prefight entertainment at a heavyweight championship bout between Jack Dempsey and Gene Tunney, serenaded Queen Marie of Rumania, and marched in Franklin Roosevelt's inaugural parade.

Hoxie began sending trained assistants out across the country to spread the mouth organ gospel to the nation's youth. "I'm sure they kept a lot of kids off the street," notes LaFell. "When a kid picks up a harmonica and he hears a group playing, he wants to play like that." The children of Chicago certainly did; more than 150 harmonica youth orchestras were organized in the Windy City. In Dayton, Ohio, nearly twelve hundred children received weekly instruction on the mouth organ. Between 1927 and 1937, 115,127 schoolchildren enrolled in Los Angeles' harmonica band program. It has been estimated that over two thousand harmonica bands were formed in the United States during the Depression.

Like many other youth organizations launched during this period, the Hoxie band had militaristic overtones. Again, Leon LaFell: "The band was modeled on a military organization. We had captains, lieutenants, sergeants, corporals, and so forth. We always performed in full uniform. They were beautiful outfits, with Sam Browne belts, dark blue jackets, and light blue pants with a gold stripe up the side. We had special leather pouches made for our harmonicas and a special insignia on our caps. Hoxie wore the same uniform when he led the band in parades, even though he was quite rotund." John Philip Sousa's military parade bands had been the inspiration for groups like Hoxie's, and the March King (who was rumored to be a closet harmonica player) gave a nod to the mouth organ bands by composing a rousing march entitled "The Harmonica Wizard." Boy Scouts could earn merit badges by achieving proficiency on the harmonica. Hohner unveiled a Scout model with a compass built into it and a slew of other instruments aimed at the youth movement, including the Boys Brigade, the School Band, the Song Band, and the Trumpet Call. To help youngsters learn to play these models, RCA Victor released an instructional record, "How to Play the Harmonica," which gave "full instruction for the playing of the scale, utilizing the Marine Band harmonica," and provided "a rendition on the harmonica of 'Old Black Joe,' with piano accompaniment."

The mouth organ took the stage—and a big step toward legitimacy—thanks to an aggressive hustler named Borrah Minevitch, who mixed pathos, comedy, and music to create the Harmonica Rascals, which for twenty-five years was one of vaudeville's biggest draws. The next mouth organ phenomenon to emerge from the wings was a remarkable soloist named Larry Adler, who matched Minevitch for drive and charisma but outdistanced the bandleader by a considerable margin in the talent department. Both these dynamos were proponents of the new chromatic harmonica, but while Minevitch focused on slapstick and popular songs, Adler performed in formal attire and came to adopt a repertoire more suited to the concert hall. Despite their differences, the careers of these two tireless self-promoters ensured that a whole generation of harmonica players would grow up feeling that a professional career was possible and that no musical genre was off-limits to them.

Hollywood was also doing its part. The Harmonica Rascals, Larry Adler, the Cappy Barra Harmonica Ensemble, Murray Lane's Harmonica Scamps, the Philharmonicas, Leo Diamond, and other harmonica acts were showcased in film features or shorts, and the mouth organ became standard equipment for celluloid cowboys in countless Hollywood westerns.

A new form of show business—radio—was helping the mouth organ reach an even larger audience. Individual performers like Adler and John Sebastian, and groups like the Harmonica Rascals, the Harmonica Harlequins, and the Cappy Barra Harmonica Ensemble, made regular appearances over the nation's airwaves. It was radio that exposed the existence of a large audience hungry for country music and the blues and thus made millions aware of the prominent role played by the mouth organ in these previously parochial art forms. The harmonica had become the most popular instrument in America.

The onset of World War II in Europe put the brakes on the American harmonica craze. After 1940, German-made Hohner instruments were no longer available; the youth groups disbanded and school music programs stopped using the harmonica. The instrument's built-in obsolescence suddenly became a serious liability for professional players, who began taking crash courses in harmonica repair and hoarding Hohners. "During the war I had several hundred harmonicas in a bank vault in New York," Larry Adler told me.

Ironically, the mouth organ got a boost when the United States entered the war. When home-front rationing was introduced, the shellac industry, which supplied the raw material for phonograph records, was put under military control. The American Federation of Musicians, which had been trying for years to negotiate a better agreement with the record companies, saw an opening and announced a total ban on commercial recording by its members. The boycott lasted for two years, and until it was lifted, record labels were forced to release discs showcasing singers (most of whom were stage performers and thus members of AGVA, the American Guild of Variety Artists) or musicians performing on miscellaneous, nonunion instruments. The AF of M had never attempted to recruit professional harmonica players, who were almost exclusively AGVA performers, and mouth organists suddenly found themselves in great demand, along with ukulele virtuosos and musical saw artists.

There was still the problem of acquiring quality harmonicas during the war. There were at least a dozen stateside harmonica manufacturers, but many produced substandard instruments, and their level of production never came close to meeting the domestic demand. (More than 30 million harmonicas had been imported into the United States between 1936 and 1939.) The most successful of the American harmonica makers, both financially and in terms of the quality of their instruments, were the William Kratt Company of New Jersey, launched by former Hohner employees, and the George P. Regan Harmonica Company in California.

Few players were lastingly converted to American harmonicas. Within three years after V-J day, Hohner's superior instruments were again streaming into the country, and the firm was on its way to reclaiming its monolithic control of the mouth organ industry. "In the middle of 1948, Hohner came back with a bang," remembers former Regan employee and ex–Harmonica Rascal Ray Tankersley. "They had the cheap labor—ten cents on the dollar against American labor. We talked about fighting them, but we decided to keep what we had made and close the doors."

With the return of the GIs from overseas, Americans regained their domesticity with a vengeance. A new national nesting instinct and the advent of television sounded the death knell for vaudeville. The large harmonica groups gave way to smaller, more economic combos— most often trios consisting of a lead chromatic, a chord, and a bass. This concept was plied most successfully by a Chicago-based threesome, the Harmonicats, whose echo-laden recording of "Peg o' My Heart" was the surprise number one record of 1947. The 1950s saw Richard Hayman achieve popular success with his recordings of "Ruby" and "The Theme From the Threepenny Opera" and the occupation of the White House by an enthusiastic harmonica devotee, Dwight Eisenhower.

Chromatic harmonica soloists were becoming increasingly drawn to classical music. Larry Adler's popularity had led several modern composers, including Darius Milhaud and Benjamin Arnold, to write new works expressly for the mouth organ. The baroque interpretations of John Sebastian, the first harmonicist to devote himself exclusively to the classical repertoire, were simultaneously confounding and pleasing audiences in the nation's concert halls.

On the rawer stages on Chicago's South Side, the harmonica was entering the electronic age. In a 1951 recording session, twenty-one-year-old Walter Jacobs blew his harmonica into a cheap public address microphone plugged into a guitar amplifier and unleashed a raw, intense, and—above all—exciting torrent of swooping bent notes and slashing phrases. Bluesmen like Jacobs were a primary source of inspiration for Elvis Presley and the small army of performers that followed his lead, but the harmonica was left off the menu during rock and roll's salad days.

That changed in 1963 when "Love Me Do," an engaging pop record driven by a harmonica hook, led to a remarkable reshuffling of the cultural deck that put an English group in the rock and roll driver's seat. Within months Hohner, which had suffered declining sales for years, was offering a Beatles model diatonic harmonica. An even stranger musical twist followed when most of British bands that followed up on the Fab Four's success in the United States (most notably the Rolling Stones, their stiffest competition) were revealed to be blues disciples intent on selling white American teenagers remakes—often featuring the harmonica—of the rhythm and blues standards that had been created in their new fans' own backyard. Taking the cue, many white American teenagers began to seek out the black blues artists who were only a subculture away. Some become activists. In the early 1960s, a Chicago University student named Paul Butterfield began singing and playing the harmonica in the blues bars on the South Side, eventually forming a mixed-race rock/blues group whose 1965 debut album helped—in a literal fashion that would have been impossible a decade earlier—to bridge the gap between the white rockers and the blues players. It was Butterfield's band that Bob Dylan—who had already entranced folk music aficionados with his combination of a dense lyricism with an utterly basic sound punctuated by bursts of untamed harmonica playing— asked to accompany him when he began to remake himself as a rock star in the mid-1960s.

Harmonica sales in the United States surged, increasing by 66 percent in the single year between 1965 and 1966. Hohner unveiled a Blues Harp diatonic model. The chromatic harmonica still had occasional flashes of glory—Henry Mancini's recording of "Moon River," one of the monster pop hits of the decade, was framed around a George Fields solo—but the post-Butterfield hipsters were discovering blues players like James Cotton and Junior Wells while country music fans were getting reacquainted with the harmonica thanks to the hundreds of recordings that featured the diatonic virtuosity of Nashville session legend Charlie McCoy.

On December 16, 1965, the harmonica became the first instrument heard in outer space when one of the more dedicated of these amateurs, astronaut Wally Schirra, serenaded the planet with a tiny, four-hole Hohner Little Lady during the *Gemini VI* mission. "I started fooling around with the harmonica as a boy," recalls Schirra. "Just a couple of the people at NASA knew that I planned on taking a harmonica with me. It was pretty close to Christmas, so I played 'Jingle Bells.' It came out quite well. People all over the world sent me harmonicas. They put me in the Atlanta musicians' union." (Schirra's Little Lady can be seen on display at the Air and Space Museum in Washington, D.C.) By the end of the 1960s it was estimated that 40 million Americans had attempted to play the mouth organ.

On a less astral plane, the American fascination with the harmonica continued to broaden. The Society for the Preservation and the Advancement of the Harmonica (SPAH), which was formed in 1962 by a group of harmonica boosters in the Detroit area, flourished, and the organization now boasts a worldwide membership and has inspired the founding of twenty-four regional harmonica clubs in the United States. A survey taken in the early 1970s found that one-half of the records on the American pop charts had harmonica parts on them. A 1979 Gallup poll found that within the United States there were 1,549,000 people who seriously claimed to be "experts" on the harmonica.

The harmonica's reputation as the instrument of choice for leaders of the republic was enhanced in 1981 when Pres. Ronald Reagan was reported to have entertained himself by playing "Red River Valley" on a gift harmonica as he recovered from a near-fatal gunshot wound. Even from his hospital bed, the Great Communicator was flexing his greatest talent—the ability to tap into American myth.

Frank Hohner, Matthias's grandson, ended his twenty-year stewardship of the Hohner Company's American branch when he retired in 1980, just as a swelling market was encouraging fresh challenges to his firm's dominance from two new American harmonica manufacturers, Lee Oskar and Huang. These upstarts offer competitively priced instruments and some intriguing technical innovations, such as Oskar's removable reed plates, though Hohner still sells over 1 million harmonicas each year in the United States. But it has been the players, and not the instrument makers, who have continually upped the ante since the harmonica first reached America.

The Harmonicats. From left to right:
Al Fiore, Jerry Murad, Don Les.

The Bands

The harmonica first went professional in America on the stages of the vaudeville theaters that were the heart of the country's entertainment scene from the late 1880s until the end of World War II. In 1928, vaudeville's zenith, there were over a thousand of these playhouses. Contemporary critics tended to consider vaudeville a second-rate form of entertainment, but its mission was not to edify the elite but to provide the public with a vast variety of affordable, popular entertainment. Even during the worst valleys of the Depression, a night at the vaudeville theater was a bargain. A single dollar ensured hours of diversion that typically included a Fox Movietone newsreel, a cartoon or a comedy short, a feature-length film, and ten live acts topped by a well-known headliner and a full orchestra.

The harmonica first appeared on these stages as a feature of "Dutch acts," Germanic minstrel shows that were popular around the turn of the century. By the early 1930s, when the first headlining vaudeville act to feature the mouth organ, Borrah Minevitch's Harmonica Rascals, became popular, fierce competition from motion pictures and radio was precipitating vaudeville's decline. In 1933 there were only a handful of Palaces and Orpheums left, but the genre held on tenaciously until the start of World War II. Nearly all of the American entertainers who began their careers before 1940 were products of this incomparable training ground, and mouth organists were no exception.

Borrah Minevitch (1902–55) and the Harmonica Rascals

"Half the world plays the harmonica, and the other half wishes it could." This was Borrah Minevitch's battle cry during his heyday between the wars, and if there was any truth in the claim, it was due in no small part to him. As a young man Minevitch conceived an ambition—to be a mouth organ impresario—so beyond the pale that it was unique to himself. He molded a raw crew of players, most of whom were still in their teens when they joined him, into one of the most successful show business acts of his day. Harmonically speaking, Minevitch's band was paramount for more than two decades and served as the proving ground for most of the great mouth organists who came of age between the wars.

But to the beardless prodigies he hired, life could be chilly in the Minevitch shadow. A profane, sour-tempered skinflint offstage, Minevitch worked a perverse, lifelong con that could have been lifted straight off the pages of one of Dickens's sagas of urban lowlife. A show business Nosferatu whose feeding ground was the vast reservoir of talent spawned by the harmonica band movement, Minevitch shuttled dozens of underage players through his act for nearly thirty years, working them mercilessly and paying them next to nothing.

Even the musical legacy of Minevitch's Harmonica Rascals is bittersweet. The Rascals' ranks always included several of the country's best mouth organists, but for the most part their stage routine was a cyclone of slapstick, in the eye of which was the group's talented comic, Johnny Puleo. Minevitch and his talented youngsters created an entirely new concept—the professional harmonica stage band—that allowed them to chart miles of new musical territory, but they also ensured that for years afterward the harmonica would be indelibly linked with juvenile comedy.

Born in the Russian city of Kiev as the last of seven children, Borrah Minevitch was ten when the family emigrated to the United States. The Minevitches had only just settled into a new life in Boston when Borrah's father died, and the family struggled. To help out, Borrah peddled newspapers in Scollay Square. Minevitch already showed a fondness for music ("The sound of a hurdy-gurdy always made me drop everything"), and he pestered his mother to buy him a violin; he was given a new harmonica instead. Inspired by the mouth organ skills of a fellow newsboy, Minevitch was soon giving impromptu sidewalk concerts. Minevitch's other boyhood passion was the movies; he spent countless hours slouched in the seats of the local theater, devouring the comedies of Mack Sennett, Harold Lloyd, and Charlie Chaplin.

When an older brother moved to New York City, Borrah followed him, enrolling at City College but spending most of his time at the Clare Tree Major School for Dramatic Acting. The chromatic harmonica had made its debut, and Minevitch experimented with the display model in his neighborhood music store so often that he eventually broke it.

Minevitch dropped out of college and took a job manning the notions counter on the second floor of the Wurlitzer store on Forty-second Street. He began luring young customers to his counter by serenading them on his harmonica from the top of the stairs. Notions sales surged. Howard Wurlitzer increased his young salesman's salary and finagled him a one-shot engagement as a guest harmonica soloist with Dr. Hugo Reisenfeld's orchestra at the Rivoli Theater on Broadway, a performance that Minevitch later claimed was highlighted by a spectacular entrance that culminated with him pitching headlong into the orchestra pit. A college thesis Minevitch had written on the harmonica came to the attention of the Hohner Company, which distributed thousands of reprints of the piece and hired its author as a mouth organ publicist.

Minevitch was more enthusiastic about promoting himself. In 1925 he ran across a man named Aaron Keil who had recruited forty boys from a junior high school in the Bronx to form a harmonica band. Minevitch enlisted twenty-five of these youngsters, christened them the Symphonic Harmonica Ensemble, and began booking them into vaudeville houses. Live, the ensemble gave earnest performances of jazz and classical numbers, but for their first recording Minevitch chose a number entitled "Hayseed Rag." He was showing signs of cruder, more commercial instincts.

Nineteen twenty-seven marked a critical juncture for Minevitch. The Symphonic Harmonica Ensemble became the first mouth organ group to appear at the Metropolitan Opera House and followed up this triumph by making a splash on Broadway in the Ziegfeld musical *Sunny*. And that year, at a harmonica contest held in Boston, Minevitch met a diminutive fourteen-year-old mouth organist named Johnny Puleo. The four-foot-one-inch Puleo was widely assumed to be a dwarf, but according to his friend Hugh McCaskey, "Johnny was normal at birth. He grew up in the ghetto and came down with rickets, so his arms and legs never grew." Puleo had a plastic face and large, soulful eyes, and Minevitch was quick to realize that the boy was a natural pantomimist. The Symphonic Harmonica Ensemble was about to become transformed.

Minevitch left the Hohner Company and pared his group down to a more manageable nine players. His publicity handouts made much of his humble newsboy origins, and Minevitch decided that his troupe should have a striking visual identity that would personify this romantic version of his own urban boyhood—he made them over as the Harmonica Rascals, an anarchistic but lovable pack of big-city ragamuffins. Minevitch, by contrast, became a spectacular parody of a Broadway dandy, adopting a stage costume that included a bright yellow checkerboard jacket, a purple shirt, white spats, and a light gray bowler hat perched at a steep angle. The tightly arranged musical offerings that Minevitch's troupe specialized in gradually became eclipsed by the chaotic chemistry that developed from onstage improvisations between Minevitch and Puleo, whose lack of height was emphasized by having his abbreviated legs encased in cowboy chaps. The act became an avalanche of nonstop slapstick that focused on the physical abuse of the group's tiny silent comic (Puleo remained mute onstage for his entire career) and on Minevitch's bizarre pseudoconducting style, which consisted largely of rubber-armed gestures and spastic body language.

It was the Three Stooges with mouth organs, and audiences loved it. The Rascals became one of vaudeville's most popular acts. With Minevitch grossing over $3,000 a week, other street-urchin harmonica bands began springing from the wings of theaters around the country. The Rascals signed with Decca Records and during the next ten years appeared in a number of films. Minevitch often faked other players' solos on-screen, but he was not an outstanding mouth organist.

"He learned to play a very fast, clean chromatic scale that made an impression on people, but he wasn't really that good a harmonica player," says former Rascal Pete Pedersen. "But he could play three notes on a harmonica and tear you apart with his body English. He was an incredible showman. There's never been another like him."

With success came the unleashing of the full force of Minevitch's genius for self-promotion. He once engineered his own "disappearance," emerging after a few days in a flood of publicity with the claim that he had been kidnapped by Corsican sailors off the coast of France. Minevitch's press releases were unabashedly florid: "His last ten years typify the journey from rags to riches which pertains to all civilized countries. . . . Minevitch placed his faith in the universal appeal of a simple instrument, which, somehow, had become the stepchild of music. No one ever had plumbed its possibilities." When the Rascals landed their own weekly radio program, Minevitch used the airwaves to promote the Borrah Minevitch Harmonica Institute of America in New York City. Fledgling players that responded—125,000 in the school's first year—received an eight-page booklet entitled "Harmonica Secrets of Borrah Minevitch—The Inside Story."

In the early years, the Rascals traveled with steamer trunks full of Hohner harmonicas, but after Minevitch began marketing his own line of mouth organs, most of them adopted the Minevitch Technique Tone ten-hole chromatic models, which came in a "stage key" (the key of C) and a "radio key" (the key of A). Some Rascals, including Hugh McCaskey, continued to play Hohners: "The Minevitch harmonicas weren't very good. They had a very thin reed and they were easy to bend, but you couldn't keep them in tune." The Minevitch harmonicas were originally made by Klingenthal, a German company, but the bandleader eventually built his own factory in southern California. Minevitch's mouth organs never posed much of an economic threat to Hohner, but the instrumental possibilities offered by the harmonica group concept led the German company to develop several new models.

To add a bottom to the harmonica group sound, Hohner created the bass harmonica. Like the chord harmonica, the bass harmonica is a pair of mouth organs joined together; the lower half of the instrument contains the natural notes of the scale while the upper half offers the player sharps and flats. The #265 model offers the two octaves between Contra E and small e, and the larger #268 model allows the player to achieve the almost three-octave range between Contra E and Contra C. There are no draw notes on these instruments. Two heavy, stiff reeds were placed in each hole to boost the bass harmonica's volume. In the recording studio, bass harmonicist Mike Chimes encased his instrument in a cigar box outfitted with two phonograph megaphones and augmented it with a string bass.

The limited number of chords available on the diatonic and chromatic mouth organs did not go far enough in answering Minevitch's need for a rhythm section. Rascal Fuzzy Feldman solved the problem by learning to play several Hohner Autovalve diatonic harmonicas wedged between his fingers. Sam Scheckter, a member of Carl Freed's rival harmonica group, recalls that the Autovalves "didn't give Fuzzy all chords, but he used to choke them so that even though he wouldn't get the actual clear chord, it gave him a rhythm." Meanwhile, Hohner developed a true chord harmonica, its model #267, with advice from Mike Chimes. The largest mouth organ, the two-foot chord harmonica, is actually two instruments hinged together. Twenty-four four-note chords (twelve blown and twelve drawn) with double reeds in every hole are built into each, resulting in 384 total reeds in ninety-six double holes for a total of forty-eight possible chords. Feldman, the inspiration for the instrument, never played it. "He didn't like it," says Scheckter. "He cut it up into small segments and used sections of it."

Before the advent of the chord harmonica, the longest mouth organ had been the polyphonia, a Hohner model designed for playing glissandos, fills, and trills that were difficult or impossible on diatonic or chromatic mouth organs. The notes of the polyphonia are arranged chromatically so that a complete chromatic scale can be achieved by simply playing all the blow notes or, on some models, all the draw notes as well. Over the years, Hohner has offered seven different versions of the polyphonia, the most popular being the three-octave models, the #261 and the #263. Minevitch insisted that Johnny Puleo play the polyphonia; having the smallest member of the band play the largest instrument made for the best sight gag.

Musically, the 1934 Harmonica Rascals were perhaps the most impressive of Minevitch's many groups; nearly half of the recordings made by the Rascals over their long history were cut that year. The Rascals' music had a buoyant drive to it, thanks in no small part to Fuzzy Feldman's propulsive rhythm playing. The Rascals often abandoned an ensemble approach in favor of dense layers of incessant individual riffing by the core section of chromatic players (Leo Diamond, Abe Diamond, and Alex Novelle), a fracturization that made for a busy sound. Their arrangements often consisted of dozens of sudden, brief phrases linked by great waves of rippling glissandos, and the Rascals had a collective penchant for freakish sound effects—everything from exaggerated hand effects to growls, trills, clucks, gulps, and birdcalls.

Leo Diamond played lead and wrote most of the arrangements for the group during this era. A product of New York's Hebrew Orphan Asylum, by the time he was in his teens Leo was not only an excellent harmonica player who could write and arrange music but a talented multi-instrumentalist who could find his way around on the saxophone, flute, piccolo, and clarinet. After winning a Central Park harmonica contest at the age of fourteen, Diamond joined the Rascals and was pressed into service to furnish the band with fresh material, a grind he kept up for a dozen years.

"Leo Diamond *was* the Minevitch sound," claimed Hugh McCaskey. "He was the Guy Lombardo of the harmonica and the real key to their success." Other Rascal alumni contend that it was Minevitch who made the band's musical approach such a schmaltzy one. "He insisted on everything sounding like Guy Lombardo," contends Eddy Manson, "and he undid so many fine things that Leo wrote." Abe Diamond has confirmed that his brother and Minevitch "were mutually fond of each other, so much so that in the early years Borrah wanted to legally adopt him. The only disputes they had revolved around music. Minevitch always wanted to add 'showmanship' touches. These went against Leo's musical senses and did cause friction, but the dynamics between them is what made the Rascals what they were." Hugh McCaskey: "Leo was the musical conductor. In the beginning no one read music, so Leo would write the arrangements and then teach the guys how to play it using the blow/draw system."

Eventually Minevitch began to feel that the lack of bona fide readers in the band was keeping the Rascals from getting the critical appreciation that they deserved. "Someone had pointed out to Minevitch that we couldn't read music," remembers Eddy Manson, "so he decided that we would all learn to read and that we would do a whole show from written music." In 1936 the Minevitch Rascals presented what was billed as the first evening of serious harmonica music at Queen's Hall in London.

Twenty-year-old Leo Diamond put together a challenging program, including an original concerto, Ravel's *Bolero,* Gershwin's *Rhapsody in Blue* and *An American in Paris, The Grand Canyon Suite,* and the premiere of a work written especially for the group by British composer Eric Coates.

"That was a big night," says Eddy Manson. "We were all dressed up and we had music stands in front of us. Minevitch was standing there, conducting with a baton from the score—he didn't know how to read note one. We went through the whole program letter perfect. Everything was just great; it came off beautifully. All the critics came up and congratulated us. What they didn't realize was that we had pulled the greatest musicianly stunt of all. Not one of us was reading a single note. We had all memorized every damn number in the show."

One of the most intriguing players in the long cast of characters who went through the Minevitch band was Ernie Morris, a Rascal for nearly twenty years. Morris, an African American, was much older than his teenaged colleagues. He usually handled the low harmony part, but it was his tone that had the biggest influence on the group's sound. "Ernie was the first one who ever got that big, fat throat vibrato," contended McCaskey. "The story was that he was just doing it one day and Minevitch put his ear up to Ernie's harmonica and he took the harmonica away from him and gave him another one. Between shows Minevitch had the harmonica apart and was holding it up to the light and looking at it to see what was going on. He ended up having Ernie show the other guys how to do that." This heavy throat vibrato became the Rascal's musical trademark.

Morris's influence extended beyond the Rascals. "The player who impressed me most was Ernie Morris," says Larry Adler. "No one has yet duplicated his tone." Larry's brother Jerry concurs. "Ernie Morris was an absolutely fabulous player. When that guy played blues, he put Sonny Terry and everyone else to shame." Alan "Blackie" Schackner remembers trying several methods to duplicate Morris's tone, including wrapping his harmonica in cellophane and playing through a megaphone.

"Ernie Morris had the greatest tone of all," offers the Harmonicats'

Al Fiore. "When he put that harmonica to his lips, he did something unbelievable with it. If you listen to some of the old Minevitch recordings, you'll hear some amazing effects in there, and that's all Ernie Morris." According to former Rascal Pete Pedersen, "There were two things that made the Minevitch band: Ernie Morris and Fuzzy Feldman. Ernie was one of the most unique harmonica players. Ernie had the most gorgeous tone in the world. He would get some little funky solo things going, rhythm and blues–type things."

As a black man, Morris was inexorably called upon to shuffle and grin his way through the Rascals' comedy bits. The racial climate in some parts of the country led Morris to assume even more perverse roles; during theater appearances in the South and the Midwest, where audiences tended to react negatively to mixed-race acts, Morris was forced to perform in blackface. Morris left the Rascals in 1944 and thereafter worked out of New York as a soloist. Pete Pedersen recalls that "after Ernie left the band he didn't have too easy a time. He got to drinking a little bit more than he should have and over the years kind of wasted himself." Morris died in the 1950s.

The Harmonica Rascals' success failed to take the edge off Minevitch's personality. If anything, he became more abrasive. "When Minevitch got angry, everybody was 'boy,'" remembers Abe Diamond, "and that's when we stayed clear of him." Addressed by all of his players as "Mr. Minevitch," he was constantly warning his employees not to associate with the members of other harmonica bands. The Rascals' remuneration was pitiful. From a typical weekly take of $3,200, Minevitch paid the indispensable Leo Diamond $40 a week, out of which Diamond had to pay rent on a hotel room that served as not only his living quarters but as the band's rehearsal space. Hugh McCaskey remembered the paydays when he and the other Rascals would attempt to waylay Minevitch backstage: "Everybody would be waiting to see Minevitch because they all wanted to ask for a raise. Then he'd come in and fire you. It was difficult to ask for a raise if he'd just fired you. He knew his psychology." The Rascals' lineup became more fluid, and Minevitch constantly recruited new talent on the road.

One of youngest players ever to enlist in the Rascals was Eddy Manson, who as a fifteen-year-old trekked from Brooklyn to Radio City to audition for Minevitch. "I sat there with a lot of other players. One by one the guys go in. About five-thirty, all of a sudden they call out my name. I walked into this luscious office, beautifully decorated with nothing but busts and paintings of Borrah Minevitch. This, apparently, was God's office. All of a sudden I hear a voice say, 'All right, boy. Play, boy, play.' I look over and sure enough, there's a john. And God was on the john. So I walked over and stood on the tile floor and played for him. And he offered me a job—at fifteen dollars every two weeks."

Jerry Adler remembers trying out for Minevitch as a thirteen-year-old when the Rascals came through Baltimore one year. "I played for him and he said, 'Okay, kid, you're hired. Go check it out with your parents.' Well, I was in seventh heaven. Johnny Puleo pulled me over to one side and said, 'Look, kid, don't do it. You're too good to be with this guy, and if you sign with him, you're married to him for the rest of your life.' I thought he was jealous. While I was on my way home, Johnny called my father, and when I got home, my father said, 'No, you're going to stay in school.' Thank God he did. Minevitch was probably the most rotten, meanest individual I've ever met in my life."

By the end of the 1930s, Minevitch was appearing only occasionally with the group. "He quit doing the one-nighters and the week-enders and the three-a-day and five-a-day vaudeville," says Ray Tankersley. "Minevitch only came out then for the big appearances—the movies and so forth." Taking a stab at legitimate acting, in 1940 Minevitch reprised a role originated by Harpo Marx in the hit stage play *The Man Who Came to Dinner*.

In the early 1940s, Johnny Puleo, who had been unhappy for years over Minevitch's refusal to renegotiate his original long-term contract, left the band to start his own group. Minevitch's response was to slap an injunction on his diminutive star, and he and Puleo wrangled legally for some months before Puleo was forced to return to the act.

The Diamond brothers were the next to leave. "Leo left Minevitch when he became tired of doing the same routine for so many years," says Abe Diamond. "The band was being regrouped after Johnny quit, and apparently he and Minevitch could not agree on a future course." Hugh McCaskey, Carl Ford, and Dave Doucette were recruited to take the Diamonds' places. McCaskey recalled his first rehearsal with Minevitch. "He asked me to play for him, and I played 'Flight of the Bumblebee.' Then he said, 'Play something technical.' "

For all his orneriness, Minevitch had the best harmonica band in the country, and prospective players fought desperately for a spot in the group. Pete Pedersen was a teenager in Chicago when he joined up with the Harmonica Madcaps, a group that included Jerry Murad.

"We were doing Benny Goodman and Glenn Miller arrangements and had gotten real avant-garde with some Raymond Scott things. When the Rascals appeared at the Oriental Theater in 1942, we decided that we would go down there and show those cornballs what a real harmonica band should sound like. Well, we got backstage and the first thing I heard was Pud McCaskey warming up by playing 'Flight of the Bumblebee.' Then Carl Ford came down playing some other incredible thing. And then Dave Doucette started in. And it didn't take us long to decide, well, maybe we had made a mistake. But we were there, so we decided to do it anyhow. We were playing our second or third song when the door opens and there's Borrah Minevitch. Minevitch listened to us and then he got names and addresses. I was so shook up from the whole thing that the first thing I did when I got home was to throw up. He had said that he was going to hire us, and we thought he meant tomorrow. The following December, Jerry Murad and I got money orders and telegrams telling us to meet the Rascals in California." "It was my biggest thrill," admits Jerry Murad. "Not financially, of course."

For several years Minevitch had been able to keep as many as three Harmonica Rascal units busy, but after the drastic alterations in the American entertainment landscape brought about by the end of World War II, he cut back to a single troupe built around Puleo and began looking for new enterprises. According to Hugh McCaskey, "Minevitch moved to France in the mid-1940s and married a young woman over there, a model. He was living in the suburbs of Paris. He was into French television and movie production and a number of other business ventures, but it seems that they all failed except for the Harmonica Rascals. Your salary would come by telegram."

In June of 1955, at the age of fifty-two, Borrah Minevitch died in Paris. The newspapers reported that he had died of a heart attack while driving his car, but the Rascals were privately told a different version of their leader's demise. As one recalled later, "What they told the band was that he came home a night early and caught his new bride with her boyfriend in his bed. There was a little scuffle. They were at the top of the stairs and Minevitch rolled backwards down the stairs and broke his neck."

Hugh McCaskey recalled the denouement. "Minevitch had a daughter, Lydia. When Minevitch died, Johnny Puleo thought he was finally going to get away from Minevitch, but Lydia said no, she had the estate and now Johnny would work for her. Johnny said there was no way he was going to do it. She told him he couldn't use the name Harmonica Rascals, so Johnny decided to use Harmonica Gang. In the meantime, a man from New Jersey named Irving Levine—a player who had tried and failed several times to get with the band as a player—did a title search and found that nobody owned the name Harmonica Rascals. So he copyrighted the name, changed his name to Paul Baron, and started his own Rascals. And he's still at it."

Johnny Puleo (1913–83) and His Harmonica Gang

Johnny Puleo, the soul of the Harmonica Rascals, had sold his own to Borrah Minevitch when he signed a long-term contract upon joining the troupe. A salary that had appeared princely to a show business neophyte seemed less auspicious as the years went by and the group's popularity skyrocketed, and Puleo repeatedly tried to escape from Minevitch's clutches.

The most serious of his many flights to freedom occurred in 1942, when Puleo left the Rascals, went into hiding, and secretly formed a group with Dave Doucette, Ray Tankersley, Don Henry, Hugh Farr, and Hugh McCaskey. The group was in the middle of rehearsals at Puleo's house in Washington, D.C., when the long arm of Minevitch arrived in the mail in the form of a court-ordered injunction—Puleo's contract with his tightfisted bandleader still had seven years left to run on it, and the talented comic had no choice but to rejoin the Rascals.

After Borrah Minevitch's death, Puleo immediately formed his own troupe, The Harmonica Gang, whose founding members included Eddie Gordon, Dom and Tony Sgro, and the indefatigable Dave Doucette, who during the next six years of constant touring would somehow find the time to arrange all the material for seven albums on the Audio Fidelity label. Though the days when harmonica bands could command big money had passed while Puleo was serving out his sentence with the Rascals, The Harmonica Gang was successful. They appeared on television with Milton Berle, Dean Martin, and Perry Como. They played top showcases like the Latin Quarter in New York and did twenty-six weeks in one year at the Stardust in Las Vegas. Puleo also did some film acting without his harmonica—he had a featured role in the 1956 movie *Trapeze* that starred Gina Lollobrigida and Burt Lancaster—that helped keep his famous profile in front of the public. He retired in 1973.

While some who should know claim that Puleo was an excellent harmonica player—Jerry Adler, for one, insists that "Johnny Puleo was one of the best players ever, in my opinion"—most agree that his great talent was for comedy, not music.

The prosperity of the Harmonica Rascals inspired the formation of several similar outfits. The second harmonica bandleader to gain a foothold in vaudeville was Charles Snow, who built his act around Charley Bennington, a talented dancer whose wooden leg made him somewhat unique in his profession. The young harmonica group that backed him up was billed as Charles Snow's Broadway Pirates. Snow had the Pirates' harmonicas outfitted with trombone bells, and the finish of their act was the enactment of a shipboard mutiny. Such creative staging notwithstanding, the Broadway Pirates somehow failed to capture the imagination of the public, and by 1935 Snow and Bennington had come back full circle to the Minevitch concept, dressing their players in street-urchin outfits and calling the group Charley Bennington's Newsboy Band.

Murray Lane's group, the Harmonica Scamps, was from its inception in the early 1930s a carbon copy of the Minevitch Rascals; Lane's only original touch was to hire a black midget for his group. Still, the Scamps were a successful draw for a few years, and several excellent players, including Alan "Blackie" Schackner, Nat Bergman, George Fields, and Stan Harper, did stints with the band. But the group that raised the most successful challenge to Minevitch was Carl Freed's Harmonica Harlequins.

Carl Freed (1896–1984) and the Harmonica Harlequins

Turkish-born Carl Freed got his start in show business in the early 1930s as the leader of a small vaudeville orchestra. In 1934, Freed decided to form a harmonica band, but he had the sense not to challenge the Rascals head-on. Instead of dressing his group in rags,

Freed called his band the Harmonica Harlequins and outfitted them in garish clown outfits.

Musically, the act consisted of straight-faced renditions of popular tunes, with Freed contributing some blues on the Marine Band and serving as the emcee and conductor. The group's trademark was its solid section work. Their overall sound was more focused and less dense than the Rascals', and they were innovative. Harlequin Sam Scheckter introduced the chord harmonica to American audiences thanks to his friendship with the Rascals' Mike Chimes. "Mike brought the chord to us and told Freed that I knew chords because I could play the guitar. So I ended up the first chord player on the very first chord harmonica that was sent over from Europe."

Freed managed to convince Chimes to leave the Rascals and join the Harlequins as its lead soloist and arranger; his experience had an immediate impact on the group. Scheckter took over the second chromatic part and Phil Solomon was brought in to play chord. Nat Bergman played the third part, Milton Freeman played bass, and Sid Gold was hired to tell jokes and play some Marine Band. Soon two alumni of the Hoxie band were brought in to fill out the group: Joe Mullendore, a precocious arranger who contributed a fourth chromatic part, and Leon LaFell, an affecting tenor singer and one of the few harmonicists to master the polyphonia.

"I became really intrigued with it, to the point where I didn't even bother with the chromatic anymore," says LaFell. "Nobody had really thought to play this thing. It was used for tricks—little fill-ins and glissandos. Johnny Puleo used to hit Minevitch in the leg with it. But I became really serious about playing solos on it."

Freed was a stylish entertainer, and Scheckter remembers the memorable entrance Freed devised for the group: "We had a special backdrop with a huge clown face painted on it. At a certain part of our introduction music, a stagehand would pull on a rope, the clown's mouth would open, and we would appear inside it. We would jump out, run towards the front of the stage, and line up in a V formation. Freed would then jump out, and we'd go up front and do our act. On my first show with Freed I caught my foot on the lip of the clown's mouth, took a flop, and bent my chord in half. I got a good laugh. Freed wanted me to leave it in, but I ignored him."

In 1935 the Harlequins were signed by Hohner to do a thirteen-week radio show over station WOR in New York and recorded a 78 for Decca. One side featured a jump tune by Chimes, "Riding the

Reeds," which featured some hot solo work by the composer; the reverse was Mullendore's fine arrangement of his own "Spring Tonic." The Harlequins' bookings were steady; the group crisscrossed the country in three large Ford touring sedans. But the young players were frustrated. "I was making forty dollars a week," offers Scheckter. "In 1935, that was not bad money, but Freed was grossing fifteen hundred to two thousand dollars a week. We had heard of legitimate bands that had formed cooperatives, like Glenn Gray's Casa Loma Orchestra, so we decided to do the same." In 1935 all the members except for Mike Chimes and Sid Gold left to start another group in which each member would have an equal share in the profits.

Freed quickly regrouped. His new act, the Harmonica Lads, featured the chromatic playing of Chimes and Saul Webber and Sid Gold's gags. In 1940, Chimes and Gold left the Lads; they were replaced by Byron Bouchard and Pete Blasberg. The next year found Freed and the Harmonica Lads touring Mexico; they returned reincarnated as Senor Carlos and his Caballeros. A few months later, the Caballeros, like so many musical groups, dissolved in the aftermath of Pearl Harbor.

The Cappy Barra Harmonica Ensemble

"It was like starting all over again," recalls Sam Scheckter about the period after 1935 when he and his fellow ex-Harlequins were putting together a new act. Bass player Milton Freeman left the group to get married and was replaced by Don Ripps. Phil King was recruited to inject some comic relief. Sam Sperling also joined the band; he and Joe Mullendore adopted the Hohner twelve-hole tenor chromatic, which was tuned an octave lower than the standard model.

Their personnel in place, the former Harlequins turned to Maurice Duke, a high-powered hustler who had developed numerous show business contacts as the leader of a New York Democratic club. According to Leon LaFell, "Duke was a short fellow who had been left badly crippled after a bout with polio. He had to walk in a brace with a cane, but he was a very dynamic individual, an absolute riot. Duke had absolutely no inhibitions. What he wanted to do, he did. What he wanted to say, he said. When he wanted to act crazy, he'd act crazy.

He could get in and speak with people in the business that nobody else could get access to."

While Duke busied himself lining up publicity opportunities, the players were struggling with a new musical identity for their group. "Our approach was the opposite of the Rascals'," says LaFell. "We played big band music. We copied the big bands and did their arrangements. We worked and worked and worked. The group was really good, but nothing was happening for us. One day, we all took a walk through Central Park and went to the zoo there. We came to this cage and found ourselves gazing at this horrible-looking capybara, the largest rodent in the world. Duke says, 'Hold it! This would make a great name for the band.' We took out our harmonicas and started playing, and Duke ran for the nearest phone. He called the papers and said, 'Hey, come down to the zoo! There's a bunch of kooks playing harmonicas in front of a rat's cage!' The papers picked up on it, and we got a lot of free publicity and our first real break, a date at the Roxy Theater.

"The Roxy was the biggest vaudeville theater in the world at the time. Our music was classy and we wanted our image to match it. We borrowed money and bought white ties and tails for the evening shows and morning and afternoon formals. It was a real shock to come out onto a stage that size. The orchestra had to vamp our introduction twice before we got all the way out there. We went over terrifically. From that point on, we had no trouble getting bookings. In a few months *Billboard* rated us the fifth most popular vaudeville act."

In 1937 the Cappy Barras appeared in a Biograph movie short, *Musical Airways,* and did a twenty-six-week stint on NBC radio. They also cut two records for the Master label and became the first harmonica group to get a booking at fabled Radio City Music Hall. The following year Maurice Duke went to Hollywood to line up some film work for the group, a trip that paid off when the Cappy Barras were cast in a big-budget Universal feature, *Mad About Music,* which starred Deanna Durbin and Herbert Marshall.

The influence of the big bands showed itself in the attention that the Cappy Barras gave to perfecting their section work. Nat Bergman's lead playing was often devilishly fast and always precise, but his solos were always placed within a solid group concept anchored by the playing of Phil Solomon, the first great master of the chord harmonica.

Joe Mullendore's arrangements were a big step forward for harmonica band music. "It was just a fluke," claims Mullendore. "Nobody would have ever started out to arrange music for a harmonica band. I just happened to be able to do it. I think you really ought to be able to play the harmonica to arrange for it, because you know the difficulties and how to avoid them."

Leon LaFell's unique polyphonia work was an integral part of the group's sound. He also had a pleasing tenor voice, and his vocals gave the Cappy Barra Harmonica Ensemble an added dimension. (While he was with the Cappy Barra group, LaFell recorded four vocal sides under his own name with Johnny Hodges on alto sax and Duke Ellington at the piano.)

In 1940, Sam Scheckter and Sam Sperling both left the band; George Fields replaced Sheckter. The group was cast in another feature film, *Bowery Boy*. Soon after, the act split into two groups. The first unit, which worked primarily in the Chicago area, included LaFell, Nat Bergman, Phil Solomon, and Don Ripps. A second unit, based in New York, was formed around Phil King and featured several outstanding young newcomers, including Fields, Charles Leighton, Alan Greene, and Pro Robbins.

In 1941 the first unit worked on a movie called *Pot o' Gold* that starred Jimmy Stewart and Paulette Goddard. While the group did not appear in the film, the Cappy Barra Boys and Jerry Adler performed several tunes for the film's sound track backed by Horace Heidt's orchestra.

Don Ripps succumbed to the lure of matrimony and a home life in late 1941, and the first Cappy Barra unit was reduced to a trio. "We were on a train traveling to the next job when we heard about Pearl Harbor," remembers LaFell, "and we decided that was it. We all enlisted."

The remaining Cappa Barra Boys worked steadily in vaudeville and in nightclubs through most of the war years. George Fields left in 1941 to move to California; musically, the group became a trio with Leighton handling the lead, Alan Greene playing chord and singing, and Pro Robbins on bass. Phil King, who booked the band and owned the touring car the group traveled in, inserted an occasional fill on the polyphonia, handled the comedy bits, and generally fronted the outfit, which finally disbanded in 1944.

The Philharmonicas

In 1935 one of the instructors at Borrah Minevitch's Harmonica Institute in New York, Dave Macklin, organized the most promising of his young charges into a group that he dubbed the Philharmonicas. It was the big band era, and the Philharmonicas were one of the first harmonica bands to show its influence. Harry Halicki, Joe Jass, Charles Leighton, Frank Mitkowski, Victor Pankowitz, and the Pitello brothers, Charles and Joe, were all teenagers who were thoroughly immersed in the big band sound. Jass shared lead duties with Leighton and created most of the group's arrangements by spending hours spinning the records of bands like Glen Miller's and Artie Shaw's on a windup Victrola, picking out the individual strains of the groups' dense harmonies by ear and transposing them to the chromatic harmonica.

One of the most popular radio programs of the period was "Major Bowes' Amateur Hour" on CBS. Neophyte musicians would perform and then listeners would anoint the most popular by phoning in their votes. The Philharmonicas appeared on the "Amateur Hour" in 1936 and emerged as the winning entrants. They joined Major Bowes' Second Anniversary Review and spent the next nine months appearing around the country. The seasoned teenagers then began performing on their own in theaters and nightclubs; they also made several movie shorts.

The Philharmonicas never recorded commercially, but their privately pressed recordings, their film appearances, and their live performances greatly influenced their peers. The group broke up for good at the onset of World War II. The Pitello brothers and Harry Halicki joined the coast guard and formed the Philharmonica Trio. This threesome made several excellent recordings for Columbia.

Johnny O'Brien (1902–91) and the Harmonica Hi-Hats

The most successful harmonica acts grew out of the deep reservoir of East Coast mouth organ talent, and when San Francisco–based vaudevillian Johnny O'Brien decided to put together a mouth organ band in 1937, he placed a persuasive phone call to Dave Doucette in New York. The ex-Rascal arranger and lead player had just put together a band called the Harmonica Kings, which was floundering despite its excellent musicianship, when O'Brien called with an offer of two radio shows a week and a guaranteed string of theater performances on the West Coast.

A few weeks later, the Harmonica Kings were getting used to both their new home in the Bay Area and a new name: the Harmonica Hi-Hats. They were an impressive group. Doucette played lead, Lenny Schwartz played second, Alan Pogson took the third part, Sam Blanco blew chord, and Carl Friedman played bass. Johnny O'Brien was more than just a connoisseur of talent; he was also a first-rate jazz player on the diatonic—a niche he had all to himself in those days. "Johnny could play chromatic scales up and down the Marine Band," recalls Stan Harper. Doucette went to work writing arrangements for their radio broadcasts; during the next ten months, he produced 359 charts.

The Hi-Hats spent 1938 touring back and forth between San Francisco and Chicago. That year two more great East Coast players, Eddy Manson and Sid Goodman, joined the group. When Sam Blanco parted company with the band, Alan Pogson picked up the chord.

Despite their appearances in several movie shorts, the West Coast did not prove to be a fertile enough territory, and the Harmonica Hi-Hats disbanded in 1940. Johnny O'Brien continued in show business as a folksy humorist and harmonica player. "He generally was regarded as one of the greatest artists—if not *the* greatest artist—on the diatonic instrument," Eddy Manson has noted. "He was easily the best I ever heard, and a terrific performer to boot."

Jerry Murad (1915–) and The Harmonicats

The cofounder of the Harmonicats, the most popular harmonica group ever, was born in Constantinople, Turkey. Jerry Murad's family emigrated to the United States in 1921, finally settling in Chicago.

"My mom bought me a Marine Band for a quarter when I was nine," recounts Murad. "Shortly thereafter I was able to pick out a simple melody. I soon found out that the diatonic harmonica could not give me all the notes I needed, so my mom graduated me to a small, ten-hole chromatic." Murad's real inspiration came when he saw the Harmonica Rascals in a Chicago vaudeville theater. "That was the greatest music I had ever heard."

Pete Pedersen was a boyhood friend of Murad's. "Somehow Jerry Murad appeared on the scene one day with a chromatic harmonica. It was the first time I'd ever seen one. I had been trying to play the song 'Wabash Blues,' and there was a note in the melody that I could never get on the diatonic. Jerry let me play his chromatic, and all I had to do was push the button to get that note. That was the biggest revelation I've ever had in music."

There would be other discoveries. Murad and Pedersen were both enlightened when they heard a fellow teenager named Al Fiore tear into a chord harmonica solo one night in a city park concert, and in 1937 the Harmonica Madcaps—with Murad on lead, Pedersen on harmony, Fiore on chord, and Bob Hadamik on bass—were formed. There were two amateur shows on Chicago radio at the time, both sponsored by jewelers, and the Madcaps were perennial contestants. "The winner always won a Benrus watch," remembers Pedersen. "We were always on the damn show because all the contestants who showed up were singers. So we appeared every time under a different name, and we'd always win. But we only got one watch for four guys." When Pedersen and Murad got the call to join Minevitch, the Harmonica Madcaps disbanded.

"Jerry didn't stay that long with Minevitch. He fought with him," says Pete Pedersen. "Jerry wasn't happy with Minevitch," recalls Fiore, "and I suggested that we form a group. He left the Rascals and came back to Chicago."

Murad quickly contacted Don Les. "He had been playing bass harmonica with the number two Minevitch group while I was with the number one group and our paths crossed," says Murad. "I had never heard anyone play the bass harmonica like him." Les was in the middle of a painful divorce and was relieved to come to Chicago and move in with Murad. "Jimmy Mulcay renamed us the Quintones, added a girl vocalist, and started producing us," says Al Fiore. "We didn't last a year, and so we went back to the trio thing."

They now called themselves the Harmonicats, a name supplied by Les. "We suffered for a while," he recalls. "I went to work in a department store and Al was helping his father in his shoemaker's shop. So

Jerry sort of took over the leadership of the group because he had the time to see the agents."

In 1947 the Harmonicats did a stint at the Tic Toc Club in Milwaukee. After one of their shows a man got up from a table and introduced himself to Don Les. "My name is Bill Putnam," he said. "If you ever think of recording something, let me know."

The Harmonicats got a break when they managed to get a week's booking at Helsing's Vodvil Lounge in Chicago, a proving ground for new acts. Their stint stretched into six months, during which time they shared the stage with numerous other new faces, including George Gobel and Patti Page. Their agent, who was trying to build on the group's success at Helsing's, urged the trio to go into a studio and put something on vinyl that he could play for club owners. The Harmonicats called Putnam and arranged to meet him at Universal Recording Studios on the forty-second floor of Chicago's Civic Opera Building in the wee hours of the morning after their last set at Helsing's. The trio arrived with a guitarist and bass player in tow and recorded four songs: "Peg o' My Heart," "September Song," "Harmonica Boogie," and "Fantasie Impromptu."

"Peg o' My Heart," a sentimental vaudeville chestnut that had been around since 1913, featured Fiore's chord playing. "Alan Pogson had been doing 'Peg o' My Heart' with the Minevitch group for quite a while," admits Fiore. "When I used to sub for him in the band, I had to learn his solo. All I did was change a couple of chords in the bridge. I've always given him the credit for it."

"I'm going to try something," said Bill Putnam as the Harmonicats prepared to run through their first take of "Peg." That "something" was to be one of the first uses of an echo chamber on a recording session.

"It wasn't done electronically," reveals Fiore. "Bill put a speaker in the men's washroom down the hall, which was wall-to-wall marble tiles, and ran a wire from it into the studio. Then he put another microphone in front of the speaker. Our sound went from the studio to the speaker in the washroom, where it created an echo effect that was rerecorded by the other microphone." The combination of putting the chord harmonica out front and adding a heavy echo effect made for a startling, new sound. "I was very much surprised, as it was the first time that I had heard my chord harmonica recorded professionally," recalls Al Fiore. "It was very pleasing to the ear." "We cut this little record and thought nothing of it," says Les.

A 78 was issued on the Universal label. The Harmonicats were convinced that "Fantasie Impromptu" would prove to be the most popular with audiences, so it went on the A side of the release. The B side was filled out with "Peg o' My Heart."

"Putnam gave the record to a disc jockey named Eddie Hubbard," says Don Les. "The first time he played 'Peg' he got two hundred calls." To the amazement of everyone involved, "Peg o' My Heart" became a hit record in the Chicago area almost overnight and was quickly rereleased on Putnam's new label, Vitacoustic. "The first sightings of flying saucers had occurred about that time," recalls Al Fiore. "To promote the record, they had a plane fly over Chicago and drop these cardboard Harmonicats records all over the city."

"Peg o' My Heart" became a national smash, riding the Hit Parade for twenty-six weeks and narrowly edging out Frankie Laine's recording of "That's My Desire" for the number one hit of 1947. "The record ended up being the biggest single hit of all time behind 'White Chrismas,'" contends Don Les, "which doesn't count because it's a seasonal thing." According to Jerry Murad, " 'Peg' has sold well over twenty million copies to date. In the Detroit area alone between 1947 and 1950, it sold over one and a half million copies."

" 'Peg o' My Heart' was different," contends Don Les. "We had a unique style. Today, all groups sound the same. I'd break my guitars onstage, too, if I couldn't play. But in those days, they tried to make every record different. There were whistling records, all kinds of gimmicks. We were one of the first to use the echo effect. It had been done before we did it; I had already heard it on a Benny Goodman record. But we got the credit because we had the hit record. To me, what really made the difference was the amplified guitar we used, which gave it a certain touch. It was a combination of three different ingredients. Any one of them might have made a hit record, but when you put them all together—the guitar, the echo chamber, and the fact that it was not only a harmonica but a *chord* harmonica out front— you really had something. Nothing could have held it back."

"The timing was important," says Fiore. "The guys were just back from the war and sentimental things were popular."

The Harmonicats agree that they couldn't have done it without Bill Putnam. "Bill Putnam *made* the Harmonicats," contends Al Fiore. "People couldn't believe what they were hearing. He was our genius, and he was the man who made the money for us." " 'Peg' made Bill

Putnam the biggest engineer in the country," says Don Les. "He went on to become Frank Sinatra's chief engineer for many years."

The Harmonicats were a hot property. They expanded to a four-piece with the addition of Cappy Barra alumnus Leon LaFell on polyphonia, who stayed with the group for two years. In 1948 the group's recording of "Hair of Gold" reached number fifteen on the charts. The Harmonicats signed with Mercury and went back into the studio, again with Putnam. "We tried to come right out with another hit," recalls Al Fiore. "I cut other chord solos similar to 'Peg o' My Heart,' but they didn't mean a damn thing." Jerry Murad recorded the harmonica solo for a recording of Miklos Rosa's film theme "The Story of Three Loves," which reached number fourteen in 1953, and the Harmonicats' recordings of "Bewitched," "Charmaine," "Malaguena," "The Harmonica Player," "Just One More Chance," and "Hora Staccato" all sold well.

"I didn't learn to read music until we formed the Harmonicats," claims Al Fiore. "We did things the hard way; everything was self-taught. We helped each other. Prior to recording, breathing techniques were practiced in order to minimize the 'grunting' effect in the microphones."

For the first decade of their existence, the Harmonicats shared a single microphone onstage, but the desire to re-create their reverb-laden studio sound in live performances led them to start using Fender amplifiers in 1955. "We wore chestplates that held Shure ribbon microphones in front of us," remembers Fiore. "We played right in front of these microphones and through the amplifiers. Don and I eventually recorded that way in the studio; Jerry recorded through a regular ribbon microphone."

The Harmonicats switched labels in 1960, moving to Columbia. Within a year they had their second big single, a reworking of the Perez Prado hit, "Cherry Pink and Apple Blossom White." An album of the same title became the number seventeen LP of that year.

Murad, Fiore, and Les all agree that their next album, a classical recording entitled *Harmonica Rhapsody,* was the trio's best studio effort. Pete Pedersen contributed some fine arrangements to the album and sat in on harmonica as well. The record was a commercial disappointment, however, and the group returned to their practice of offering up solid if unexciting mouth organ versions of popular tunes. Al Fiore contends that the group was in effect the artistic victim of its own commercial success. "We learned a lesson recording very technical tunes that the average public didn't understand. The songs didn't sell. So we were forced to play very commercial numbers, which I know didn't please a majority of the harmonica players."

When there was no successful follow-up to "Cherry Pink," personality conflicts in the group grew more pronounced, and in 1972, Don Les left the band and was replaced by Dick Gardner. Al Fiore recalls Les's departure with regret. "There was a lot of dissension in the group. I think it was the biggest mistake the Harmonicats ever made." Les teamed up with chromatic ace Mildred Mulcay and formed the Don Les Harmonicats.

Al Fiore retired in 1982 and was succeeded by Bob Bauer. Both Bauer and Dick Gardner are top-rank players, and the group lost little musical ground after Les and Fiore left, which is saying something given the stature and reputations of the departing players.

After forty years fronting the band, Jerry Murad is officially retired now, but the Harmonicats still perform occasionally. Murad was never an improviser, but his rock-solid playing was perfectly suited to the Harmonicats' traditional approach to their repertoire of standards. "I played the old-style wooden body #280 or 64 type for fifty years," notes Murad, "but I recently switched to the new fourteen-hole Meisterklasse chromatic. I like it very much and find that I can do without the first two holes of the #280."

"There is nothing like the sound of a harmonica," says Murad. "You are the complete master of it. It is very soulful, and with vibrato it is beautiful. They will never build a synthesizer to duplicate its unique sound. There are limitations with the harmonica compared to instruments that are fingered, but then on the other hand it works the other way around, so it would not be fair to compare. The harmonica is now an accepted part of the music scene all over the world. My group thinks like instruments, not like harmonicas. As far as my own playing goes, I copy no one and play my own style."

The Mulcays

The professional harmonica realm is unrelentingly male. Many women had taken up the mouth organ as children thanks to the harmonica programs offered by the public schools during the 1930s, but professional careers for female instrumentalists of any kind were rare—a scarcity that unfortunately continues to this day. Murray Lane put a fresh twist on the Minevitch formula by putting together the first all-female mouth organ troupe, the Harmonicuties, complete with midgette. Visitors to the Country Music Hall of Fame in Nashville can view a film clip from the 1930s in which popular vaudeville comedienne Lynn Mayberry performs a compelling train imitation on the diatonic harmonica. And Big Mama Thornton was not only one of the greatest of the female blues singers but an excellent blues harmonica player. But in the pop field, Mildred Mulcay stands alone.

Mildred Mulcay had grown up playing several instruments, and after World War II she joined an all-female jazz band as a saxophonist. One night in Hollywood the group shared the bill with several other acts, including a dapper New Yorker named Jimmy Mulcay, who tap-danced and played the Marine Band. Twelve weeks later Jimmy and Mildred were married.

Mildred became what she calls "a backstage wife" while Jimmy hoofed on the Midwest theater circuit. At one stop the promoter had inadvertently booked an all-male show; he convinced Mildred to play piano behind her husband's dance routine to add a female presence to the evening's entertainment, and from that day on the Mulcays were a duo.

Jimmy Mulcay decided to switch from the diatonic to the 64 Chromonica. An "ear" player, he struggled with the transition. The musically schooled Mildred began assisting her husband in picking out melodies and before long was learning her way around the chromatic harmonica herself, a task that she found simple enough once she had mastered the art of tongue blocking. Jimmy yielded in the face of his wife's superior musicianship, switched to the chord harmonica, and the Mulcays became a mouth organ act.

Mildred Mulcay developed into a strong soloist with a full-bodied tone. She claims that the Mulcays were the first pop harmonica act to use amplifiers. One of their most popular nightclub numbers was "My Happiness," and in 1953 the Mulcays sent a transcription of their version to the song's publisher, who released it on Cardinal Records. It went on to become a million seller; their follow-up, "Alabamy Bound," also sold well. The Mulcays eventually recorded for MGM, Dot, Coral, Jubilee, Somerset, and GNP. According to Mildred, the duo played "everything from Radio City Music Hall on down." They toured with Bing Crosby, Bob Hope, and Red Skelton and appeared on television with Ed Sullivan and Jack Benny.

Jimmy and Mildred eventually settled in the Hollywood hills and concentrated on playing dates on the West Coast. Jimmy Mulcay died in 1968, and Mildred spent the next ten years fronting the Don Les Harmonicats. She then returned to the West Coast and worked cruise ships until retiring to Las Vegas. She has "many happy memories of my career as an unusual musician—a female harmonica player."

The Stagg McMann Trio

The Stagg McMann Trio (the group's name was an attempt to blend the last names of members Paul Steigerwald, Hugh McCaskey, and Manny Smith) had the same stripped-down instrumentation pioneered by the Harmonicats, but they are generally regarded to have been more daring and original. Al Fiore, for one, was an admiring fan of the group. "The greatest harmonica trio ever, in my opinion, was the Stagg McMann Trio. They played arrangements that are still fantastic in today's jazz music. Their classical interpretations were superb, too."

McCaskey, Steigerwald, and Smith were all alumni of various harmonica bands that were active during the 1930s in Lancaster, Pennsylvania. In 1940 the threesome, all recent high school graduates, traveled to New York. After a year's apprenticeship on the national vaudeville circuit playing behind former Harmonica Rascal Alex Novelle, the trio went on their own for a season. The wartime draft broke up the group in 1941, and McCaskey, who had been turned down by the army because of poor eyesight, worked throughout the war years with the Minevitch troupe.

The Stagg McMann Trio regrouped after the war and resumed playing the country's top theaters and nightclubs, including the Roxy, Loew's State, and Palace theaters in New York, and the Oriental and State Lake theaters in Chicago. There were tours with Mickey Rooney, Vic Damone, and the Ink Spots, and television appearances on programs hosted by Milton Berle, Ed Sullivan, Steve Allen, and Jackie Gleason. In 1950 the Stagg McMann Trio recorded a self-produced album that featured their radical approach to the trio concept, a record that ranks as possibly the finest studio effort ever by a harmonica threesome. Unfortunately, Paul Steigerwald left the group soon after, and within a year Manny Smith left to go to television repair school on the GI bill. McCaskey persevered. A natural comedian, he polished that side of his talent and developed a successful solo act that mixed gags with his incomparable harmonica playing. One of the great chromatic players, McCaskey remained busy as an entertainer until his death in 1989.

Interview With Hugh McCaskey

I first became aware of the harmonica through the early movies I saw as a boy. I saw some of the early Minevitch things, the shorts and features like *One in a Million* with Sonja Henie. I remember seeing *The Singing Marine* with Larry Adler when I was about twelve; I was so impressed that I wanted to be a harmonica player. I inherited an old Koch chromatic harmonica from an uncle and taught myself to play it. My mother was a piano player who had been a rehearsal pianist for the Philadelphia opera company, and she taught me to read music.

The WPA was sponsoring harmonica bands in the playgrounds in Lancaster. The pastor of our church invited all the harmonica groups to join together as the St. Mary's Harmonica Band, which eventually became a nine-hundred-member band, and from that I met Paul Steigerwald and Manny Smith. We played Marine Bands in unison. It made for an awful sound.

After high school Paul, Manny, and I went to New York on our summer vacation. They were holding amateur nights in the theaters, and we won first prize in one. And then we went into another and won first prize again. The management approached us and told us that we could win *every* night if we took less money. We said, "No way!" We had it by the tail—we were going to win *everywhere*. So we never won again. That was life—we just didn't know about it yet.

We were hired to back up Alex Novelle, the ex-Rascal, who was playing small-time theaters. The pay was fifty dollars for the three of us, and for that we did five vaudeville shows a day and traveled a couple of hundred miles overnight in Manny's car to get to the next town.

It was 1940 and they were drafting people. Novelle left to go into the service and we worked without him as the Stagg McMann Trio. Manny and Paul got drafted in '41 and I got recommended to Johnny Puleo, who was hiding from Minevitch and trying to start his own act. I went to Washington in the summer of '42 and lived in the basement of Johnny's house with Dave Doucette, Ray Tankersley, Don Henry, and Hugh Farr. But Minevitch found out about it and got an injunction against us. Johnny said we weren't going to be able to work, so he sent Dave and me home. The day I got home I got a telegram from Minevitch offering me a job. I called Johnny and asked him what to do, and he said he couldn't hold out much longer. He said to take the job and he'd see me when he got back with the band.

The Rascals were out in L.A. working a few theaters. Carl Ford, Dave Doucette, and I came in to replace the Leo Diamond trio with that unit. We were all lead players, so Minevitch said, "Who wants to play what?" And Carl said, "I'll play lead." I guess he had been through the Rascals politics before. I didn't see much of Minevitch. He only conducted one show that I was on. That was fine because I didn't like him.

I was with the Rascals when I got drafted in '43. I figured I wasn't going to be drafted—I have very bad vision—so of course I was. The guy at the induction station said, "You shouldn't be in the army." I said, "Well, how do I get out?" He said, "I shouldn't be here either."

The Stagg McMann Trio regrouped after the war. We did an album in 1950. It still holds up somehow. We didn't use the standard trio concept of "oompah oompah" with the chord and bass. The arrangements were different. The chord was used for comping purposes and for section work with the lead harmonica, something that had just never been done before. For a straight-four rhythm, Manny did a brush effect where he'd let a little air escape when he played the push beat. A kid named Tony Luisi did the arrangements.

After the Stagg McMann Trio broke up in 1951, I went back to Minevitch. Later that year I got a single act together. I started using the name Stagg McMann. There were a lot of nightclubs then, so I was able to earn a living. I did a straight act for the first year or so, but then I started doing a misfit clothing comedy act. I had a fright wig made up, a balding wig with wild hair off to the side. I'd take it off during the act and my hair underneath would be the same. I would make my entrance on a pogo stick, which could be dangerous. They had some rotten stages in Spokane and I went in right up to my armpits in one. In Seattle I fell right on my tailbone on a marble floor and couldn't get up. So I ditched the pogo stick.

I went down to San Francisco and got into the Purple Onion club, where I developed an act that was about half comedy and half harmonica. I was at the Purple Onion about six months with Phyllis Diller, the Kingston Trio, a piano player, and a bass player. And they had a budget of $550 a week—for everybody. We'd do four or five shows a night. There was a twenty-five-cent cover charge to keep out the riffraff. Then I went across the street and was the opening act at the Hungry i for a couple of years. That was a better deal, but you had to stand in back of the bookkeeper when they made their deposit, because they had so many liens against them that you had trouble getting your money.

My manager sent me on a tour of Australia in 1962, and when I came back, there was just nothing. The well had gone dry. I was out of the business for three months. That was the only time that I got an honest job.

In about '64 or '65 I ended up in Chicago. Don Les had a heart attack and I subbed for him on bass with the Harmonicats. Jerry liked the interlude of talk and jokes that I was doing in the act, so when Don came back I switched over to harmonetta and did the jokes. We would work an hour show and we would do twenty-five minutes of quartet and then the other guys would leave the stage for twenty minutes and I'd do my thing. Then we'd finish up with the quartet. I guess I subbed three or four times for Al on chord when he was sick.

In 1976 I did a multiple-track of big band arrangements—mostly Glen Miller, Tommy Dorsey, and Artie Shaw things—in my office at home on a four-channel Teac machine. I usually overdubbed twelve tracks. It took a long time, but some of the things are surprisingly cohesive. It was first released on an eight-track tape and then on the Happy Harmonica series that I was doing with Jerry Murad. Sunnyvale Records had a Happy series: Happy Organ, Happy Guitar, Happy Harmonica. They never credited anybody on the albums. Jerry and I did two albums together overdubbing. Jerry came to me with the concept: we'd split it down the middle and we'd each play half of the parts. But I could never get him to show up and tape. After we started, he wanted to play lead on everything. He didn't want to do the drudgery of the background parts and stuff. So that only lasted a couple of albums.

I've been married since 1945. I have two kids. We didn't miss any meals. We never had all the expensive toys that I would have liked to have had, but I earned a living doing what I loved to do, so I think I'm very fortunate. The lack of recognition doesn't bother me. The last ten years I've been doing the cruise ships, which has been most satisfying.

I like to listen to jazz, but I can't play it. I'm one of those old traditional, Minevitch-type players. I don't think my style is anything unique. I just try to play as musically as I'm able to. I use the Super 64. They have bigger, heavier reeds and last longer. The Larry Adler models are twelve-hole chromatics that have the long-thrust reeds. They'll outlast the short reeds three to one. Some of the harmonicas I use now I used in the forties. I don't play very loud; I let the microphone do it. And I fix them and do my own tuning. I'm not a very good customer of Hohner's. I guess I've spent maybe four hundred dollars on harmonicas in the last fifty years.

I don't think the harmonica is limited at all. I like it the way it is. That's why I don't bother with the Millioniser and all those other things. Because that's not a harmonica. I'm selling the harmonica and the harmonica sound. If I'm going to play a synthesizer, I'll get a keyboard.

There hasn't been a commercial hit by a harmonica group for decades, although several bands have managed to keep viable.

Wellsville, Ohio's Sgro brothers, Dominic and Tony, broke into the big time with Johnny Puleo's Harmonica Gang and have since worked as a duo. They've recorded for RCA, performed with the likes of Frank Sinatra, Perry Como, Dean Martin, Tennessee Ernie Ford, Andy Williams, Spike Jones, Steve Allen, Milton Berle, and Johnny Carson, and claim to have been the first Italians to appear on the Grand Ole Opry.

In 1968, Dave Doucette formed a quintet in Las Vegas called the Stereomonics with Eddie Gordon, an outstanding musician at home on all the harmonicas whom Doucette often cited as the finest chord player ever. As their name implied, the group's trademark was a heavily amplified sound. Doucette and Gordon even coaxed Johnny O'Brien to come out of retirement and join them briefly, but by the end of 1969 the Stereomonics were down to a trio. After an eight-week stint at Las Vegas' Frontier Hotel ended with no other bookings in sight, Doucette went back to work behind the bar.

In 1975, Doucette was contacted by Tom Stryker, a talented player from California who had helped to organize a group in San Jose called the Big Harp that was successfully reviving the seven- or eight-piece harmonica group sound and using Doucette's old arrangements. Stryker invited Doucette to appear as a special guest at the Big Harp's annual Christmas party and sent him an airline ticket.

This was the beginning of a new phase in Doucette's long and remarkable career, for he stayed on in San Jose to become the Big Harp's musical director. He was soon working with several California harmonica bands, and in his typical workmanlike fashion, Doucette was inspired to produce several new original harmonica compositions over the next few years, including "Le Petit Overture." He died in 1983.

Paul Draper soars while Larry Adler solos.

The Soloists

Along with the harmonica groups, vaudeville spawned many individual performers on the mouth organ. Some were comedians who used the harmonica as a convenient prop. There was the popular Britt Wood, a funnyman who between gags treated audiences to renditions of maudlin tunes like the syrupy "My Buddy" on his Marine Band. The performances of Lynn Mayberry, a well-known comedienne on American stages who patterned her act after Fanny Brice's, always featured her diatonic playing.

The most successful of the harmonica-playing vaudeville humorists was Herb Shriner. A folksy comedian and monologist in the vein of Will Rogers, Shriner used the harmonica primarily for laughs; onstage he would produce a variety of trick instruments, including a harmonica that housed an electric shaver and another with a neon tube hidden inside it that would light up in his hands while he played. At the height of his popularity Hohner issued Herb Shriner diatonic and chromatic models. Shriner had a genuine love for the harmonica and valued the company of virtuoso players. In the early 1950s he assembled the cream of the New York harmonicists for a recording session. An all-star lineup including Charles Leighton, Alan "Blackie" Schackner, Cham-Ber Huang, Don Henry, Frank Mitkowski, and Alan Pogson recorded several sides that were issued on Columbia.

By the 1930s there were several serious mouth organists working in vaudeville, including Bob Coffey and Stan Robinson, a black instrumentalist and bandleader who performed in white tie and tails and whose act was climaxed by a frenetic version of "Tiger Rag" played on an assortment of polyphonias. Another of the earliest—and by far the most successful—professional harmonica soloists in America was Larry Adler.

Larry Adler (1914–)

Neville Cardus of the *Manchester Guardian* has unblinkingly compared Larry Adler with Paganini, stating firmly that "it would be hard to prove that anybody playing any instrument in the world of music today plays with more than Mr. Adler's art and virtuosity."

"Many people don't realize that Larry is the granddaddy of them all," says Jerry Adler. "He created the whole field. He made the breakthrough when the harmonica was considered a toy; it was a major chore for him to get anyone to listen to him seriously."

Adler's musical talent is matched, if not exceeded, by a keen ambition. Adler decided as a boy that stardom awaited him, and he stalked it ruthlessly. Other harmonica players have derided his towering ego ("He won't be satisfied until he dies in his own arms," goes one gibe), but complaining about Adler's self-absorption is not unlike criticizing the landing gear of the Wright brothers' first airplane. The salient point is that Adler was the first harmonica soloist to get off the ground, and he took his instrument with him.

"Baltimore was an awful place to be born and I spent my first fourteen years plotting my escape," Adler writes in his autobiography. "My parents didn't have exceptionally musical dispositions," Adler told Albert Raisner, "but their Jewish faith led to me being immersed in religious music." As a boy Adler briefly studied piano at Baltimore's Peabody Conservatory of Music; legend has it he was expelled at the age of ten for not being able to resist a perverse urge to play "Yes, We Have No Bananas" at a piano recital. Adler's own recollection is that "I was rejected because of my total absence of aptitude and an incorrigibly bad ear."

"I have told and written that my first experience with the harmonica was when Fred Sonnen formed the Baltimore Harmonica Band when I was about twelve," Adler told me. "But I've also since found a press clipping that shows me at the age of nine in a harmonica contest. I don't remember that at all. What I wanted to be was a concert pianist; I was very much impressed by Rachmaninoff. But I was the only student ever expelled from the Peabody Conservatory. Once you get expelled from music school, you realize that somebody is trying to tell you something. When I read about this harmonica band being formed, I just went down there and got in the band."

Within a year Adler managed to win a mouth organ contest sponsored by the *Baltimore Sun*. Adler's resolutely individualistic approach was already conspicuous: his winning effort was a performance on the chromatic harmonica of Beethoven's Minuet in G, a choice that stood in marked contrast to the popular tunes offered up by the other youthful contestants. "When I read in the *Baltimore Sun*, 'Lawrence Cecil Adler is Baltimore's best harmonica player,'" admits Adler, "it went to my head." In the full flush of this first triumph, Adler decided that his future was on the stage. A friend had once introduced him to Nat Brusilof, a staff violinist with the NBC orchestra, and the fourteen-year-old Adler went to New York with $35 in his pocket and headed straight for the unsuspecting Brusilof's apartment.

The violinist finagled an audition for Adler with Borrah Minevitch. "I played my heart out because to me Minevitch was God. When I finished playing, Minevitch said, 'Kid, you stink.' I started to cry. Johnny Puleo said, 'Aw, why don't you let the kid come onstage with us for one show?' and Minevitch said, 'Get him outta here.'" It is difficult to imagine a chronic iconoclast such as Adler being part of any group effort, much less one led by the tyrannical Minevitch, and Adler has

pointed out that eventually there would have been a musical collision. "I didn't produce the Minevitch sound, which depended on a
throat vibrato. I never liked that sound, I wouldn't use it, and I never
would have fit in."

Brusilof came through again, this time helping Adler get a job playing on the sound track of a cartoon short. The recording session was
held in the Paramount Theater Building, and afterward Adler sought
out the headliner there, bandleader Paul Ash, and auditioned for him
on the spot. The result was the start of Adler's vaudeville career. First
came a cross-country tour with a Paramount unit during which the
young mouth organist was introduced to audiences in each city as a
local boy who had been discovered just minutes before by the master
of ceremonies playing outside the stage door. Then there was another
road trip, this time with Adler playing the mouth organ while two
men wrestled a bear.

"No show then had amplification," recalls Adler. "I played without a
microphone, accompanied by a full pit orchestra, and they *heard* me.
Maybe in those days people simply listened. But I still can't figure out
how they could hear a little mouth organ in a large theater. I wouldn't
dare play under those conditions today."

Adler made his recording debut about this time—his version of the
event has him being kidnapped by singer Ruth Etting's mobster
boyfriend for a session. At sixteen, Adler landed a part on Broadway
in Flo Ziegfeld's *Smile* and found himself befriended by the show's
star, Eddie Cantor, with whom he shared a striking physical resem-
blance. Adler met many of the right people in Broadway's rarified circle through Cantor.

Thanks to his rejection by Minevitch, Adler was a soloist from the
beginning, but in the early years Adler usually performed in ragamuffin garb à la the Harmonica Rascals. His repertoire at this stage of his
career consisted mostly of popular tunes; his big numbers were
"Smoke Gets in Your Eyes" and a rousing version of Ravel's *Bolero*.

Adler broke into films in 1934 when he was signed by Paramount
to appear in the film *Many Happy Returns*. He arrived on the set already grousing about the $300 he was earning for his cameo appear-
ance, then balked absolutely when he learned that Guy Lombardo
and His Royal Canadians were slated to accompany him. The twenty-
year-old Hollywood newcomer announced that Lombardo's music
was not to his taste and demanded that a more suitable orchestra be
retained to accompany him. After a week-long standoff, Adler point-

edly mentioned to the studio head that Duke Ellington was filming on an adjacent lot, and a few days later the scene was filmed with Ellington's orchestra backing up Adler.

Adler had come to the attention of the famed English impresario Charles Cochran, who arranged a 1934 tour of Great Britain that was a major breakthrough for the harmonica-playing dynamo. Under Cochran's guidance, Adler sought to upgrade his image. The Huck Finn stage attire was discarded in favor of formal evening dress, and Adler worked feverishly at expanding his classical repertoire.

Cochran had arranged Adler's schedule of appearances as if his protégé were the typical promising young classical performer. Adler needed to become identified with fresh material: Cochran commissioned Cyril Scott to write a serenade for harmonica and piano. Adler needed to appear with a full orchestra: a concert with Australia's Sydney Symphony was arranged. There was the matter of the obligatory debut recital: Cochran booked Adler in London's prestigious Wigmore Hall, where the mouth organist performed an ambitious program that included several Bach pieces, the slow movement from Mozart's Oboe Quartet, K. 370, and pieces by Debussy, Ravel, Falla, Stravinsky, Bartók, Poulenc, and Walton. The reviews the next day were uniformly positive. Larry Adler had placed the harmonica firmly on the legitimate concert stage.

Adler's first commercial recording, "Smoke Gets in Your Eyes," sold 200,000 copies. When Hohner announced that they planned to bring out a Larry Adler chromatic model, there were 360,000 advance sales. English composer William Walton declared that there were only two great instrumentalists in the world—Yehudi Menuhin and Larry Adler. During the late 1930s Adler played extensively in Europe, South Africa, and Australia. He returned to the United States in 1938 to find that he had been essentially forgotten here.

A series of concerts with the Chicago Symphony resurrected his career in America, and Adler signed a recording contract with RCA Victor. His recording of an abbreviated version of Ravel's *Bolero*—Adler gave such a physical performance during the recording session that he broke a tooth—became a best-seller in Europe and the United States. (Adler was once summoned to meet the composer after performing the piece in Paris. After listening to Adler's recording, Ravel seemed uncomfortable; his only comment was a plaintive, "Why don't you play it all?")

Although he routinely improvises when playing popular material,

Adler has admitted that "I am not now, nor have I ever been, a jazz musician. This does not disbar me, happily, either from liking jazz or from the pleasure of making music with jazz musicians." Adler's most successful brush with jazz occurred during a stay in Paris in the spring of 1938. Sitting in the audience at a concert by the Quintette du Hot Club, an outstanding group led by the legendary gypsy guitarist Django Reinhardt, Adler was called onstage by the master of ceremonies. When Adler explained that he had not brought a harmonica with him, Django said, "I've got one," and pulled a chromatic out of his pocket. This encounter led to Reinhardt's group backing Adler at a recording session for Columbia. Four sides—"Body and Soul," "Lover Come Back to Me," "My Melancholy Baby," and "I Got Rhythm"—were issued; they are stunning improvisations, with Adler, no doubt inspired by the caliber of his accompaniment, running phenomenal solos over the quintet's propulsive vamping. "No artist flings a word like *genius* around lightly, particularly about a fellow artist," Adler says, "but Django is the one person I wouldn't hesitate to call a genius. Playing with him didn't mean just a few hours of excitement, but a few far too short hours when I really felt I'd learnt something."

After the United States entered World War II, Adler attempted to enlist but was turned down because of his poor eyesight. He volunteered his services to the USO, for whom he made many appearances while keeping up a demanding personal schedule. In 1941 alone, he performed with the Bronx Symphony, the Cleveland Symphony, the Philadelphia Summer Symphony, and the New York Philharmonic. Sandwiched in between were movie appearances, record dates, vaudeville shows, and radio performances.

In November of 1941, Adler premiered a concerto for harmonica and orchestra written for him by Jean Berger. Adler had never learned to read music ("I always learned my scores completely by ear, and it was usually sufficient to hear a piece twice to be able to play it back"), but now that contemporary composers were writing complex works for him, Adler had to step up to the challenge of deciphering musical notation.

He was soon put to the test. In 1943, after a performance with the San Francisco Symphony, Adler was visited backstage by the French composer Darius Milhaud. Adler asked Milhaud to compose a work for him. The result was *Suite for Harmonica and String Orchestra,* the first piece that Adler learned wholly from written notation. In his autobiography, Milhaud mentions how he tried to ensure that his work would outlive Adler's career. "Fearing . . . that the suite might never be played again, once the soloist's exclusive rights had lapsed, I wrote another version for violin and orchestra."

Milhaud's music was celebrated for its complexity, and Adler struggled with the piece. ("I could not understand it, could not grasp it.") Milhaud's *Suite* was finally premiered in Paris in May 1947. Adler may have overprepared; midway through the first movement his concentration failed him and he lost his place. He desperately faked typically Milhaudian phrases until regaining his footing. "In my panic I had a vision," Adler recalled later. "I saw in front of me a review of the concert as it would appear next day in the *New York Herald Tribune*. It made uncomfortable reading."

Adler was more cheered by the reviews garnered by his next project, a partnership with dancer Paul Draper. "Paul was the first to combine ballet and tap dancing. I got the idea of trying a classical recital with him. He would do his solo and I would do my solo and we would perform together at the end of each half of the concert. And at the end of the second half, we would have the audience call out things and I would play a medley of their requests and Paul would dance to it. This was a very, very successful combination. I think that at one point we were the highest-paid concert attraction in the world."

The early 1950s marked both the high point in Adler's career—he was making over $150,000 a year—and the peak of cold-war political conservatism in America. Adler was an outspoken and caustic leftist. In 1954, a society matron named Hester McCullough attempted to stop a scheduled appearance by Adler at a Greenwich, Connecticut, nightclub because of what she claimed were the harmonicist's connections with "Red-front organizations." Adler claims that his managers at the William Morris Agency told him that he could either sign a non-Communist affidavit or sue Ms. McCullough for libel. Adler chose the courtroom, and the resulting trial was a donnybrook that received a good deal of publicity before ending in a hung jury and with Adler becoming a victim of the blacklisting plague of the McCarthy era. He was branded, in his words, as "the greatest subversive, Communist, left-wing, agitating, revolutionary character since Zinoviev tried to overthrow the British government, only I was doing the whole thing with a mouth organ." Adler had always been a hit with English audiences, and he and his wife decided to relocate to London with their three children. Adler denied harboring any bitterness toward his native country, although he did not hesitate to criticize specific individuals. Except for a year's stay in the United States in 1959, he has made London his home and professional base since 1949.

In England, Adler met the composer Ralph Vaughan Williams, who asked Adler if the fact that the mouth organist must alternate between exhales and inhales made a true legato impossible. Adler responded by playing a Bach concerto on the spot and challenging the composer to distinguish which notes were blown and which were drawn. Vaughan Williams left the soiree asking for a technical sheet on the dos and don'ts for the harmonica. Three months later, Adler received the completed solo part to a one-movement Vaughan Williams work entitled *Romance in D*. Adler previewed the piece in a New York concert. Irving Kolodin of the *Saturday Review* was there: "One may say that the harmonica is an instrument against all music, as it is understood in any manifestations connected with the names of Bach, Vaughan Williams, etc. That Larry Adler, at his recent appearance in Town Hall, managed to fascinate the attention and sometimes please the ear is the musical happening of the winter most soundly entitled to the term 'phenomenal.'"

Kolodin found Adler's physical performing style disconcerting, however: "The best way to listen to the harmonica . . . is to close the eyes and disassociate the sight from the sound. In the round, with Adler teetering on tiptoes to reach a reluctant reed, opening and closing his cupped hands to approximate the swell box of the organ, throwing in body English where all other resources failed, it seemed too much a losing battle for any reasonable enjoyment. . . . Like any fanatic Adler is so attached to his perpetual headache that he has invited some of the best contemporary minds to devise ways of writing even more difficult music for it, and thus defying generations yet unborn to match his attainment of the unattainable."

Adler officially debuted Vaughan William's *Romance* at a London Promenade Concert in August 1952. At a celebratory party afterward, the composer insisted that his colleague Arthur Benjamin be the author of the next work expressly written for the mouth organ star. In July 1953, Benjamin completed his *Harmonica Concerto*, a piece specifically crafted to show that the harmonica could handle all the standard concerto formulas. A month later Adler premiered for the third consecutive year a new work written expressly for harmonica and orchestra at one of London's Promenade programs. This time it was Malcom Arnold's *Harmonica Concerto, Op. 46.*

Adler, who had turned forty, began to explore other musical avenues. He spent more time at the piano. "Larry happens to be an extremely fine pianist—totally self-taught," contends Jerry Adler. "I was with Larry at a rehearsal for a benefit concert many years ago. He was playing this piano and Vladimir Horowitz walked up to him and said, 'Larry, why don't you throw that little thing that you play down the toilet and stick to the piano?' "

After a year spent studying composition and theory, Adler scored his first motion picture, the 1953 British movie *Geneviève,* which became a surprise hit in Europe and America. Adler found himself nominated for an Academy Award under a pseudonym. ("I was blacklisted at the time, and my name was taken off the film.") He lost out to Dimitri Tiomkin's music for *The High and the Mighty,* but Adler went on to score fifteen films, including *King and Country* and *High Wind in Jamaica.* He has also written music for many BBC television programs. It has been a remarkable output for a musician who did not learn to read music until midcareer.

After he signed a recording contract with RCA Victor in 1967, Adler became a more frequent visitor to his native country. He was featured in concert with the New York Philharmonic for the first time in more than twenty years, but an article in *Time* magazine displayed the same prejudices that had always bedeviled his career: "His tongue-twisting technique and feathery phrasing have dazzled concert audiences for more than a quarter century; but purists still dismiss his performances of classical music as gimmickry, akin to playing horn concertos on a length of garden hose." He told *Time* that he was depressed over the thought of the uniqueness of his legacy. "What I know is likely to die with me. At the moment I feel I'm a kind of footnote in musical history. I've put something into concert music that wasn't there before." In February 1977, Adler commissioned an *Armenian Rhapsody for Mouth Organ and Orchestra* from Aram Khachaturian, who thus became the thirteenth composer to write a piece for the harmonicist.

In a 1960 interview with Albert Raisner, Adler confessed that "in twenty-five years in show business, I have used every trick imaginable to make the harmonica more attractive, to better 'sell' my music. I would be happy to do without all this at the present and to let my conscience guide me instead of the reaction of the public. The essential thing is to play good music on your instrument . . . it is not necessary to put music to the service of the harmonica, but the harmonica to the service of music."

For years Adler played the twelve-hole #270 Chromonica, but he eventually adopted the Silver Concerto model. "I now find that this may have been a mistake, because it is so heavy that I think it has militated against my technique. If you are doing a two-hour recital, you feel it by the end. I think I prefer the original twelve-hole chromatic. I was fooled by the fact that I could get a rather mellower sound on the Silver Concerto. But if I can find some good, early twelve-hole mouth organs, I may go back to them."

Larry Adler recently celebrated his fiftieth anniversary in show business. He continues to perform, although rarely, and he's not shy about expressing his profound disinterest in modern popular music. "Few musicians today are attracted by the meretricious product that passes for music in this Age of the Gimmick," he wrote in the liner notes to a recent album. "Every one of the songs [here] have lyrics fashioned by men who respected the English language and I wish that I could sing them on my harmonica. I think that the harmonica is, in fact, a singing instrument but it does tend to mess up its consonants."

"I consider myself a classical player," Adler told me. "When I'm with good jazz musicians, I love playing jazz, but I think I'm basically a classical player. That has been my main interest since I heard Rachmaninoff as a boy.

"The technical limitations of the harmonica are considerable. I can't get all of the intervals and chords that a violin can get, and there are a lot of violin passages I can't play, but even Jascha Heifetz once recommended certain violin pieces to me that he felt could be better played on the harmonica. What is great about the mouth organ is the singing tone that you can get from it. You can get a sound that is very near the *vox humana,* the human voice. I love it for that reason."

Charles Newman (1915–)

It was 1942, and Charles Leighton of the Cappy Barra Harmonica Gentlemen was relaxing between shows in the wings of a Los Angeles vaudeville theater, mentally critiquing the performance of a well-known exotic dancer. "She used a parrot in her act," recalls Leighton, "that had been trained to remove bits of her clothing." This would have been remarkable enough, but during her finale a man, stripped to the waist and wearing a turban, appeared on the stage apron and squatted behind a tom-tom as the pit orchestra launched into Ravel's *Bolero.* While the dancer—with the parrot's assistance—stripped, the man pulled out a chromatic harmonica and began playing Ravel's well-known theme on it while simultaneously beating out an insistent rhythm on the tom-tom with his other hand.

"I suddenly realized that it was Charles Newman," remembers Leighton. "He was one of the first harmonica soloists and had done a lot of radio. I was very curious to meet him. We must have played a week on the same bill with Newman, and after every show we would go looking for him backstage. We never did find him."

Charles Newman started playing the harmonica as a boy in Phoenix, Arizona. By the time he was nineteen he was broadcasting over KFRC in San Francisco, exposure that led to stints with the society orchestras of Horace Heidt and Paul Whiteman.

In 1934, Newman's chromatic playing was being featured on bandleader Fred Waring's nationwide radio broadcasts. "I did a virtuoso act that featured a lot of fast, startling runs," he recalls. Newman had developed a dense technique characterized by chords, double stops, tongue switching, and a heavy use of bass accompaniment. His challenging repertoire favored well-known classical violin pieces and a stunning interpretation of Chopin's *Fantasie Impromptu.* Newman tried to interest Waring in adding some jazz numbers to the program, but the bandleader was not receptive to the new music. After Waring's radio show was cancelled, Newman spent some time in England before returning to the United States and launching a career as a soloist in vaudeville.

In the late 1930s, a new record label, Decca, jolted the phonograph industry by releasing some Bing Crosby 78s whose remarkable quality was the result of a new electrical recording process. One of the next beneficiaries of this superior technology was Charles Newman, who in 1938 recorded eight sides for Decca, including a masterful version of Sarasate's *Zieguenerweisen,* that ranked as the finest harmonica recordings available at the time. "I remember hearing Charles Newman's records when I was a kid." says Don Les. "He was perfection on records, absolute perfection."

After the demise of vaudeville, Newman settled in southern California and concentrated on playing jazz on the chromatic harmonica, the harmonetta, and the guitar in local clubs. ("When I first heard Toots Thielemans on record, I thought perhaps it was me playing— that's how much we sounded alike," he claims.) Still active in his late seventies, Newman prides himself in being able to serve up jazz in all its forms, from traditional to bebop to the most current stylings.

Leo Diamond (1915–66)

Leo Diamond continued his feverish professional pace even after he and his brother Abe stepped off the Minevitch treadmill in the early 1940s. The Diamonds made for Hollywood, where they convinced Richard Hayman to join them in a group called the Harmonica Solidaires. When Hayman left the group after adding quite a few arrangements to their book, George Fields was called in from the East Coast to take his place. The Solidaires worked steadily in films and television and on radio for several years.

Ever since his earliest days with Minevitch, Leo Diamond had been obsessed with finding new sounds and settings for the harmonica, and he stepped up his search now that he had complete creative control. The Solidaires were one of the first harmonica groups to use amplified harmonicas. (Diamond's group was originally outfitted with contact mikes placed on the players' throats; they later used one of the first electronic pickups made for the harmonica.)

Leo Diamond began making frequent trips to the Hollywood studios to do session work on the sound tracks of feature films and some original scoring for George Pal's cartoons. When Abe Diamond left show business to open a music store, Leo concentrated on his career as a session player and began recording as a soloist.

During the 1950s, record labels were busy hyping "high fidelity," a new recording technique that was a precursor to true stereo, by releasing a slew of sound-effects records. Diamond's penchant for such experiments made this period in the record business a very successful one for him; he recorded many single releases and a dozen albums for such labels as RCA, Roulette, ABC, and Reprise. In 1953, Diamond resurrected a twenty-year-old original tune called "Off Shore" and recorded an echo-laden version of it that became one of the rare solo harmonica hit recordings.

The most atmospheric of Diamond's many compositions was his

tone poem "The Skin Diver Suite," which he recorded for RCA. As a publicity stunt that hinted of his training in the Minevitch organization, Diamond researched the piece by submerging himself in a tank at Marineland, from where, he told reporters, he would "listen to the sounds of the deep."

In Pete Pedersen's opinion, "Leo was very much ahead of his time with the harmonica. What he accomplished was the first really organized harmonica music. Few people have ever come up to his level as far as harmonica arranging is concerned." According to Richard Hayman, Diamond "got more sounds out of the harmonica than anyone else. He had a sweeter tone. He perfected the idea of vibrato."

A bona fide workaholic, Diamond was trying to establish a harmonica workshop studio and writing an instruction method at the time of his death.

Mike Chimes (1914–84)

With the disintegration of vaudeville, his professional base for more than twenty years, Mike Chimes returned to his native New York City. He became a top session player there, lending his talents to innumerable commercials and sound tracks, and performing and recording with Frank Sinatra, Neil Diamond, Johnny Mathis, Perry Como, Harry Belafonte, Pete Seeger, André Kostelanetz, and Gladys Knight, among others. During the 1950s and 1960s, he teamed with his wife and two young sons in an act called—appropriately—The Chimes Family.

One of the most respected and well-liked of the harmonica veterans, Chimes continued to gig steadily as a guitarist and harmonicist in nightclubs and also wrote an instruction method for the harmonica.

Pete Pedersen (1925–)

After his eight-year stint with the Minevitch Rascals, Pete Pedersen maintained his link with the harmonica world by doing most of the arranging for the Harmonicats' many recordings. "He is the best in the world for writing for groups or anything else," claims Jerry Murad.

After leaving the Rascals, Pedersen joined Fuzzy Feldman and Don

Henry in the Don Henry Trio; the group recorded several excellent sides for Regent, including a hit version of "The Saber Dance." After three years with Henry, Pedersen and Feldman spent nearly a decade together as a duo. a period highlighted by the pair's eight appearances on "The Ed Sullivan Show." Pedersen eventually moved to Memphis and began working as a composer for "the world's largest jingle factory."

In 1976, Pedersen was hired by Butterfly Records, a subsidiary of Polygram, to travel to Canada and produce a disco record. The resulting single, "Too Hot for Love," was a huge hit, reaching number one on the U.S. dance charts for a brief period. Pedersen decided to stay in Canada, but during the five years he spent there "the disco business when right down the tube" and he went back to his career as a free-lance music writer. "When I decided to get serious about working again," says Pedersen, "I came back to Memphis," where today he and a partner own a successful music production company.

Pedersen still performs as a harmonicist, and his skills as both a player and as an emcee keep him in demand at harmonica functions around the country. A beautiful performance by Pedersen of his own excellent arrangement of Gershwin's *An American in Paris* was featured recently on a harmonica sampler album, *Heavy Duty Harpin'*, distributed by Hohner. He is one of the most thoroughly musical of the great chromatic harmonica soloists.

In recent years Pedersen has become active in a promotional campaign behind the Millioniser, an electronic synthesizer designed by Swiss harmonica player Walt Miller. "You can't consider the Millioniser a harmonica," admits Pedersen. "That's the biggest mistake you could make. It's a high-tech synthesizer. There's an advantage in that a harmonica player can play it. You can get a kind of expression out of it that you can't get out of a keyboard synthesizer. It has a great vocabulary of sounds and an incredible range of something like eleven octaves. You can get a tuba sound, you can get a violin sound, you can play chords, you can hook it up to any number of MIDI instruments and play them as well as your own sounds simultaneously.

"Now harmonica players don't have to worry about competing with anybody. You can go out there and bang it out with any kind of instrument. You're really playing in the big leagues now. But you have to play it musically in order to make it happen. The instrument and the instrumentalist are two different things."

• • •

Richard Hayman (1920–)

After the Diamond brothers bolted from the Harmonica Rascals, one of the group's members, twenty-year-old Richard Hayman, became its principal arranger. Although Hayman had not had any formal musical training, he had learned to play the harmonica, guitar, and accordion as a boy and had gained his first experience as a musical director teaching his schoolboy harmonica band, The Harmonica Sparklers, to read music. He joined the Harmonica Rascals right out of high school, eventually leaving Minevitch to play and arrange with Leo Diamond's Harmonica Solidaires.

By the time Hayman parted company with Diamond, he was determined to make a career as a writer and arranger, and he began working with various singers and performers in Las Vegas and Hollywood. George Stoll, then the musical director for MGM, was an early mentor; he put Hayman to work on such films as *Girl Crazy, Meet Me in St. Louis,* and *As Thousands Cheer.*

In 1952, Hayman was hired to arrange the score for the film *Ruby Gentry,* which featured George Field's rendition of the title theme. He recorded a harmonica version of the song that same year that became a major hit and resulted in a resurgence in the mouth organ's popularity.

Hayman spent the next twelve years as musical director of Mercury Records. He also began arranging for Arthur Fiedler's Boston Pops orchestra, an association that has lasted for three decadess. He parlayed this experience into a chance to become a pops conductor in his own right; he is currently the principal pops conductor with the St. Louis Symphony, the Detroit Symphony, the Alabama Symphony, the Hartford Symphony, and the Calgary Philharmonic and has appeared as guest conductor with, among others, the Boston Pops, the Buffalo Philharmonic, the Pittsburgh Symphony, the Indianapolis Symphony, the Dallas Symphony, the Atlanta Symphony, and the Vancouver Symphony.

Hayman's affinity for singers has made him a popular musical director for touring shows; he has traveled as musical director for such stars as Bob Hope, Tom Jones, Engelbert Humperdinck, Red Skelton, The Carpenters, The Osmonds, Roy Clark, Pat Boone, Bobby Vinton, and Mike Douglas.

Hayman has recorded under his own name since the early 1950s and currently has over fifty albums to his credit. Perhaps the most unusual of these was recorded during the mid-1950s, when Hayman assembled the best of the New York harmonica elite, including Charles Leighton, Blackie Schackner, and Eddy Manson, for a session as "Richard Hayman's Harmonica Orchestra." Hayman was an early booster of pop groups like the Beatles, and in the late 1960s he released an album, *The Genuine Electric Latin Love Machine,* that featured his harmonica fed through a Moog synthesizer accompanied by electric organ and electric harpsichord. As a player, Hayman is noted for his strong vibrato, his clean phrasing, and for his preference for the #270 chromatic tuned to A instead of to the more usual key of C.

Hayman has also somehow found time to compose. He has written extensively for television, including the arranging for a nine-part PBS series on Mark Twain. Several of his compositions have become standard pieces in the repertoires of orchestras and bands throughout the world. In 1978 he premiered his own *Concerto No. 1 for Harmonica and Orchestra* with the Detroit Symphony.

Alan "Blackie" Schackner (1917–)

"No matter how good you play, it gets boring. You've got to give them a little breath. And then give them something different. And then hit them again." Classic show business wisdom from a streetwise oracle named Alan "Blackie" Schackner.

Schackner started playing the harmonica as a child with Murray Lane's group. He was a member of the original Broadway cast of William Saroyan's Pulitzer Prize–winning play, *The Time of Your Life,* and a regular on radio's "The Kate Smith Hour" in the early 1940s. After honing his talents on the stages of the borscht belt resorts, Schackner toured for a time with Milton Berle and joined the cast of Arthur Godfrey's television show. Between engagements, he managed to graduate from the New York College of Music and to squeeze in further study at New York University, training that enabled him to compose original music for several motion picture and theater productions and to become a sought-after New York session player.

The only harmonica player to have been celebrated in *Ripley's Believe It or Not* ("Harmonica Virtuoso Can Play the Famous Violin Solo Hora Staccato—A Total of 1,096 Notes—In 90 Seconds!"), Schackner has appeared in concert with the likes of Robert Merrill and Sergio Franchi. He realized a lifelong ambition by giving a recital in New

York's Town Hall with Cy Coleman, the composer, accompanying him. A frequent television performer, Blackie has appeared on the "Ed Sullivan Show," the "David Frost Show," and "What's My Line" (on which he taught Beverly Sills and Gene Shalit how to play the harmonica), and he has written five best-selling instruction books.

These days, Blackie talks about the physical demands of being on the road several times a year playing resorts and cruise ships (a lifestyle symbolized by his compact traveling case efficiently broken down into separate compartments for his harmonicas, his file folders stuffed with arrangements, and a pair of gleaming, patent-leather stage shoes), but it is impossible to imagine him out of harness. Despite his technical credentials, Blackie would no doubt prefer to have his résumé filed under *entertainer*.

Interview With Blackie Schackner

I grew up on the Lower East Side in New York. I guess you could say I had a colorful childhood. My father, a wonderful man, was a hustler who ran gambling joints.

I became very interested in the harmonica because an older friend played it. I used to sleep with it under my pillow. Victor Pankowitz, who pioneered a lot of harmonica techniques, was a boyhood friend. He turned me on to tongue switching—playing out of both sides of your mouth. For some pieces, that technique comes in very handy. I eventually appeared on the "Horn and Hardart Children's Hour." I did a different song each week; it was good training. Paul Douglas, who later became a big star in the movies, was the announcer. He was the one who gave me the nickname Blackie, because I was always getting sunburned from swimming in the East River in the summer.

I went from high school into the Murray Lane Harmonica Band. It was a marvelous group. There were a lot of harmonica bands then. Larry Adler was big, and there was a lot of work. After my stint with Murray Lane, I got a wonderful job at the Academy of Music and stayed there for several years. I would play in between films with this organist, a woman named Louise Rush, who taught me quite a bit about music. I did so well there that I got a second job at the Jefferson Theater, which was also on Fourteenth Street. They had it set up so the organist at the Jefferson would go on a half an hour before the organist at the Academy of Music.

I was shuttling back and forth and making $125 a week, which was more than my father was making at the time. I was a big man in the neighborhood in those days. Later, when these jobs fizzled out, my mother came to me and said, "You're going to be a bum. There's not enough work in show business. You'll have to get a regular job." I passed a civil service test and got a job for about $25 a week.

After about a year, I passed an audition and got a job with the Broadway production of William Saroyan's *The Time of Your Life*, which ended up winning the Pulitzer. I played a newsboy who wanted to be a great singer. I didn't play any harmonica onstage, but they had a scene where a young kid named Gene Kelly danced while an old Arab played a harmonica. The guy who played the Arab faked it and I actually played the harmonica offstage. I worked that show for two years.

I lost three years out of my life because of World War II. I was a tank man; I taught hand-to-hand combat. After the war, I started working the borscht belt. There was a lot of work in the Catskills at the time. I still hold the all-time record for most appearances at the famous Concord Hotel. I had the kind of act—straight down the middle—that worked for the convention crowds. I even do some Beatles tunes in my act.

I always worked as a solo, accompanied by whatever orchestra would be there. If you get a good orchestra or a good pianist, that's a big thrill. Sometimes you work and you get some really lousy musicians—then it's ulcer time. Since you have to depend on your arrangements, I write them myself, so I know what's in them. When I work, I try to reach the people, to communicate. After playing the virtuoso stuff, I'll get down to earth. You keep them entertained as well as give them good music. That's the name of the game; that's why people will hire you.

One of my favorite projects was writing the original music for the film *Portrait of Jennie*. A song of mine, "The Happy Cobbler," was successful for me. I've done concerts with many fine entertainers, including Bob Hope and Bob Newhart. I did an evening with the Washington Symphony where I played and conducted. That was a big thrill for me.

In 1956, I wrote an instruction book called *Anyone Can Play the Harmonica* that was put out with an accompanying record. I've also written a book on blues harp. I'll play a little diatonic occasionally. I can bend all the notes and everything, but I don't like to play the Marine Band because it screws me up when I go back to the chromatic. A lot of diatonic players can't play the chromatic; it's a more involved instrument, and they don't want to take the time to learn it.

In the old days, there were so many places to work. A lot of the guys are in trouble now because they have nowhere to work. The recording business is down now. I love session work because recording musicians are generally the very best. I mostly play and read on a C chromatic, but I carry the others in case they want some double stops that work better in another key.

I'm a Hohner man most of the time. I play the #270. It feels like it's part of you; it fits nicely in the hand. You can do anything on it. The 64 Chromonica is too big, and the low notes hang up on it. To my mind, the #270 has more guts. Hohner makes it in two different configurations; one has longer reeds. I prefer that model because it usually lasts longer.

If you play a chromatic tuned to 440, right away you're out of tune, because very often the piano is tuned a little brilliant, so the whole orchestra is slightly sharp. And they'll say, "Oh, those damn harmonicas." I usually play 443s. On recording dates I'll bring a 440, a 443, and a 445. You have to order them from the factory.

Frankly, it's surprising that the harmonica sounds as good as it does, considering its size. I would like to see a chromatic with a wooden comb like the #270, nuts and bolts fasteners for the reeds, screws to tighten the plates, some slight changes to the mouthpiece, and a good, solid chrome plate. That, to me, would be an ideal harmonica.

I practice every day. I hate it, but I do it because I have to. I can't start to slip. If anything, I try to get better. But to very honest, I'd much rather be out in the garden growing the vegetables. All that puffing is physically hard. At my age, I should be taking it easy, but whatever it was that drove you in the first place to be better than the next guy is the same thing that continues to drive me.

You have to do your job. You have to learn your business. There are a lot of so-called harmonica players who just learn one or two songs and consider themselves virtuosos. Thankfully, there are quite a few players around who are legitimate pioneers and excellent players. Toots Thielemans plays a very fine grade of jazz. Eddy Manson and Charley Leighton are fine players. Richard Hayman is not only a great player but a good conductor as well. Stan Harper is a very good player. These guys elevate the harmonica's status—they don't bring it down.

Sonny Terry

Folk Music

The harmonica was first and foremost a folk instrument. The German craftsmen who created the mouth organ in the early 1800s had in mind a musical novelty that would appeal to the masses, not an instrument that would compete against the likes of the piano or the violin. They made their harmonica small, adopted a diatonic scale instead of a fully chromatic scheme, and arranged its notes so that players could easily achieve the major tonic and the minor sixth, which could be substituted for the dominant seventh so common in folk melodies.

Contemporary folk musicians in America tend to gravitate to the traditional music of the South, which was the first folk music to be commercially recorded. The conventional wisdom has long held that the folk music developed there mirrored its segregated social system—that there were two separate-but-equal strains, one created by blacks (which led to the blues) and the other the product of whites (which formed the basis for commercial country music)—but this notion is simplistic. In Dixie the two races not only worked and lived in close proximity but also shared their musical repertoires. Musical boundaries were more often based on class than race: the gulf between the music played in the drawing rooms of the homes of the Southern elite and that played on the back porches of rural folk (black or white) was far greater than the relatively narrow breach between country music and the blues. African American banjoists and fiddlers who played jigs and reels were common in the South at the turn of the century, and white musicians were quick to appreciate—and imitate—the unique approach and feeling that blacks brought to their adopted instruments.

The early record companies were slow to define their markets along racial lines. The most successful of them, the Victor Talking Machine Company, did not record black blues singers until 1920; prior to this the label had concentrated on trying to interest African Americans in its Red Seal classical recordings. When record companies began to actively seek out folk talent in the 1920s, they were more interested in the material than in the racial background of the performers. Victor released DeFord Bailey's version of "John Henry" (a song popular with both blacks and whites) coupled with another harmonica instrumental, "Chester Blues," performed by an excellent white mouth harpist named D. H. "Bert" Bilbro. A comparison of the two recordings clearly shows that the two players were spawned from a biracial harmonica tradition that included imitations of fox-and-hound chases and locomotives. Dozens of these ventriloquial tours de force were recorded.

One of the finest of the train imitators was Palmer McAbee, who recorded "McAbee's Railroad Piece" and "Lost Boy Blues" in Atlanta in February of 1928. The sounds of the steam locomotive—the hissing boilers; the haunting whistle; the clamorous rhythm of the wheels against the tracks; the sudden muting of the machine's roar as it enters a tunnel; the squeal of air brakes—all are beautifully depicted in McAbee's solo piece.

In 1929 harmonica player Freeman Stowers recorded several sides in Indiana for Gennett. The label dubbed him "The Cotton Belt

Porter," and his train piece, "Railroad Blues," may have been based on personal experience. "Railroad Blues"—one of the rare first-position harmonica train songs—re-creates a journey by rail to St. Louis. Stowers wastes as little time as possible depicting the train's departure and its arrival, preferring to showcase his masterful imitations of an onrushing locomotive and the split tones of the steam whistle, achieved by playing a cluster of notes and simultaneously moaning into his harmonica. In his riotous variation on the fox-and-hounds motif, "Texas Wild Cat Blues," Stowers acts out the chase of a wildcat by two men and their dogs, complete with canine yelping and the desperate snarling of their cornered prey. On his recording "Sunrise on the Farm," Stowers imitates a barnyard full of farm animals.

Without vocal references, attributing these instrumental performances to black or white performers is often a matter of conjecture. Freeman Stowers was most likely a black performer, but among his recordings is a "Medley of Blues," which includes "Hog in the Mountain," a hillbilly tune. Palmer McAbee was probably white, but he recorded a blues number. "Race" records for black audiences were introduced in the early 1920s. For several years inclusion in such catalogs was based more on a performer's musical style than on his or her color, but in 1927 the Allen Brothers, white players whose records showed a pronounced blues influence, filed an unsuccessful, $250,000 lawsuit against Columbia when one of their recordings was issued on that label's race series. As the lines became drawn, rural musicians of both races drifted toward their appointed genres: blues and country music.

By the early 1940s the commercialization of such styles had come far enough to inspire a reaction. A loose aggregation of performers—made up for the most part of educated urbanites but also including genuine products of the soil such as the singing guitarist Leadbelly and the master of the talking blues, Woody Guthrie—who shared a taste for traditional music and progressive politics came together in New York City's Greenwich Village. Within a few years, one of these purists' own groups, the Weavers, were recording stars, and the seeds were sown for a folk music revival that reached its peak in the hootenannies of the early 1960s. A charter member of this original New York contingent was a harmonica player named Sonny Terry.

Sonny Terry (1911–86)

Sonny Terry was born Terrell Saunders in Greensboro, Georgia. His sharecropper father was a talented mouth organist with a taste for stunts like playing the harp without using his hands. "He used to play harmonica at them Saturday-night fish fries and some such things. He didn't never do no blues. . . . He done buckdances, reels, and jigs, stuff as that you could dance to."

When not in use, his father's sole harmonica was kept on the fireplace mantel, but by the time Terry was eight he would stand on a chair and reach for it whenever his father was away. After the inevitable discovery, his even-tempered father requested that the boy play him a tune. He must have been suitably impressed; soon after he got the boy a mouth organ of his own, and not long afterward Sonny was playing the harp in church.

Eleven-year-old Terry was amusing himself one day by beating a stick on the kitchen table when a sliver sheared off and lodged in his eye; Sonny lost half his sight. Five years later, a playmate struck him in the head with a chunk of iron and he lost the sight in his good eye. For the rest of his life Terry was only able to distinguish light and dark and vague shapes.

He retreated into his music. "I wouldn't go out of the house because I was ashamed. The only thing I had any interest in was playing my harmonica, and I kept on it night and day. . . . In them days I just as soon died—except for my harmonica. It was a friend who didn't give a damn if I could see or not." All told, he was housebound for two years.

The Saunders moved to Shelby, North Carolina, and it was there that Terry heard his first blues. "I never heard no blues until I was about eighteen years old. . . . The blues seemed to give me more room for my moods. I guess the blues was just part of me, even before I knew it." His father, anxious to see his son make a future for himself, encouraged Terry to think of himself as a professional musician. Terry started playing in the streets and in local harmonica contests, occasionally joining transient medicine shows. Terry remembers listening to DeFord Bailey on the Grand Ole Opry broadcasts. "He was good, but our styles was different 'cause he played more like country western. I was surprised to hear that he had a 'Fox Chase,' too, but he took the hunter part while I took the dogs. I learned

'Alcoholic Blues' from him and some other licks."

Terry was developing his own riffs, too. He taught himself cross harp and came to prefer playing Marine Bands in the keys of A or Bb. Terry discovered early on that he could achieve some unique effects on his small instrument by using his large hands. "I found out . . . that by slappin' my palm against my harmonica hard, I could cut the wind off and get a pumping sound." Terry would later stun urban folk audiences by generating a riveting, seamless interplay between his falsetto voice and his Marine Band, but this was a common style among both black and white backwoods harmonica players. Henry Whitter, Alfred Lewis, and Noah Lewis used this kind of call-and-response motif in their fox-chase recordings, all of which were made before 1930. Train songs, coon dog imitations, chestnuts like "Lost John"—all were part of Terry's repertoire. His playing was cleaner and less dense than that of his peers, for he chorded much less often. His mastery of the blues, his beautiful tone, and his irrepressible rhythmic drive gave him a wider range than any of his contemporaries in either the old-timey or blues camps.

Terry settled in Durham, where he joined forces with a guitar virtuoso and fine singer named Blind Boy Fuller. In 1938, Vocalion released the first recordings of Fuller and Terry. They impressed record producer John Hammond, who invited Terry to New York for an appearance at a "Spirituals to Swing" concert held in Carnegie Hall, where the harmonica master found himself sharing the stage with the likes of Count Basie, Benny Goodman, and Lester Young. Terry's performance was a highlight of the program, but soon he was back in Durham, playing in the streets with Fuller.

Fuller died suddenly in 1940 and Terry teamed up with another singing guitarist, Brownie McGhee. The pair visited New York City in the early 1940s, where they roomed with Huddie Leadbetter, a blues shouter and convicted murderer from Louisiana who had successfully re-created himself as "Leadbelly," folksinger to white urbanites. Leadbelly introduced McGhee and Terry to Woody Guthrie and his other friends in the burgeoning New York folk music scene, and the pair eventually decided to move north; Terry shared an apartment on East Ninth Street with Leadbelly for two years.

Terry and McGhee struggled; for a time in 1943 they were reduced to playing on the streets of Harlem. Their personal relationship became frayed, and McGhee moved to New Jersey to start a small band of his own. Left to his own devices, Terry began working on his singing. (Until then, he had limited his singing to falsetto seconding behind Fuller or McGhee.)

Good fortune appeared in the guise of actor Paul Robeson, who recommended Sonny for a part in a new Broadway musical, *Finian's Rainbow*. At his first rehearsal, Terry balked when he was told that he would have to perform the same tunes in the same way at each performance, but he quickly changed his mind after being told that his salary would be several hundred dollars a week. The show ran for five years.

In 1950, Terry again joined forces with Brownie McGhee. Their playing created a sensation at the Leadbelly Memorial Concert at New York's Town Hall in New York that January, but this first reunion gig was to be their high-water mark for the next five years, and they were soon reduced to playing in small clubs for $5 apiece.

Then Broadway called again, this time with an offer to appear in the debut production of Tennessee Williams's *Cat on a Hot Tin Roof*. McGhee and Terry both appeared in this show during its three-year run. That success was followed by a tour of Europe and a string of U.S. appearances with Pete Seeger. In 1962, McGhee and Terry went out on the road with Harry Belafonte. They signed with a legitimate booking agency for the first time in their careers and finally achieved the professional stability that had eluded them for so long.

McGhee and Terry fought continually on and off stage—by the 1980s they were each playing separate sets—but they were fixtures on the folk circuit for more than two decades. Sonny Terry's profoundly physical approach to the harmonica and his ability to seemingly play and sing simultaneously was never forgotten by anyone who came in contact with it. His live appearances and his many recordings (especially those on the Folkways label) inspired countless neophytes to take up the mouth organ.

Harmonica Frank Floyd (1908–84)

Mississippian "Harmonica Frank" Floyd always contended that he had been sprung from the most basic of circumstances. He had never been given a formal first name, he insisted—"Frank" had been his own idea. As a thirteen-year-old Frank fell under the spell of the records of blues yodeler Jimmie Rodgers, and a year later he began a thirty-year odyssey as a hobo who sang, played the guitar, and blew his harmonica with medicine shows and carnivals, on street corners, in poolrooms, and in town squares throughout the South.

Floyd's music became more influenced by the blues as he grew older. "I just liked blues," he told *Living Blues*. "There was a lot of colored people and all of them played blues. . . . The one I liked at first was Blind Lemon Jefferson. I have one of his records and wouldn't part with it for nothin'. . . . Now the harp players, from days gone by there was El Watson, Palmer McAbee, and William McCoy. In later years, Wayne Raney was the best of all."

Floyd developed a flexible approach that mixed talking blues, hillbilly music, and pop standards with a histrionic stage presence. His first instrument was the harmonica; the guitar came later. Disdaining the usual practice of placing the mouth organ in a holder, he opted instead for sticking it straight into his mouth like a cigar. "I learned to play harp the way I do when I went out to a place in Louisiana and lost my rack. I tried to balance it on the guitar or to have somebody hold it for me, but I finally worked that way out and I've hardly ever used a rack. I believe I'm the only one that's ever played that way." Floyd's ability to sing out of the side of his mouth and to interject melodic mouth harp riffs made for a memorable effect. "Back in my day," Floyd once said in a radio interview, "if you couldn't almost do the impossible, there wasn't nobody who wouldn't give you a penny."

It was a hard life. "You say a white man can't know the blues," Floyd later said. "During the Depression I'd sleep in ditches and know if I died that night, no one would know who I was or where I come from." In 1932, Floyd made a brief side trip to Mexico before ending up in Hollywood, broadcasting over KELW with Buster Steele and the Log Cabin Wranglers. In between spates of hoboing, Floyd would cool his heels performing at radio stations like KLCN in Blytheville, Arkansas, and KTHS in Hot Springs. In 1949, Floyd had a radio program on a Valdosta, Georgia, station.

The following year found Floyd in Memphis, splitting his time between pig farming and sitting in with the Eddie Hill band on broadcasts over WNIC. On July 15, 1951, he became the first white performer to be recorded by legendary producer Sam Phillips, who remembers Floyd as a "very humble" man who was still apt to go off on an occasional spree of rail riding. Some of the cuts recorded at Phillips's studio were leased to the Chess label; two others—"The Great Medical Menagerist" and "Rockin' Chair Daddy"—were eventually issued on Phillips's Sun label, but not until 1954. "Rockin' Chair

Daddy," the result of a request by Phillips for an up-tempo tune, has a distinct rockabilly feel and is held up by some as one of the first rock and roll recordings. But Floyd's fling in the studio was not a satisfying experience for him; years later he complained that Phillips "never give me one penny for my Sun release. Chess sent me one check for one hundred dollars—that was all." Phillips later admitted that he had been at a loss as to how best to exploit Floyd's talents. "Here was a musician I was very much into. He was a modern-day hobo. It was difficult to find a market for him because people appreciated what he did without buying his records that much. He was really out of the old school—a one-man band. . . . If I had been able to spend the money on Frank Floyd, I think he could have become an institution."

Floyd's material was richly varied—he could effortlessly move from talking blues to humorous narratives to comic vaudeville routines to pop tunes to lively, uptempo material—but derivative. "The Great Medical Menagerist" was taken from Chris Bouchillon's "Born In Hard Luck," recorded in the 1920s; Floyd's repertoire included songs based on recordings by bluesmen like Jim Jackson, Blind Boy Fuller, and Bo Carter.

After his stint with Sun, Floyd issued another record on his own label and then moved to Dallas, where he sold ice cream. He was living in Cincinnati when he was tracked down by blues collector Steve LaVere in 1972, a rediscovery that led to a new career playing the college and folk festival circuits.

Floyd was not shy about his place in the scheme of things. He often claimed that he had invented rock and roll, but his opinion of the form was mixed. "Once in a while one of these groups will sound like a dyin' calf in a hailstorm," he noted, "but music's music." He was just as realistic about his own talent. "I learned two styles of music— blues, country or western acts—because I love both styles, but I don't like grand opera at all," he wrote in the liner notes for a 1976 album on Adelphi. "I play my harp in my mouth, in-wise, like a cigar, sing, pick the guitar at the same time. Also, I do lots of imitations with my mouth: chickens, dog, mule, crow, goose, duck."

Peg Leg Sam (1911–77)

The careers of Arthur "Peg Leg Sam" Jackson and Frank Floyd were as similar as their repertoires, further evidence of the common ground between black and white mouth harpists in the rural South between the wars. Jackson grew up in South Carolina hearing his mother play religious music on the organ and accordian and learning the rudiments of the harmonica and tunes like "Lost John" from neighbors. In the 1920s he met Elmon Bell, who taught him a more modern and bluesier style.

From the age of twelve on, Jackson was on the road more often than he was home. His preferred means of transportation was the freight train until 1930, when he lost his right leg in a railroading accident. Jackson carved himself a wooden leg, made his way to New York, and spent the next few years crewing on steamer ships that cruised the Caribbean. He left the sea in 1936 and began broadcasting over the radio in Rocky Mount, North Carolina, while the tobacco market was in session, a seasonal job he continued to hold down for the next twenty-five years on both radio and television.

The rest of each year would be spent on the road with medicine shows and carnivals, although Jackson always pointed out that he preferred busking for tips on street corners. ("I'd rather do that than anything I know.") As a member of the Emmett Smith medicine show in the 1940s, Jackson met Leo Kahdot, a pitchman who called himself Chief Thundercloud; the two were still working together thirty years later, although by that time the medicine show had been pared down to just the two of them: Chief Thundercloud would give the audience the bill of goods about whatever product he was currently selling while Jackson provided the entertainment.

Peg Leg Sam Jackson was an orchestra and sideshow in a single package. In 1960 he had been shot in the face, emerging from the hospital months later with most of his right ear and part of his jaw gone, and a deep, horrible scar that ran from his ear to his mouth. Jackson parted company with Chief Thundercloud in 1973. He bought a small piece of land and began showing up at outdoor music festivals, where his skills were immediately appreciated. Word of him spread, especially after his performance at the Philadelphia Folk Festival was shown on public television. British blues enthusiast Pete Lowry recorded an album's worth of Jackson performances for Trix Records in 1973; before he died there were Peg Leg Sam releases on Flyright and Blue Labor as well. These are invaluable records of the medicine show formula plied by the likes of Jackson and Frank Floyd, a fascinating grab bag that included blues numbers, old-timey songs, toasts, and humorous recitations.

Mel Lyman (?–?)

In the early 1960s the folk boom was surging all over America, and many of the most fervent fans of this genre congregated at Boston's fabled folkspot, the Club 47. One of the most successful acts to come out of the Boston scene was the Jim Kweskin Jug Band, which recorded four albums for Vanguard between 1963 and 1967 and later recorded for Reprise. One of its founding members was a banjoist and harmonica player named Mel Lyman.

Lyman had a mystique about him from the beginning. He made vague references to having hoboed around the country and about learning much of his music during a stay in the hills of North Carolina, but most of his past was a mystery to his bandmates. Lyman rented a room in Jim Kweskin's house, a highly social headquarters for endless parties and trips to the Club 47 to listen to music, but Lyman preferred to closet himself in his room and play Ray Charles records for hours on end. "I asked him once why he never listened to any other kind of music," Kweskin told writer Jim Rooney. "He said, 'Ray Charles contains all music.'" Washtub bass player Fritz Richmond recalls that Lyman was a little out of place in the lively jug band setting, that he was much more at home with slow country blues than with up-tempo jazz numbers. Onstage, Lyman could become so involved in the music that the Jug Band felt the need to structure their sets so that the slower, more emotional tunes that he was partial to were not followed by jump numbers that would break his mood. "When I play, I am a mouth harp," he told Tony Glover. "People who play the harmonica are hung up."

Lyman was establishing himself as a moral and artistic presence within the Jug Band, and his bandmates began paying more attention to his preachings about the power of astrology and the benefits of a macrobiotic diet. One memorable day Lyman announced that he had gotten "a flash" that his wife and four children—who were in Eureka, California—were in danger, and he and Geoff Muldaur drove a van across the country and brought his family back to Cambridge. Within days the newspapers were full of articles about how Eureka had been badly damaged by a tsunami caused by an Alaskan earthquake, and word began to spread around Boston about Lyman's quiet but profound personal aura.

Maria Muldaur has recalled her experiences with Lyman in Jim Rooney and Eric Von Schmidt's excellent book on the Boston folk scene, *Baby Let Me Follow You Down:* "Me and Geoff and Mel Lyman went across the country together. We had lots of adventures. Mel kept a hundred-pound sack of brown rice in his VW bus. He was already on a macrobiotic diet, into astrology, had taken acid, morning glory seeds, and a lot of pot. . . . Mel was getting a reputation as a guru—someone who knew something. Today you can go to the local Rexall and get 'I Ching' books and Tarot cards, but he was one of the first guys to be putting all that together. He was in on one of the first 'if-if' experiments—Leary and Alpert's first acid experiments. So people were starting to come to Mel. . . . He was our spiritual leader, while Jim was our show business leader."

Lyman left the Kweskin band after their first appearance at the 1964 Newport Folk Festival. Maria Muldaur: "I had only been with the Jug Band for a couple of months. . . . So how was I to know in my basic tremulous condition of facing seventeen thousand people that Mel Lyman was so into his harp solo that he wanted to blow at least one, if not two, more choruses. I was not musically and cosmically and sensitively aware of this. So after he did a very lovely solo, I came back in and sang the last verse. . . . That so crimped his musical soul, and I guess he felt we were really going show biz to the point where he quit the band at the end of that weekend."

When Bob Dylan arrived backstage at the 1965 Newport Festival just prior to his first performance in public with an amplified backing group, several people, including Lyman, tried to lecture the unruly troubadour about his responsibility to folk music. As the last notes of Dylan's high-volume set died out, Lyman took it upon himself to soothe the emotions that were running high among the audience as well as backstage, bringing the festival to a close with a solo harmon- ica rendition of "Rock of Ages." By the following year, even Lyman had made at least a qualified peace with commercialism; the program from the 1966 festival included an ad featuring Mel's endorsement of the Hohner Blues Harp.

Lyman had become involved with Jesse Benton, a talented singer and the daughter of the painter Thomas Hart Benton. They bought some property in the Fort Hill section of Boston with a commanding view of the city, and as others joined them, a community began taking shape. The Fort Hill group helped to found Boston's first underground newspaper, *Avatar,* which spread Lyman's teachings—including the notion that folk music was a gift from God that had to be preserved and nurtured—within the counterculture.

"We'd go visit," says Maria Muldaur, "because Mel really had taught us a lot and we loved him. . . . But the people who started surrounding Mel were too rigid and just on too many trips. . . . They invited Geoff to play on a session . . . and at a certain point he said, 'Hey, I love Mel because he's a great guy, not because he's God.' I wasn't there, but apparently a deadly hush fell over the thing, and the next thing he knew he was 'out.' . . . I think that Mel started out as a guy who was truly looking for the truth and thought he had found some answers . . . but the trip of him being worshiped corrupted his best intentions. . . . It started being the 'inner circle' and the 'outer peons,' and you couldn't get in to see Mel, and things got more and more mysterious, and there were more and more slaves on the periphery actually drilling with arms and so on."

Mel Lyman eventually moved to California. He seems to have died there sometime in the 1970s, but his followers—who continue to flourish cooperatively as The Lyman Family—have been known to answer queries about his demise with the asserion that Lyman is currently busy orbiting the earth.

The Newport Folk Festivals of the 1960s allowed several other notable harmonica players to connect with the public, if in a less cosmic manner than Mel Lyman. Bob Dylan's early mentor Tony Glover formed a disorderly but highly talented acoustic trio with guitarists "Spider" John Koerner and Dave Ray that made three best-selling albums for Vanguard *(Blues, Rags & Hollers; More Blues, Rags & Hollers;* and *The Return of Koerner, Ray & Glover)* between 1963 and 1965. (They reunited in the 1970s for two albums on the Mill label.) Countless aspiring harp players have gained their first real clues about the instrument from Glover's relentlessly hip and highly entertaining 1965 instruction manual.

Doc Watson, who came out of Deep Gap, North Carolina, to become the toast of the 1963 Newport Folk Festival, is rightly regarded as the foremost flatpicking guitarist working today, a measure of fame that has obscured the fact that he is also one of the finest traditional harmonica players around. Watson got his first mouth organ when he was five; thereafter family tradition dictated that a new harmonica would be his each Christmas. He grew up listening to the Opry broadcasts, which led to a lifelong love of the music of the Delmore Brothers; his harmonica playing is very much in the Wayne Raney/Lonnie Glosson mold.

John Hammond made his Newport Folk Festival debut in 1963 just prior to the release of his first album on Vanguard. Hammond had committed himself to mastering blues guitar by the time he was thirteen, and by the time he recorded he had also mastered the art of playing harp in the rack. By the mid-1960s, Hammond was working in New York City with electric bands; one of his earliest backup groups was the Hawks, who were hired out from under him by Bob Dylan and who later achieved fame as The Band. There were three albums for Atlantic (his sidemen included Duane Allman) and an original acoustic sound track for the film *Little Big Man*. In 1973, Hammond seemed poised for superstardom when he joined forces with Dr. John and Mike Bloomfield to form Triumvirate, but the group was short-lived. Between 1975 and 1982, this formidable live performer recorded several albums for Rounder Records.

Mark Graham (1953–)

Many of the traditional harmonica pieces being carried on by players like Doc Watson, including the train song and the fox-and-hounds chase, had previously been staples in the stock fiddler repertoire. In recent years there has been a strong surge in interest in traditional Irish fiddle music among American folk musicians; these thickly ornamented numbers are often performed at blistering tempos and are as technically challenging as any in traditional music. This style has attracted many harmonica players in recent years, including the Northwest's Mark Graham, whose remarkable talent is difficult to pigeonhole. He is a walking gold mine of harmonica lore, having mastered several folk blues styles as well as Irish music, and a superbly sardonic songwriter who enjoys skewering contemporary subjects like religious cults, transsexuals, the New Age movement, and vegetarians. Graham's studio work (especially on his own standout album *Natural Selections* and on Kevin Burke's *Open House*) and live performances show how satisfying his commingling of traditional harmonica wizardry with hilarious, offbeat songwriting can be. And in a field littered with soloists, Graham's marvelous skill at playing in harness with other instruments stands out.

Interview With Mark Graham

I grew up in Renton, Washington. My folks liked music, but it was about as middle of the road as you could probably get—white-line music. There was the odd record of Scottish bagpipe music or something like that. My uncle got a Johnny Horton record when I was about seven and I listened to that a lot. The one that really got me was "Sink the Bismarck."

When I was about eight years old some friends of mine played me a Homer and Jethro record and I went out and bought it. I learned everything on that record—all the lines, every piece of music, the words to every song. Their stuff was really funny and the music was fantastic. I was really into the humor aspect; I had a lot of Smothers Brothers records, too.

I played clarinet in the school band, but when I got to be thirteen or so it was uncool to carry anything to school, so I quit. I really didn't do anything musically until my last year of high school. I played a little bit of harmonica. My high school librarian showed me how to play the banjo some and I started hanging around with the people who were playing old-time music around Seattle.

In 1971 or so I went to a concert of Kenny Hall, the mandolin player, and I heard this echo of everything going on behind me, and it turned out to be this guy named Chuck Pliske sitting in the audience playing the harp note for note along with the fiddle. I thought, "Hell, that's great. I've got a harmonica somewhere. I'm going to do that." So I went home, dug it out of the baseball cards and fishing gear, and started trying to learn some of the stuff I already knew on the banjo.

I was playing a lot of music on the street at that time. I made my living in 1971 and 1972 sitting in front of the post office on University Avenue in Seattle, playing and singing. Making about ten or fifteen dollars *a day*. That was enough to live in a place with fifty dollars a month rent; I probably spent ten dollars or less a week on food. I even managed to save up enough money to go to Europe. I was playing the harp a little bit then, but not much. I played the mandolin for a while and learned how to play the concertina and the fiddle and some guitar. I'd get to the point where I could play a little bit and then I would just sell it. The only things I kept were the banjo and the harmonica. I finally got rid of the banjo about 1980. The harp was so versatile.

When I started playing, I was playing all straight harp. If I did any cross harp it was just so I could get the flat seventh. I wasn't working much on tone or rhythm—mostly learning melodies. Then in 1976 I started listening to a little bit more of Doc Watson's playing. He is a great harp player; his tone is so beautiful. I was interested in Doc, the Crook Brothers, Humphrey Bate, DeFord Bailey. I listened a lot to *Picking and Blowing* with George Pegram and Red Parham on Riverside. I was real interested in that stuff, but I really didn't know how to even get started. Instead of concentrating on fiddle music, I started listening to more banjo tunes, which had less of a pronounced melody and more rhythmic action going on. I got more into cross harp and started trying to come up with a kind of a hybrid of rhythm and melody—trying to be less concerned about the actual melody and more about the tone and rhythm and attack. I'd put together a little bit of Doc Watson, a little bit of Charlie McCoy, and some of my own approach. I developed kind of a Charlie McCoy style but with a different set of licks. From there I started listening to more blues and a *lot* of Sonny Terry. I've listened to Sonny Terry over and over and over and over and over and over. I've taken a lot of the things he used on his up-tempo stuff and kind of incorporated it into my playing of old-time music because it fills it up and gives you something to do other than play the melody. You don't even need a guitar player because it's so rhythmically energizing.

About 1973 I started playing with Frank Ferrel and Dudley Hill in the Irish American String Band. One of the people I met during that period was Benny Thomasson, the fiddler, who showed me that there was really no one way to play a tune, which was liberating. I would go to the national fiddlers' championships in Weiser, Idaho, where I met a harmonica player named Sam Hinton, who records for Folkways. He doesn't even use the rack, he just shoves the thing in his mouth and plays this fast fiddle music. He spits it out and catches it in his hand when he wants to sing. I ran into another player named Rick Epping in 1973. His harp playing just fried me, it was so cool. He has a beautiful tone. He is a good country blues player and also plays a lot of Irish music. I heard him play this Irish version of the fox chase that is kind of derived from bagpipe playing, and it's astounding.

I joined another old-time band who were all living on Vashon Island in Puget Sound. We were picking apples and being hippies and getting pretty ludicrous. That's when I started getting into Irish music. I went to Ireland in 1975 with that band and played over there. It was really humbling. You go over there and you think you know something, and you meet little kids that can play *everything*. We met this guy on the street so destroyed by drink and life that he couldn't even hardly open his eyes or lift his head off the sidewalk, but he could just play the hell out of the tin whistle. Accordion bands, tin whistle bands—people just playing all this amazing music. Most of the harmonica players in Ireland play the chromatic. What they do is they take the slide and turn it over so that the high row is exposed. With that type of a setup you can kind of imitate the fiddle ornamentation—the rolls and triplets and stuff like that. There are a few really hot practitioners of that approach: Eddie Clarke, who's really quite something, Ciaron Hanrahan, and the Murphy family.

After I got back home, I was playing some Irish music on the diatonic harps, and then a friend of mine gave me a chromatic harmonica that he had taken apart once and hadn't gotten together right. He had accidentally flipped the slide over. I started noodling around on it, playing some of these tunes, and it was just like a new world coming. I had hardly ever played the chromatic before that.

After playing with some Irish bands in Seattle I got together with a banjo player named Jerry Gallaher and we put together The Hurricane Ridgerunners with Armin Barnett on fiddle and Paul Kotapish on guitar and mandolin. We did one record for Topaz and then everybody got bummed out by the Reagan era and decided they were going to have to make some money or get run over. I continued playing music and making no money, but I also had a job as a glassblower.

By 1979 I was at a low economic ebb. My folks had a little trailer out on Vashon Island and I decided to spend the winter there. And, man, you're talking bleak. It was gray, rainy winter and I had a car that kept breaking down all the time so I had to walk or hitchhike everywhere. But that's where I started writing my own tunes.

I moved to Massachusetts in 1983. I was chasing girls and moved up to Quebec for a while. That's a whole can of worms up there. There must be about twenty or thirty diatonic harmonica players who have recorded records of fiddle music up there. Some of them are really great but they're *all* good. A couple—Robert Legault, Wilfred Boivin and Yves Lambert—are outstanding.

Then I moved to Boston for a few years. I was playing in a band called the Chicken Chokers, and through them I got to meet most of the younger old-time players on the East Coast, and I spent more time messing with my rhythm and tone. There was so much melody going on anyway; I just wanted to find a place to be useful. I spent a lot of time doing research, listening to old records and trying to adapt some of the blues stuff I knew. I played on a record with the Chicken Chokers on Rounder, and then I did a record of my own for Front Hall Records, *Natural Selections*. There's a lot of humor on the record. It wasn't so much a conscious decision as just the kind of stuff that comes out when I sit down to write. I'm interested in a lot of things, and I can't stand to say something that I know has already been said a million times. And there are so many kind of weird things you run into in your life. You read a few R. Crumb comics and you have a bunch of weird friends and you have a bunch of weird things happen to you, and after a while your head starts filling up with some pretty strange stuff.

I play the Marine Band in the keys of G and A; otherwise, I use Special 20s. I've been playing a lot of chromatic lately. I recorded an album on Green Linnet with a fiddle player named Kevin Burke, and we get a kind of twin fiddle sound because I play in a lower register—the same register as the fiddle—and imitate those fiddle ornaments. I play the twelve-hole chromatics. Years ago I figured out from listening to Eddie Clarke's records that if the two rows of reeds on the G chromatic were tuned to G and F# instead of the usual G and G#, you could play with the G row open. I used to buy the regular G chromatics and then retune the whole damn thing—that's about the closest to being a psychotic that I've ever been—but now I have them made up for me. I still hate chromatics, and if I wasn't playing with a fiddle player, I wouldn't even think of touching them, really. Unless you learn to work on them, you can spend the gross national product of a small country playing them.

Phil Wiggins (1954–)

Two years after the death of Sonny Terry, Flying Fish Records released the first album by the blues duo John Cephas and Phil Wiggins, and fans of the Piedmont blues style began to feel the warmth from a torch being passed. The Piedmont approach is a melodic brand of blues developed in the Southeast that is associated with a sophisticated guitar style in which the melody is fingerpicked on the treble strings while a steady bass pattern is kept up with the thumb. It was introduced in the 1920s and 1930s by Blind Blake and Blind Boy Fuller, two of the most accomplished guitarists in the history of the blues; its most successful proselytizers were Terry and Brownie McGhee.

Phil Wiggins was introduced to the harmonica as a high school student in Virginia, and before long he was deciphering the styles of Sonny Terry, Little Walter, and Rice Miller. He met John Cephas, a guitarist and singer, in 1976, and the two played with Chief Ellis in the Barrelhouse Rockers, a popular Washington, D.C.–based group.

When Ellis died, Cephas and Wiggins joined forces as an acoustic duo and began admirably filling the gap left by the demise of the supremely popular Terry/McGhee partnership; they can now claim a worldwide audience. Cephas and Wiggins captured two W. C. Handy awards—the blues' equivalent of an Oscar—in 1988; their *Dog Days of August* album, a wonderfully relaxed session taped in Cephas's home, won the award for Best Traditional Blues Album of the Year, and the duo were named Blues Entertainers of the Year, an honor that had traditionally been claimed by electric blues artists.

The Piedmont approach may be the most challenging and tuneful of the blues variations, and Wiggins has put together a lively and technically sophisticated style that allows him to match Cephas's often brisk tempos and emphasis on melody. He and Cephas are also fine interpreters of the classic Delta style, but their success is due in large part to their insistence on mixing up traditional formulas. The pair's dynamic stage presence, their gospel influences, their recordings with jazz combos and brass bands, and Wiggins's fine songwriting have injected an essential vitality and freshness into the magnificent genre that is the country blues.

Wayne Raney

Country Music

I f you're a fan of the harmonica and country music, raise a glass at the next appropriate occasion in tribute to Henry Whitter, the man who started it all. In March 1923, Whitter, a Virginia textile worker, strode purposefully into the New York offices of Okeh Records executive Ralph Peer and introduced himself as "the world's greatest harmonica player." After Whitter ignored several attempts by Peer to show him to the door, Peer agreed to audition him. "I took him down to the recording studio," Peer recalled, "and we ran off a half dozen of these things, and he *was* a great harmonica player, no doubt about that." There is no record that any of these recordings—all mouth organ solos—were ever issued, but when Okeh released its first hillbilly record, two sides by Fiddlin' John Carson, soon afterward, the company was stunned at the phenomenal sales that resulted and Peer called Whitter back to New York to record several more tunes. Whitter's second session produced two cross-harp instrumentals ("Old Time Fox Chase," probably the first of dozens of spirited mouth organ recreations of fox-and-hounds hunts to be recorded, and "Lost Train Blues") and several vocal numbers, one of which, "The Wreck of the Old 97," became a nationwide sensation.

The success of the Carson and Whitter 78s led to a rush of recordings of traditional, down-home music in which harmonica pieces figured prominently. Some date the birth of country music to a week-long 1927 session held in a hotel room in Bristol, Tennessee, during which Peer, by this time working for Victor, produced the debut recordings by future legends Jimmie Rodgers and the Carter Family. The first performer Peer recorded in Bristol was a fine harmonica player named El Watson. There may also have been a personal basis for the mouth organ's high profile on early recordings of country music—historian Charles Wolfe has noted that Peer had a special liking for harmonica music and that his chief rival, the Columbia Phonograph Company's talent scout Frank Walker, was himself a mouth organist.

In recording traditional music, the record companies were following the lead of radio, another new medium that had an impact on American life, especially in isolated rural areas, that is impossible to exaggerate. As country music historian Bill Malone has pointed out, the first American commercial music, both on radio and on records, was urban, but accidental or incidental broadcasts and recordings of country music in the early 1920s brought surprisingly strong audience response. "Country" music was probably first broadcast over an Atlanta station in 1923. Within a year, Chicago's WLS took aim at the thousands of Southerners who had migrated to that city and began broadcasting its "National Barn Dance" program. October of 1925 saw the debut of a new Nashville station, WSM, whose station director, George D. Hay, had been the staff announcer for the "National Barn Dance." By the end of the year Hay had established a regular Saturday-night country music show patterned closely on the Chicago program. For the first few years, WSM's "Barn Dance" broadcasts were casual affairs—in Hay's phrase, "good-natured riots." The local musicians were rarely paid, but—galvanized by the thought of reaching an unimaginably large audience—they streamed out of the hills. All four of Nashville's radio stations were programming traditional music, and there seemed to be enough airtime for everyone.

Country music is most often associated with the guitar, banjo, or steel guitar, but in the early days of WSM's "Barn Dance" the fiddle and the harmonica were the most prominently featured instruments, an emphasis that reflected the instrumental tastes of the local population. According to Opry historian Charles Wolfe, the central Tennessee area produced "a host of superb harp players," including Charlie "the French Harp King" Melton, Hilary Marable, Grady and Clarence Gill, and Gwen Foster, who recorded in the 1920s as both a solo harp player and as a member of the Blue Ridge Mountain Entertainers. "At no place in the South was the harmonica as popular as it was in Middle Tennessee," contends Wolfe. One of the most popular of these early Nashville mouth harpists was a genial country physician named Humphrey Bate.

Dr. Humphrey Bate (1875–1936)

Throughout the early part of this century Dr. Humphrey Bate attended to the medical needs of the residents of Castalian Springs, Tennessee, most of whom were also familiar with Bate's other incarnation as a talented amateur musician who had played the harmonica and guitar in local bands since boyhood. Bate was fond of playing light classics on the mouth organ, but his passion was the old fiddle tunes of his boyhood, many of which he had learned from former slaves on his father's farm. Despite his thriving medical practice, by the advent of World War I Bate was managing three musical groups, booking them for every imaginable rural function and for appearances in silent movie theaters.

It was Bate's band, the Possum Hunters, that was featured on the first old-time music program aired on Nashville radio, a 1925 broadcast over WDAD. The Possum Hunters were a talented group whose trademark was the alternating of the lead between the fiddle and Bate's harmonica; they regularly opened the WSM "Barn Dance" broadcasts. Despite their popularity, the Possum Hunters had only one recording session, held in Atlanta in 1928; one of the resulting 78s, "My Wife Died on Saturday Night," became their most-requested number. The first Opry band to go on the road, the Possum Hunters toured the RKO vaudeville circuit in the Midwest and upper South under WSM's sponsorship and functioned as a unit until Bate's death in 1936. "WSM lost the dean of its Grand Ole Opry," noted George Hay.

"History has tended to overlook Dr. Bate's important role in starting the Opry," Charles Wolfe has written. "It was Dr. Bate who, even before Hay came to Nashville, saw the potential for using radio as a medium for country music. It was Dr. Bate whose vocation and reputation lent old-time music a much needed air of respectability. And it was Dr. Bate who, as much as anyone, gave to the 'Barn Dance' a charming sense of informality and comradeship—a trait that the modern Opry still endeavors to preserve."

Herman Crook (1898–1988)

One Saturday night in the spring of 1988 I stood in the wings of the main auditorium at Nashville's Opryland and watched Herman Crook go to work. It was ten-thirty—not a particularly productive time of day for most eighty-nine-year-olds—but Crook launched himself from the stage apron with a determined if somewhat halting step and made for the same space he had first filled on another Saturday in July of 1926—center stage at the Grand Ole Opry.

The applause had only just risen up from the seats after a singer's last tune, and bows were still being taken, but Crook's seemingly premature entrance had more to do with the deceleration that comes with age than it did with ego. The Opry is a well-oiled machine—television monitors displaying the time down to the second are strewn all over the lip of the stage—and Herman knew from experience that his early departure from the wings would give him just enough time to reach his microphone before Roy Acuff, host of this segment of the Opry show, began his introduction of the Crook Brothers band.

Acuff was the living symbol of the Grand Ole Opry's golden era, but his preamble to the Crook Brothers' segment was properly deferential; after all, when Acuff came to Nashville to join the Opry's regular cast in 1938, Herman Crook was already a twelve-year veteran of the program. After a few words Acuff surrendered the microphone, and Herman Crook led his group into an up-tempo instrumental, just as he had done nearly every Saturday night for sixty-two years.

Herman Crook knew his place in history. "I am the oldest man on the Opry and I've been there longer than anybody else," he told me later in a backstage dressing room. "I play every Saturday night. I never have played on a Friday night," he remarked, puzzled, as if this oddity had just occurred to him. "They never did ask me."

The marathon of Saturday-night Crook Brothers shows ended on June 10, 1988, when a heart attack brought down the quiet, courtly mouth organ player who had personally witnessed the entire history of country music's preeminent showcase. Watching Crook onstage at the glitzy Opryland hall that spring evening, it was almost impossible to imagine that he had been a contemporary and peer of shadowy legends like Uncle Dave Macon, the Delmore Brothers, and DeFord Bailey. In the early days, the Opry had revolved around groups like the Gully Jumpers, the Dixie Clodhoppers, and the Fruit Jar Drinkers. Sixty years later, only the Crook Brothers were still regularly dispensing the unadorned string-band music that had launched the Opry.

Herman Crook seems to have been satisfied with his role as an Opry stalwart. He married the pianist in his first band and settled with her in Nashville to raise seven children. Crook did not depend on music as a livelihood—he worked for many years as a tobacco twister—and his band rarely traveled outside the Nashville area. Despite their protracted history, the Crook Brothers made only a few recordings. After some unsuccessful sides for Victor in the late 1920s (Herman Crook's verdict was that "they weren't very good"), thirty-five years went by before the group appeared on a joint album with Sam and Kirk McGhee in the early 1960s. But for more than six decades countless Opry visitors and listeners thrilled to Crook's prowess as an instrumentalist, and his band's nonpareil record for job security in a precarious business is testimony to both the group's high musical standards and to Crook's talents as a bandleader.

"All of my folks came from up in DeKalb County, about sixty or seventy miles from here," Crook told me. "We lived in the country. I don't remember my daddy—he was killed by a tree when I was two or three years old. I've been trying to play the harmonica since I was a boy. For about eighty years, I reckon. I had an uncle that played the harmonica, and my older brother Matthew played. You could buy them for twenty-five cents then. We called them French harps."

Even as youngsters Herman and Matthew were already assembling a repertoire of old-time songs and appearing at local functions and house parties. The brothers played twin harmonicas in unison in a style heavily influenced by the back-bowing techniques of country fiddlers, an approach they naturally developed as teenagers that became the trademark of the group the brothers formed in the early 1920s.

The Crook Brothers began making regular broadcasts over Nashville's WLAC, but they were eventually lured to WSM. In 1925 they became charter members of a new country music program developed for the station.

"When this show first started, it was called the 'Nashville Barn Dance,'" Crook explained to me. "We played it for two years for nothin'. Back in them days, people thought that if they got to play over the radio, that was really somethin'. When they decided to pay, we happened to be one of the lucky bands they picked out. They started us out at five dollars each for a Saturday-night show. I been on there ever since."

Matthew Crook turned his back on music in 1930 to join Nashville's police force. Another Crook—Lewis, a banjoist—joined the band; he was no relation, but his presence allowed Herman to feel comfortable about continuing to bill the group as the Crook Brothers. The group settled into its role as one of the Opry house bands, eventually achieving a collective longevity that dwarfs the extended tenures of such revered Opry fixtures as Ernest Tubb, Minnie Pearl, and Little Jimmy Dickens. The same year a rawboned young howler from Alabama named Hank Williams made his spectacular debut on the Opry, Herman Crook was celebrating his first quarter of a century on the program.

As Herman and I talked backstage at Opryland in the comfortable rehearsal room that the Crook Brothers band shared with Little Jimmy Dickens, I mentioned that the spacious quarters were a long way from the cramped, Spartan dressing rooms in the old Ryman Auditorium, the Opry's home from 1943 until 1974.

"I like the new place fine," agreed Crook. "It's a larger place—accommodates more people. And it's filled every Saturday night. We have our own lockers and a place to rehearse, and if you want a cup of coffee or an orange drink, it won't cost you a penny. They treat me all right. I just got a raise last week. I've even talked to the big boy—I forget his name, but he's the owner of everything. I shook hands with him and told him, 'I've been on here sixty-two years.'"

Herman was firm about his musical loyalties: "Country music—that's my kind of music. Good old breakdowns, sacred numbers, and good songs." Sitting ramrod straight in his chair, he raised his voice as Jimmy Dickens's guitarist and steel player plugged into an amplifier on the other side of the rehearsal room to work out an instrumental break. "All the years I've been on the Opry, there've been a lot of changes," Herman noted as his flinty eyes roved over the electronic paraphernalia. "If I was manager of the Opry, there'd be a change in it. I'd be just like George D. Hay. I wouldn't have a drum on that stage at all on Saturday night. A drum is just somethin' with a lot of noise— ain't got a good sound to it at all. George Hay didn't want a drum and he didn't want no electric instruments. He just wanted the pure, down-to-earth country music on a guitar, banjo, fiddle, harmonica, and a piano. You want no kind of a horn."

Satisfied that his point was well-taken, Herman described his current working arrangement with the Opry as his band members began to arrive and unpack their instruments. "We just do two turns a night. We play breakdown numbers for the square dancers. Every once in a while Roy Acuff will call me up there to play a solo number—'Lost John' or 'Amazing Grace.' I just stand out there and do the best I can.

"The harmonica's the only instrument I play. I get as much music out of that as the others get out of what they play. The harmonica is good for playin' breakdown numbers and for playin' chokin' numbers like 'Lost John.' You can make a tune sound pretty lonesome on the harmonica."

Occasionally, a sideways gleam would surface in Crook's eyes and his sly, backwoods humor would surface. Fifty-seven-year Opry veteran Lewis Crook was introduced as "the youngster that plays banjo for me." Fiddler Earl White chuckled—he'd obviously heard all of this before—as Herman solemnly outlined his impeccable moral credentials: "I've never had a drink of beer or whiskey in my life. Never smoked a cigarette in my life. I never used a curse word in my life. I've never touched a woman besides my wife. Of course"—here he leaned forward with the punch line—"I *am* a *Crook.*"

About fifteen minutes before he was due onstage for his slot on the second Saturday-night show, Crook made his way backstage, accepting the hellos of stagehands, fans, and musicians as he took his customary spot in the wings near announcer Grant Turner's lectern. "I'm not in the Country Music Hall of Fame, but I should've been," Herman stated purposefully as he eyed the progress of the show. "They got one of my harmonicas that I gave 'em. My goodness, if anybody deserves to be in the Hall of Fame, I oughta be in it—anybody that's been around as long as I have."

Moments later Herman was standing in the spotlight with a Hohner Marine Band in his palm as Roy Acuff informed the audience that the elderly gentleman to his left was the all-time Opry veteran. Then Herman Crook's unerring harp filled the hall as he led the Crook Brothers band into "Sally Goodin"—a tune he had mastered before the Archduke Ferdinand was bushwhacked and all the able men in DeKalb County had gone off to the First World War—and the stage quickly filled with a pack of high-stepping square dancers.

Two months later, I spotted Herman Crook's obituary in the Sunday newspaper. That night I replayed the tape of the conversation we'd had that night in the Opry rehearsal room.

"I'll be ninety if I live until next December second," Crook said at one point. "I ain't as good a man as I used to be, but I still have good wind when it comes to playin' harp. I wouldn't mind makin' some more records if I got the chance. I got a letter from a fella way off yonder somewheres who said I was the best harmonica player in the world. I told my wife, 'Boy, he's coverin' a lot of territory, isn't he?' "

DeFord Bailey (1899–1982)

One gray afternoon in November 1977, I parked my car at a street corner on Edgehill Road in a black neighborhood in Nashville. The man I was looking for had managed a shoeshine stand on that corner as recently as six years before, but now there was no sign of it. I walked into a nearby drugstore that had obviously been there for years and asked the pharmacist behind the counter if he might know where I could find DeFord Bailey. He obligingly pointed out a high-rise apartment building across the street.

I walked into a lobby furnished with chairs filled with old men and women reading newspapers and conversing quietly and found Bailey's name and apartment number listed in a tenant directory on the wall. A few minutes later, I was knocking on the door of number 30, which swung open to reveal a tiny, white-haired black man, impeccably turned out in a white brocaded shirt, sharply creased pants, and gleaming patent-leather shoes. I stammered out an introduction and, stretching the truth only a little, said that I was a harmonica player who had traveled across the country just to meet the man who had recorded "Ice Water Blues." Smiling, Bailey welcomed me in a quiet voice, stepped aside, and ushered me into his apartment, a small place filled with photographs and train memorabilia in which time seemed suspended somewhere between the world wars.

We talked about his songs and DeFord produced a tape recorder containing a cassette of his old recordings. I had heard that Bailey would play his harmonica only on a cash basis, so I placed a twenty-dollar bill on a nearby table as discreetly as I could and told him how much it would mean to me to hear the sound of his mouth organ in person.

"I play the banjo, you know," he responded, and produced a five-string from somewhere and began fingerpicking it left-handed. After a time I steered the conversation back to the harmonica again.

"I play the guitar, too," he volunteered, and in a minute he was cradling a guitar and picking out a melody in a subdued, tuneful style reminiscent of Mississippi John Hurt's.

I decided to force the issue by pulling out a Marine Band and attempting my own version of my host's "Ice Water Blues." I stewed in my embarrassment as he pondered my playing. "You got some of that in there pretty good," he finally said. "Keep practicing, son— keep practicing. I've been playing harmonica for seventy-five years. You know I must know *something.*"

Bailey carefully opened a box containing a Marine Band in the key of G, confiding that the A and G models were the best for his songs but that he could get by with a Bb if he had to. He cradled the harmonica in his right hand, brought it to his mouth, and for the next few minutes his remarkable playing filled the small room.

We listened to the tape of Bailey's old recordings and discussed the finer technical points of harmonica playing. After a lesson from DeFord on how to play the bones properly, I asked him if I could have a picture taken with him. He agreed, but saying that he would like to change his clothes, he politely excused himself and disappeared behind a curtain that divided the single room into a parlor and a bedroom. A few minutes later he reappeared, this time in a black frock coat, string tie, and a Stetson hat that looked as if it were enjoying its first trip out of the box. He posed with me, we shook hands, I tried to tell him what his records had meant to me and how much I appreciated his kindness, and then I was walking down a stairwell, trying to imagine Bailey as a young man in the WSM studios, perched on a

Coca-Cola crate in front of a microphone, harmonica in hand, waiting for George Hay's introduction.

At the close of the NBC "Music Appreciation Hour" on the night of December 10, 1927, host Walter Damrosch commented stiffly that "while most artists realize that there is no place in the classics for realism, I am going to break one of my rules and present a composition by a young composer from Iowa. This young man has sent us his latest number, which depicts the onrush of a locomotive."

After the stirring orchestral train imitation was finished, those listening to the network broadcast over Nashville's WSM heard George Hay follow Damrosch's lead. Promising his audience "nothing but realism, down-to-earth for the earthy," he called on DeFord Bailey, "The Harmonica Wizard," to perform *his* train piece, "Pan American Blues." After Bailey's artificial steam had dissipated, Hay reminded listeners that "for the past hour we have been listening to music taken largely from the Grand Opera, but from now on we will present the Grand Ole Opry."

DeFord Bailey, despite his undeniable genius, was an unlikely candidate to become the most popular of the many fine harmonica players in the early days of country music. He was a quiet man, a tiny hunchback barely four feet ten inches tall. And he was black.

Bailey was born on his parents' farm near Bellwood, Tennessee. "Everybody in my family played music," he told Bengt Olsson. His mother and his aunt both played the guitar, his brother was a banjoist, and his father and his grandfather were fine fiddlers. Bailey claimed that one of his uncles was the best black banjo player he had ever heard. Two of DeFord's uncles played the harmonica; one, Albert, had quite a local reputation. DeFord remembered his family as being known as "the best musicians since slavery times."

Bailey's physical shortcomings were the result of a bout with polio at the age of three. Bedridden for a year, he spent his convalescence trying to unravel the mysteries of the harmonica and the mandolin. "I tried to learn more about my harp from other people when I was a boy," Bailey told David Morton, "but I didn't learn very much. . . . I was in a different class." Bailey told me that as a child he was so obsessed with perfecting a train imitation that he would spend whole days sitting under a nearby railroad trestle, studying the shuddering roar of passing locomotives. He later became justly famous for his harmonica train pieces, which were so accurate that a railroad engineer once visited the WSM studios for the express purpose of congratulating the mouth organist on his achievement and to suggest a few subtle corrections to DeFord's whistle pattern for crossings.

Bailey's physical problems, the racial climate of his day, and his talent for music all helped to give him an introverted, dreamy character. "I've always been like a child," he told Bengt Olsson. "I have a very vivid imagination: I think like a child and I feel like a child. People say I drive them crazy after a while." Bailey confided to David Morton that his schooling was sketchy: "I didn't study nothing else but my harp." When the white family for whom he did chores moved to Nashville in 1918, DeFord went with them.

His solitary personality notwithstanding, Bailey sought the musical spotlight. Preposterously, he teamed up with a mirror image of himself—another diminutive, crippled African American harmonica player named Bob Lee—and together they played around Nashville. Bailey also worked as an elevator operator, playing his harmonica between stops for passengers, one of whom encouraged him to make his first radio appearance as a contestant in a harmonica contest sponsored by WDAD. A description of the competition in the Nashville *Tennessean* reported that "the first prize in the French Harp contest was won by J. T. Bland who played 'Lost John.' The second prize was won by DeFord Bailey, a negro boy, who played 'It Ain't Gonna Rain No Mo'.'"

Dr. Bate brought Bailey to an Opry broadcast, introducing him to Hay as "the dangdest harmonica player that ever lived" and convincing the announcer to put DeFord on the air that same night. Bailey was made an Opry regular in 1926 and within a year had become the most popular member of its cast with his own regular fifteen-minute segment.

There is no hard evidence that the Opry tried to keep DeFord's race a secret from the Opry audience. Bailey rarely spoke during the broadcasts, but this may have been in keeping with DeFord's essentially shy nature, and he did sing occasionally on the air. While Bailey was the only black regular on the Opry, other African American gospel singers, guitarists, and blues performers appeared on the program. Whatever notions the Opry audience had about DeFord's background, they responded enthusiastically to his performances; his fan mail was sizable. According to Charles Wolfe, "it wasn't at all uncommon for DeFord to appear for two or even three sets in a single Saturday-night show." Opry scholar Richard Peterson has documented that in 1928 Bailey performed almost twice as often on the Opry as any other performer.

In 1927, Bailey traveled to Atlanta and cut two sides for Columbia that were never issued. Two weeks later, Bailey was on a train for New York, where he recorded eight tunes in two sessions for the Brunswick label. On October 2, 1928, Bailey was the focus of the first recording session held in Nashville, during which he cut eight sides for Victor.

At the time, record companies had a practice of issuing blues recordings—then aimed solely at black audiences—as "race" records; recordings of white country music performers were sold as "hillbilly" discs. Bailey's race, his status as a star of the Grand Ole Opry, and the fact that his purely instrumental music reflected the overlapping musical repertoires of blacks and whites in the Tennessee hill country (Bailey himself always contended that he played "black hillbilly" music) enabled Victor to release his recordings in both series. DeFord Bailey had become the first crossover star in country music.

As Paul Oliver's research has shown, the material that Bailey recorded was not especially original. "Old Hen Cackle" was a traditional fiddle tune, "John Henry" was a well-known favorite of both blacks and whites, "Ice Water Blues" was based on a tune called "The Preacher and the Bear," and "Davidson County Blues" was a reworking of the piano showcase "Cow Cow Blues." Bailey's recordings, however, do not reveal the full measure of his range, which included blues, pop, sacred, and jazz numbers as well as traditional tunes.

What they do give us is solid evidence of his genius. His tone is unfailingly beautiful and astonishingly full, and his numbers are strongly melodic and cleverly conceived. What puts Bailey squarely in the ranks of the greatest of harmonica players is his polyrhythmic brilliance, which has never been equalled. In tunes like "Ice Water Blues" (a popular record that was reissued three times), Bailey effortlessly juxtaposes a melody line against two or three rhythmically distinct cadences that somehow dovetail seamlessly. Bailey once tried to describe to David Morton what distinguished his style from that of other players: "My timing is different from theirs. . . . I got a double sound. I can't play single. It doesn't sound good to me. . . . I add time to vacant space." He took great pride in the clarity of his playing, and he liked to inject something unique (he called it "throwing a little judo") into each of his pieces.

Bailey often headlined touring package shows featuring Opry stars that drew large audiences. "When I first came to town, he was one of the top stars and was much in demand for personal appearances," Roy Acuff admitted. "I carried him on my band. I wasn't known and he drew a crowd. . . . He helped get me where I am."

"Rabon and I used DeFord on a lot of our personal appearances," wrote Alton Delmore of the Delmore Brothers. "[He] was a pioneer in the field of playing the harmonica. When we joined the Opry we saw a lot of DeFord and he was a real friendly fellow and we liked him very much. So did the rest of the entertainers on the Opry. . . . We all thought just as much of DeFord as we did our white friends. He was a little fellow who commanded our admiration and respect."

On the road, Bailey was no longer sheltered by the faceless anonymity offered by radio. He usually could not eat at the same restaurants as his Opry colleagues. Although he suffered some indignities at the hands of his fellow performers on these road trips (on one tour DeFord was wheeled out onstage at each performance in an oversize baby buggy), many of them were particularly solicitous of his welfare. When he toured with Uncle Dave Macon, Macon would often claim that Bailey was his valet so that the harmonicist could room with him. Most of the time, however, Bailey had to scour black neighborhoods in each town for lodging. As Bill Monroe told writer Jim Rooney, "We'd walk the streets together, two, three o'clock in the morning, nobody out, in the roughest parts of town we'd be down there getting him a place to stay. . . . Then he would get in the room and lock the door and stay there until I went to get him the next day." Bailey slept with a pistol under his head while on these tours.

A trend toward modernization at the Opry led to the steady reduction of Bailey's airtime, which by 1935 had shrunk to five minutes. By the early 1940s he was called on to play only if time permitted. Bailey's close friend David Morton feels that Bailey was a victim of a publishing battle between ASCAP, which published most of his repertoire, and BMI. WSM had invested in BMI and pressured its cast of regulars to write new songs that would be published in the BMI catalog.

Bailey was finally given his notice by Hay in 1941. In a souvenir pamphlet published four years later, Hay commented on the end of

Bailey's Opry career: "That brings us to DeFord Bailey, a little crippled colored boy who was a bright feature of our show for about fifteen years. Like some members of his race and other races DeFord was lazy. He knew about a dozen numbers, which he put on the air and recorded for a major company, but he refused to learn more, even though his reward was great. He was our mascot and is still loved by the entire company. We gave him a whole year's notice to learn some new tunes, but he would not. When we were forced to give him his final notice, DeFord said, without malice: 'I knowed it wuz comin', Judge, I knowed it wuz comin'.'" Bailey himself, however, was steadfastly bitter about his firing, claiming that he never got paid more than five dollars for an Opry performance and that his treatment had not been on a par with that received by other performers.

Bailey had started a shoeshine parlor with an uncle in 1931, and he went to work there after leaving the Opry. When the parlor became a casualty of a 1971 urban renewal program, he moved into a nearby housing project for the elderly. He steadfastly resisted offers from the Newport Folk Festival, for album projects alone and with folksinger Pete Seeger, for network television appearances, and for a cameo appearance in the Burt Reynolds film *W. W. and the Dixie Dancekings*. When the Opry called, however, Bailey still answered; he stole the show at an Old Timer's Night at the old Ryman Auditorium in 1974 and played at the new Opryland complex on his seventy-fifth birthday. He would occasionally talk about recording again, but never did.

In 1982, Bailey spent several weeks in the cardiac care unit of Nashville's Baptist Hospital for treatment of heart disease. Shortly after his release, on July 2, Bailey was rushed to the hospital's emergency room, where he was pronounced dead on arrival from kidney failure and heart congestion.

The Hohner Company formally petitioned the Country Music Hall of Fame to induct Bailey. Minnie Pearl and Alcyone Beasley, Humphrey Bates's daughter, urged his selection, but Roy Acuff told *The New York Times* that Bailey did not deserve a place in the Hall of Fame, saying that the harmonica player's contributions had done nothing to further country music.

Thanks to the tireless efforts of David Morton, June 23, 1983, was declared DeFord Bailey Day in Nashville. A striking granite headstone, engraved with a diatonic harmonica and the words *Harmonica*

Wizard, was unveiled in a ceremony at Nashville's Greenwood Cemetery. Roy Acuff, Bill Monroe, and Herman Crook were among the crowd. Acuff was still smarting from the criticism he had received over his comments concerning Bailey's qualifications for the Country Music Hall of Fame. "If his name is ever put on the ballot," he told reporters, "he will have a vote from Roy Acuff."

Bailey would have enjoyed the occasion. The Crook Brothers played two of his favorite breakdowns, "Sugar in the Gourd" and "Grey Eagle," Bill Monroe played Bailey's "Evening Prayer Blues" on the mandolin, and James Talley contributed a version of "John Henry." After the headstone was unveiled, Herman Crook brought the observance to a close with a solo harmonica rendition of "Amazing Grace." Some of those in attendance then drove to the Country Music Hall of Fame, where several Bailey artifacts—three hats, some shoes, a folding cane chair, and two of his megaphones—were donated to the Country Music Museum.

Lonnie Glosson (1908–)

While still a teenager, Arkansas native Lonnie Glosson rode the freight trains to Chicago to audition as a guitarist, singer, and mouth organist for the WLS "National Barn Dance" program. He got the job and worked on that program alongside many top country entertainers, including Gene Autry, who tried to persuade Glosson to go with him to Hollywood to make western movies. Glosson stayed in Chicago instead, joining the WJJD "Suppertime Frolic" program.

Glosson moved to California in 1934 to work for a Los Angeles radio station, but he soon returned to the Midwest, serving as emcee and featured performer on the "Renfro Valley Barn Dance." His 1936 recording of "Arkansas Hard Luck Blues" was one of the first recorded examples of the "talking blues" style later perfected by Woody Guthrie and popularized by Bob Dylan. In 1949, Glosson became one of the first country performers to work in television when he hosted a program for station WSB in Atlanta. His extended on-again, off-again radio partnership with fellow harmonica player Wayne Raney began during this period. Eventually, Glosson concentrated on giving public-school concerts, a circuit he continues to travel. Now in his eighties, Glosson is a regular on the folk festival circuit and recently toured the Netherlands.

Interview With Lonnie Glosson

I remember hearing my mother play the harmonica when I was two years old. She played numbers like "Red Wing." That fascinated me very, very much. I started to play when I was about ten or twelve years old. My mama learned me to play "Home Sweet Home" on the harmonica, just one note at a time. I picked it up from there.

I guess we must have played Hohners, but I don't remember. I bought them in a drugstore. Old Standbys were a quarter, the Marine Band was thirty-five cents. When I was a boy, I never heard of a "harmonica." We called it the "French harp," but I don't know why.

When I was a teenager, I used to ride the freight trains all everywhere. I'd go into these cities like Little Rock and go to the barbershop and I'd play and take up a collection. At night, I'd go to the fire station. They always had a bed or two empty, and after I'd play the harmonica, they'd let me stay all night.

I was playing just the harmonica then, little old tunes like "Turkey in the Straw." There was a brakeman one time who showed me how to blow the train, and after I'd learned that train whistle, I picked up everything on my own, choking. I call it cross-harp "choking." I learned to play with the tongue block; I call that a "second." I picked up the guitar back in 1932 or '33. After I learned chords, I got me a harmonica holder.

I didn't start playing professionally until I went on KMOX in St. Louis in 1925. That was the first time I went on radio. I went up to the radio station and the manager asked me, "What can I do for you?" I says, "I play the French harp." He said, "Would you like to play on the radio?" I said, "I sure would."

He took me in the studio and set me down. He said, "Now, you sit right there," and put a big old mike in front of me and said, "Now you watch that light up there. When that red light comes on, you start playing." So I set there, and I had my eyes glued. He didn't tell me that it would be about twenty minutes before I played. When that light turned red, man, my mouth was so dry, I could hardly play, but I played the train and "Lost John."

Every afternoon I went on WIL in St. Louis, and then I'd go over to the studios at KMOX. You didn't make any money out of it, but it got my name around. That's the way I got started. Everybody listened to the radio back then.

This was back in the days when everything was dry. I didn't drink myself, but I'd go down to where they sold it in these private homes and sit there on Saturday night and play the harmonica and take up a collection. One night, the police chopped the door down and took everybody to jail. They took everything out of my pocket except the harmonica. When I got in my cell, I started playing "Lost John." A policeman come back there and he said, "Boy, what's your name?" I told him and he hollered at the turnkey, "Let that boy outta here. That's Lonnie Glosson. We listen to him every afternoon on KMOX. Give that kid his stuff back and let him go home." And they did.

My first recording I did for Sears Roebuck back in 1930. It didn't go too good. It was a long time before I made another record, for Decca back in 1946. I tried to get them to put out a harmonica album, but they wanted me to sing. Then I got with Mercury after that, and they wanted me to do singing, too. You couldn't tell them crazy guys that I was a harmonica player and not a singer. My voice just wasn't commercial enough to sell records.

I first met Wayne Raney back in 1938. In 1950 we got together and just fell in naturally playing together. Me and Wayne was on two hundred stations across the United States, Mexico, and Canada at one time. You just couldn't tune in to any kind of a radio at night back then without hearing our program. Wayne, he played harmony on the harp and I led and played the guitar. He would play harmony in the same key harp—he choked the harmonica just like I do.We sold somewhere around 4 or 5 million harmonicas over the radio. We were selling harmonicas for a company in Chicago, and we told them they would have to get a good harmonica or we couldn't sell them. Kratt put us out a good one. You could brag about them and live up to your guarantee. They was just as good as Hohners. Kratt was the president of Hohner whenever Hitler took over. He left Germany to come to the United States. He lived to be a hundred and some years old. He was 103 when they arrested him for drunk driving. These days I play Hohners. They got all kinds of them out, but the insides are the same, like the Marine Band. The Pro Harps are good—easy blowing.

Me and Wayne parted company about 1960. I hit the road again. I played school assembly shows. When I was younger, I could play about four shows a day. I covered a lot of territory. I'm still doing it. I drive myself around in a van and do my own business. I play a lot of colleges and big bluegrass festivals. I'm going to keep going until I can't go. I'd go crazy if I quit. Did you ever notice that when most of these people retire, in a few days they're dead? It's very boring to sit around and not do a thing.

I don't know what it is about the sound of the harmonica. It being such a little instrument, and getting so much out of it. My harmonica playing is absolutely, completely different from anybody else's harmonica playing. I play the harmonica just like you was throwing your voice. The sound and everything comes from way down deep in the throat.

Wayne Raney (1920–93)

Wayne Raney measured all of show business's angles. As a disc jockey, singer, harp player, guitarist, studio owner, producer, songwriter, and recording artist, his influence was extensive. Johnny Cash has claimed that listening to Raney's radio broadcasts as a young boy in Dyess, Arkansas, inspired him to pursue music as a career. As a harmonica booster, Raney had few peers; over the years he was responsible for the sale of millions of mouth organs.

An Arkansas native, Raney's earliest musical memories were of listening to the Delmore Brothers on the Grand Ole Opry broadcasts. As a five-year-old, Raney became excited after listening to a one-armed hobo play the harmonica on the street. ("I said then that I would learn to make it sound like that.") His parents sold eggs to buy him his first mouth organ, a Hotz diatonic, and within a year he had taught himself the rudiments of the cross-harp style. Born with a crippled foot, Raney was excused from many of the chores on his family farm; he taught himself the harmonica and guitar, listened to Lonnie Glosson over KMOX, and dreamed of becoming a professional musician.

Despite the protests of his parents, he began leaving home for extended periods of time, hitchhiking from one radio station to another, trying to make a name for himself. Raney was fourteen years old when the manager of radio station XEPN heard him playing in a pool hall in Eagle Pass, Texas, and gave him his own program. In 1934, Raney made his first recordings for Victor's Bluebird label. Two years later Raney met his idol Lonnie Glosson when he won second place in one of Glosson's harmonica contests. The two became friends, and when Glosson's band broke up in 1938, they began broadcasting over KARK in Little Rock. "I developed my own style of playing harmony that would fit his lead style," said Raney. Glosson and Raney would play together off and on for the next twenty-five years.

Glosson was a born rambler who tended to strike out for greener pastures at regular intervals, and Raney worked at becoming a successful radio personality, hosting a program for KFWB in Hollywood, California, in 1941. Later that year Raney moved to Cincinnati and settled in for a long stretch with Glosson at WCKY, performing, spinning records, and selling mail-order Kratt "talking harmonicas." "They sold for a dollar sixty-nine," recalled Raney. "We did taped shows for two hundred thirty different radio stations, and in a five-year stretch we sold over five million harmonicas."

In 1945, Raney returned to Texas to broadcast over KRLD in Dallas. He then moved on to WMC in Memphis, where he was again reunited with Lonnie Glosson. The pair began playing with the Delmore Brothers, who had been fired from the Opry and were trying to resurrect their careers with a new sound based on a boogie-woogie guitar style that Alton Delmore had perfected. The lonesome harmonicas of Raney and Glosson meshed beautifully with the Delmores' fresh approach, and they were asked to join the brothers' radio show. The four also put together a successful touring show that featured Raney's harmonica specialities, "Fox Chase" and "A Race With a Model T Ford," and Glosson's "talking harmonica" act.

Beginning in 1946, the Delmore Brothers began recording for King Records, often using Raney and Glosson on harmonicas. Raney offered to play a session for free if King would release a record by him, and at the end of a Delmore Brothers session Raney recorded his first two sides, "The Fox Chase" and "Green River Valley." Raney and the Delmores continued to play on each other's records for four more years; their "country boogie" style laid the groundwork for the rockabilly craze of the 1950s. In 1949 the Delmores hit it big with "Blues Stay Away From Me" (which featured the twin harmonicas of Glosson and Raney), but Raney topped them with his number one country hit, "Why Don't You Haul Off and Love Me," which sold over a million copies and earned him a call from the Grand Ole Opry. That same year Raney accompanied Lonnie Glosson on a session for Mercury; in 1950 he cut four sides for London Records as "Lonesome Willie Evans."

The recording partnership of Raney and the Delmores ended with the death of Rabon Delmore in December of 1952, and Raney became a member of NBC's "California Hayride." In 1954 he joined the band of honky-tonk troubadour Lefty Frizzell, singing harmony and playing the harmonica. "I recorded with him and also toured with him," notes Raney. "I played harmonica on Lefty's album of Jimmie Rodgers songs." Raney left Frizzell to become a regular member of the cast of Wheeling, West Virginia's "WWVA Jamboree."

Raney's association with King Records ended in 1955. He flirted briefly with rockabilly, recording material in that vein for Decca before beginning another five-year stint at WCKY. Raney began spending less time performing and more on the business end of music, founding Poor Boy Records in 1958 before settling in Concord, Arkansas, where he opened up a recording studio and founded a second label, Rimrock.

Raney's last recording session as a performer was for Starday Records in 1964. When Stax Records bought his studio and pressing plant a decade later, Raney retired from show business. Interest in his career surged again in the mid-1980s after an English label, Charly, released two albums' worth of Raney's recordings.

Raney loyally professed his preference for the Kratt diatonics over any of the Hohners. "What appeals to me about the harmonica," he told me, "is the sound of loneliness that fits everybody at certain times." Wayne Raney died on January 23, 1993.

Jimmie Riddle (1918–82)

Jimmie Riddle spent twenty-five years with Roy Acuff's Smokey Mountain Boys, and his boss and fellow band members never really knew what to make of him. "Jimmie is an extraordinary fellow. He will beat a mean hillbilly tune onstage and then go home, rig up his hi-fi outfit with two hours of jazz, classical, and semiclassical music, and enjoy every minute of it," Acuff once commented wonderingly. Riddle's passion for astronomy ranked just behind his love of music and of hunting frogs at night. In the early years with Acuff's troops, band members ridiculed him unmercifully for asserting that men would someday walk on the moon. Riddle's interests ranged from the Greek philosophers to reincarnation to the macro-micro cosmic theory, which speculates that the universe might simply be a flea on the back of a dog. In short, Riddle was just the sort of freewheeling individualist who made for a good harmonica player, and he was in fact one of the most thoroughly musical mouth organists ever to work in country music.

Jimmie Riddle grew up in Memphis. "My first recollection I have at all playing the harmonica was actually when I had learned to play it, because my mother told me I was three and a half years old," Riddle said in an interview with *Country Heritage* magazine. "And her father—my grandfather—John L. Boone, played the old harmonica. All he played was the old country tunes—breakdowns and everything. Mama told me I was just fascinated with it. She said he handed me the harmonica—never had one in my mouth—and I took that thing and played a tune on it!" His first public performance was a rendition of "That's My Weakness Now" for his fellow first-graders; before long he was playing for nickels on Beale Street.

Riddle's only formal musical instruction came from a neighbor who taught him some basic guitar chords when he was ten. Within two years, he was teaching himself piano and accordion. Riddle's grades suffered as he became more involved with music. "I'll bet I've had five hundred dollars' worth of harmonicas taken away from me while I was going to school," he once confessed. At sixteen he started playing the beer joints with older musicians, and during the next four years, he played with many Memphis groups, most notably local favorites Uncle Rube Turnipseed and His Pea Ridge Ramblers. He eventually adopted the chromatic harmonica as his instrument of choice, a rare preference for a country player.

Riddle first saw the inside of a recording studio as a member of the Swift Jewel Cowboys, for whom he played guitar, accordion, bass fiddle, and harmonica. In 1939 they recorded at the Gayoso Hotel in Memphis. Riddle played boogie-woogie-style chromatic harmonica on "Dill Pickle Rag," "Kansas City Blues," "Raggin' the Rails," and "Fan It."

Later that year Riddle moved to Houston to join the Crustine Ranch Boys, a western swing band, taking a day job in the shipyards to avoid the draft. In 1943, the Crustine Ranch Boys opened a show for Roy Acuff, who heard Riddle jamming backstage and offered him a job. (Acuff had played the harmonica as a boy and had always been a fan of the instrument; an earlier version of his group had included Sam "Dynamite" Hatcher, a fine singer, guitarist, and mouth organist.) Despite his worries about the draft, Riddle decided to join Acuff as a harmonica player and accordionist. About this time he recorded two sides (including "I Want My Mama," his take on the "talking harmonica" motif) on his own for Decca, who billed him as the "Harmonica Wizard." Riddle was drafted in late 1944 and served in the army until the summer of 1946, rejoining Acuff as soon as he was demobilized.

Onstage with Acuff, Riddle would serve up a blistering harmonica fox chase and show off his mouth organ talent on "Shotgun Boogie," "Thirty Days," "Chiquita Banana," "I'm Walkin'," and "Yes, Sir." A favorite number of the band's was a spoof of classical music built around Riddle's harmonica playing. On the road, Riddle made all the onstage introductions, handled the band's correspondence, signed contracts, and even wrote press releases. When the group toured Europe, Riddle proved to be a voracious sightseer, especially enjoying a trip to the Hohner factory in Germany.

In the late 1940s, Riddle began playing more piano with the Smokey Mountain Boys, explaining that "Roy needs the piano to hold the rhythm, and when we don't have one, it makes a difference. I've had twenty-five years up front so I don't mind. Besides, I get a chance to sit down during the shows." Riddle found himself spending even more time at the keyboard after harmonica player Onie Wheeler began appearing regularly with the band in the mid-1960s.

Riddle also worked as a studio musician in Nashville, where he and Wheeler were top session harmonicists. Besides backing up such country artists as Johnny Horton, Red Foley, Bill Anderson, Rex Allen, Johnny Bond, Jim Reeves, and Jimmy Dean, Riddle played behind mainstream pop singers like Joni James, Johnny Ray, Anita Bryant, Connie Francis, and the Four Guys.

Riddle recorded only two solo albums during his long career. The first, *Country Harmonica,* released on Cumberland Records, featured his chromatic playing and is a lively collection of jazz, country, and boogie-woogie tunes. The second, *Let's Go* on Briar, was recorded in 1964 and shows Riddle as a solid diatonic player; surprisingly, most of the material is heavily influenced by the blues harp style of Slim Harpo and Jimmy Reed.

Riddle was a sound-effects genius who on the road could enliven an otherwise boring piece of highway by perfectly mimicking a tire blowout. Onstage, he would provide the train whistle for the "Wabash Cannonball" and occasionally perform "The William Tell Overture" by tapping on his throat. Riddle's mastery of a hiccuping vocal trick called "eephin'," which his uncle Ralph Boone taught him when he was six, rejuvenated his solo career after he performed it on a 1969 "Hee Haw" appearance. Riddle made dozens of "eephin' " appearances on the show, began making club appearances, and recorded a single for Decca that paired "Wildwood Eeph" with "Yackety Eeph." "All I know is my uncle Ralph called it 'hoodlin'.' That was the original name of it. . . . There's no tellin' how far back it goes," Riddle told *Country Heritage*. "Seems like it might have been something the old slaves would do, like a little chant. . . . There are variations on it. You can put a syncopated lick in it. You can get a rhumba lick. My son taught me a five/four lick."

About his harmonica playing, Riddle told writer Elizabeth Schlappi that "I was just born with it. I really think we are all instruments of God, and He plays through us, and this is the way He chose to play through me." Riddle had a collection of several hundred Hohner harmonicas. He was best known for his mastery of the twelve-hole #270 chromatic, but was also at home on the Old Standby and Marine Band diatonics.

"I heard an old saying one time: 'For every tuxedo, there's a thousand pair of overalls,'" Riddle once said. "The country people, they're the ones that like the country music, and ninety percent of the people are really country-music-minded at heart. Some of these musicians play too much stuff and the people don't know what they're doing. They just want to hear the plain old melody. I like *all* types of music: country, classical, pop, jazz, bluegrass—any facet of it. But the people who listen to country music, they don't know what a jazz musician is doing. In fact, most musicians don't know what he's doing, unless they happen to be jazz musicians themselves. . . . I really enjoy playing country music because it is the easiest kind of music to play. When you get off on that jazz and stuff like that—I like to listen to it, but I can't really play it."

Onie Wheeler (1921–83)

Onie Wheeler, a talented harmonica player, singer, and songwriter (his tunes have been recorded by George Jones, Merle Haggard, Lefty Frizzell, and Roy Acuff, among others) was one of the most active harmonica players in country music during the 1950s and '60s. Raised on a Missouri homestead, Wheeler pursued farming as a young man, but throughout the 1940s he was also developing his skills as a musician and singer on radio stations throughout Missouri and Arkansas.

By 1950, Wheeler was hosting a regular program for station KWOC in Pine Bluff, Arkansas, and earning a local reputation that enabled him to form his first band, the Ozark Cowboys. After a recording debut on Agana Records, Wheeler was signed to the Okeh label in 1953. His contract was later assumed by Okeh's parent label, Columbia, and Wheeler began touring widely, hitting the road in 1954 with a newcomer named Elvis Presley. Wheeler's style had been modeled after the approach of classic honky-tonk singers like Hank Williams and Lefty Frizzell, but after his tour with Presley his records began to show a shift toward the "country boogie" style. Wheeler always contended that this change in direction was something that he—as a longtime fan of the Delmore Brothers and Wayne Raney—had been looking to make for some time. Whatever its genesis, Wheeler's new approach—and Elvis's new status as a musical superstar—was the basis for his 1956 hit, "Onie's Bop," a novelty number designed to give Wheeler the opportunity not only to poke fun at Presley but to offer up impersonations of various well-known country singers. While "Onie's Bop" was a vocal showcase, many of Wheeler's other records—especially "Onie's French Harp Boogie"—showed off his first-rate harmonica playing.

Wheeler recorded briefly for Sun Records before moving to Nashville, where over the years he recorded for several labels, including Starday, Musicor, Scottie, United Artists, Epic, K-Arc, Papa Joe, and Brylen. He did many sessions in the 1950s and '60s for Columbia as a harmonica sideman, lending his talents to the studio efforts of Sonny James and others.

In 1965, Wheeler began playing harmonica in Roy Acuff's band. He did tours of Vietnam with Acuff and as the leader of his own band and had a modest hit on Royal American in 1972. Like many country performers, Wheeler became popular in Europe, eventually touring there twice each year.

Charlie McCoy (1941–)

Charlie McCoy is undoubtedly the most recorded harmonica player in history. For decades now, three or four times a day, five days a week, Charlie McCoy has been helping the singers who pass through Nashville's fabled studios sound better. Since 1960, McCoy has played behind hundreds of artists, including Tammy Wynette, Joan Baez, Simon and Garfunkel, Ringo Starr, and Bob Dylan, and recorded several best-selling solo harmonica albums, thereby reintroducing the country music audience to the mouth organ and becoming one of the most influential and widely imitated harmonica players ever.

The mouth organ was his first love, but by the time he was in high school he was playing trumpet and guitar in rhythm and blues groups. McCoy's first trip to Nashville as an eighteen-year-old singing guitarist was a disappointment, but a year later he returned and began a career as a session stalwart. His fabled style, with its bell-like single notes, its remarkably melodic approach, its speed and precision, and its unerring sense of economy and placement, was sharply distinct from the wide-open, down-home style of his predecessors.

In the mid-1960s, McCoy played bass and guitar on three of Bob Dylan's landmark rock albums. McCoy was the same age as Dylan, and he was associated with a group of younger Nashville session men who enjoyed occasional escapes from the Nashville pop/country formulas they were being paid to bring to life in the studios. In the late 1960s, McCoy became one of the founding members of Area Code 615, a loose coalition of Nashville musicians who recorded two excellent albums of rock-influenced instrumentals. Rock groups like The Byrds and The Flying Burrito Brothers had made a stir by releasing country-influenced albums, and the possibility of an alliance between these country rockers and the younger Nashville session men was an intriguing one. But the cultural differences between the two camps were too great, and a disappointing experience at the Fillmore, San Francisco's rock headquarters, hastened the demise of Area Code 615 and delayed the realization of such an unlikely musical brotherhood until Waylon Jennings and Willie Nelson accomplished it a decade later.

In the mid-1970s, McCoy signed a contract with Monument Records for a series of solo harmonica albums. The first release, *The Real McCoy,* was the top-selling country album for five weeks that year. He had four top-ten hits in the seventies and twice won the Country Music Association's Instrumentalist of the Year award. In 1977, McCoy took over the position of music director for the popular country music television program "Hee Haw," a job he still enjoys.

Interview With Charlie McCoy

I'm originally from West Virginia. My mom and dad divorced when I was pretty young, and because of a minor health condition the doctors decided it would be good for me to spend the winters in Florida with my dad and summers in West Virginia with my mother. The summer I was eight years old I saw an ad in a comic book—fifty cents and a box top, buy a harmonica, you know. I conned my mother out of fifty cents and it finally came. I probably got on my mother's nerves pretty bad, but I was able to look at the instructions—blow hole four, draw hole five—and figure out the four songs—there was "Swanee River," "Oh Susannah," "Polly Wolly Doodle," and "My Country 'Tis of Thee"—by looking at the charts. I must have had a better-than-average ear.

I was hot on the harp for a while, but then I put it away. I went back to Florida to start back to school and my dad was unpacking my luggage and said, "Hey, where'd you get this?" And he picked my harmonica up and started to play. I didn't know he could play. So I got interested again for a week or two.

Shortly after that I got a guitar. I turned fifteen in 1956 and rock and roll was here and everybody wanted to be Elvis. I definitely had my mind set in the area of guitar playing and singing. Growing up in Florida, the radio down there was kind of segregated, so we didn't hear any r&b down there. So I go back to West Virginia in the summer, and of course at that age, all the guys are talking about music and learning how to dance and discovering girls and all that. So we started talking music and I said, "Yeah, man, I dig 'Long Tall Sally.' That's a great record by Pat Boone." They said to me, "*Pat Boone?* What in the world have you been listening to?" I said, "What do you mean?" And they said, "Haven't you ever heard of Little Richard?" I said, "No." They played me the Little Richard version and I said, "Oh, yeah, yeah, this is it. There *is* a definite difference."

So I went back to Florida that year and tried to tell everybody about Little Richard and nobody knew what I was talking about. I started roaming the radio looking for stations. I found an r&b station down there and I heard a Jimmy Reed record, and that just got to me real bad. My dad worked in a furniture store right on the edge of the black section of Miami, and one Saturday I went to work with him and I snuck out and found a record shop. I bought "You Got Me Dizzy" by Jimmy Reed and I brought it home and played it. My dad just freaked. He said, "I can take Elvis, but this is too much." So I was confined to playing my Jimmy Reed when he wasn't at home.

I got an earphone jack on my clock radio and an old pair of earphones. Late at night I'd lay in bed listening to the radio and my dad couldn't hear it. I finally found WLAC in Nashville. They were playing some heavyweight r&b, with lots of harmonica music. I thought Jimmy Reed was it, but when I heard Little Walter, I said, "Whoa, wait a minute. There's more." I was just really digging it, and one day like a bolt out of the blue I said, "Wait a minute, I've got a harmonica. Why can't I do this?" That's when my whole focus changed. I started experimenting and trying to figure out what Jimmy Reed and Little Walter and Sonny Boy and all those guys were doing. I didn't know anything about cross harp, but I finally figured out that they weren't blowing on this thing, they were drawing on it.

I started playing guitar and singing at a place in Miami. I was hired to play rock and roll fifteen minutes an hour. One night Mel Tillis came in and heard me and told me that if I'd come to Nashville, his manager could get me a record contract tomorrow. I was seventeen years old and I said, "Oh, yeah, man, great!" So that summer I went to Nashville and auditioned for everybody—Chet Atkins, Owen Bradley—playing Chuck Berry guitar and singing. They said, "Well, I guess he's pretty good, but we don't know what to do with him." I went back to Florida, tail between my legs, and started studying music at the University of Miami.

I went to school about a year and got sick of it. I loved the music, but the other stuff—the English and the history—was so hard for me that I found I didn't have any time to spend on the music, and I really got frustrated by it. I kept thinking about Nashville and how everybody up there had been so nice. While I was there in 1959, I saw Brenda Lee record "Sweet Nuthin's." I'd seen that session, and all those musicians. Nobody had charts—they just played—and I thought, gosh, this is great.

After a year I finally got up enough nerve to tell my dad that I wanted to drop out of college, and I came to Nashville and got a job as a drummer. It was either take that job or go home and lose face, so I took it and one thing led to another. Jim Denny got me a contract with Cadence Records as a singer. My first single was called "Cherry Berry Wine" and it went to number 99 in *Billboard* before it dropped out. I had already started playing recording sessions. My second record bombed and then Cadence went out of business. I signed with Monument and did something like nine rock and roll vocal singles for them that did nothing.

Jim Denny started letting me play on demo sessions. He was using Grady Martin and Hank Garland and Harold Bradley on his demos, so there was no need for me to play the guitar. He said, "Play that harmonica. That'll be different." I played on a demo and he called me in one day and said, "Chet Atkins heard this demo you played on and he wants to record this song on a new artist named Ann-Margret, and he wants you to do exactly what you did on the demo." The record was called "I Just Don't Understand" and it ended up a top-twenty pop record. One of the guys on the session said, "I really dig what you're doing. You want to do a session with Roy Orbison this week?" Roy Orbison was one of my heroes. So we did the record "Candy Man," which was also a hit. So I played on two top-twenty records in the first week. It was what you call being in the right place at the right time. After that it was session city all the way.

The harmonica was almost nonexistent in country music when I got to Nashville. Jimmie Riddle had a couple of records that he played on, and Onie Wheeler played on a few, but there was a long dry spell in there. The blues revival may have helped me, because the first records I did had a kind of a bluesy feel to them. At the time I did "Candy Man," I wasn't really influenced by country music because I had just come into town. At first the blues thing was a real novelty because nobody in town was doing it, but it wore off on people real quick. They liked the instrument but they wanted to hear it done a different way, I guess.

One of the biggest helps to me in creating whatever it is that people call my style was Grady Martin, who was the greatest session leader I ever worked with. He had this uncanny ability to know what something was going to sound like before he played it. Almost every time they would run a song down, his first idea was what he went with, and it was always right. One time we were on a session and running a song down. I was just feeling my oats and playing, and I looked down and I caught Grady just giving me the evil eye real bad. After we finished one take I went over to him and said, "Am I doing something wrong?" He said, "You're playing too much. Listen to the words and get in between 'em." That really stuck with me.

I learned a lot from other instruments. Steel guitar always impressed me. I'd be on a session and the steel player would play a lick and I'd say to myself, "I wonder if I can play that same lick." Then we started doing a lot of unison stuff on sessions—steel and harp, Dobro and harp, fiddle and harp. Producers started asking me, "Could you play the melody more and not play so funky?" All of this was leading me into this style I developed, and I was getting a lot of work. Jimmie Riddle would laugh and tell me, "Man, just keep it up. Every once in a while somebody calls and you're busy, and I get a little work from it."

A songwriter named Bob Johnston had come to Nashville and he started using me on his demos. He was kind of a radical guy for Nashville, and nobody there thought much of him, but he took his demos to New York, and the head of CBS at the time, Bob Mercy, said, "Who produced these demos?" Johnston said, "I did. I made them in Nashville." Mercy said, "How would you like to produce a record for us?" And he said, "Sure." So they gave him Patti Page, who at that time was the coldest artist they had. Johnston had some connections in L.A. and got her the title cut on the movie *Hush . . . Hush, Sweet Charlotte,* which revived her whole career. They thought, "Hey, this guy's a genius. We've got this artist over here that nobody can work with. Let's see if Johnston can." And the artist was Bob Dylan.

In 1965 I went up to New York to go to the World's Fair. Johnston had told me, "If you ever come to New York, call me. I'll get you Broadway tickets." I called him up and he said, "What are you doing this afternoon? Come on by CBS. I'm gonna record with Bob Dylan and he wants to say hello to you." So I went over there and it was just him and this upright bass player there. Johnston introduced me to Dylan and he blew me away. He said, "I've got one of your records." I couldn't believe it—it was one of my old rock records. He said, "Hey, you want to play?" And I said, "I didn't bring any harps." He said, "No, don't play harp—get that acoustic guitar over there and play." We did a song called "Desolation Row." And after that session, Johnston talked him into coming to Nashville. So we did the albums *Blonde on Blonde, John Wesley Harding,* and *Nashville Skyline.* I remember doing one song ["Rainy Day Women #12 & 35"] and playing bass with one hand and trumpet with the other. I used to do that in rock bands. All I could do was play simple riffs, and on the song it sounded like a drunk Salvation Army band, but that's what Dylan was after.

Dylan was pretty cool. He had very little to say. If you'd ask what he thought about something, his answer was always, "I don't know, what do you think?" Apparently, we were doing the right things, because he never told us not to do what we were doing.

Then Johnston got Simon and Garfunkel, and I played bass harmonica on "The Boxer." I know now why the group broke up. When they would be in the studio together, every time Garfunkel would have a suggestion, it was always, "No, Artie, that won't work." That was Simon's pat answer for everything. Later I went to New York and did one cut playing bass on Simon's first solo album. He drove me nuts. We worked for like five hours on sixteen bars. It was a terrible thing. He's a genius, you know, but if you're going to work for him, you're definitely going to march to his drummer.

About 1968 five Nashville players—Kenny Buttrey, David Briggs, Wayne Moss, Mac Gayden, and Norbert Putnam—decided that they wanted to go into the studio and create their own thing. They went in the studio a couple of times, but they didn't think they were coming up with anything, so they brought myself, Weldon Myrick, Bobby Thompson, and Buddy Spicher in. The first couple of times we went into the studio, nothing happened. We'd all try to play real rock and that didn't work, and if we'd all play real country, that didn't prove anything. Finally Bobby and Buddy came in and they'd worked up a thing on "Hey Jude" with just a fiddle and a banjo. Everybody kind of fell in playing. The bass and drum were just like the Beatles' record, but the people on top were kind of playing country and bluegrass, and it was kind of a magical thing, that it all melded together like that. We did a couple of other songs, and this guy from New York, Elliott Mazer, heard some of it and went off to Polydor and got them interested in the project. So we put out an album calling ourselves Area Code 615.

We went to the Fillmore West and did four nights there. That was the only appearance we ever made. Looking back on it, we were at a disadvantage right away because to the people who went to the Fillmore, we probably looked like insurance salesmen. That was the time when Haight-Ashbury and all that stuff was really happening, and we must have really looked like IRS guys. They dug the music, I think, but our appearance was just a little too much for them. We did a second album, but the record company wanted us to go on the road, and all of the guys in the band were heavy into sessions and so the thing fell apart.

Of course, I was plenty busy. I had a fifteen-year stretch where I did over four hundred sessions a year. You might think that that kind of schedule would be instant burnout, but you know, if you can find a great song, you can always get inspired again. Out of all my sessions, "Candy Man" is real close to me. I like to go away from a session and think to myself, "Man, I played exactly what that song needed." One of the few times I really got that feeling was on "He Stopped Loving Her Today" by George Jones. All I did was four licks in that record and I felt that I really did what needed to be done.

I kept wanting to be a singer, but finally in 1968 I put out an instrumental record and was finally introduced to country music as an artist. Two years later, this station down in Pensacola started playing a cut off that album, "Today I Started Loving You Again." The album had been taken off the market, so the whole thing had to be re-pressed, reissued, and everything. That got the ball rolling and I did several more instrumental albums for Monument. Our total sales were over a million and a quarter before the label went bankrupt, and I got a lot of awards as an instrumentalist.

I also started touring. I loved it. After all those years of just going downtown and making a great living, all of a sudden I wanted to go out on the road because there's fuel out there, man, and it pumps you up and gets you excited. The only thing a studio can tell you is exactly what you played—it won't tell you if it liked it or not. Once you play for a live audience and they get turned on, there's nothing like it.

I've been associated with the "Hee Haw" television program for nineteen years. I started out as just a sideman. They hired me because at that time most of the acts that came on used the house band, and there were so many people coming on with records that I had played on. I was at the peak of my session thing then, and it was a real tough choice for me to do that show because it involved pretty much all your time two months of the year. After a couple of years they asked me to be music director, and that's been a real great thing. I've just been tickled to be associated with it. I'm really pretty busy out there. If somebody doesn't like the mix, I'm the one they come after. And I'm in charge of the house band and I represent the musician's union on the set.

Jimmie Riddle and I worked together on "Hee Haw" for about ten years. He was just a great guy. He basically played chromatic, but he didn't play any kind of jazz or anything. He could do "Clarinet Polka" and stuff like that—he did all those old, tricky, technical things. The strange thing about Jimmie was that he was a keyboard player, but he played the harp upside down. He had the high notes on the left, and of course the piano is just the opposite. That used to blow my mind. I used to wonder, how in the world does he think like that?

I got Herman Crook on "Hee Haw" once, and I got Wayne Raney and Lonnie Glosson on there another time. The producer didn't have any idea of who they were, and I said, "Man, I'm telling you, all the real old-time country music fans remember these guys because they used to be on that powerhouse radio station in Cincinnati and they used to sell harmonicas like hotcakes." Lonnie didn't seem to be the least bit affected by television. He just jumped out there and did it to it.

There was a guy in Nashville who was trying to get me to collaborate with DeFord Bailey on something. I talked to DeFord about it, but he was skeptical and it didn't happen. It would've been great. DeFord had that one thing, but it was really something.

There are a lot of good young harp players in Nashville. Terry McMillan's done some good stuff with George Jones and Tanya Tucker and Lacey J. Dalton. There's another guy named Kirk "Jelly Roll" Johnson—he's done all the Judds' records and the Randy Travis things. And there's a kid that tours with Loretta Lynn named Mike Caldwell who plays so fast it's blinding—there oughta be a radar gun on him. I thought I played pretty fast, but boy, he can burn it. Buddy Green, who used to tour with Jerry Reed, and Phil Gazell—they're both good players.

In 1975 I recorded with a big French artist named Eddie Mitchell. Two years later he brought a couple of us over to do a tour all over France and Belgium. In 1987 I was doing a session with a Danish artist, and his producer said to me, "Would you consider doing a couple of albums with us?" Monument had gone bankrupt, so I said, "Why not?" I did a couple of albums with this Danish company, and a booking agent over there said, "I believe I can book you in Denmark if you want to work." I said, "I'd love to work, but what about my band?" And he said, "I've got a band over here that I think you'll be very happy with." Well, reluctantly I went and I was amazed. This band he put me with was absolutely fantastic. One of the guys in the band was French, and he had some connections and we kind of filtered into France. Since then I've been spending a lot of time in Europe. It's a different mentality over there. When it's time to break for dinner or to drink wine, that's it. Nothing else takes precedence. There's no stress over there, either.

As far as the different types of harmonicas go, it's hard to explain why you pick one over another. For the longest time I played the Old Standby. I liked the feel of it. It was a little smaller, and whenever I played onstage, it had that little embossed figure so I could always tell which side was up without looking at it. Hohner used to make them in seven keys, but I think they only make them in two keys now. I've probably got enough of them to last me the rest of my life. So on seven keys I used the Old Standby, and on the other five keys I had the Marine Band. I play the Special 20 now and I'll use Vest Pocket harps, too. The Vest Pocket has a high G and a high A, and Hohner made me a couple of special G#s.

I know a bunch of guys that play all kinds of strange positions, but I more or less just stay with straight cross harp. The only special tuning I really use much is raising the fifth draw reed to the major seventh. Now I pretty much play that raised fifth draw reed all the time because I can always choke the seventh back on it. For country music, melodically speaking, that major seventh is everywhere. To me, it seems like I can do a whole lot more things. That tuning was shown to me. I used to have an office down on Music Row, and one day my secretary came back and said, "There's a fan of yours out front who wants to talk to you." I said, "Send him on back." This older gentleman came in and said, "My name is Duane Parker. I'm a harmonica player from Watertown, New York. I've played chromatic all my life until I heard your records. I've got your albums and I'm trying to learn. But there's one song I'm really having problems with—'Danny Boy.'" Now my curiosity's up, but I'm not saying a thing. He said, "The only way that you could have done this song is to have tuned this fifth reed up." He pulled out a harp with the fifth reed tuned up and played the song and said, "That's the way you done it, isn't it?" And I said, "No, but that's the way I'm gonna do it from now on." What I had done in the studio was use different harps for the verse and the chorus.

I hold the harp wrong. I know I don't hold it the way they tell you to in the books. Since I've been doing so many personal appearances, I've gotten into more of a vibrato with the throat, because with these sound systems, you've got to eat the mike to get heard. I play right on the mike in person, but not on sessions.

I play the chromatic some, but I don't do much. I have one album I cut for a Danish label that's primarily chromatic, but about all I'm doing is playing melodies. I love it when those chromatic players get that great big tone. It sounds like a freight train. Larry Adler has that kind of sound.

There have been times when the limitations of the diatonic have frustrated me. We had this spot we did for five or six years on "Hee Haw" called the Million Dollar Band with Chet Atkins and Boots Randolph, and they always wanted to play bebop or swing tunes where the melody goes rambling off through the chord changes. You can't really do it on the diatonic, and I used to get really frustrated by that.

You'd just have to find a place in the song where you could ad-lib a little bit. But most of the commercial music that the masses get into can be done on the diatonic, and that's what I'm into—playing for the masses. The only jazz I know is a basketball team in Utah. Rock and roll and country is about it for me.

As far as other players go, I like Little Walter—he's *it* as far as I'm concerned. Then there are Toots Thielemans and Stevie Wonder. And Howard Levy—I think he's probably an alien. I did a little demo with him a couple of years ago. A British songwriter and harp player named Julian Dawson came to town and he got Jelly Roll, myself, Randy Singer, and Howard to demo this song he wrote especially about harmonicas that went through all these different styles. Of course, I did the country style. They got to this place where the song opened up into kind of a free-form jazz swing thing, and Howard not only went in and did the piano behind it, he went in there and absolutely just blew us all away. He was showing me how to do that overblow thing and I still don't have it down. He told me that he landed on it by accident. I told him, "Man, I don't believe you're from around here. I think you probably came in on a spaceship from somewhere." It's inhuman what he can do.

I can't really tell you what drew me to the harmonica. An eight-year-old kid reads a comic book and sees an ad—there's no logic to that. But since then I've found that there are a whole lot of things I like about it. Number one, it probably is closer to the human voice than any other instrument. It's also obviously easy to carry around. If you watch audiences, a harp really catches people's ear. To me, there are four instruments that really get to people: the harp, the fiddle, the banjo, and the sax. I believe when those four instruments are played well, audiences just really go for it.

I've got a new album out called *Out on a Limb,* and it's probably the most versatile thing I've done. I have this great fiddle player in my European band, and he's heavy into Irish music. We've got two Irish things on this album that were really hard to learn to play but that I'm nuts about. I'm really trying hard to hook up with some kind of a substantial recording deal in Europe. I'm still working for "Hee Haw" and doing a few road things and a session or two here and there. My session work is way down from what it used to be, but some of it's by choice because I'm going out of the country a lot. But I'm sure enjoying it now. Every time I have a session I'm fired up. Of course, I'm not thirty years old anymore. I don't think I could take the pace we used to do. In four years, if I want to, I can take my retirement from the union. I've got a heck of a retirement with all those years of sessions, but that doesn't mean I'm going to quit. I'm playing now just as much or more than I ever have.

I have to thank Nashville for letting me make it. It's been a heck of a trip, I'll tell you. Somebody recently asked me, "Have you been playing that thing all your life?" And I said, "Not yet."

Don Brooks (1947–)

Don Brooks, who may possess the most soulful tone of any harp player in country music, had the good fortune to be born in the state of Texas, one of the choicest musical arenas in a country justly celebrated for its cultural crossbreeding. Like countless harmonica players of his generation, Brooks was led to the instrument through a fascination with the blues.

Brooks played cornet and guitar as a boy ("I was a horrible guitar player") and developed an adolescent craving for black rock and roll. One evening, listening to a Dallas radio show called "Cat's Caravan," Brooks was electrified by a Sonny Terry record. After a friend gave him a harmonica, Brooks began a long, frustrating attempt to copy Terry's cross-harp playing in first position. Brooks started performing in Dallas coffeehouses, playing with anyone who would let him onstage, regardless of their musical orientation. He now feels that his willingness to feel his way through the disparate styles offered up by these players gave his playing a melodic thrust that few young harmonica players attain.

The period around 1965 ("the Dylan phase," he calls it) found Brooks playing with the likes of his friend Johnny Vanderver and more established singers such as Jerry Jeff Walker, country blues ace Mance Lipscomb, and singer/guitarist Michael Murphy, who also played the harmonica and was curious about Brooks's predilection for first position. When Brooks professed ignorance about cross harp, Murphy gave him his first introduction to second position, and Brooks never looked back. "I can't even play any first position now," he claims.

Brooks followed a girlfriend to New York City in 1967. Jerry Jeff Walker was a neighbor, and he was Brooks's passport to the Greenwich Village folk scene that radiated from clubs like Gerde's Folk City.

"I came to New York as a blues player," says Brooks, "and ended up in the folk scene." His circle of musical partners included David Bromberg, Eric Weissberg, Paul Siebel, and John Hammond. In 1968, Jerry Jeff Walker hired Brooks as a featured player on an album project, and after the success of a cut from that record, "Mr. Bojangles," he and Walker began touring widely. Brooks's reputation was growing; he began to work occasionally with Harry Belafonte.

In 1973 he and Jerry Jeff opened a show for Waylon Jennings at the Troubador in L.A., and Jennings asked Brooks to contribute to his upcoming recording project. *Honky Tonk Heroes,* an album on which Waylon's best musical instincts were enhanced by the absence of the usual Nashville production clichés, made "outlaw" country music the hottest new phenomenon that genre had seen in many years. Within a year, Jennings and his longtime friend Willie Nelson, both fronting groups featuring harmonica players, were not only dominating the country field but had become two of the top acts in pop music. Waylon was brought to New York to bring country music to Max's Kansas City, a notorious punk pantheon. His dazzling band, led by Brooks and pedal steel player Ralph Mooney, set a standard that subsequent alternative country bands found difficult to meet.

Don Brooks had made some simultaneous commitments to songstress Judy Collins, which led him to miss occasional shows with Jennings. Brooks felt somewhat removed from the rest of the band, but when the full group was assembled for shows, it was a powerful congregation. "Waylon had an unbeatable rhythm section," Brooks recalls. "We slayed people everywhere we went. I expect that's the most amazing musical experience I'll ever have." Brooks offered up some beautiful playing on Jennings's next album, *This Time,* including a performance on the title cut that he and many of his admirers point to as the epitome of his full-bodied tone and his compelling rhythmic drive.

Brooks eventually ended his working relationship with Jennings and continued touring and recording with Judy Collins. He also went on the road with Guy Clark, Jerry Jeff Walker, and Harry Belafonte. The role of accompanist is one Brooks seeks out. "I've always been a sideman. My job was always to make them sound good. I don't even know any solo material." Brooks continued to make his home in New York City, eventually becoming that city's most asked-for diatonic session musician. His Marine Band work can be heard on recordings by such artists as Carly Simon, The Bee Gees, Ringo Starr, Yoko Ono, Bette Midler, Rita Coolidge, Diana Ross, and Billy Joel.

In 1985, Brooks landed a job on Broadway with *Big River,* Roger Miller's musical version of Mark Twain's Huckleberry Finn saga that won several Tony Awards that season. Brooks appeared onstage as well as in the pit band in the production, and his playing (including some fine bass harmonica work) was prominently featured on the cast album on MCA.

For the most part, Brooks plays the Hohner Marine Band model. "The draw three hole is the single most important note on a diatonic," he contends. "It's the link between going up and down on the harp." He studied the chromatic for a time with Robert Bonfiglio, but was never able to develop a real rapport with the instrument. Like many studio players, Brooks has experimented with some special tunings for his diatonics; his favorite is one on which the blow three note is tuned to a major second and the draw five note is changed to a major seventh.

His major influences are the melodic bluesman Lonnie Johnson and Mance Lipscomb. As far as other harp players go, Brooks unhesitatingly states, "I revere Paul Butterfield's playing. He took that Chicago style and took it somewhere else, made it into something his own that was very exciting." Asked about his own style, he says, "I think that my bluesy tone and my rhythm playing are the things that are uniquely mine. The thing that's helped me was playing with *everybody* in the old days. Hopefully, I didn't change my style to suit the material. The music will tell you where to go. It's there, you just have to find it. I never had to figure out how to play country music. I was playing country music from a country blues background. Everything I do—everything I play—is blues.

"There's an interesting contradiction with the harmonica. The harp can span the whole range of American music, and yet it's so personal that it's hard to find a venue for it. I'm the luckiest harmonica player in the world to have worked so much."

Mickey Raphael (1951–)

Because of his association with the universally popular Willie Nelson, Mickey Raphael has probably enjoyed a larger worldwide audience than any other harmonicist with the exception of Stevie Wonder. Prominently featured on Nelson's impressive 1975 breakthrough album, *The Red-Headed Stranger,* Raphael continues to record and tour with country music's biggest crossover phenomenon, and his intelligent playing has become a hallmark of Nelson's sound.

Raphael gravitated toward the Dallas folk music scene as a teenager and fell under the spell of Don Brooks. "I went to this little coffeehouse one night and saw him playing, and it just impressed me so much," Raphael recalls. "He had moved to New York and was kind of a legend around Dallas. He sat me down one night after a show and showed me this little lick that went all the way up and down the harmonica, just a little pattern. Right away I just jumped about twenty steps from the little I already knew about the harp." Raphael also mentions being impressed by Jimmie Fadden's playing with The Nitty Gritty Dirt Band around this time.

Raphael eventually joined singer B. W. Stephenson's band. One of his most enthusiastic boosters was University of Texas football coach Darrell Royal, a passionate fan of country music. One night in 1973, Royal invited Raphael to a postgame party in a Dallas hotel room and asked him to bring along his harps. The resulting informal jam session included Charley Pride and Willie Nelson, who passed around a guitar and took turns singing. "I played a little with Willie and he asked me to come and sit in with him sometime. A while later he played a firemen's benefit in a high school gym somewhere outside of Dallas, and I showed up and played a little. Later we were sitting there talking and he said, 'Why don't you come to New York with me in a couple of months—we're going to play Max's Kansas City.' So I went up there and played with Willie. He really wasn't touring that much then; it was still a couple of years before he left Texas again on real tours."

Raphael moved from Dallas to Austin, Nelson's home base, and began a crash course in country music. "When I joined Willie's band, I really didn't know *anything* about country music. I'd never listened to it at all. I was a folk blues player. I just wanted to play in a country band and ride around in a bus. Charlie McCoy was the first guy I really listened to as far as playing country music. For that style—and Charlie plays great blues, too—he's technically perfect."

After two years spent playing weekend dances all over the sprawling expanse of the Lone Star State, Willie Nelson went into a studio in Garland in 1975 and recorded *The Red Headed Stranger,* a concept album full of segues linked by a cowboy narrative that showcased Nelson's arresting voice and distinctive gut-string guitar playing amidst a deceptively casual backing by his road band. The hit single culled from the record, the old Fred Rose ballad "Blue Eyes Crying in the Rain," featured some subtle echo harmonica work by Raphael and marked the beginning of Nelson's climb to worldwide ascendancy after years of workmanlike obscurity.

Ironically, counterculture artists such as Nelson, Waylon Jennings, and Jerry Jeff Walker were used by the country music industry to breathe new life into a genre long stifled by the rigid Nashville formula. Austin's musical community suddenly found itself the focus of international media attention, and Willie Nelson became the uncrowned king of Texas music. Raphael's growing reputation led to his appearing as a supporting musician on many albums by promising young country singers, most notably Emmylou Harris and Rodney Crowell, and for a time he regularly commuted to Los Angeles for studio work. He still occasionally lends his talents to other projects—an uncredited harmonica solo by Raphael on a Mötley Crüe album won the group's lead singer one rock magazine's award for Instrumentalist of the Year.

"For my money, the best harp is the Marine Band," says Raphael. "I'm really sold on them." He also has a fondness for Hohner's Pocket Pal model. "They sound great and they really sing, but they're only good for one or two sessions." Raphael has also been impressed with the old Hohner Navy Band model and with an Echo Vamper built along the lines of a Marine Band that he bought on a tour of Australia.

Raphael has been intrigued by some of the recent changes in harmonica design and has a few suggestions of his own. "I'd love to see a Marine Band where you could just pop out the plates when they go flat. With Lee Oskar harps you can change the plates, which is cool because you can take the top plate and the bottom plate and have two different keys, so you can get Dorian modes and the like."

Raphael lists Paul Butterfield and rhythm and blues saxophone genius King Curtis as two of his biggest influences. He constantly works on making his playing more melodic; he credits Grady Martin, currently playing guitar with Nelson, with impressing upon him the importance of tunefulness. "That's one reason I've been impressed with Lee Oskar's minor harps. Like on 'Georgia on My Mind,' which is in the key of C, I use a D-minor harp—it's a natural minor scale—and I can play the melody line just the way Willie sings it, whereas on an F Marine Band, I'm really just playing licks along with the song. It's hard to play melody—to keep it simple. That's one thing about chromatic: you can play melody. I don't really play chromatic; I'm working on learning my scales on it. You have to have a good understanding of theory to play the chromatic. I jammed with a harmonica group in Detroit once called the Strnad Brothers. They did some great stuff. I had never played with a bass harmonica or a chord harmonica before. It'd be great to put a harmonica band together and do a cruise or something.

"The harmonica is something that everyone can play—sort of. Everybody's had one. But the sound itself—you either love it or hate it. It's very difficult to become a great player, but in some ways it *is* an easy instrument. Once you figure out the tricks, you can really just fake it. I mean, you could be playing terrible and people will love it. On the other hand, you could be playing great and nobody will notice. It's rare that someone will hire just a harmonica player—you've got to double on guitar or piano or something. It's just not used all the time in all music, like some instruments. I've recently begun playing the diatonic accordion onstage with Willie.

"The sound of the harmonica stands out so much that it would get too repetitious or boring if you heard it on every song. With Willie I try to play a lot of rhythm stuff and a lot of string-line things behind him, so that it's not just hot licks, so that you don't get burned out on it. I do play on every song onstage, but I don't solo on every tune.I like those echo harps. It's another thing to keep it from being tedious."

Raphael sees no end in sight to his association with Nelson. "We work all the time. He has a loyal band because he in turn is very supportive of the people he works with. He's not like other touring pros who hire a new band all the time."

As for the future of his instrument, Raphael sees the harmonica as not being immune to the influence of electronics. "Things are getting so complex. I love some computerized music, but I still like the human factor. I prefer having a real drummer, for instance. But I'm waiting until they synthesize the harmonica. The problem is that some of those sounds come close to the tone of harp, but you don't have that personal feeling. I've heard about a voice tracker that works off a microphone, so technically it should work for harp. You can link it up with a DX7 or any kind of computer. You play the harp into the microphone, and then you hear the saxophone or whatever you've got it sampled with. I'm not sure how it would handle bent notes; that might confuse the signal. As soon as it becomes available, I'll have one and mess everybody up."

Little Walter Jacobs

Val Wilmer.

The Blues

If you want to map the outer limits of American influence, try charting regions where the blues is unknown. In its own right, and as the common foundation for some of our most popular cultural exports—jazz, much of Tin Pan Alley's output, country music—the blues has been universally celebrated.

In a sense, the blues is a triumph of style over form. Slaveowners in North America suppressed the native culture of their human property much more fiercely than did their counterparts in Latin and South America. Ethnomusicologists who have attempted to identify aspects of blues and jazz as being specific holdovers from the music of West Africa—the home of most of the black slaves brought to

North America—have been persistently frustrated. Forced to adopt Western instruments, African Americans eventually developed a music—including the compelling twelve-bar, three-chord blues progression that appeared at the beginning of the twentieth century—that in structure was more European than African.

But while the framework of the blues may be uniquely American, Africanisms abound in its delivery. The history of Western music is marked by a search for clarity and purity of tone, and European instruments were designed with this quest in mind. African musicians inherit quite different sensibilities and tools. Blues researcher Paul Oliver has noted that "West African instrumentalists have a dislike of 'pure' notes or tones." In the Western tradition, overtones, buzzing noises, rattles, and droning effects are the worst of musical sins, but in West Africa musicians are judged on their ability to achieve just these same effects. The same characteristics of the harmonica's sound that have not always endeared it to Western music critics—its impure overtones, its reedy whine, and its ability to play "between the notes"—had great appeal to the descendants of these West Africans.

Denied access to the world of formal instruction, African Americans were free to develop novel and radical techniques on their adopted instruments that allowed them to express their musical predilections. New tuning schemes for the guitar were devised, and knife blades and the necks of bottles were pressed against the strings to create a dense, stinging drone. The fronts of upright pianos were removed, newspaper was wedged behind the strikers to dampen their attack, and inspired but unorthodox fingering systems and keyboard stylings were developed. The vibrato and damping effects possible on the harmonica through the use of hand techniques were elevated to a high art, and if African Americans did not invent the cross-harp style, they certainly perfected it.

The note bending available in cross harp allowed players to achieve the minor thirds, flattened fifths, and minor sevenths that characterize the "blue" scale, but it was the harmonica's talent for vocalizing that ensured it a leading role in the blues. The West African slaves brought with them a passion for singing that was first channeled by their New World masters toward the rendition of English hymns and later surfaced in the work song—a rhythmic, a cappella field chant—and then the blues. The blues can be mastered and appreciated instrumentally, but take away the highly personalized vocal style and storytelling power that has become associated with it and it is just another seductive chord progression. It is the mouth organ's ability to give voice to a language beyond words that has made it the quintessential blues instrument.

Musicologist Michael Licht contends that the mouth organ was a fixture in African American folk music by the 1870s. Many blues artists associated with other instruments got their musical baptism through boyhood experiences with the mouth organ. Robert Johnson, the Mississippi Delta singer and guitarist whose chilling brilliance and premature death has made him the most celebrated blues figure ever, played his first paying gig as a teenaged harp player. "I started playing what they call the French harp at home, the harmonica," Muddy Waters recounted in Robert Palmer's *Deep Blues*. "Now when I was nine, I was getting a sound out of the French harp. When I was thirteen, I was very, very good. I was playin' it . . . at fish fries, picnics, and things. I should never have given it up! But when I was seventeen, I put the harp down and switched to the guitar." Waters gained his first glimpse of what lay beyond his native Mississippi on a brief Southern tour as a harp player with a minstrel show. The first inkling that the world at large had of the blues harmonica style was gained through the phonograph.

Jaybird Coleman (1896–1950)

One of the earliest and most arresting blues harpists to appear on record was Gainesville, Alabama's Burl "Jaybird" Coleman. His family were sharecroppers, and Coleman's childhood was filled with hard, physical labor. Coleman picked up the harmonica at the age of twelve; his parents encouraged his musical attempts, hoping that he might manage to avoid their own wearying occupation.

Like many rural Americans of his generation, Coleman's first trip away from home came after he joined the army at the outbreak of World War I. If he expected to see the world, he was disappointed; he never left his native state. Nevertheless, Coleman was mustered out of the army with not only his first experience as a performer—he had made a reputation for himself entertaining his fellow doughboys—but his nickname, supposedly inspired by his stubborn disinterest in army regulations.

Coleman returned briefly to Gainesville when the war ended, but after a few months working as a farm laborer he moved to Bessemer,

Alabama, and began playing music full-time. In 1922 he teamed with guitarist and singer Big Joe Williams; he later spent two years traveling through the South with the Rabbit Foot Minstrels, a popular tent show. Returning to Bessemer, Coleman married a popular local singer, and the couple supported themselves by entertaining at local parties and church suppers. The Colemans were regular churchgoers who were well-known in the black community for their powerful singing of spirituals. In his alter ego as a blues singer and harp player, Jaybird was equally popular among blacks and whites. He would often stroll through the city streets playing and singing, his harmonica audible for several blocks and a swelling crowd following in his wake.

In 1927, Coleman expanded his audience considerably by recording as a solo performer for the Gennett, Silvertone, and Black Patti labels, and as a member of the Bessemer Blues Pickers. His records seem to have sold reasonably well, but Coleman always asserted that he was never paid for them. Despite his treatment at the hands of white-owned record companies, for several years Coleman allowed his career to be managed by the local Ku Klux Klan chapter, who booked him throughout the South.

Jaybird Coleman sang and played the purest brand of blues, usually without accompaniment, in a stark, emotional style rooted in the work songs and hollers of his childhood. He would sing a lyric in a powerful, impassioned voice and then closely second the slurred, moaning melody on the harmonica. He favored the high-pitched E and D harps and played them in a heavily choked, cross-harp style marked by a tense, rapid hand vibrato.

During the 1930s, Coleman was loosely associated with the Birmingham Jug Band, a group he helped to form. In 1930 he recorded with them for Okeh and Columbia, playing harmonica and jug. That same year Coleman made a solo recording, "Coffee Grinder Blues," for Columbia, but he feuded with the label over money and blocked its release. Not surprisingly, it was his last session, and thereafter Coleman worked mostly outside of music, although he continued to play with various jug bands and on the streets of Bessemer and Birmingham until his death.

The Memphis Jug Bands

The jug bands were down-home aggregations that provided a link between country blues and early jazz. So called because they usually featured players who blew into empty jugs to provide a bass accompaniment, these small string bands specialized in a kind of rural jump music. By 1915 they were common in Louisville, Kentucky, and in Cincinnati, Ohio.

The jug band sound was introduced in Memphis, Tennessee, by the mid-1920s, and within a few years several such groups were working steadily in that city. In those days Memphis was a wide-open city, the New Orleans of the upper South, and its musicians were a busy lot. At night there were the clubs on Beale Street, a raw avenue even by red-light district standards; during the day bluesmen and jug band performers working singly or in pairs attracted large crowds in the streets or in Handy Park.

The Memphis jug bands were loosely organized outfits whose personnel constantly turned over, but there was so much work that most of them employed professional booking agents who often fielded two units under the same name so that a band could be booked for more than one job on a given night. Harmonica players figured prominently in the Memphis jug bands, and three of them—Will Shade, Noah Lewis, and Jed Davenport—led popular recording groups and thus exerted an influence that stretched far beyond Beale Street.

Will Shade (1894–1966)

Known to his friends as "Son Brimmer," Will Shade turned to music for his livelihood after too much heavy, physical work as a young man left him unable to hold a job as a laborer. The first instrument Shade mastered was the guitar, but he became a solid jug blower and a first-rate harp player as well. In the mid-1920s, Shade formed the Memphis Jug Band, an extremely popular group that spawned many imitators.

When an RCA Victor mobile recording unit arrived in Memphis in 1927 looking for local musical talent, the first group it recorded was the Memphis Jug Band. Victor released two sides, "Sun [*sic*] Brimmer's Blues" and "Stingy Woman Blues"; they proved so successful that in June the group was brought to Chicago to record four more titles. Shade's outfit was in the studio more often than any other jug band; between 1927 and 1934 the band recorded seventy-three titles.

Shade was a strict musical perfectionist with a head for business who imposed a regular rehearsal schedule and arranged his own bookings. He was a talented arranger, and his ability to constantly drum up fresh material was a key factor in the consistent sales of his group's recordings. Musically, the Memphis Jug Band was more versatile and sophisticated than its competitors; the group frequently featured fiddlers and was known for its harmony singing. The jug bands played for both white and black audiences—often on the same day—and the recordings by the Memphis Jug Band testify to the ease with which its members played both sides of the musical fence. While they produced fine versions of blues tunes like "Kansas City Blues," "Memphis Yo-Yo Blues," "KC Moan," and "Stealin'," the group also recorded waltzes and familiar white tavern material like "I'm Looking for the Bully of the Town" and "He's in the Jailhouse Now."

Will Shade also recorded several sides with Memphis Minnie, one of the finest of the female blues singers. He continued to perform in and around Memphis long after the end of the jug band era. The ripples of the folk music boom of the 1950s somehow managed to reach him, and in 1956, Folkways Records reunited him with Memphis Jug Band guitarist Charlie Burse and Gus Cannon to record an album. In 1960, Decca released Shade's "Newport News Blues," on which he sang and played guitar.

Harmonica player Charlie Musselwhite first met Will Shade in the early 1960s. "He and his wife, Jennie Mae, lived up on Fourth Street, right off Beale, in the funkiest place you could imagine," remembers Musselwhite. "All the musicians who had played during the heyday of Beale Street and the jug bands when everything was happening would stop by, and Son would hold court in his room there. He'd say, 'You going to the store? Bring me back some milk, now.' Of course, he wasn't talking about *milk*. He showed me some stuff. Shade told me that his mother taught him the harmonica, that she grew up in slavery. The first songs he learned from her were the first songs he taught me. They were just little wails and things—they had no name."

• • •

Noah Lewis (1895–1961)

In 1928 a young banjoist named Gus Cannon auditioned in Memphis as a solo performer for an RCA Victor talent. Cannon was told that he might have a shot at a recording session, but only if he was part of a larger group. A few days later Cannon returned, this time as the leader of Cannon's Jug Stompers, a hastily organized trio filled out by guitarist Ashley Thompson and a brilliant harp player named Noah Lewis.

Lewis had learned to play the harmonica as a child on his family's farm in Henning, Tennessee. The tracks of the Illinois Central ran through his hometown, and Lewis may have begun fashioning at a tender age the train pieces for which he would later become justly celebrated. In 1912 his family moved to Ripley, where Lewis worked as a field hand and spent his evenings playing at local functions for tips.

It wasn't until 1926 that Lewis began working seriously at music, appearing—most often alone but occasionally as a member of the Memphis Jug Band—at an endless round of dances, frolics, picnics, parties, craps games, and suppers. When Gus Cannon recruited him for the 1928 session with the Jug Stompers, Lewis brought with him an original tune, "Minglewood Blues"; his playing on this number made such an impression that Victor had him record three harmonica solos at the end of the session, including "Chickasaw Special," one of the most phenomenal of the many mouth organ tributes to the steam train.

A small, slight man, Lewis was nonetheless a powerfully pneumatic harp player who regularly performed with brass bands. "Lord, he used to blow the hell outta that harp," Cannon recalled years later. "He could play two harps at the same time . . . through his mouth and nose, same key and same melody. . . . Noah, he was so full of cocaine all the time—I reckon that's why he could play so loud and, aw, he was good."

As a Jug Stomper, Lewis made more records for Victor in 1929 and 1930. In 1930 he recorded four sides for the label as the leader of his own group, but after this Lewis worked mostly as a farmhand. Weakened by the collective toll of his personal excesses, he slipped into inactivity, musically and otherwise, after a serious illness in the 1950s, eventually being reduced to living in a cramped, decrepit shack.

Lewis was admitted to a local hospital in the winter of 1961 suffering from frostbite. "Noah froze his feet," a friend recalled. "He had stayed out all night and lost his track somehow. He couldn't find the way back home. He was in bad shape when he was found." Surgeons amputated both his feet, but within days Noah Lewis was dead from blood poisoning.

Jed Davenport (?-?)

Jed Davenport seems to have been a native of Mississippi. He arrived in Memphis in the 1920s and began a forty-year career playing in the clubs and on the streets of that city and making occasional forays into the countryside with various medicine shows.

Davenport's first recording session was held under the auspices of Vocalion Records at Memphis's Peabody Hotel in 1929. More versatile and musically schooled than most of his colleagues, Davenport not only played the harmonica on these sessions but also contributed some jug and trumpet playing. The following year he recorded sides with the Beale Street Jug Band and with Memphis Minnie. His early harmonica work was typically rural, but his cross-harp playing—usually on his favorite E Marine Band—became more influenced by the early jazz stylings; he perfected the use of the cupping hand to achieve a wah-wah effect.

Davenport worked frequently as a member of a five-piece band that included saxophone, bass, drums, and piano, and he appeared often in the pit bands of tent shows when they passed through Memphis. After 1937 his instrument of choice was the trumpet, which he played with local jazz bands. Jed Davenport seems to have left Memphis in the early 1940s, only to return years later. He was still working the streets of that city for tips into the 1960s, which is the last mention we have of him.

The jug band mouth organists in Memphis played a pivotal role in the harmonica's progress. It was they who expanded on the coon-chase and locomotive solo traditions and showed that the mouth organ could hold its own as a lead melodic instrument in a group setting. It would be up to another Tennessean, John Lee Williamson, to capitalize on their work and place the harmonica at the forefront of modern blues.

The Chicago Players

John Lee Williamson (1914–48)

John Lee "Sonny Boy" Williamson took up the harmonica as a boy in Jackson, Tennessee. Before he was out of his teens, he was a prominent member of a local blues fraternity that revolved around such local performers as Yank Rachell, Robert Lee McCoy, Big Joe Williams, and Sleepy John Estes (a haunting singer who often recorded and performed with his son-in-law, the talented harp player Hammie Nixon). Although Williamson performed regularly in Memphis and no doubt came under the influence of the jug band virtuosos who haunted Handy Park and Beale Street, he preferred to work with one or two guitarists and favored the country blues. His contemporaries claim that the singing and playing style that would make Williamson famous was fully formed by 1934, when he migrated to Chicago, a place where the careers of many of the blues' finest artists were launched in the clubs that sprang up on its black South Side.

This northerly passage had become commonplace for Southern blacks decades earlier, and their migration became a flood as the sharecropping system in the South buckled under the catastrophic effects of the Depression. The prospect of achieving racial dignity in the big city was also a strong magnet. As harp player Jazz Gillum told an interviewer, "I wanted to go somewhere if somebody hits you, you can hit 'em back. In Mississippi, if somebody hits you, you got to run."

RCA Victor's blues recordings were issued on its budget label, Bluebird. Bluebird's resident producer and talent scout in Chicago was a hard-boiled character named Lester Melrose, who during the Depression signed many top blues artists to the label. In 1937 he arranged for a recording session for twenty-three-year-old John Lee Williamson at the Victor studios in Aurora, Illinois.

It was a powerful debut. Sonny Boy's first stint in front of a microphone yielded three songs that were to become blues standards: "Good Morning Little School Girl," "Bluebird Blues," and "Sugar Mama Blues." The sides show little evidence that Williamson had spent the previous three years in Chicago. Perhaps in an effort to make his first session as comfortable as possible, Yank Rachell and Big Joe Williams were brought up from Tennessee to accompany him, and these performances are stellar examples of the rural string-band style they had perfected years before. The records sold well, especially in the deep South.

After a series of successful sessions steeped in a countrified atmosphere, Melrose gambled on modernizing Williamson's sound. Singer/guitarist Big Bill Broonzy had been using a string bassist and a drummer on his Victor sessions, and in 1940, Melrose hired Broonzy's backup band to meld Sonny Boy's telling vocals and intimate harp playing with the thudding pulse of a modern rhythm section. The results were recordings produced with the jukebox in mind that popularized a sound and a pattern of arrangement that, in the hands of successors like Muddy Waters, would become known as the "Chicago blues" sound.

John Lee Williamson didn't have a particularly forceful voice or a special mastery of the harmonica, but he had other gifts essential to the making of a first-rank blues artist. He was simple and direct; he could turn a catchy phrase; his warm, personable singing—in which the lyrics were slightly slurred or hummed, perhaps because of his tendency to stutter—was absolutely credible; and he seamlessly punctuated his vocal lines with trademark mouth organ fills in an irresistible call and response that made him the first blues harmonica star.

Williamson seems to have been even more ingratiating in person than he was behind a microphone. "He was a good-hearted boy, and freehanded as he could be. He would give you the shirt off his back to his friend, and he had a lot of them, too," was how Broonzy recalled him. Billy Boy Arnold, who would later become a well-known harmonica player himself, was just a boy when he was befriended by Williamson. In Arnold's version, Sonny Boy takes on seraphic proportions: "He was 'bout one of the finest fellers I know. . . . He worked to keep the people with somethin' to eat and somethin' to drink. He was just good." Sonny Boy was also known for the encouragement that he gave up-and-coming bluesmen; Muddy Waters's first paying gig in

Chicago was as a sideman for Williamson. But Sonny Boy was locked in a chronic struggle with alcohol, and when he was drunk, he was often aggressive and foolhardy.

Around two A.M. on the evening of June 1, 1948, Williamson parted company with friends a few blocks from the Plantation Club, where he had just finished performing. Half an hour later his wife found him struggling to open the door of their apartment and bleeding heavily from a head wound and a gash near his left eye; someone had attacked him with an ice pick. His harmonicas, wristwatch, and wallet were missing.

"Lord have mercy," he managed to moan. He lapsed into a coma and died a few hours later in the hospital; his body was shipped south to Tennessee for burial. He was thirty-four years old. No one was ever charged with his murder.

Jazz Gillum (1904–66)

William McKinley "Jazz" Gillum was another Lester Melrose discovery. Gillum was born in Indianola, Mississippi, and after his parents died when he was young, he was raised by his uncle, a local church deacon. He had his first experience performing in public playing the harmonium—the harmonica's distant cousin—in his uncle's church. Gillum may have chafed in this righteous atmosphere; at the age of seven he moved to Charleston, Mississippi, to live with other relatives. By 1918 he was earning pocket money by playing the harmonica on the streets.

Gillum moved to Chicago in 1923 and worked sporadically with Big Bill Broonzy during the next decade. He spent the first half of the 1930s playing in Chicago clubs, recording as a sideman and perfecting a lively, tuneful approach to both the straight and cross-harp styles that relied heavily on tongue-blocked octaves. Gillum's fondness for the high end of the harmonica set him apart from other blues harpists. In 1934 he made his first recordings under his own name for Melrose and Bluebird, and between 1936 and 1942 he recorded several more sides for Victor and Vocalion. After serving in the army between 1942 and 1945, Gillum resumed his association with Bluebird; among the thirty numbers he recorded for that label was "Look on Yonder Wall," a tune that has since become a blues classic.

Gillum left music in the 1950s, but in 1961 he resurfaced to record an album on Folkways with singer/pianist Memphis Slim. He began appearing in Chicago nightspots again, but his comeback came to an abrupt end when he was killed in a shooting.

Rice Miller (Sonny Boy Williamson II) (1897–1965)

The man's music was unvarnished and upright, but Rice Miller's public life was largely spent perpetuating a sinuous falsehood.

"When you cross your heart to someone," he once sang in a voice quaking with injury, "you're not supposed to tell a lie." Yet Miller's own acquiescence in a heavy-handed piece of fraudulence at the outset of his recording career and his insistent, ill-tempered defense of it afterward have been scrutinized by blues commentators to the point where his ethical lapses have threatened to overshadow his triumphs as an artist, which were considerable.

Even his real name is disputed: Willie Williams, Willie Williamson, Rice Miller, Willie Miller, Little Boy Blue, Sonny Boy Williamson—all were aliases he embraced at one time or another. He was most likely born Alex Miller in Glendora, Mississippi. Raised by his mother and a stepfather, he was called Rice from infancy. As an old man, Miller hinted darkly that he had had a raw start in life, but he seems in fact to have come from a home stable enough to hold him until he was in his thirties. When he finally struck out on his own in 1928, Miller was already an experienced harp player (he later claimed that while in Glendora he had only played church music), and he discovered that he could use the instrument to make his way in the wider world.

It was a circuitous passage. For the next fifteen years, Miller lived off his wits and his sizable talent as he crisscrossed the backwaters of the deep South. More than one bluesman who grew up in the regions frequented by Miller during this period has recounted vivid childhood memories of a musical snake charmer bisected by a belt lined with harmonicas who tramped the back roads in rubber boots cut off at the ankles, occasionally pausing long enough to separate the locals from their money with his reedy magnetism. As a traveling blues salesman, Rice Miller was irresistible. He would park his harp in his lips and play while clapping his hands or snapping his fingers to keep time, blow into a Marine Band stuck lengthwise in his mouth as if it were a cigar, or coax tunes out of a tiny harmonica hidden in his cheeks. Years spent wheedling money from strangers left him with a repertoire that roamed widely. Blues, pop tunes, spirituals, hillbilly numbers—they all flowed from his harp.

The year 1941 found Miller traveling in the company of a young guitarist named Robert Lockwood. They approached Sam Anderson, the owner of radio station KFFA in Helena, Arkansas, about playing on the air. Anderson listened to a hasty audition, convinced a local flour company to sponsor a program, "King Biscuit Time," featuring the duo, and overnight Miller and Lockwood were transformed from musical vagabonds into the King Biscuit Entertainers.

"King Biscuit Time" put the forty-four-year-old Miller on the professional map, but it also led to his becoming mired in a piece of professional subterfuge when he allowed KFFA to bill him as "Sonny Boy Williamson." Miller was twenty years older than the Chicago performer of the same name, but his reputation was decidedly local. John Lee Williamson's records were well-known in the Arkansas Delta, and there is no doubt that the ruse was engineered to trade on the younger singer's commercial appeal. There was nothing subtle about the duplicity; "King Biscuit Time"s' announcers even urged listeners to buy "Sonny Boy's" records at their local stores. (Miller had yet to make his first record.) The fact that John Lee Williamson was five hundred miles away in Chicago must have made Miller and Anderson breathe easier, but there are stories that the real Sonny Boy made a special trip to the area in an unsuccessful attempt to stop KFFA from using his name.

Augmented by a pianist and a drummer, the King Biscuit Entertainers made regular forays into the countryside, performing from the back of a flatbed truck. The steady touring and the radio exposure made them perhaps the most popular blues group in the South. Their sound, a unique blend of Miller's down-home style and the young Lockwood's jazzy playing, exerted a profound influence on other bluesmen. The young B. B. King listened faithfully to "King Biscuit Time," soaking up Lockwood's advanced chordal ideas. Miller influenced another future star on a more personal level. Blues shouter Howlin' Wolf once confessed that Miller had taught him how to play the harmonica: "He married my sister Mary in the thirties. That's when I met him. He was just loafing around, blowing his harp. He could blow, though. But he lived too fast. . . . He used to come there and sit up half the night and blow the harp to Mary. I liked the harp, so I'd fool around, and while he's kissing Mary, I'd try to get him to show me a couple of chords. I'd go round the house then and I'd work on it."

After Robert Lockwood left Helena in 1945, Miller had brief partnerships with guitarists Elmore James and Arthur Crudup. By then divorced from Howlin' Wolf's sister, Miller fell into a romantic entanglement strong enough to cause him to remarry, quit music, and take a job driving a tractor, a turn of events that shocked all who knew him. The fifty-year-old Miller was past the point of no return, however, and he was soon pushing Hadacol tonic on a West Memphis radio station.

Remarkably, Rice Miller didn't make a record until he was in his midfifties, when he cut several sides for the Jackson, Mississippi-based Trumpet label, still billing himself as "Sonny Boy Williamson." These stunning 78s included the surpassingly beautiful "Mighty Long Time," which sold a healthy sixty thousand copies.

Miller's solid regional success was duly noted by Chicago's Chess brothers, Phil and Leonard, who regularly scouted Southern talent as the owners of a small, independent record company that had become the leading producer of the new, amplified blues approach pioneered by artists like Muddy Waters. In 1955 they brought Rice Miller to Chicago. Backed by Muddy Waters and his group, Miller recorded a typically sassy shuffle, "Don't Start Me Talkin'." The song made it into the top ten on the rhythm and blues charts; Miller was nearly sixty. Eight years of Chess sessions followed. Miller recruited Robert Lockwood as a regular sideman, and they became fixtures on the Chicago club circuit.

Miller rarely played through an amplifier, preferring to display his amazing repertoire of acoustic harmonica voices. In his hands, the diatonic could chortle, sputter in outrage, slice like a razor, or purr like a sated tiger. "I want to get close to you, baby, like white on rice," he once sang in what could have served as a description of the coupling of his voice and his instrument, both of which were perpetually driven by his rhythmic genius. Miller's lyrics went straight to the bone and were filled with startling imagery.

Many of the Chicago bluesmen had been friends of John Lee Williamson, and Miller was increasingly challenged by them and by blues chroniclers to explain his claim that he was "the original Sonny Boy." Little Walter Jacobs, for one, was disgusted: "It was like thievin'. There was one Sonny Boy and that's it, just one, and I don't mean that second one! Man, I'll never know how he could take people's money."

In 1963, Miller toured Europe as a featured member of a traveling blues package show. His colleagues recall him swilling nonstop from a hip flask and brandishing knives on the tour bus, but his onstage performances were the high points of the concert series, and he played the role of the aging bluesman to the hilt. No one was more amazed at Miller's reception on the Continent than the grizzled harp wizard himself. When the official tour ended, he and pianist Memphis Slim remained behind. The English rock groups—who in a few months would overwhelm the American musical scene—lionized Miller, and he made a series of performances and recording sessions with bands like the Animals and the Yardbirds. Within weeks the aging Mississippian had become a confirmed Anglophile who occasionally affected a British accent and who had taken to wearing Saville Row suits, bowler hats, and kid gloves.

And then suddenly he was back in West Helena, bragging to disbelieving locals about his European triumphs and hosting a resurrected "King Biscuit Time" radio show. Sonny Payne, the program's announcer, told writer Robert Palmer about the time he asked Miller why he had returned to the backwaters of the Arkansas Delta after tasting such phenomenal success overseas. "I just come home to die," Miller answered. "I know I'm sick. We're just like elephants. We knows."

Miller had friends drive him around the area that he had obviously come to think of as some kind of home after all the years of restless wandering. In the months before his death, he spent hours fishing on the banks of the Mississippi, lost in his memories.

Little Walter Jacobs (1930–68)

The legacy of Marion "Little Walter" Jacobs is a musical mirror so brilliant and expansive that today it is impossible to find a blues harp player who is not seen most clearly when reflected in it. "Probably the single most innovative performer in the history of the blues," is Peter Guralnick's summation. A self-assured, supremely cool soloist onstage and in the studio, behind the scenes Jacobs was a man in a hurry. By the time he was twenty-five, he had completely transformed blues harmonica; a dozen years later he was dead.

Jacobs own version of his early years had him leaving his Alexandria, Louisiana, home when he was eight. At twelve he was surviving off the money he made playing popular numbers and jump tunes on his harmonica in the clubs and on the streets of New Orleans. "A lot of them big shows would have bands, you know," Jacobs once explained. "The band would come off and I'd go up and blow my harp. They'd throw tips on the bandstand. . . . I had never had no group together."

Three years later Jacobs was in West Helena, Arkansas, sleeping on pool tables and working hard at mastering John Lee Williamson's style before falling under the spell of Rice Miller, who seems to have been unusually kind to him. Before long Walter had something of a local following. After the demise of "King Biscuit Time," Robert Lockwood had been hosting his own local radio show, and when he left town, Little Walter took his place. Backed by a pianist, the fifteen-year-old did more than hold his own; his show's fan mail soon outstripped that of "King Biscuit Time."

The young harp star was already advancing a radical approach to his instrument. "Walter had a sound that didn't nobody else have," recalled guitarist Honeyboy Edwards, who first met Jacobs during this period. "He could play then with as good a punch as when he was recording later."

Edwards and Jacobs teamed up and were pleased enough with the results to try their luck in Chicago. They surfaced first on the sidewalks of Maxwell Street, the South Side's prime shopping district and a profitable showcase for bluesmen on weekend afternoons. In 1947 the owner of a Maxwell Street radio and record store recruited the seventeen-year-old Jacobs and a singing guitarist named Othum Brown for a recording session. The resulting 78, issued on the Ora Nelle label, featured Brown singing "Ora Nelle Blues" and Jacobs's voice and driving harmonica on "I Just Keep Loving Her."

This debut recording shows that Walter was a seasoned blues performer well before he came of age, and that his youth and his wide-ranging taste in music was an advantage instead of a liability. As a youngster, Jacobs prided himself on his ability to play polkas and waltzes; as he grew older, he was drawn to the novelty jump tunes of Louis Jordan and to swing bands like Count Basie's. His blues playing, which early on was a sort of souped-up version of John Lee Williamson's approach, began to show signs of a swinging complexity and daring that reflected the influence of jazz soloists, particularly jump tenor virtuosos like Arnett Cobb.

After eight years of peripheral hustling, Little Walter Jacobs was anxious to make his mark. "I had a little setup on the street . . . start out about nine in the morning, quit about four in the evening. So I would keep going, have a few coins until I got of age, and then I started playing with some of the older fellas, you know, that was in the clubs." One of these more experienced players was a singer and guitarist named McKinley Morganfield. Better known as Muddy Waters, he and Jacobs began an association that became one of the great partnerships in American music.

Waters had left Mississippi for Chicago in 1943 and had been haunting the South Side's nightspots, playing and singing whenever he could and searching for a sound that would set him apart. As he told writer Jim Rooney, "One thing I knew I wanted was that harp sound. I guess I loved the harp 'cause that's the first thing I learned on. . . . When I run up on Little Walter, he just fitted me." Waters, Jacobs, and guitarist Jimmy Rogers made a regular practice of clambering onstage between other performers' sets and stealing their thunder; people began calling them "the headhunters."

The three were not only awesomely talented; they were committed to putting in long hours shaping their ensemble sound. As Jimmy Rogers put it, "We'd do a lot of rehearsing during that time. The three of us. And Walter wanted to learn. His ears were open. . . . He was mostly playing between Rice Miller and that saxophone sound of Louis Jordan; after he came with us, we developed him mostly into a harder sound." To Muddy Waters, Jacobs was "a man who was always thinking of something. His mind just kept going, learning more and more and more."

Little Walter was already getting a reputation for volatility; some, including Muddy Waters, hypothesized that Creole blood was the root cause of his feral nature. Waters's quiet, firm dignity—an aura that would later make him the blues' most successful ambassador to the world—served as a calming influence on Jacobs. "He was a good boy, but he had that bad, mean temper, that kind of thing, like, 'You don't mess with me too much,'" was the way Waters remembered it. "Then when we got together, I found out that I was the only somebody that could do anything with him when he really got out of hand."

In 1948, Muddy Waters began recording for Chess, a label that spurned the casual, if not downright anarchistic, production methods employed by most of its competitors. Jimmy Rogers has vividly recalled Leonard Chess's creative focus: "You were supposed to make, I think, it were four sessions a year. . . . We'd go in at nine o'clock at night, and it was maybe three or four o'clock before we'd leave out. Leonard worked hard, he really would work hard—sometimes he overworked! You didn't go in there too often and make a number right away, you know—he'd be turning it around there quite a while trying to get the best you have." This was an ideal working environment for a creative dervish like Little Walter. Muddy remembered him literally running around the studio, occasionally getting underfoot but always throwing out a stream of suggestions.

On a Muddy Waters recording session on July 11, 1951, Little Walter plugged a microphone into a guitar amplifier, cupped his harp over it, and took the blues to the edge of a new musical territory. On three of the tunes recorded that day ("Country Boy," "My Fault," and "She Moves Me"), Jacobs unwrapped a harmonica technique that made the most of the amplifier's cutting power and sustain. Little Walter was probably not the first harp player to go electric, but he had been using amplifiers from his earliest days on Maxwell Street, where shopowners rented musicians access to their electrical outlets. In 1952, Chess released Waters's recording of "Standing Around Crying," on which Walter's tube-driven harp was put out front to shadow Muddy's powerful vocal note for note, the swooping bent notes seeming to leap off the vinyl.

Jacobs attacked the limits of this new concept relentlessly. In the clubs he began using a National amplifier with two speaker cabinets placed on opposite sides of the stage for a fuller sound and cheap public-address microphones such as the JT30 model made by the Astatic Company. A squat, bullet-shaped unit, the JT30 had a broad face that accommodated nearly the full length of a diatonic harmonica and thus allowed a wide range of tonal effects.

In a 1967 interview with *Living Blues* magazine, Little Walter talked about his style: "All my best records, I made them with an amplifier. . . . I'm controlling my own sound for the purpose of benefit. But he [the engineer] don't understand that, he figured that I could just take an ordinary mike that he had and go 'womp, womp, womp, womp, womp.' Just play out in the open and nobody could hear, couldn't even hear myself and the band can't hear. . . . Once you cut through with workin' that mike and harp, you got it made. You cup that harp right on that mike and make noise. . . . Lot of things you got to know about that mike. That mike is tricky. . . . It's not too heavy, it won't be flyin' out of your hand and you tryin' to blow. . . . You can go to strainin' and it'll kill you. I don't be blowin' too hard. That's the reason I snuggle up to that mike, see, 'cause I can keep a whole lot of wind in that harp. I don't have to do nothin' but navigate with it then." Jacobs also featured the chromatic harmonica on several of his recordings. Although he favored playing in the key of D on a C chromatic—the nearest equivalent to the cross-harp approach on the diatonic—and rarely touched the slide, Walter was the first blues player to use the larger instrument effectively.

The high-voltage sound pioneered by Jacobs broke down all barriers for blues harmonica. Jimmy Rogers remembers being told by a club owner in 1945 that he wouldn't hire a harp player, but by the early 1950s blues combos that didn't feature the "Mississippi saxophone" were hurting. Billy Boy Arnold contends that in 1952 "saxophone players were starving, piano players weren't working at all. In fact at that time you couldn't get a job without a harmonica player."

Leonard Chess began having Little Walter record his own tunes at the end of Muddy Waters's sessions. In May of 1952, Jacobs recorded an instrumental called "Juke" that he and Muddy had been using as a theme song in club appearances, and Chess issued the record under Little Walter's name. Jacobs had always aimed to be a star in his own right, and one afternoon in Shreveport, Louisiana, while on tour with Waters, he became so agitated after hearing "Juke" played continuously on a local jukebox that he deserted the band and caught the first train back to Chicago. "Juke" eventually outsold all of Chess's previous releases. Through the kind of incestuous arrangement common to Chicago blues groups, harp player Junior Wells headed south to join Muddy while Little Walter took over Wells's Chicago band, the Aces.

The Aces were the ideal band to help Jacobs fully realize his swing tendencies. Guitarist Louis Myers had a wide-open, chordal style, and converted jazz drummer Fred Below's mastery of the loping shuffle helped Little Walter chart a new course for Chicago blues bands. "At the time we had a sound that the other cats didn't have," remembers Myers. "Everywhere we went, boy, they called us hell and destruction."

"Walter was simply a person you could always learn something from, just by being around him," said Below. "He was always calling rehearsals for us to go over new tunes or tighten up our old ones. And the funny thing was, nobody ever complained about the time spent rehearsing. We were learning. See? It was like Walter was running a school where you could really learn something you were interested in. The beautiful thing was that you could check out what you learned each day by playing it in the club that night." Louis Myers became a fine harmonica player himself under Jacobs's tutelage.

Little Walter and the Aces were the first Chicago blues outfit that could successfully share the same bill with big, horn-laden rhythm and blues outfits like those led by B. B. King and Ray Charles. (In fact, he was influencing them; white bandleader Buddy Morrow recorded a big-band version of Jacobs's harmonica instrumental "Off the Wall" for Mercury in the mid-1950s that copied the original note for note.) They were enthusiastically received by the hard-to-please audience at New York's Apollo Theater, who had reacted coolly to Muddy Waters's appearances. Jacobs's popular follow-up to "Juke" was the chillingly beautiful "Blues With a Feeling," which again highlighted his ringing tone and his startling melodic gifts.

In 1954, Little Walter had one of the most creative and successful years in rhythm and blues history. "You're So Fine" hit the charts first, followed by "Oh Baby," which stayed on the hit list for four months and received a *Cash Box* award. "You Better Watch Yourself" was another winner for Walter, who closed out the year with the best-selling "Last Night." Jacobs also managed to play on three hit records by Muddy Waters; Leonard Chess was still insisting that Walter accompany Waters at recording sessions.

It was the storm before the calm. In 1955, Chess struck gold with the initial releases of Chuck Berry and Bo Diddley, who were helping to create rock and roll. The long hours that Leonard Chess had spent perfecting the sound of his blues performers were now more often invested in overseeing Berry and Diddley sessions. Many of the label's blues acts were neglected or quietly dropped. Muddy Waters and Little Walter, having been the most popular Chess artists, suffered the most. Jacobs was not to have another hit record for two years.

Little Walter was not yet thirty. He had helped Muddy Waters perfect one blues style before permanently redirecting the genre himself. At his peak, he had been one of the most successful blues recording stars in history, and when his decline was prematurely hastened by the advent of rock and roll, Jacobs resented it. He had never had much patience with the notion of paying one's show business dues. "Wait till the man get maybe fifty or sixty years old. Hell, he's walloped then. They use him for a gimmick," he complained bitterly to *Living Blues*.

With his career in limbo and without the steadying influence of Muddy Waters, Little Walter's naturally cocky personality became even more mercurial, and he often clashed with his band members. Louis Myers was the first of the Aces to give notice. Robert Junior Lockwood was recruited to take his place, and for a time his presence even improved the band musically. In 1956, Luther Tucker, a first-rate guitarist barely out of his teens, joined Walter's band, and while Little Walter's heavy drinking was beginning to affect his performances, his group was still an impressive outfit. "It was a pretty heavy band," Tucker told Robert Neff. "We always got an encore. It was an amazing thing what that cat could do with a harmonica. . . . We used to jam with sax players, and each note they blew, Walter could turn it around. . . . We disputed over money, and that's why we left him, one by one."

Jacobs made two trips to England in the mid-1960s, but his performances were uneven. He was often drunk onstage, but he blamed his erratic performances on his backup musicians. "I'd been better with nothin'," he groused to journalists. "I set all them patterns, see? Then they all listened and took it from me." Jacobs felt better about a short tour on which he was backed up by a young English group, the Rolling Stones, who had taken their name from a Muddy Waters recording on which Walter had played. "Them Rolling Stones better than the Beatles, man," he told *Living Blues*.

By the late 1960s, Little Walter had become old before his time. He had no regular home; he often stayed in the basement of Muddy Waters's house. He was unable to keep a steady band, partly due to his penchant for waving loaded pistols onstage. On February 15, 1968, Jacobs died after being struck on the head during a street brawl.

"He had a thing on the harp that nobody had," Muddy Waters told Jim Rooney. "And today they're still trying for it, but they can't come up to it. . . . He knew what to put in there and when to put it in there. So all I can say is that he is the greatest I've ever heard."

Walter Horton (1918–81)

Walter Horton was born to blow. Johnny Shines, the fine blues singer and guitarist, has told writer Peter Guralnick about meeting the fabled harp player when Horton was only thirteen: "He would be sitting on the porch, blowing in tin cans . . . and he'd get sounds out of these things. You see, this harmonica playing is really sort of a mark for Walter, it's not something he picked up. . . . And he's gonna do that as long as he has breath in him. . . . I believe he'd crack tomorrow, he'd crack with a harp in his hand and he'd keep it in his hand. And probably you could never take that harp away from him."

Walter Horton was another Memphis product. His father gave him his first harmonica when he was five, and after winning a local talent contest, Walter began spending all his free time with Memphis Jug Band leader and harmonicist Will Shade. As a child Horton was a familiar figure at the impromptu concerts in Handy Park. Boyhood friend Eddie Taylor remembered playing with Horton at parties for "big shots, like Mayor Crump." Some blues researchers claim that Horton recorded with the Memphis Jug Band in 1927, when he would have been only nine years old; Horton himself told interviewers that he toured with the group that year as part of a traveling show hosted by blues shouter Ma Rainey.

Walter took to the road in the 1930s, traversing the Southern backwaters with several guitarists, including Big Joe Williams and Floyd Jones. He and Jones lived in Chicago for a short period in 1938 (during which Horton later claimed to have first begun playing amplified harmonica), but he was back in Memphis the following year, recording there with Little Buddy Doyle. Johnny Shines contends that Rice Miller met Horton about this time and actually took some instruction from the much younger player.

At the age of twenty-two, Walter Horton gave up music because of fragile health. For the next nine years he worked at whatever odd job came his way, but by 1948 the gangly, soft-spoken harp player was again appearing in Chicago's blues clubs. Two years later he was back in Memphis, hauling ice and broadcasting regularly on WDAI.

A local disc jockey named Sam Phillips had created a profitable sideline for himself by recording the efforts of Memphis's finest bluesmen and selling the masters to established rhythm and blues labels like Chess and Modern. Horton later claimed that Phillips had heard him blowing his harp in Handy Park, and when Horton happened to walk past his recording studio a few days later, Phillips had invited him in and asked him if he wanted to record. The session took place in January 1950; two sides from that date, "Little Boy Blue" and "Now Tell Me Baby," were leased to Modern Records. Phillips later started up his own label, Sun, which in 1953 released another of his Horton masters, a harmonica instrumental entitled "Easy." The tune, based on Ivory Joe Hunter's vocal hit from about the same time, "Since I Lost

My Baby," was an aggressive, amplified performance that has become a harmonica cult classic.

Eddie Taylor had put together a band in Chicago with a young singer named Jimmy Reed, and in 1952 he made a special trip to Memphis to recruit Horton for the group. Horton made the move, but two weeks after he arrived in Chicago, Junior Wells, who had recently taken over the harp chair in Muddy Waters's band from Little Walter, was drafted into the army and Muddy enlisted Horton to take his place. It was a short stint; Horton missed a job and was fired.

Johnny Shines and Horton recorded as a duo for JOB Records in 1952, an effort that resulted in some soaring harp playing from Horton on "Evening Sun" and "Brutal Hearted Woman." Shines gave Horton free rein on these classic sides, and they show every facet of Walter's genius, from his startling phrasing to his uncanny tone. Horton's best solos are masterpieces of power, feeling, and the element of musical surprise. He was a master at filling the harp with air; his playing had a full-throated resonance that has never been surpassed.

In 1954, Jimmy Rogers broke from Muddy Waters to carve out his own career as a front man, and Horton joined Rogers's group. In 1956, Chess released Rogers's "Walkin' by Myself," a melodic blues shuffle dominated by Horton's most famous recorded solo. Walter also contributed to several Muddy Waters sessions during this period, playing especially impressive harp on "Forty Days and Forty Nights" and "Just to Be With You."

Horton was not confident in his singing abilities, and as a result his solo career was fitful. In 1954 the States label released a record by Big Walter and His Combo entitled "Hard Hearted Woman," a solidly arranged tune centered around some beautiful straight-harp playing, a Horton speciality. Two years later Horton recorded a pair of excellent original tunes—"Need My Baby" and "Have a Good Time"—for Cobra. Throughout the 1950s, Horton worked regularly in various bands and as a sideman on countless studio sessions, mostly for the Chess and Cobra labels. His brilliant playing enhanced recordings by Johnny Young, Willie Dixon, Otis Rush, J. B. Hutto, Floyd Jones, and Wild Child Butler, among others.

In 1964, Willie Dixon produced a full-fledged album project for Horton on Chess Records, an uneven effort called *The King of the Blues Harmonica*. Dixon's heavy hand was everywhere; he wrote several of the tunes and even did most of the singing. Horton's taste for unconventional material—probably a legacy from his jug band days—is shown in his spirited version of "La Cucaracha."

The 1960s saw Horton touring widely, both in the United States and in Europe. Besides appearing with his own groups, he was a regular member of Willie Dixon's All Stars. In 1965, Walter recorded for Testament Records and was featured with Johnny Shines and Johnny Young on two Vanguard LPs. In 1969 he was finally allowed to produce himself, and the result was a first-rate solo album for Alligator Records with old friend Eddie Taylor serving up perfectly sympathetic backup on guitar and Horton's protégé, Carey Bell, joining Walter on several harmonica duets.

In the mid-1970s, Horton teamed up with John Nicholas, a talented young guitarist from Boston, and the two recorded extensively for the Blind Pig label. In 1980, Horton's intense visage was seen in movie theaters throughout the world in a cameo appearance with John Lee Hooker in the movie *The Blues Brothers*. Right up until his death, Walter Horton's shimmering tone was still the envy of the blues harp world.

Junior Wells (1934–)

Amos "Junior" Wells, a Memphis native, moved with his mother to Chicago in 1946. To hear Wells tell it, his adolescence was a prolonged struggle to get through the doors of Chicago's nightspots. If denied access to the clubs, the teenaged Wells would park himself on the sidewalk and give an impromptu performance for spare change while keeping one ear cocked to catch any music that would leak out from inside.

The South Side house parties—neighborhood functions complete with cover charges, well-stocked bars, and hired musicians that were hosted by apartment dwellers to subsidize their rent payments—were easier to infiltrate. At one of these events Wells fell in with two young guitarists, Louis and Dave Myers. Wells's age notwithstanding, the trio landed a job playing seven nights a week at the Hollywood Rendezvous and began calling themselves the Aces.

In 1952, Little Walter, on fire with the realization that his first recording was a national hit, bolted from a Southern tour with Muddy Waters and suddenly resurfaced in Chicago. In a few days the Aces were out on the road with Jacobs and Junior Wells was on a train to Louisiana and into the harp chair in the Muddy Waters band.

The next year Wells made his first records, for Leonard Allen's States label. He was obviously being groomed to follow in Little Walter's substantial wake; Wells's harp playing on these sides owes a great deal to Jacobs's style, and the Aces, Muddy Waters, and Otis Spann—all of whom had recently appeared on Little Walter's recordings—were brought in to serve up the accompaniment. Wells's third release, a remake of John Lee Williamson's "Hoodoo Man," was a big seller; the song became his signature tune. After a troubled stint in the army (he went AWOL to attend a 1954 recording session), Wells married and resumed his musical career. There were singles for the Chief label in the late 1950s and early 1960s. When soul music exploded on the scene, Wells enthusiastically incorporated the new sound in his 1962 recording of "Messin' With the Kid."

By the middle of the decade, Wells was usually appearing in tandem with the brilliant young guitarist Buddy Guy. In 1965 blues enthusiast Bob Koester, who had just launched his own label, Delmark Records, arranged for Guy, Wells, and their backup band to record an album's worth of material in the wee hours of the morning after a full night's work at Theresa's Lounge, a South Side blues venue. The resulting LP, *Hoodoo Man Blues,* successfully captured the ever-funky spontaneity of Chicago's blues clubs and won *Jazz* magazine's vote as best blues album of the year. One of the great modern blues recordings, *Hoodoo Man Blues* captures Wells's unique concept, soulful singing, and punchy, economical harmonica style at their peak.

A 1966 single, "Up in Heah," was a number one local chartbuster for Wells, and he signed a profitable deal with Mercury Records. His blending of traditional blues and modern funk made Wells a natural for the blues revival circuit in the late 1960s, and during that period and into the next decade Junior recorded several singles for various labels as well as albums for Delmark, Vanguard, Mercury, and Atlantic. Twenty years later, neither his talents nor his schedule show any sign of diminishing.

Interview With Junior Wells

My recollection of the harmonica goes way back because I was a professional musician when I was twelve years old. I remember they had a radio program that came out of Randy's Record Shop in Nashville when I was young. At that time, we didn't have electric lights. We would hook up a car battery to a radio.

My father was a preacher, but that wasn't my style. I went to church, but I also had a little old friend named Ike. He had a board and put a nail in it and strung a wire on it and played it down in the woods. We had the little girls jumping up and down.

I was playin' harp then. I used to live in the dark. You know what a vampire is? I used to sit there and listen and fantasize. I was listening to Sonny Boy Williamson's records and I would close my eyes and I could visualize myself playing the harp.

Rice Miller was not the original Sonny Boy—John Lee Williamson was. I met John Lee Williamson in 1944, after we'd moved to Chicago. Nice man. He was doing a thing with Tampa Red and Big Maceo. I went by the club and I couldn't get in—I was ten years old. I was sitting outside blowin' a harp. They said, "Heeyyyy, kid. Sounds good. Come on inside." They got me in.

I was cuttin' school and working on the pop truck. The pop truck would come through the neighborhood and the man would pick me up. I worked all week and he gave me a dollar. I went down on Harrison Street in Chicago and I saw a Marine Band in a pawn shop. I went in and told the owner about it. He said, "I got an Old Standby in the window." "I want the Marine Band," I said. "Why you got to have that?" I said, "Because Sonny Boy told me that was the type of harp to buy." I asked him if I could get credit and pay him the rest later. He walked away to talk to somebody and I put my dollar down and walked out the door with the harp. I was walkin' down the street blowin'. And you would have thought I had robbed a damn bank. Detectives came from everywhere.

The judge asked me, "Did you steal this harmonica?" I said, "No. I told him that I would bring him the other money in two days." The judge said, "Well, did he give you permission to leave the premises with it?" I said, "No," and he said, "Well, if he didn't give you permission, then you stole it." The judge asked the pawnbroker, "If I give you the money, will you please drop this case?" He said, "All I want is my dollar." The judge said, "Here, I'm going to give you five. That way, if he ever comes in there again, you're covered." He told me, "Now, if you ever make a record, I want the first copy of it." But he died before I made my first record.

I met Little Walter when I was twelve years old. Muddy and the band played a matinee over at the union hall. A police officer, a friend of my sister's, took me over there. The club owner told him he was responsible for me. Muddy asked me if I knew my time and I said, "I think so." They pushed the issue on me, and I went on up to the bandstand. Walter looked down at me. "He gonna blow a harmonica? A pip-squeak?" I made seventy or eighty dollars in tips. Muddy was making fifteen dollars; sidemen were making eight fifty.

I just think that I'm a very fortunate person, to have known all the older blues artists who took so much time with me. Because I probably would have been in the penitentiary or dead as of today. I was a gang leader when I was young. This was my way of thinkin' of how to get ahead. One time when I was up before the judge, he told me, "I'm tired of lookin' at you. I'm going to put you in jail until you're twenty-one. You'll find out how the boys play in the big house." Mama brought Sunnyland Slim, Big Maceo, Tampa Red, and Muddy Waters down to keep my black ass out of prison. They spoke up in my behalf. They let me go. I went back to the gang. The second-in-command was my age. I told him, "It's your gang now. I'm gone." Two weeks after that—well, they couldn't even open up the casket, he was shot up so bad.

I met the Aces at a house party in Chicago across the street from where I was living. They said, "Hey, let's try to put something together." We didn't have no drummer at first. There wasn't even a Fender bass. Dave was playing a guitar bass type thing. When I first joined the union, I was too young to go into the clubs. This woman wanted me to play on a Sunday matinee thing at her club. We couldn't be in there because we were too young, but she put us in the union so that we could play.

"Juke" was the Aces' theme song. We'd play it coming up and coming off the bandstand. When Muddy did a song called "Just Make Love to Me" in the studio, Leonard Chess said, "Well, okay, that's great, but what else you got? You can't put out a one-sided record. You gotta play an instrumental or something." So Walter blew our theme song for Leonard Chess and pow! We couldn't do nothin' about it because we didn't have anything copyrighted. Didn't even know anything about that kind of stuff. Walter come to me and said, "Hey, man, I know you got a good band. Let's me and you do a duet." But I knew Walter's head. He was hot in the head and I was, too. You can't have two hotheads together. And then Muddy wanted me to do a thing with him, so I went with Muddy.

I talked to Chess about recording. Chess said, "No, you're not ready. I'll let you know when you're ready. You just stay back there and be a sideman." I went out on the road with Muddy. He had to leave for a couple of weeks, and I carried the show for him. At that time you had to pay union taxes, and when Muddy came back, he asked me, "Did you put your tax in there?" I said, "No." He said, "I got to have it." I gave it to him. When we finished the gig that night, I said, "I quit." He said, "Okay, go on home." Which I did. After that, they come through Arkansas and picked up James Cotton.

I recorded first with States Records. I did "Hoodoo Man" for them. But they didn't push it. But when I did it for Delmark—it won't stop sellin'. I can't explain it.

I remember when the Rolling Stones first come to Chicago. Chess called me and said, "I want y'all to come down here. I got Sonny Boy and Walter down here recordin', and they're cussin' each other and pullin' knives out and everything. And I know what's goin' on, but we got the Stones in here and they're pinned to the damn wall." Mick was blowin' the harp. I was showin' him some stuff. He was sayin', "I can't get that." I said, "You can get anything you want. It just takes time." So, boom, the next thing I know they had them on Ed Sullivan.

But Ed Sullivan wouldn't put us on. Why? Because he thought the blues was nothing in the first place. It goes way back the same way. I was at Sun Records in Memphis, Tennessee, when the guy there said, "Hey, you go get me a white boy who can shake his ass and move like a"—he didn't say "like a black man," he said "like a *nigger*"—"and we gonna get rich." When Elvis Presley came out, he wasn't what they call rock and roll. When he came out, he was doing Big Boy Crudup's stuff. Then *boom*. It's a cycle. When the Rolling Stones came out, they were doing Wolf's tunes, Muddy Waters's tunes—on Ed Sullivan. What the black performers were doing, they called it rhythm and blues. Then they changed it to rock and roll when the white kids got into it. Now, I'm not prejudiced. I remember when the Grateful Dead used to open shows for me. Bonnie Raitt proved something about the blues when she won all those Grammys. I played on her first record and toured with her. She's a very beautiful young lady. She deserves it.

When the Stones came over, they told the newspapers that we were their heroes. That's what I love about the Stones—they never denied anything. I did one tour with them in 1970. It was great. They're a great bunch of people. But when they first started doing their thing, they were wild. Back then, they couldn't get in half the hotels because they were throwing the televisions out the windows. Mick's a good man. He's nobody's fool. Bill Wyman is a stone dude. He turned me on to a lot of things.

You got so many young blues guys now. The blues doesn't know just one nationality or color. Everybody has the blues. You'd be surprised at the response around the world. I've been everyplace but Russia. I did a trip to Africa—it was beautiful. You don't see harp players over there—you got more brass and guitars and drums in Africa.

The greatest thing I ever did was to go up two times for a Grammy Award. The last time they asked me to play on the show. That's when it meant something to me, because out of the thirtysome-odd years, they never had the blues live on the Grammy Awards. That made me feel so good. For years they never gave the blues any respect at all. So I feel like I'm doing a thing for older blues players that didn't get a chance. What I'm doing is what I feel and what keeps me alive. The recording companies are trying to get me to change my style, but I can't do it, because I know that anything I can't feel, I can't play. I know if they had as many radio stations playin' blues as they have playin' rock and roll, it'd be all over. Because the blues touches everybody.

I endorse Lee Oskars because they're a hell of a harp. I love them. You won't blow them out. I'm a Marine Band man also. There are different techniques. I can't really explain how you do it. The more you get into it, you hear the slight differences in the sound of the harp. I don't know what it is about the harp that gets to people. I can't answer that. I just know what it feels like to me.

James Cotton (1935—)

"Very few kids," James Cotton once admitted in a severe understatement, "came up the way I did."

He was born in Tunica, Mississippi, as the last of nine children. His mother would occasionally entertain her children with train and chicken imitations on the harmonica, and it was she who presented James with his first harp as a Christmas present when he was six. While turning the dial of his sisters' radio one afternoon, Cotton accidentally tuned in to "King Biscuit Time" on KFFA and heard Rice Miller's harp slithering across the airwaves. The boy was mesmerized. "I never knew it was supposed to sound like that! I listened to that show every day I guess for a couple of years."

Cotton did his initial experimenting with the harp in the fields behind his house because his father, a Baptist minister, frowned on blues playing. "It just grew on me more and more," Cotton recalls. "I got more interested in it, I did get better, and when I got to play with a band, that really did something to me."

Cotton fell under the persuasive spell of an uncle who introduced the boy to his windup Victrola, on which James would listen to John Lee Williamson's records for hours on end, thinking that he was listening to Rice Miller. One Saturday night his uncle watched as the nine-year-old Cotton played his harmonica on the steps of the local juke joint and made $45 in half an hour. "My uncle said, 'If you can do that, it's time to leave here now.'" Three weeks later James Cotton was in West Helena, Arkansas, listening as his uncle introduced him to Rice Miller. "I said, 'I come up to play with you,' and I pulled my harp out of my jeans and blowed him a tune right there," is the way Cotton recalled their first meeting for *Living Blues*.

Cotton spent the next six years as a member of Miller's rough-and-tumble household, absorbing a wealth of harmonica instruction and no doubt many other lessons in life. One night in a roadhouse Cotton gave his first paid performance perched on Miller's knee. When Cotton was fifteen, Miller suddenly announced that he was moving to Milwaukee. "He just laid the band on me," Cotton told Robert Neff, "and said, 'Well, you make it for yourself.' The band went to my head. . . . I went crazy. I screwed up everything! . . . Those guys had been playing as long as I was old, and every time they tried to tell me, they couldn't tell me nothing. So they finally just left. . . . I suffered for a while. I got a job driving a dump truck, hauling gravel. I had some time to realize what had happened."

A wiser Cotton eventually made a new start in Memphis as the leader of James Cotton and His Rhythm Playmates; he also played with Howlin' Wolf, Elmore James, and Junior Parker. In 1953, Sam Phillips's eagle eye focused on him and Cotton was brought to the Sun studios to record two sides that went nowhere. The following year, however, he recorded again for Phillips, and this time the results included "Cotton Crop Blues," one of the best of Sun's blues releases. A few months later Muddy Waters came through Memphis and asked Cotton to sit in, a weekend gig that proved to be the beginning of a long association and a deep, mutual admiration.

"He brought me to Chicago and I stayed in the band with him for twelve years," Cotton has said. "I tried to be helpful to the band. I wanted to work with him because I respected him." By 1957, Cotton had even replaced Little Walter as Muddy's harp player in the studio, a compliment of the highest order. Cotton recorded dozens of tunes with Waters during the next ten years, including the original version of Muddy's signature tune, "Got My Mojo Working."

As Waters got older, he began to pare down his time onstage, and Cotton and pianist Otis Spann were increasingly called upon to front the band. Cotton responded by developing into a fine singer. Sam Charters recorded an album by the Waters band without their leader in 1965 that prominently featured Cotton's singing and harp playing. In 1966, Cotton took the obvious next step, forming his own band and signing a contract with Verve.

Cotton's timing was deliberate. His close friend Paul Butterfield and other white blues players were opening up vast new commercial territories for the genre, and Cotton wanted to have a share in it. "I had a black band, but because of people like Paul Butterfield and Mike Bloomfield I got released in a white field," says Cotton candidly. "I got on tour with Janis Joplin for a while, Blood, Sweat and Tears for a while, and things started opening up for us." Cotton's signing of a management contract with Albert Grossman—the front man for top-rank rock acts such as Bob Dylan, the Butterfield Blues Band, and The Band—put him in position to capitalize on the blues revival that took place in the later 1960s. His excellent band, which included ex–Little Walter sideman Luther Tucker on guitar, was a powerful unit—Cotton today rates it as his favorite among the many groups he's led over the years—and Cotton's onstage histrionics (including midsolo somersaults) made for a memorable stage show.

There were two excellent albums for Verve (*The James Cotton Blues Band* and *Pure Cotton*) and an LP for Vanguard that surrounded Cotton with several of San Francisco's best players. Ace rock producer Todd Rundgren supervised a Cotton album for Capitol. Two recording projects for Buddah Records, including one recorded at Allen Toussaint's fabled New Orleans studio, followed.

Cotton still spends the greater part of each year on a grueling touring schedule. *Mighty Long Time,* a recent album on the Antone's label, finds him surrounded by one of his finest supporting casts and shows once again the rich, full tone and warm singing style that have earned him a place in the gallery of blues legends.

• • •

Jimmy Reed (1925–76)

Jimmy Reed's father was a harmonica-playing Mississippi delta sharecropper who encouraged his son's early interest in music. Eddie Taylor was a childhood playmate of Jimmy's, and he showed Reed enough on the guitar to set him on his way. Jimmy worked at the instrument at every opportunity. In 1943, Reed left Mississippi to try his luck in Chicago; he was all of eighteen. He could play the harmonica and the guitar, but the spelling of his own name was a mystery to him. Ten years later he would be one of the most popular blues stylists in the country.

Reed enlisted in the navy and remained in the service until 1948. He returned to Mississippi and made a brief stab at farming, but soon moved north again, this time to Gary, Indiana, where he worked in the steel foundries and played the blues clubs at night. After a year of this numbing grind, Reed had mastered the difficult task of playing harmonica in a holder draped around his neck while strumming his own accompaniment on the guitar and was determined to establish himself as a full-time entertainer.

Eddie Taylor was also living in Gary, and the two old friends naturally gravitated to each other. In 1949 they recruited a drummer and began working as a trio. The band seems to have been conceived in the beginning as a showcase for Taylor, who was light-years ahead of Reed in terms of musicianship and experience, but Taylor's stage presence was somewhat muted and he was not a confident singer. As more of the vocal chores fell to Reed, he began to overshadow Taylor onstage.

The band auditioned for Leonard Chess, who passed on them. In 1953 they were picked up by a new Chicago rhythm and blues label, Vee Jay. The group's first two singles, released under Reed's name, caused little reaction, but their third record, "You Don't Have to Go," suddenly soared to number nine on the r&b charts. Nearly every record Reed released between 1955 and 1960 was a solid hit. Infectious send-ups such as "Honest I Do," "Big Boss Man," "Ain't That Lovin' You Baby," and "Bright Lights, Big City" were right at home on the playlists of the early rock and roll radio stations; between 1957 and 1963 Reed had twelve of his r&b hits cross over to the pop charts, and many of Reed's tunes were covered by white performers.

Jimmy Reed's style was irresistibly simple. The title of his first record—"High and Lonesome"—aptly describes both his personal inclinations and his overall sound. When Reed's trademark boogie-woogie rhythm guitar pattern (a loping riff played on the low E and A strings) was combined with a basic but insistent drum sound, the result was a no-frills, bottom-heavy approach tailor-made for the jukebox. Eddie Taylor contributed lead guitar fills that meshed seamlessly with Reed's engaging, relaxed vocals.

Jimmy Reed's novel harmonica style was also a key to his successful sound. Although he was a fine cross-harp player, Reed favored straight harp in the keys of A and Bb and the top four holes on the harp, a zone avoided by most players because of the difficulty of manipulating the small reeds. Playing in first position let Reed do most of his high-end work with blow notes, which tend to be more pliable than the draw notes at that end of the instrument. Reed's high-note technique produced greasy, slippery squeals that contrasted beautifully with his bassy guitar accompaniment. Unique at the time he introduced it, Reed's harmonica concept has become widely imitated.

Reed began suffering from epileptic attacks in 1957, an affliction that was not eased by his chronic drinking. Had it not been for his personal tribulations and his precarious health, Reed might have been in a better position than any other black bluesman to cash in on the r&b revival of the mid-1960s. The prime movers behind the blues renaissance, the English blues/rock bands, had a particular passion for Reed's music. The Rolling Stones' first album included their version of Reed's "Honest I Do." Over the years, Reed's infectiously simple compositions have been covered by countless rock groups, including the Byrds, Little Richard, Elvis Presley, Eric Clapton, the Grateful Dead, and Steve Miller. Reed's records sold relatively well into the 1970s, and he continued to tour sporadically until his death.

Charlie Musselwhite (1944–)

In 1963, the only thing rarer than a white face in a South Side blues club was the same complexion behind a harmonica on the bandstand. In those days such a countenance could only belong to either Paul Butterfield or Charlie Musselwhite, two very different personalities who shared a passion for the blues and the nerve to clamber onstage with the likes of Muddy Waters, Little Walter, Walter Horton, and Rice Miller. Even before he left his Memphis home at eighteen,

Musselwhite had been searching out the blues, spending time with Will Shade, Furry Lewis, and Gus Cannon. Musselwhite was only twenty-two when Vanguard released the first of his many albums, 1967's *Stand Back! Here Comes Charley Musselwhite's Southside Blues Band,* but he had already been recorded in a supporting role behind Walter Horton, Tracey Nelson, and John Hammond.

Musselwhite moved to California in the late 1960s. He has been one of the most prolific of blues recording artists, producing records for several labels, including Paramount and Arhoolie. Lately he is enjoying a resurgence (his most recent recordings for Alligator show a rejuvenated Musselwhite, strong material, and fine supporting musicians) and easing into the role of elder blues statesman, a title that suits a man with sly humor and Southern charm.

Interview With Charlie Mussselwhite

I was born in Mississippi, right on the Natchez Trace. My father played guitar and harmonica, and my grandmother played the piano. I always had harps as toys when I was a kid, so I was always honking on them. I was listening to everything. I just loved the sound of the blues; I'd always been hearing it on the radio. We moved to Memphis in 1947. I really liked to go downtown and listen to these blues guys play on the streets. I was twelve or something, looking at these people and wondering who they were.

I went to Chicago in '62. I was eighteen. I didn't know nobody. I just knew that you could get a job in a factory making *three* dollars an hour. So I went up there and finally I found a job with an exterminating company. I would be driving all around Chicago, and there'd be a sign that would say "Little Walter—Wednesday Through Sunday" or something. I had heard these guys on records, but I had no idea these people were in Chicago. Somebody had once told me that anybody who was successful lived in New York, so I thought that all the musicians who made records lived in New York. There I am in Chicago, man, and *everybody* was there. It was just like going to heaven.

I didn't give a damn about being white. I was brazen—I didn't give a damn about nothing. I was from Mississippi, and everybody in Chicago was from down south somewhere. I was just there to have a good time, and people sense that about you. I was just in the swing of life, having a *hell* of a good time.

Matthias Hohner, harmonica maker to the world.
From the Peter Kassan Collection, Smithsonian Institution, Washington, D.C.
Photo by Eric Long

Matthias Hohner's Trossingen home and workshop, 1857–1880.
Courtesy of Martin Häffner

clockwise from upper left: Hohnerette, two Rollmonicas with music roll, Hohner Harmonetta, Hohner centennial medallion. *From the Peter Kassan Collection, Smithsonian Institution, Washington, D.C. Photo by Eric Long*

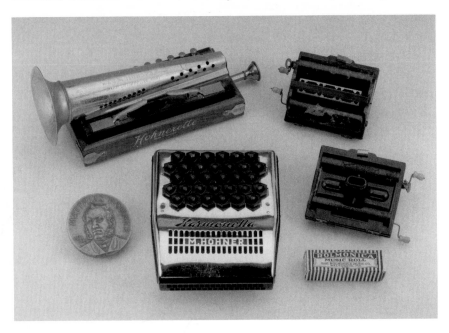

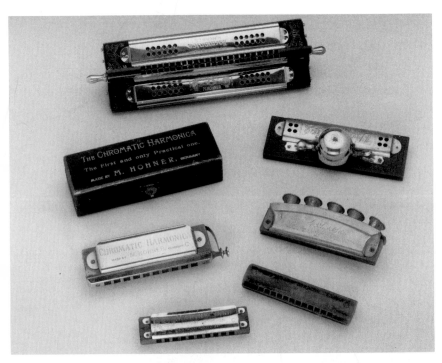

clockwise from top: Hohner Tremolo, circa 1900; F. A. Böhm's Violin King model, circa 1900; C.A. Sydel Söhne's Fluteophone, circa 1900; handmade wooden harmonica, circa 1880; Hohner Marine Band, circa 1900; Hohner's original chromatic harmonica, circa 1925. *From the Peter Kassan Collection, Smithsonian Institution, Washington, D.C. Photo by Eric Long*

The Hohner 64
Chromonica #280.
*Courtesy of
M. Hohner, Inc.*

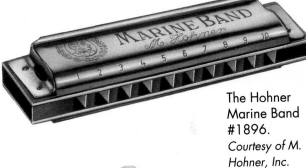

The Hohner
Marine Band
#1896.
*Courtesy of M.
Hohner, Inc.*

The Hohner Double
Bass #265.
*Courtesy of M.
Hohner, Inc.*

The Hohner 48-
Chord Harmonica
#267.
*Courtesy of M.
Hohner, Inc.*

Albert Hoxie's Philadelphia Harmonica Band, circa 1934. *Courtesy of Sam Scheckter*

Carl Freed's Harmonica Harlequins. Carl Freed, center. *Clockwise from left:* Leon LaFell, Nat Bergman, Joe Mullendore, Phil Solomon, Milton Freeman, Sid Gould, Sam Scheckter, Mike Chimes. *Courtesy of Sam Scheckter*

Borrah Minevitch (in checked jacket) surrounded by his Harmonica Rascals, circa 1934. *From left to right:* Abe Diamond, Johnny Puleo, Irvin Crane, Leo Diamond, Hal Leighton, unidentified stagehand, Al Furbish, Mike Chimes, Fuzzy Feldman, Ernie Morris. *Courtesy of Richard Bain*

Jimmy and Mildred Mulcay share a microphone with Bob Hope. *Courtesy of Dave Zaval*

Hugh McCaskey.

The Cappy Barra Harmonica Gentlemen. *Top, left to right:* Sam Sperling, Leon LaFell, Nat Bergman. *Bottom, left to right:* Phil King, Don Ripps, Sam Scheckter, Phil Solomon. *Courtesy of Sam Scheckter*

DeFord Bailey. *Les Leverett Collection*

The Crook Brothers Band. *Top:* Herman Crook, Lewis Crook. *Bottom:*
Blythe Poteet, Kirk McGhee, Bill Stone. *Les Leverett Collection*

Jimmie Riddle and Onie Wheeler. *Les Leverett Collection*

Charlie McCoy.

Mickey Raphael.
Mike Manuel

John Lee
Williamson,
circa 1940.
*Mimosa Records
Productions, Inc.*

Junior Wells gives Mick Jagger a harp lesson, 1970. *Dick Waterman*

LITTLE BOY BLUE
PHONE 728

Broadcasting Over WEBQ on

MONDAYS--6:00 a. m. and 10:45 a. m.

WEDNESDAYS--10:45 a. m.

THURSDAYS--6:00 a. m.

FRIDAYS--11:45 a. m.

Price--25c

Rice Miller handbill, circa 1940. *Courtesy of Carrie Wilkins, Mimosa Records Productions, Inc.*

Walter Horton. *Ray Flerlage*

James Cotton. *Val Wilmer*

Paul Butterfield.
Michael Ochs Archives

Bob Dylan.
Michael Ochs Archive

Charlie Musselwhite. *Peter Amft.*

George Smith and Kim Wilson at the 1978 San Francisco Blues Festival. *Jeff Fereday*

Howard Levy.

Jean "Toots" Thielemans.

Tommy Reilly.
Courtesy of Sigmund Groven

William Galison.
Mark Ferri

At first I was just hanging out. And people would come up: "Why are you here?" "Well, I love the music and I play a little bit." "Oh, you play a little bit, huh?" It'd be that simple. "Hey, so and so. He says he plays harmonica." "Oh, yeah?" Then I'd just get called up. That would happen just over and over again. I'd be sitting in all the time, and then I started to get offers. "Hey, we're going up to Milwaukee. Why don't you come work with us?" And I'd go.

You know, all white people look alike. Lots of times I'd be in some place and somebody'd say, "Hey, Paul!" "That's not my name." "Yeah, I saw you two weeks ago over at such and such a place." "I've never been there." "Yeah, I saw you, man! We talked. I bought you a drink." It didn't take long for me to figure out that there was some guy around named Paul that was playing. So that was my introduction to Butterfield. As far as I know, we were the only two white guys on the South Side. Me and Paul were just there, on our own hook, by ourselves. I admired that about him. He was a great player, too, in those days. Before he was recording, to me he was tops. Later it changed somehow, and it didn't appeal to me as much—his whole attitude. But he was tough.

Little Walter really looked out for me. He would walk me to the bus stop and wait until the bus came, or drive me home. Walter was always a scrapper. He was short, but pound for pound, that was one tough little guy. Louis Myers told me about how he and Walter once met these two women wrestlers. Walter invited them back to the motel room. Well, this woman didn't like Walter's approach, he was trying to be too fast, so she just started throwing him all over the place. Louis said Walter had his footprints on the ceiling. And he's hollering, "Oh, baby, let go of me!" And she'd be throwing him up in air and bouncing him off the wall. Louis was crying, he was laughing so hard.

Things happened to Walter where he became ashamed of himself. When he left Muddy and went out on his own, he found himself playing in places he wasn't used to, like the Apollo Theater in New York. He'd be backstage and the stagehands would be making little comments to him about how he was just a country boy. They really messed Walter's head up. I remember walking into a club and Walter was sitting there in a chair with his mike in one hand and his harp in the other hand and he was staring at the floor; the band was playing, waiting on him to do something. I remember asking him, "What's going on?" "Oh, hell, I don't know," he said. He had bad habits, but so did a lot of people. They didn't get their heads turned around like it happened with Walter. Then the "black is beautiful" movement came along. Everyone is talking about soul food and blues and the black heritage. And Walter's going, "Oh, yeah, I was right all along." Walter started blasting again. He was playing just *great*. That was just a little bit before he died.

Me and Big Joe Williams was living together, and somebody offered him a job in a little neighborhood tavern on the North Side called Big John's. He asked me to come with him, and they sold so many drinks that night that they decided to keep it going. Mike Bloomfield started playing piano with us. Big Joe decided he was going to leave town, so Mike started playing guitar and we looked around and got a drummer and a bass player. In a matter of months Big John's turned into like *the* place to go.

We got a better offer in another club, so we told Paul, "Come on and take this," and he moved right in. Somewhere along in there Elektra offered Paul a contract. I'd already known Sam Charters, who was with Vanguard, which was sort of the competition for Elektra at that time. He'd come through town and would want to know what was happening, and I'd take him around to see different people. He was behind the *Chicago the Blues Today* record that I did with Walter Horton. I remember I took the day off from a factory job to do that. Vanguard had gotten into folk music and now they decided, "Well, we need a white harp player." I was the only other choice, I guess. So that's how my first record happened.

The Vanguard record got around pretty good. In 1967 I got this offer to work at the Fillmore in California. I didn't know what all that stuff was about. When I left Chicago, it was cold, unpleasant. I got off the plane, it was sunny, people were *very* pleasant. "Have a nice day!" Whoa! So I just decided, "I'm not going back." There were so many clubs around. And California was just real conducive to life, I thought. Chicago was just such a bad-news, dead-end, bad-luck, rough motherfucker. I had great times there, though. I remember one time out on Roosevelt Road—*that* was a night. Earl Hooker, Freddie Roulette, Buddy Guy was there, Carey Bell was on harmonica. It was just one of those nights; it just never stopped. Earl was just *incredible*. You'd just keep thinking, "It *can't* get any better than this," and it would just get better and better and better. I remember Buddy Guy at the bar just jumping up and down, screaming at Earl Hooker—"Yeah! *Yeah!*"

As far as harps go, I like the Old Standbys, especially the Bb. There used to be a wooden harp called the Echolux that had stars painted on it. It was a regular ten-hole, and it was the best harp. I had an A Echolux for eleven years, and it just got better and better.

I play the Lee Oskars. They're real convenient. You can buy extra reed plates, and when they go flat, you can just pop some other reeds in there. When you're out on the road, in the middle of nowhere, where they don't know about these things, you can't be looking for help because it won't be there.

I can't pin down my influences. Both Walters, I guess. I was closer to Walter Horton than to Little Walter. I just listen to phrases. To me, being a phraser is where it's at. Take your time, pick your notes. I'd rather underplay than overplay. Melody counts to me. With a lot of people, it's how many notes can you cram into eight bars, which I think misses the whole point. Especially when you're playing blues—that has nothing to do with how many notes you can play. All it has to do with is feeling. If you can play just one note and get it across, that's all it takes. *Tone.*

It was RCA Victor's Lester Melrose who first exposed the depth of Chicago's blues talent and who helped John Lee Williamson and Big Bill Broonzy piece together the rudiments of a new urban blues style. The homegrown Chess label infused this style with the intensity of Mississippi delta natives such as Muddy Waters and Willie Dixon and perfected the classic Chicago blues sound. Their lead was followed by other Windy City record companies such as States, Cobra, and Vee Jay, who mined the same rich vein of talent. As Chicago became the commercial blues mecca, many of the best Dixie-based bluesmen, including Howlin' Wolf and Rice Miller, moved north to where the money and studios were. When it comes to blues harmonica, over the years the city on Lake Michigan has offered up an embarrassment of riches.

The Holy Grail for Chicago blowers was the harp chair in Muddy Waters's band; they measured their worth and status in terms of that seat in the same way that tenor saxophonists of the swing era lusted after a slot in Count Basie's orchestra. Although there were exceptional harp players who were never called—John Lee Henley, Little Willie Foster, Snooky Pryor, Billy Boy Arnold, to name a few—the struggle for blues harmonica supremacy in Chicago can be traced by following the personnel shifts in Waters's band.

When Walter Horton left Muddy's group in 1952, a young player named Henry Strong ("He was the best harp blower in Chicago next to me," claimed Little Walter, who was not one for compliments) moved in. Strong was stabbed to death in 1954, and his entire recorded output consists of a few sides playing behind pianist Henry Gray and a pair of Muddy Waters tunes ("Sad, Sad Day" and "She's Alright"). Waters turned next to George Smith, whose singing was just as strong as his full-bodied harp playing. Smith's stay with Waters was a short one; he moved to Kansas City in 1954 and cut some great records there for RPM (including the phenomenal "Blues in the Dark" and "Telephone Blues") before moving on to Los Angeles, where he lived until his death in 1983. He recorded for small California labels in the 1960s and put together an album of Little Walter tunes for ABC Bluesway in 1969. His talent was extraordinary—he had one of the fattest harmonica tones ever—but his career was haphazard and unfocused; he recorded as "Little Walter, Jr.," the "Harmonica King," and "George Allen" more often then he did under his real name. Although Smith's recorded legacy is slimmer than that of most players of his caliber, his influence lives on in the playing of a quartet of premier harpists who came under his spell as young players: Rod Piazza, Kim Wilson, William Clarke, and James Harman.

It was James Cotton who got the nod when Smith left Waters, and not long after Cotton's long tenure ended, Muddy surprised a lot of people by hiring a young white player from New York City, Paul Oscher. Perhaps the first white harpist to completely master the quintessential Chicago harp style, Oscher is a brilliant player who had the misfortune of having his time in Waters's group coincide with the artistic low point of Muddy's career, when, acceding to pressure from Chess, the blues master recorded a pair of unfortunate "psychedelic" albums that, perversely, sold well. Most of Oscher's studio work in support of Waters was buried in a wash of wah-wah guitars and other misguided studio effects, but a hint of his fine playing can be heard on several songs on Muddy's *Live at Mister Kelly's* LP. An outstanding slide guitarist, talented pianist, and accordionist as well as a harp master, Oscher continues to perform as Brooklyn Slim.

Oscher stayed with Muddy for four years and was succeeded briefly by Carey Bell before Mojo Buford settled in during the early 1970s. In 1974, a young harp player named Jerry Portnoy got a phone call from Waters's manager. "Time stopped for me," recalls Portnoy. "There was only one reason in the world for this guy to call me, and it was so heavy I couldn't even deal with it. 'Muddy wants you to call him. He's home right now.' I dialed Muddy's number. 'You ready to travel?' he asked. 'We start May twenty-fifth in Indianapolis. The boys are playin' down at Queen Bee's Lounge this weekend. Go down there and play with them and get used to them.' I didn't know what to say. After we finished talking I checked with Muddy's manager, who told me to get a passport because they were going to Paris that month.

"I hung up the phone and I lost it. I went bananas. If you want to be a brain surgeon, well, there is a course of action you can take—go to medical school, study, and become a brain surgeon. But for blues harp players, there was only one job, and the planets had to align pretty good for it to happen. When I hung up the phone, I ran out of that house and didn't even close the door. I was filled with this nervous energy and I just ran right up the street to a friend's record store and burst in the door and said, 'Muddy Waters just hired me.' I was running around in circles. Man, it was the greatest moment of my life, except for maybe when my children were born.

"The next day I was on the bus. I was still ten feet off the ground. There was this old woman there with a shopping cart and I was just looking at her wondering, 'Did this person ever have a dream in her life that ever happened for her?' I had just achieved this phenomenal thing. I'll never forget the first time I walked out onto a stage with that band at a baseball stadium in Indianapolis. The announcer said, 'Ladies and gentlemen—the Muddy Waters Blues Band,' and the thrill that went up me was unbelievable. No matter what else I do in my life, when they lay me in the ground, the first line on the obit will be, 'Jerry Portnoy, former member of the Muddy Waters Blues Band. . . .'" Portnoy and most of Muddy's band went out on their own in the late 1970s as the Legendary Blues Band; more recently, he has been working out of the Boston area and solidifying his reputation as one of the most genuine keepers of the Chicago flame.

Currently carrying the torch in the Windy City are Dave Waldman, another master of the traditional harp style, and two young African American harpists, Billy Branch and Sugar Blue, both of whom have made their marks by stretching the traditional blues harmonica formula. Branch picked up the mouth organ as a boy, but didn't become committed to the instrument until he moved to Chicago to attend college and fell into the blues scene there. He prefers to mix blues with "a lot of heavy rhythmic stuff, like some War pieces." Branch paid his dues as a member of several Chicago bands, including the Willie Dixon All Stars. In 1991 he was featured on Alligator Records' "Harp Attack," where he shared equal billing with his mentors Junior Wells and James Cotton.

Chicago-based James Whiting, aka Sugar Blue, won a Grammy for Best Traditional Blues Recording in 1986 for his version of "Another Man Done Gone" recorded live at the Montreux Festival. Blue lived for a time in France, where he recorded two albums and met Mick Jagger, who asked him to contribute some harmonica to two Rolling Stones albums, *Some Girls* and *Emotional Rescue*. *The New York Times* has called him "an extraordinarily lyrical young harmonica player." Although *Downbeat* hailed Whiting as "a remarkable blues harmonica virtuoso," his playing also shows a strong jazz influence.

The Southern Players

Not all the Southern blues artists moved north; many resisted the lure of Chicago and were content to build their careers south of the Mason-Dixon line. Most recorded for small, regional labels and never received the attention given the Chicago-based performers, but their ranks include several influential harp players.

Memphis's celebrated blues harmonica legacy survived the defections of John Lee Williamson, Walter Horton, and James Cotton to be carried on by Joe Hill Louis and Dr. (Isaiah) Ross (The Harmonica Boss). Both were among the finest—and last—representatives of the one-man-band species, self-contained powerhouses who simultaneously sang, picked the guitar, played the mouth organ in the rack, and provided a basic rhythmic accompaniment by playing high-hat cymbals and bass drums with their feet. Both began their recording careers thanks to Sam Phillips, champion of the unorthodox; Louis recorded several raw sides for Sun in the 1950s, and Ross also recorded for the label before moving to Flint, Michigan, in the late 1950s and establishing himself as a popular performer in Europe.

Mississippi has continued to produce harmonica masters, the most notable of which are Jerry McCain and Sam Myers. McCain, whose first recording, a 1961 single for the Rex label that coupled the jukebox gem "She's Tough" with "Steady," one of the great blues harp instrumentals, has seen his career resurrected after his tunes were covered by rock bands like the Fabulous Thunderbirds. Sam Myers, who recorded for Ace, Fury, and Soft in the 1950s and '60s, was best known for his brilliant backup harp on Elmore James's 1961 recording of "Look on Yonders Wall" until he began appearing and recording with Anson Funderburgh and the Rockets in the mid-1980s. Myers is also a topflight blues singer; his resurgence has been one of the most welcome developments in recent blues history.

Louisiana has been home to some excellent harp players, including the spellbinding Papa (Alexander) Lightfoot, whose slim recorded output included an incendiary session for Imperial in 1954 that produced "Mean Old Train" and a wild version of "When the Saints Go Marching In," two sides that showed a no-holds-barred approach to amplified harmonica and a unique approach to phrasing that betrayed Lightfoot's New Orleans roots.

Leslie Johnson, better known as Lazy Lester, seems to have developed a proficiency on the harmonica more quickly than most. "I was working in a grocery store in Baton Rouge," he told writer John Broven, "and I bought a harmonica and a record while I was working there. I was sitting on the back of the bus going home and I revved the harp up a bit. By the time I got off the bus at Scotlandville I had it tuned down the way I wanted it. The record was 'Juke' by Little Walter. Jimmy Reed was my favorite, but I've got my own style. I just kept fooling with it till I got the sound out of it that I wanted." In the late 1950s, Lester played harmonica on many of Lightnin' Slim's best records on Jay Miller's Excello label, and beginning in 1958 he recorded thirty sides of his own for Miller. Lester's playing is solidly in the Jimmy Reed mold. "Sugar Coated Love" was his best-seller, and "I Hear You Knockin'" also did passably well for him, but Lester never really had a bona fide hit. One of the few blacks in Jay Miller's stable of studio musicians, Lester played on the records of many other Excello artists, usually as a percussionist but occasionally contributing on harmonica and guitar. He moved to Pontiac, Michigan, in the 1960s and began working in the auto plants there. Thanks in no small part to the recent rerecordings of his tunes by the Fabulous Thunderbirds, Lester has begun recording and touring again.

Slim Harpo (1924–70)

The most popular Louisiana harp blower was Slim Harpo, who began life in West Baton Rouge as James Moore. Orphaned as a teenager, he worked on the docks in New Orleans and learned to play the guitar while blowing into a harmonica lodged in a metal holder hung around his neck. By the early 1940s he was playing in clubs and bars in Mississippi and Louisiana as Harmonica Slim. Harpo came to the attention of blues producer Jay Miller when he seconded Lightnin' Slim on a 1955 session. Two years later he recorded "I'm a King Bee" for Miller, which proved to be a major hit for Excello.

The adenoidal vocals, stark harmonica, and deceptively simple instrumental background that characterized Harpo's style owed a lot to that of Jimmy Reed, and Harpo had similar success in crossing over to white audiences. In 1961, Excello released his "Rainin' in My Heart," which not only climbed the r&b charts but reached number thirty-four on the pop surveys. He began touring steadily throughout the South, but he became embroiled in a contract dispute with Miller that halted his recording career until 1963, when he resumed recording with Excello. Harpo came back strong in 1966, earning a number one r&b record with the swamp blues classic "Scratch My Back," which reached number sixteen on *Billboard*'s Hot 100. He added to his string of bayou blues hits in 1967 and 1968 with "Tip On In" and "Te-Ni-Nee-Ni-Nu," respectively.

After the Rolling Stones included a version of "King Bee" on their debut album in 1964, Harpo worked hard to connect with rock audiences, recording with psychedelic backgrounds and playing the Fillmore East and the Electric Circus in New York in 1969. He was on the verge of a European tour and perhaps a commercial breakthrough when he died of a heart attack.

The economy of Slim Harpo's harmonica style beautifully set up his marvelous tone and memorable fills; witness his atmospheric "Blues Hangover" from 1960. His tunes have been reworked by many rock groups; the Rolling Stones included his "Shake Your Hips" on their 1973 *Exile on Main Street* album, and more recently the Fabulous Thunderbirds have worshiped at his altar, covering "Scratch My Back" and "Rainin' in My Heart."

The Future

Although the Holy Trinity of blues harmonica—Rice Miller, Little Walter, and Walter Horton—have all left the scene and their successors—James Cotton, Junior Wells, Carey Bell, and Sam Myers—are aging, the blue-eyed blues harp movement spearheaded by Paul Butterfield and Charlie Musselwhite has taken root in every region of the country, and the durability of the blues harmonica style shows no sign of erosion, despite this profound shift from its original cultural roots. Nearly all of the younger, white harpists made their initial reputations as masters of the Chicago approach and repertoire, but in recent years many have reached a more mature stage in their development and are making more original contributions to the blues vocabulary. Aficionados on the East Coast can slake their blues harp thirst with regular doses of the standout playing of Jerry Portnoy, Sugar Ray Norcia (who is also a fine, emotional singer), Steve Guyger, Danny Russo, and the Nighthawks' Mark Wenner. The Pacific Northwest is home to two great harpists who are also outstanding singers: Paul deLay, who has crafted a highly personal harmonica style and is an expertly soulful chromatic player, and Curtis Salgado, who played with Robert Cray and Roomful of Blues before striking out on his own. Steve Nardella and Madison Slim are two of the most accomplished harp players working out of the Midwest, and Gary Primich is advancing the blues harp tradition in Texas. California, one of the epicenters of the blues revival hurricane of the late 1960s, has spawned many blues harmonica stars. With the international success of the Sacramento-based group Little Charlie and the Nightcats, audiences around the world are realizing what California fans have known for years: that Rick Estrin is one of the most talented harp players and singers of his generation. The Bay Area has produced two of the great blues harp traditionalists, Mark Hummel and Gary Smith, while Los Angeles is home to three players who were heavily influenced by the great George Smith: Rod Piazza, an ace on both the diatonic and the chromatic harmonicas whose career began in the late 1960s with the Dirty Blues Band; William Clarke, who is maintaining a high profile these days after a string of fine albums for Alligator; and a transplanted Southerner and supremely expressive singer, James Harman.

Magic Dick

Rock and Roll

The harmonica never had its Elvis Presley. The guitar became the totem of rock and roll, largely because it was the six-string that Presley slung across his twitching shoulders. In 1955 the harmonica had all the requirements for assuming a leading role in rock except for a charismatic champion. It had the right bloodline: rock and roll began as a souped-up melding of country boogie and rhythm and blues, two genres in which the harmonica had long been the dominant wind instrument. It had the underdog status so appealing to young, rebellious rockers: like the guitar, the mouth organ had always been seen by the musical establishment as a low-class instrument. And for once, even the traditional indifference shown to the mouth organ by the music industry establishment was no hurdle, because early rock and roll was hawked by the same small, independent record companies that had already issued some of the finest harmonica work in both country music and the blues.

Before Sun struck vinyl gold with Presley, the label had released the first recordings of blues harmonica aces Walter Horton, James Cotton, Joe Hill Louis, and Isaiah "Doctor" Ross. In 1954, a few months before Elvis's first record was issued, Sun had brought out Harmonica Frank Floyd's "Rockin' Chair Daddy," often touted as one of the earliest rock and roll records. After Presley left Sun, Phillips shelved his blues projects and concentrated on grooming other white Southern rockers for stardom, including an ambitious hillbilly cat named Billy Lee Riley, who may have been the harmonica's best white hope in the early days of rock and roll. A bluesy singer, talented guitarist, and capable harmonica player, Riley was a member of the Sun house band. After scoring hits on his own with "Red Hot" and "Flying Saucer Rock and Roll," Riley put together an excellent band, The Little Green Men (they wore stage costumes sewn from green pool-table felt), and turned them into one of the wildest stage shows in rock and roll. Riley recorded two harmonica instrumentals, "Itchy" and "Thunderbird," for Sun, but they were not outstanding efforts and were for some reason released under the name of another Sun artist, Sonny Burgess. Riley dusted off his harps in the mid-1960s to record a harmonica instrumental album of Beatles tunes for Mercury.

Chess, Sun's rival to the north, was also trying to get a handle on the rock and roll revolution. The Chicago label was far removed from the greasy funkiness of the Southern rock and roll talent and put its money instead on urbane doo-wop groups like the Moonglows and the Coronets. At first the label seemed reluctant to part from its successful blues formula, calling Little Walter into the studio to add his unmistakable brand of harmonica ornamentation to a pair of tunes by the Coronets released in 1954.

The harmonica missed out on one of its best opportunities to inject itself into rock and roll when it was not included in Chuck Berry's first session at the Chess studios in May 1955. Although Berry's backup musicians were the same players used on the label's blues sessions—the drummer was Fred Below, Little Walter's timekeeper—none of Chess's stellar blues harpists were on hand. The meteoric success of a tune from this session, a spoof on country music entitled "Maybelline," catapulted Chess into the thick of the new rock and roll market. Although Berry was a seasoned blues performer who over the years recorded several straight-ahead blues numbers for Chess, he was never joined in the studio by any of the label's resident harmonica aces.

After Berry's career skyrocketed, Chess scurried to find other black performers who could offer up tunes in this new style. The label's next big rock and roll entry, hypno-voodoo shaman Bo Diddley, put the harmonica on teen jukeboxes for the first time by using such harp players as Lester Davenport, Little Willie Smith, and Billy Boy Arnold on his early records. Arnold's playing on Bo Diddley's first hit led to his being signed by Chess's rival Vee Jay, which quickly released Arnold's "I Wish You Would"; according to Billy Boy, Chess used its considerable influence to ensure that his record never got airplay. Arnold and Vee Jay continued to release sides set in rock and roll grooves, including "Rockinitis" and "Kissing at Midnight," with limited success.

Vee Jay had considerably better luck with Jimmy Reed, whose stripped-down, insistent beat proved as popular with rock and roll audiences as it did with blues fans. Reed's commercial breakthrough with tunes like "Big Boss Man" paved the way for crossover triumphs by other black blues harpists: Buster Brown's big seller of 1960, "Fannie Mae," was built around a harmonica riff, and Slim Harpo climbed the pop charts the following year with "Rainin' in My Heart" and again in 1966 with "Scratch My Back."

The original, bluesy underpinnings of rock and roll faded as the Presleys and Berrys were supplanted by confections like Fabian and Frankie Avalon, and the mouth organ's limited role in the genre was reduced to essentially the same cameo role as it had served in popular music—the quickest way to down-home funkiness (Charlie McCoy's harp signature on Roy Orbison's "Candy Man" from 1960) or sticky wistfulness (the chromatic harmonica on Brian Hyland's "Sealed With a Kiss" from 1962). The mouth organ might never have gained a real foothold in rock and roll if it had not been for a chance meeting in 1962 between the rhythm guitarist of an English pop group and a young veteran of the Texas dance halls named Delbert McClinton.

McClinton had begun singing and playing the guitar professionally as a teenager in Fort Worth, schooling himself in rhythm and blues by backing up the likes of Howling Wolf and John Lee Hooker when they swung through Texas. "One night we were backing up Buster

Brown and Jimmy Reed in the same night. I had just bought me a harmonica because they were two of the best, ya know, and I was ready to learn. Well, we were sittin' in the dressing room before the show—I didn't drink at the time—but they were both passing a quart of Old Grand-Dad, and I was sittin' in the middle helpin' 'em drink it—I never did see the show!" But McClinton proved to be a quick study on the mouth organ, and his first record, a cover of Rice Miller's "Wake Up Baby," was the first by a white artist to be played on KNOK, Fort Worth's black radio station.

It was McClinton who played the distinctive harmonica lick that helped Bruce Channel's "Hey Baby" to become an international hit in 1962. When Channel was invited to tour England that year, he took McClinton with him. McClinton was surprised to find that many British musicians were just as absorbed in the harmonica as he had been a few years earlier and that he was now cast in the role of the old master. As he later told Suzan Crane, "From the first night I was there, somebody in every band had a harmonica [and] come down to the dressing room and wanted to learn something. And this went on every night. . . . Well, one night we worked with the Beatles. They were the opening act for the Bruce Channel show, and the only thing I knew about them was this girl had said, 'I really want you to hear this band; they're the hottest band in the north of England,' and they were. They had on these nice-looking lightweight black leather suits, and whichever one I taught to play something on harp, I asked him where he got the suit, and I went into London the next day and got me a coat."

The British Bands

John Lennon was the Beatle in leather to whom McClinton had tried to explain the mysteries of cross-harp playing. Lennon, whose musical heroes were pop rockers like Buddy Holly and the Everly Brothers, sought out McClinton not as a blues maven but as someone who knew how to use the harmonica to deliver a melodic hook. Lennon's harmonica work was a cornerstone of the Beatles' early sound. The group's first three hits in Britain—"Love Me Do," "Please Please Me," and "From Me to You"—had the mouth organ front and center; all told, nearly a dozen Beatles tunes recorded between 1963 and 1965 featured the harmonica, including "I Should Have Known Better" and

"I'll Get You." During the Beatles' first tour of America, John Lennon told interviewers that his favorite musician was Sonny Terry, but by 1966 the Beatles had abandoned their original formulas, and Lennon's harmonica disappeared from their recordings.

Although the Beatles made their reputation as pop stylists, the "British invasion" of America that swept in behind them brought the first stirrings of a blues revival that would soon revitalize rock and roll. British tours by Big Bill Broonzy, Muddy Waters, and Little Walter in the early 1960s had spurred a fascination in that country with African American rhythm and blues, and by the time the Beatles signed their first recording contract, a half dozen small clubs in London had become the pulpits from which rawer British bands tried to mimic the Chicago blues sound. One of the earliest of these was formed by guitarist Alexis Korner and harmonica player Cyril Davies. The pair had begun their careers as acoustic performers, but by 1961, Davies had become enthralled with the playing of Little Walter, and he and Korner recruited drummer Charlie Watts and bassist Jack Bruce and formed an amplified band called Blues Incorporated. Early the following year Korner and Davies opened their own showcase, the Ealing Club, which attracted a devoted coterie of young fans and musicians that included Mick Jagger (who regularly fronted the group), Keith Richards, Brian Jones, Eric Burdon, and Rod Stewart (whose first recording session was as a harmonica player on Millie Small's 1964 hit "My Boy Lollipop").

Blues Incorporated split up in 1963. Davies put together the Cyril Davies All Stars, which at times included pianist Nicky Hopkins and guitarists Jimmy Page and Jeff Beck. The band recorded four sides for Pye Records and had a solid following, but on January 7, 1964—just as the amplified brand of British rhythm and blues that Korner and Davies had pioneered was becoming a popular force—Davies died of leukemia. "Cyril was a great harmonica player," Charlie Watts told Pete Goodman. "That original band really moved. . . . Mick Jagger could just get up and sing with us if he felt like it. That's how Brian [Jones] and Keith [Richards] came to sit in, too. . . . We had sessions that I've never seen bettered."

Blues Incorporated's influence among musicians nearly matched that of the Beatles. Between 1964 and 1966, it was difficult to find a British rock band without a harp player. There were the Yardbirds' Keith Relf, the Animals' Eric Burdon, Spencer Davis of the Spencer Davis Group, John Mayall of the Blues Breakers, the Kinks' Ray

Davies and Denis Payton, and Rick Huxley of the Dave Clark Five, but Mayall was the only competent soloist among this set. By far the most successful of the many musical associations that grew out of the Ealing Club's blue milieu was the Rolling Stones, a group that included two of Davies's most attentive harmonica students, Mick Jagger and Brian Jones.

Jagger and Keith Richards, the Stones' creative core, were former grade school classmates who had become reacquainted as teenagers after Richards spotted Jagger carrying a Little Walter album on a London commuter train. Months of informal jamming followed, with Richards picking at the guitar and Jagger singing and playing the harmonica. "We'd try to play some of this Little Walter stuff and Chuck Berry stuff," Keith Richards recalled in a 1971 interview. "Then we found Slim Harpo. . . . And suddenly in '62, just when we were getting together, we read this little thing about a rhythm and blues club starting in Ealing. . . . 'Let's go up to this place and find out what's happening.' There was this amazing old cat playing harp . . . Cyril Davies."

At the Ealing Club, Jagger and Richards came within the orbit of a charismatic guitarist named Brian Jones. "He was a cat who could play any instrument," Keith Richards told *Rolling Stone.* "I went out one morning and came back in the evening and Brian was *blowing harp,* man. . . . All these blue notes comin' out. 'I've learned how to do it. I've figured it out.' One day. So then he started to really work on the harp . . . the harp became his thing. He'd walk around all the time playing his harp."

In their formative years, the Stones did tours with Bo Diddley and Little Walter, whom they accompanied as well as opened for. Their first single, a cover of Chuck Berry's "Come On," had Jones's harp all over it, and their debut album included remakes of tunes by Slim Harpo and Jimmy Reed. When they visited the United States for the first time in 1964, the Stones insisted on recording at Chess's Chicago studios. Chuck Berry, Muddy Waters, Junior Wells, Rice Miller, and Willie Dixon all dropped by to watch the British band in action.

The Rolling Stones and the Beatles found themselves filling an inspirational vacuum in the home of rock and roll. The head of steam built up by Elvis and Chuck Berry had been dissipated by the one's army stint and the other's imprisonment on trumped-up morals charges, and most of the creative juice in American music was coming not from the derivative rockers who tried to follow them but from the folk scene, which had matured from a collegiate alternative to a commercial success. The advent of the British rockers caused a bitter controversy among folk music fans that widened into a genuine rift when their own crown prince decided to leave his fingerpicks behind, plug in, and sing the body electric.

Bob Dylan (1941–)

Jesse Fuller never had any trouble getting the attention of an audience. If listeners somehow failed to appreciate his fine voice, excellent material (his "San Francisco Bay Blues" has become a folk music staple), and instrumental skills, they couldn't ignore his riveting stage presence. He was a unique visual as he sang, picked a twelve-string guitar, and blew on a harmonica in a holder that also housed a microphone and a kazoo, all the while playing a high-hat cymbal with one foot and with the other manipulating a "fotdella," a percussion device of his own creation that simultaneously struck a bass drum and plucked a homemade string bass. One evening in the summer of 1960, Fuller brought his self-contained symphony to the Exodus, a Denver folk music club. During a break, Fuller was waylaid by a pale, baby-faced teenager who peppered him with questions: What brand of harp did he play? What keys did he favor? How did that harmonica holder work?

This was Bob Dylan's first real instruction on an instrument that had fascinated him since his childhood in Hibbing, Minnesota. Hank Williams had been his first inspiration, but by the time he reached his teens Dylan had steeped himself in the music of Muddy Waters, Little Walter, and Leadbelly. A Hibbing girlfriend recalls him raving about Jimmy Reed: "Bob thought he was fabulous, the best!" Although friends remember him experimenting with the harmonica by the time he was in ninth grade, Dylan didn't get anywhere with the instrument until after his run-in with Fuller.

The Bob Dylan who questioned Jesse Fuller about playing in the rack was in the grips of an all-consuming obsession with the talking blues style of Dust Bowl troubadour Woody Guthrie that was threatening his musical identity. Watching Fuller that night in Denver, Dylan must have sensed that the harmonica could help him carve out his own piece of turf, that it could add another melodic dimension to his solid but basic guitar playing, provide a bridge between his wellsprings, blues and country music ("I crossed Sonny Terry with the

Stanley Brothers," was how he later put it), and confound live audiences. ("He became the first guy to put the guitar and harmonica together, with that frame holder around his neck. Nobody had ever seen this before," claims one who was close to Dylan at the time.)

Dylan spent the fall of 1960 in Minneapolis working hard at taming the harmonica. He became close to Dave "Tony" Glover, the most talented mouth organist on the scene, who recalls introducing Dylan to the diatonic and the cross-harp concept after watching him wrestle with a chromatic harmonica. Not everyone was charmed by Dylan's early experiments on the mouth organ. "He would come over to the sorority house," a former girlfriend of Dylan's has recalled, "and he'd play his harmonica, which he didn't know how to play! And my friends would come in and they would just go, 'Uurgh! Who is this geek?' I wanted him to play guitar, which he could play well and which I knew would impress them, but he just wasn't having any of it. He was saying, 'Naw, I wanna get this.' . . . I was mortified, but he didn't give a shit."

By the winter of 1960, Dylan had settled on an unrestrained straight-harp style based on unsubtle clusters of notes. His few public comments about the development of his anarchistic harmonica technique make it sound as if it sprang from a kind of perverse willfullness. "I would blow out on the harmonica because everybody sucks in," Dylan told Pete Oppel of the *Dallas Morning News* in 1978. "The proper way to play is like Little Walter or Sonny Boy Williamson would play—which would be to cross it—and I found myself blowing out more because nobody was doing that in that area. And that's what defined the harmonica and guitar sound which I hadn't heard until that point. I just stumbled on it one day." In a 1989 interview, Dylan was more forthcoming, linking his style to his early enthusiasm for Jimmy Reed's playing: "Jimmy Reed blew out instead of sucking in. . . . He had his own style of playing . . . sometimes the whole solo would be like three notes."

In early 1961, Dylan surprised his peers in Minneapolis by moving to New York City, where he made his initial reputation not as a picker or singer but as a harmonica blower. Within days of his arrival he clambered onto the stage of the Cafe Wha?—a Greenwich Village folk club—to accompany songwriter and singer Fred Neil. The club's owner was won over: "I'd never seen that [playing mouth organ in the rack] before. I thought it was unusual and kind of kooky." Harmonica players were scarce in the Village, and Dylan became the house harp player at the Cafe Wha?

The mouth organ opened other doors for Dylan. "I met Bob Dylan at the first Indian Neck Folk Festival in May 1961," recounts Bob Neuwirth. "I remember running into Dylan because he was the only other guy with a harmonica holder around his neck." Dylan also made forays to Boston to check out the thriving folk scene there and impressed folksinger Carolyn Hester. When Hester arrived in New York in September of 1961 to begin rehearsals for her first album for Columbia, she called in Dylan—as a harmonica player. It was at a rehearsal with Hester that Dylan first met John Hammond, Sr., Columbia's legendary producer, who had already heard about Dylan from his son, John, Jr., an accomplished blues guitarist and mouth harpist. "His guitar playing, let us say charitably, was rudimentary, and his harmonica was barely passable," Hammond, Sr., later recalled, "but he had a sound and a point of view and an idea."

As Dylan was rehearsing with Hester, he sat for an interview with *New York Times* music critic Robert Shelton, whom Dylan had been courting for months. Shelton asked him about his harmonica style. "I picked up the harmonica after hearing Walter Jacobs," Dylan told Shelton. "But I play my own style of harmonica. . . . I met Jesse Fuller two years ago in Denver and studied with him." Shelton wrote a laudatory article on Dylan for the *Times,* and the folksinger handed John Hammond, Sr., a copy when he arrived at the Columbia studios for Hester's session. Not long after, Dylan signed his own contract with Columbia.

Dylan's first album was recorded in a two-day session that November. "Dylan's guitar work was strong for a twenty-year-old's debut album," claims Robert Shelton. "His harmonica work may not have been virtuoso, but it gave the album some of its flavor and texture. The mouth harp weaves the fabric of voice and guitar together, and it helped stimulate the resurgence of interest in blues harmonica in the early 1960s." Shelton interviewed Dylan again before contributing the liner notes to the album. "He linked his harmonica work to Jesse Fuller, 'Little Walter' Jacobs, and Sonny Terry. 'Now I am "blowing out" more in my own style.'" Five years later, Dylan would confess to Shelton that he felt that the best thing about his first album was his mouth organ playing.

Dylan's next visit to the recording studio came after a call from

Harry Belafonte's producer, who was searching for an "ethnic" harmonica player. Dylan earned a $50 check for playing harp on Belafonte's version of "Midnight Special." He told friends that he had been slated to play on several tunes but left after one song because he had become frustrated by Belafonte's perfectionism and insistence on recording take after take.

In early 1962, Dylan jammed several times in public with bluesman Big Joe Williams, who had made his initial recordings twenty years earlier with John Lee Williamson backing him on harp, and on March 2, 1962, they recorded six songs together—four of which featured Dylan on harmonica—for the Spivey label. Dylan, who was under an exclusive contract with Columbia, was billed as "Big Joe's Buddy." The following year Dylan hid behind the pseudonym Tedham Porterhouse to contribute some mouth harp to a Ramblin' Jack Elliott album.

During the next two years Dylan would pen the anthemic "Blowin' in the Wind" and "The Times They Are A-Changin'" and become the rough-edged darling of the folk scene. But Dylan had begun his performing career pounding piano in high school rock bands, and he kept a watchful eye on the Beatles' ascendancy; his 1965 album *Bringing It All Back Home* included several tunes recorded with an electric band. Early that summer the Byrds released their amplified version of Dylan's "Mr. Tambourine Man," and in June, Dylan recorded "Like a Rolling Stone" backed by a rock band that included guitarist Mike Bloomfield. A month later Dylan headlined the Newport Festival, where Bloomfield was appearing as a member of a band led by Chicago harp player Paul Butterfield. Dylan performed for the first time in public with a full band at the festival, having hastily put together a backup group that included Bloomfield and Butterfield's rhythm section. Folk purists were outraged; when Dylan took an electric band with him on a tour of Great Britain, some audiences tried to treat him with his own medicine. In his first electric concert in Edinburgh, *The Scottish Daily Express* reported that he had been "booed off the stage again last night. . . . Some of the audience took out mouth organs and tried to play down his singing." Dylan consoled himself by watching "Like a Rolling Stone" rise to the top of the charts. "Folk rock" became such a hot commodity that all sorts of dubious attempts at the style were inflicted on the public, which was left to grapple with such cross-cultural leaps as Bobby Darin's recording of "Me and Mr. Hohner."

Dylan the rock and roll star continued to play harmonica onstage and in the studio—as his wordplay became freer and his focus more urban, as he mixed influences as varied as Hank Williams, Chuck Berry, and Allen Ginsberg, his harmonica interludes helped keep his music elemental. The mouth harp also accentuates the pervasive loneliness of much of Dylan's music; the spooky, biblical melancholy of Dylan's remarkable 1968 album *John Wesley Harding* is largely the result of Dylan's mouth harp playing, perhaps his most melodic ever.

In recent years, Dylan has flashed his harmonica credentials sparingly. On his first appearance on the David Letterman show in 1984, he reprised Sonny Boy Williamson's first Chess recording, "Don't Start Me Talking." He seemed to rediscover the mouth organ on a 1989 tour of Europe, playing it frequently and intensely, and on his 1992 album, *Good As I Been to You*, he brought his career full circle, returning to the acoustic, harmonica-laced sound that started it all. His crude but instantly identifiable style has become such a part of the rock and roll vernacular that a crowd of rock performers have tried to co-opt it, either by calling on the man himself (Dylan has played harp on recordings by Roger McGuinn, Doug Sahm, Booker T. Jones, David Blue, Keith Green, and Sly and Robbie, among others) or by shamelessly aping him (Neil Young, Billy Joel, and Bruce Springsteen are the most prominent of the Dylan mouth organ counterfeiters).

Paul Butterfield (1942–87)

When the album appeared on record store shelves in 1965, amidst other LPs sporting colorful portraits of mop-haired, uniformed, Beatle-booted rockers, the two photographs on its cover—one capturing a trio of scruffy white hipsters and two black men at rest, slouching against the front of an urban hoodoo parlor, the other freezing the same quintet onstage in a blur of motion—proclaimed the arrival of something different: the Paul Butterfield Blues Band.

The music on the record inside the cardboard sleeve was just as distinctive—a plus in an era when the public's ears were wide open and the Beatles shared the charts with Aretha Franklin, Bob Dylan, and the Supremes. The Butterfield Blues Band never had a hit single or played the "Ed Sullivan Show," but they were as influential as any other group of their era.

They were led by twenty-three-year-old Paul Butterfield, who had grown up in Chicago listening to his father's jazz records. He was introduced to the blues by an older brother; by 1957 he and his friend Nick Gravenites were making regular forays to the blues clubs on the South Side. Butterfield began an improbable but swift transition from a flute-playing, high school track star into a brash, harp-playing singer who would at every opportunity jump onstage with living icons such as Muddy Waters, Howlin' Wolf, Robert Nighthawk, Buddy Guy, Otis Rush, Little Walter, and Magic Sam.

"I never practiced the harp in my life. Never," Butterfield admitted in a 1969 *Down Beat* interview. "I would just blow in it. I was blowing some lousy stuff. . . . We were more interested in getting high, dancing, and having ourselves some good times than anything else. . . . Muddy knows that I used to come down to him and play some nothing stuff, but nobody ever said, 'Well, man, you're not playing too well.' . . . I didn't have no plan or say, 'I'm gonna learn how to play the harp like so and so or learn how to do this or that,' y'know. I just started playing it. I mess around with any instrument I can get next to. It wasn't, 'I want to learn like Little Walter or Sonny Boy Williamson.' I just wanted to learn how to *play*. . . . One of the main reasons why I never really tried to play Little Walter's solos or Sonny Boy's or any other cat's exactly the way it was is that, in the first place, I couldn't."

By 1963, Butterfield was attending the University of Chicago, where one of his classmates was a guitarist named Elvin Bishop. Before long he and Bishop had hijacked Howlin' Wolf's rhythm section, drummer Sam Lay and bassist Jerome Arnold, and the Butterfield Blues Band settled in for a long run at Big John's club, where they were spotted in 1965 by Paul Rothchild, a producer for Elektra who sensed the commercial potential of a racially mixed band performing Chicago blues. Rothchild signed the band to Elektra and convinced Butterfield to use Mike Bloomfield on the band's debut album. Although Butterfield would later hint that in hindsight this first album had been marred by too much collective adrenaline, its high energy level and the band's absolute uniqueness as a black-and-white blues outfit helped make *The Paul Butterfield Blues Band* one of the most talked-about albums of the year.

The Butterfield contingent rolled into New York, where the most popular sounds at the time were the folk rock of the Lovin' Spoonful and the pop soul of the Young Rascals. Butterfield's shows at the Café Au Go Go in the spring of 1965 were seminal events that changed the course of pop music. This was no group of purists intent on slavishly re-creating the classic Chicago sound, but blues with an attitude. ("We suggest that you play this record at the highest possible volume in order to fully appreciate the sound of the Paul Butterfield Blues Band," read a warning on the back of their album.) Butterfield was the band's center; his confident, straight-ahead singing and harmonica playing— which was not the fat, swinging approach of Little Walter but an edgier, hot-rodded style—rode over the fiercely competitive guitar playing of Bloomfield and Bishop while the rhythmic funkiness of Lay and Arnold kept the group from sounding too polished or predictable.

Word of mouth helped the band become a last-minute addition to the Newport Folk Festival lineup that July. This annual event had a long tradition of showcasing acoustic blues acts, and Muddy Waters had performed at Newport with his full band the year before. In the interim many younger folk music fans had become captivated by the Beatles and the recent recordings Bob Dylan had made with electric instruments. The Butterfield Blues Band appeared on the opening day of the 1965 Newport festival and caused a sensation with their high-volume cockiness. When they showed up the next afternoon to play at a blues workshop, thousands were waiting. As many in the crowd danced happily, the folk zealots winced. Albert Grossman, Bob Dylan's manager, took offense at festival organizer Alan Lomax's condescending introduction of the Butterfield group and physically attacked him backstage. The last evening of the festival included another powerful performance by the Butterfield band as well as Bob Dylan's first live appearance with a band—a group that included Bloomfield, Lay, and Arnold. The Butterfield Blues Band left Newport with a national reputation and a new manager—Albert Grossman.

In 1966, Butterfield and company released their second album, *East-West,* which further expanded the group's musical territory. Although the band still played with their gloves off, there was now a more pronounced jazz influence (Butterfield had always been a jazz fan, counting among his influences Roland Kirk, Stanley Turrentine, and Gene Ammons), helped by the replacement of backbeat specialist Sam Lay with the more versatile Billy Davenport. Both sides of the album were closed out by extended, ragalike instrumental jams, which may have been inspired by the San Francisco groups that the band had heard on their highly successful tours of California. Butterfield was spearheading a national blues revival, spreading the gospel according to Muddy Waters and convincing Grossman to sign his old friend James Cotton.

When Mike Bloomfield left the band in 1967, Butterfield, a passionate admirer of big-band blues performers like Bobby Bland and Junior Parker, cagily shifted gears by bringing on board an outstanding horn section that included the young David Sanborn on alto saxophone. The next two Butterfield albums, *The Resurrection of Pigboy Crabshaw* and *In My Own Dream,* showed Butterfield concentrating on his singing and playing acoustic harmonica in a style reminiscent of Parker's. In 1969, Bloomfield and Butterfield were reunited in support of Muddy Waters on a double album on Chess, *Fathers and Sons,* a musical and commercial success that transformed Waters's career by introducing him to the rock and roll public. After recording an uninspired two-record live set in 1971, Butterfield abruptly disbanded his group, moved to Woodstock, New York, and stopped touring.

When he resurfaced two years later, it was in front of an excellent new band, Better Days, in which he shared vocal duties with Geoff Muldaur and Ronnie Barron. Better Days recorded two fine albums for Bearsville and proved to be a first-rate live act, but it disbanded within a year, partly because of Butterfield's self-destructive behavior and his by then chronically poor health. Butterfield's Woodstock neighbors included members of The Band, and he turned in a memorable performance at the group's farewell Last Waltz concert in 1976 and later that decade toured with Band alumni Levon Helm and Rick Danko. In 1980, Butterfield barely survived a bout of peritonitis brought on by a perforated intestine; he would undergo two major operations before returning to the stage the following year.

Butterfield's last metamorphosis was not an auspicious one. The self-assured bandleader of the 1960s had become an insecure, unpredictable loner saddled with a cocaine habit by the time his tattered career was resurrected by a group of New York investment bankers who formed a limited partnership to finance the comeback. The year 1986 brought a new manager, a new album (*The Legendary Paul Butterfield Rides Again),* and a television special with B. B. King and Stevie Ray Vaughan.

Butterfield's comeback trail ended in a Los Angeles motel room where police discovered his body on May 4, 1987; he had died the previous day from a drug overdose. Unpredictable to the end, he had requested a Buddhist funeral. Of all the tributes offered in the days that followed, Butterfield would no doubt have appreciated B. B.

King's verdict: "Paul was a great harmonica player, right up there with Sonny Boy Williamson, Rice Miller, and Little Walter Jacobs."

Butterfield's musical output went a long way toward bridging the musical and social chasm that had grown up between the blues and its stepchild, rock and roll—to the great benefit of both camps. On an instruction tape recorded in 1983, Butterfield tried to pin down the appeal of the mouth organ, which he liked to call "the heart's horn": "Part of the reason why I love the instrument is that it's such a pure folk instrument. It can cry better than most, and it has that magic inside. . . . That harmonica can bring out a lot of different kinds of emotions and different kinds of feelings. . . . The more sophisticated you get in your playing, the more you learn and develop, you'll find out that it really comes back to the same thing that you started out with. And that was your feeling and love for the instrument and those simple melodies."

Paul Butterfield's breakthrough and the blues revival he fronted made rock fans hungry for more; American rock was awash with harmonica during the 1960s. Like Butterfield, the best of the harp players to have successful careers in rock had strong blues backgrounds; these front-line blowers included Taj Mahal, Canned Heat's Al Wilson, Will Scarlett of Hot Tuna, and Corky Siegel of the Siegel/Schwall Blues Band (who in 1973 recorded former Stan Kenton arranger Bill Russo's unique but ill-conceived *Three Pieces for Blues Band and Orchestra* with Seijii Ozawa and the San Francisco Symphony). Many rock and rollers associated with other instruments developed enough proficiency on the instrument to add a bluesy legitimacy to their records and live performances: bass player Jack Bruce of Cream; Ron "Pig Pen" McKernan, keyboard player for the Grateful Dead; and guitarists Steve Katz of the Blues Project and Blood, Sweat and Tears, John Fogerty of Creedence Clearwater Revival, and Steve Miller are all cases in point. But some of the rock and roll harp players saw the instrument as more than just a blues vehicle, and they began adapting the cleaner, single-note approach popularized by Butterfield and applying it to chord structures that were more complex than the blues progression, stretching the diatonic harmonica melodically.

One of the first of these mavericks was Norton Buffalo, whose period of greatest visibility was the late 1970s, when he and his band the

Stampede recorded two albums for Capitol, *Lovin' in the Valley of the Moon* and *Desert Horizon*. Much of Buffalo's best playing has been done as a studio sideman; his harmonica can be heard on more than sixty-five albums by artists such as the Doobie Brothers, Elvin Bishop, Bob Welch, Kate Wolf, Johnny Cash, Spencer Brewer, David Soul, Juice Newton, Bette Midler, and Judy Collins. His solo on Bonnie Raitt's recording of "Runaway" has become a much-studied favorite of diatonic harpists, and he has worked with Steve Miller off and on for nearly two decades. Another diatonic player who has stressed a melodic approach to the instrument is Lee Oskar.

Lee Oskar (1948–)

Lee Oskar began playing the harmonica as a six-year-old in Copen-hagen: "The only source of music I had was the radio; I never had a record player. Those radio programs are why I still think of music as music, rather than as categories. They had classical music, they had middle of the road—to me it was just music. I didn't think twice about it. One time, me and Arnold Wiskey, who sang opera like Bjoerling, auditioned for a job. I'd play harmonica and he'd sing opera. I remember that somebody said to me then that I had to think about what style of music I was trying to play, but that didn't really compute."

Oskar came to the United States as an eighteen-year-old in 1966. After a period living and playing in northern California, Oskar moved to Los Angeles, determined to achieve fame as a recording artist. "I was pretty naive. I went to A&M Records and talked to the reception-ist—I thought she *was* the record company—and told her I wanted to sign a deal. I was reluctant to ask them for four hundred dollars. I thought that was a lot of money." In 1969, Oskar began playing in clubs with British rocker Eric Burdon, eventually joining forces with an established band, Night Shifts, to form a new group, War. Two al-bums with Burdon on MGM followed, and then War—and Oskar—began recording on their own for United Artists. "When I first started playing with War, that was the first time I had a record player. The first album I bought was Ray Charles's *Crying Time*, and that was a big influence on me. I never listened to harmonica records." War went on to score six top-ten singles between 1972 and 1976; over the years the group has recorded fifteen hit LPs, including *The World Is a Ghetto,* the number one album of 1972.

"I didn't even realize what it was to have a gold record, because I was still excited over being in a band. Eventually I found that there were some musical things that were natural to me but not to the chemistry of the band. I found that it was valuable to eke out time between War tours and recording to go into the studio and record and compose my own things, too." In 1976, Oskar recorded his first solo album for United Artists, which landed on the charts for twenty-four weeks and garnered Oskar Instrumental Artist of the Year awards from *Billboard, Cashbox,* and *Record World.* Oskar recorded another album, *Before the Rain,* for United Artists before signing with Elektra/Asylum, who released his *My Road, Our Road* LP in 1981. Between his own recordings and those he has made with War, Oskar has had a part in the sale of over 25 million records. His harmonica sound is very melodic and clean; in the studio, he prefers to cup a microphone in his hands and record directly into the mixing console instead of through an amplifier.

For years Oskar's instrument of choice was the Navy Band diatonic, but after the arrival of Hohner's plastic Golden Melody model in the 1970s he became intrigued with potential future uses of that material in harmonica manufacture. He began analyzing how mouth organs were built and sketching his own designs. "I was touring Japan with War. I was leaving my hotel room when I heard this harmonica. I knocked on the door of the room from where the harmonica was coming from, and a gentleman, Kan Manaka, answered the door. He didn't speak English. I didn't speak Japanese. A friend translated and told him that I was a professional harmonica player, so I got invited in. He played and I played and my friend translated. I looked at his harmonica and it was a Tombo harmonica. So there *was* an alternative. I had just been putting my harmonica ideas together because I got tired of having no harmonica alternative, tired of going to music stores and seeing all these goodies and toys and new things coming out every day for guitars and keyboards. Needless to say, I'd be lucky if they had a harmonica in the key I wanted. And who knows if it would be in tune. I told this man in the hotel room that I wanted to meet the Tombo people."

On a later trip to Japan, Oskar met with the management of the Tombo firm, which for more than seventy years had been manufacturing the tremolo mouth organs that have long been the most popular models in Asia. Oskar and Tombo agreed to begin production at the company's Tokyo factory of a new diatonic harmonica based on his designs. The first Lee Oskar harmonica debuted in early 1984.

Oskar's company, which now markets his instruments worldwide, is prospering. Several name players, including Junior Wells and Charlie Musselwhite, have endorsed his harmonicas, which offer replaceable reed plates and combs. Oskar is still pursuing new designs; he has a patent on a harmonica synthesizer. "If I can get these things out as fast I can design them," he says, "you're going to see whole stores full of stuff. It's a process. The idea is my vision, but then you have to implement it. You have to be patient." Oskar's goal is to establish a chain of harmonica departments in music stores, through which he would be able to offer not only his instruments but a full line of effects devices, microphones, and amplifiers.

Oskar's independent personality is reflected in his playing. "I started when I was six years old. It wasn't like I was a teenager when I picked it up and sat down at the drawing board. I can't help being anything but myself, so I chose the easy way. No one can sound exactly like anyone else. It's just a piece of brass with reeds that vibrate so many times a second, and it takes your aperture and your breath and your accent to make your own expression. It's not a direct electronic signal, where you just touch something and it has its own tone. It's driven by how we blow or draw into it. So the personality of ourselves gives it its character.

"There is an old joke: nobody ever gives the harmonica player in prison the electric chair—he's always the good guy. One of my quests is to change the image of the harmonica. The harmonica has a wholesome image, which doesn't do it any good in terms of being accepted musically. Number one, please yourself. Should harmonica be the thing, so be it, but play from the heart. Don't learn how to play it, just enjoy it. If you do it every day and it feels good, well, then you're bound to develop technique.

"The world of what the harmonica hasn't done, or what can be achieved, is even greater than what has been achieved. The clichés have put a frame around it, and you can break those clichés—it just depends on what the person wants to do with it."

Magic Dick (1948–)

In 1971 rock and roll received a jolting transfusion with the spirited debut album by the Boston-based J. Geils Band. The group had obvious blues roots but had put together a high-energy concept that showed the equally strong influence of sixties soul groups like Dyke and the Blazers. The J. Geils Band recorded seven more LPs for Atlantic during that decade, but the group was most renowned for its no-holds-barred stage act, which was centered around their spirited singer, Peter Wolf. The group's record sales picked up after they signed with EMI/America in 1978; their *Freeze Frame* album topped the charts for part of 1981 and produced two top-ten hits, including the number one single "Centerfold." There was a high-profile tour of Europe with the Rolling Stones in 1982, but Wolf went solo the following year and the band gave up the ghost soon after. The hands-down instrumental standout in the J. Geils Band was harmonica player Magic Dick, whose signature harmonica rave-up, "Whammer Jammer," was a highlight of the group's popular live album. While most harmonica players on the rock scene have seemed content to superimpose blues or country licks on top of contemporary arrangements, Magic Dick's work with the J. Geils Band was marked by his steadily evolving search for new ideas, sounds, and avenues for his instrument—in short, his perceptive rethinking of the whole concept of rock and roll harmonica. After ten years spent inventing and patenting new harmonicas (a line of ingenious and functional models that may prove to be the most successful of the recent mouth organ innovations), Magic Dick has begun performing again, this time as the front man for Bluestime, a group that also features J. Geils on guitar.

Interview With Magic Dick

I grew up in Pittsfield, Massachusetts, in Berkshire County. It's near Tanglewood and Lenox, which are famous for their jazz concerts and their educational centers. It was a marvelous place to grow up. The harmonica was the first instrument I actually had my hands on. I owe it all to my folks; they gave me one when I was three years old. I was just wild about it. I remember blowing and sucking on it while I was jumping up and down on the bed. I think that experience set me for life.

I played trumpet in school. I had a girlfriend in high school whose brother was in college—this was the early sixties, and there was a big folk scene then—and he was digging Sonny Terry and Brownie McGhee's records. That was the first harmonica that I heard that really put it in my face. The first time I heard blues harp playing, it really grabbed me. The first attraction was hearing that sound.

I went to college at Worcester Polytechnic Institute, majoring in physics and minoring in a lot of harmonica playing. Physics, electronics, mechanics—I was very absorbed in all of that. I still am interested in it peripherally, as it applies to the harmonica. When I was a kid, I was very curious about what made things tick. Music and my interest in art and photography—all these things grow out of the same thing.

I first learned about the Chicago blues sound at Worcester. I discovered those players from records at first, but a lot of them came through the Club 47 in Boston: Buddy Guy, Junior Wells, Muddy Waters, James Cotton. The main guy that I missed and never saw directly was Little Walter, who is without a doubt my biggest influence on the diatonic harmonica. I remember meeting Paul Oscher, who was playing some great harp with Muddy Waters back then. One night at the Club 47 he whipped out a harp and played a beautiful version of Little Walter's "Juke." It was inspiring, because he was deep into the tongue-blocking technique, which has a lot to do with getting a certain feel or a certain kind of sound on the harp.

I met J. Geils and Danny Klein at college. I was walking across campus one day and they were out on the quadrangle playing some acoustic blues. I'd only been playing harp about three months. I just sat down and started playing with them, and I've been playing ever since. We were a jug band without the jug. I played acoustic harp, J. and another guy played guitars, and Danny played washtub bass. We were a swinging little outfit. We used to play all the girls' schools and the coffeehouses. We had a great time.

I was close to getting my degree, but I was having great difficulty keeping my mind on my work. There was a lot going on, and being the young dude I was, I was easily distracted. I did a lot of thinking about what it would be like working in the corporate world as a scientist or an engineer; the reality of that was sinking in. This was during the Vietnam era. Those were wild times. A lot of people were frightened, and I felt the need for a great escape from everything I didn't like about the way things were going for me. I was waking up to the world at that point. I dug what I was studying, but it began to feel like a suit that doesn't fit you right. Eventually, I got up the courage to leave it.

The first Butterfield album had come out, and that was a big influence on us. We all decided to quit school, move to Boston, and form an electric band. Peter Wolf was already in Boston, singing with a group called the Hallucinations. He was a tough kid from Brooklyn, a record collector and a great disc jockey. We loved the blues thing, and we played it a lot. We were honing our teeth on Junior Wells's *Hoodoo Man Blues* album—that had even more of an influence on us than Butterfield's band. I emulated everything on that record for a long time. It's still a masterpiece. There's a particular harp sound on that recording which is unique. It's recorded halfway between amplified and acoustic. It fits in great with that band, and Junior got a great sound without resorting to echo techniques à la Little Walter. The Little Walter band with Freddy Below and Robert Junior Lockwood was a big role model for us.

The J. Geils Band never had the impulse to be a museum group. We learned those blues things and played them a lot live, but when it got time to get serious as a group in the studio, that material wouldn't necessarily be what we'd pick to do. It wouldn't have been the best business move to make, and it wasn't what we were doing, anyway. Wolf was coming very much from the r&b side—James Brown's early band and all of that. We were really an amalgamation of Chicago blues and the Apollo Theater groove. We had all learned and grown from these influences, and we were always exposing each other to all this different music.

We played together for about three years before we made the first record. Like most groups, we were ready for that first one. We had been playing that material for quite some time. We chose to be kind of advanced about the way we approached it. We wanted to be progressive and contemporary, but with groove and with humor. Everything that we did, we had to feel that the thing swung—that it had life—and that people could relate to it. We never got hung up in that trap of feeling that if something was commercially acceptable, it couldn't be any good. I mean, the Beatles weren't too bad.

I first picked up a lot of harp stuff on my own. There's really not a hell of a lot to work with, and if you're already a musician who's had some experience with other instruments, you get right into it. You don't want to do anything else in life—you've found your thing. I always dug the fact that the harp was so small, that you could put it in your pocket and take the damn thing anywhere. The harp is extremely physical. There's a direct connection between the air column, your body, your mouth cavity, and the instrument in your hand. You can work with the tone so much.

I love to experiment. There's so much to explore. Most of the time in the studio, I used a Fender Champ and a JT-30, sometimes with a preamp. There was a period of time when I was using an Echoplex with various guitar effects boxes. I've done a number of solos that were sort of in a Hendrix-type vein. They're rock harp solos, and they're pretty out there. But the music and the arrangement has to be right, because this kind of effect needs space to work well.

The writing and the arranging that Seth Justman did for the Geils Band featured the harp quite a bit. I don't know of any other band that used it the way we did. Everybody in the band were harp freaks. I always got great support, and they always knew what the backup requirements were for a great harp solo. In the early recordings we did, there wasn't as much overdubbing and production as we got into later. Eventually, I was creating an entire harp section playing counterpoint melodies and riffs, like a full horn section. *Nightmares and Other Tales From the Vinyl Jungle* was full of that kind of stuff.

Pierre Beauregard, another harp player based in Boston, and I have been working for a number of years on some new harmonica designs. We've come up with many different note arrangements to increase the flexibility of the instrument. Our harmonicas are more linear from top to bottom, more uniform. All the draw notes can be bent. We've used our knowledge of music theory to make the voicings fuller, to put the chords back behind the melody, and to expand the kinds of tunes that can be played, but the player can still use traditional techniques. We were recently awarded a patent for these arrangements that may be the most unique and comprehensive harmonica patent ever issued, since it deals with a strategy instead of a specific instrument. Our ideas can be applied to any harmonica—to diatonics, to slide harmonicas, to harmonicas we haven't even thought of yet. We can't wait to make them available to harp players, because eventually this is going to transform and revolutionize harmonica playing.

I played the Golden Melodys for a while, but I dislike the equally tempered tuning of them. If you play single notes, you don't notice it that much. But for blues players, equally tempered tuning doesn't make any sense. The draw chord is too rough. In natural tuning—

when the third is slightly lower than it would be in equal tuning—you have a much smoother, sweeter sound. That's the charm of the diatonic harmonica, that pure seventh chord. There are several things about the Meisterklasse diatonic that I appreciate, too, but after all is said and done I keep coming back to the Marine Band.

As far as chromatic harmonicas go, my favorite Horner instruments are the Toots Thielemans instruments—both the Hard Bopper and the Mellow Tone. And I've been impressed by the CX-12 chromatic. I like the roundness of its tone. For a 12-hole model, it has a big, mellow sound—it sounds more like the #280 than the #270. It also comes apart quickly and easily, which is great when you need to make adjustments to it. It's comfortable in the hand and the shape of the mouthpiece feels wonderful.

I remember seeing Richard Hayman once at Radio City Music Hall when I was a kid. He played over the PA system and he was damn good—a great tone. Jerry Murad is one of the best chromatic players. I saw him one night in Seattle, and man, he was something. First of all, he's a complete musician in terms of his concept of approaching the harmonica as a wind instrument and not so idiomatically harmonicalike. He plays with a tone and an execution and a power and a volume that are remarkable. He also had a concept of the instrument electronically, in the early days of recording. The Harmonicats had a really warm, electric sound for the harmonica that is unique.

I love all types of music. I play rock and roll and rhythm and blues because I love that music, but I think of myself as a jazz guy. I really think of myself as a horn player rather than as a harmonica player. Steve Lacy has been big influence on me. He's one of the world's greatest soprano sax players, an absolutely incredible musician. A great tone and a great concept. He played a lot in the early years with Thelonius Monk, who has also influenced me a lot.

I love trumpet. Roy Eldridge was my man. He was a friend for about ten years. I used to go see him every night in New York when he was playing at Jimmy Ryan's about six or seven years ago. I'd be waiting for him to come off the bandstand and we'd go out in his car and talk and then he'd drive home. He had an incredible sound, presence, and energy in his playing; he really knew how to direct that air column. I'd study him up close, watching him like a hawk. Next to Little Walter, he was the biggest change for me musically.

I've been thinking a lot about Lester Young lately. I want to get some of that relaxation and swing that Lester Young had into my own playing—the way he used space. It's difficult to get some of that sax quality on the harp, but I've learned after years of trying to go beyond limits that I thought were there that if you first form the mental concept, and keep it in mind when you play, that eventually it starts becoming a reality. You begin learning to modulate the sound in subtle ways that hint at these things. True, the harp's not as flexible as a saxophone in many respects, but I find that you can go way beyond what you ordinarily think you might be able to do with the harp.

I find the downer attitude of some blues guys kind of a drag. It's a put-on, a mask. The other thing has its masks, too, but it's closer to what everyone is involved with. To me, blues has its real place when its played by a master bluesman. I feel that I eventually mastered blues harp, in the technical sense. But it seemed like a dead end to me; I had so much more that I felt I could say, to contribute to the harp in ways that no one else has. You have to make the harmonica really musical and interesting or else it's just regurgitation. If you don't go beyond the blues retread, you can really get stuck in it. I've seen some great players get caught up in that, and I think it's a serious dead end, unless they have the creativity to write new blues things. Like Muddy Waters—he had a distinctive approach to blues and he arranged his songs carefully, so that each was distinctly different. He still sounds contemporary to me.

Music is a thing that someone experiences by degrees of quality, in the way things are played. Some people play with a lot more quality and sensitivity to overall musical values than others do. Some players have a better sense of rhythm or a better sense of melody and harmony. For me, most of what I do seems to come out of the listening I've done in jazz. I listen to a lot of Louis Armstrong. I deeply admire the way he forged the beginnings of jazz and the concept of a jazz soloist. I get a lot of compliments on my technique. A "How could he do that?" kind of response, rather than a real understanding of the style and what I'm trying to do in my music. I find that a lot of the people that appreciate the subtle things I do aren't musicians—they're just lovers of pop music of all kinds.

I'm my own worst critic. You make your own world. You're like a player in a movie that you're creating yourself. I'll forever be trying to be better at what I do. I'm never satisfied with it.

Magic Dick's reemergence as a front man is the latest example of a transformation attempted by many harmonica players over the years. Among rock players, Fingers Taylor, a versatile harpist who has maintained a high profile as a fixture of Jimmy Buffett's Coral Reefer Band since its inception in 1974 and through tours and record dates with the likes of the Eagles, Emmylou Harris, and James Taylor, has released two solid solo albums with an eye toward establishing himself as a leader. Huey Lewis had a long career as a journeyman harp player and singer before he and his band the News hit it big in 1980. The high-flying rock and roll career of Kim Wilson, the finest blues harp player of his generation, is the most successful melding of front man and harmonica virtuoso in many years.

Kim Wilson (1951–)

On the rare occasions when Muddy Waters would expound on the topic of harmonica players, the music world listened—as the ultimate groomer of harmonica legends, he was something akin to a divine oracle on the subject. In the late 1970s, Waters began giving unsolicited testimonials about the skills of a young singer and harp player he had crossed paths with at Antone's, Austin's fabled blues showcase. Kim Wilson, claimed Muddy, was the finest harmonica player he had heard since Little Walter Jacobs. This stratospheric praise was akin to an official anointment, and a lot of attention was immediately focused on the Fabulous Thunderbirds, a quartet founded by Wilson and guitarist Jimmie Vaughan.

Waters only accelerated the inevitable discovery of a remarkable talent. Wilson's playing, though solidly in the blues tradition, is so sure, so sharp, and so soulful that it has allowed him to leapfrog issues like race, originality, and musical honesty that have dogged—sometimes appropriately, sometimes not—white blues harpists. During the year I spent in Austin between 1977 and 1978, I saw on several occasions how Wilson's presence and support could elicit some truly exceptional performances from the likes of Muddy Waters and Jimmy Rogers. When you can hurdle generational and cultural gulfs to inspire musicians of that caliber, you have a rare gift. Listen to Wilson's playing on Jimmy Roger's recent *Ludella* album and you will know why Muddy Waters was moved to praise him so unequivocally.

Wilson is also a stellar singer, and for several years following the

Fabulous Thunderbirds' 1986 top-ten hit, "Tuff Enuff," his brilliant harmonica work took a back seat to his vocal prowess on the group's recordings. Success is hard to argue with; blues harp aficionados have consoled themselves with his cameo appearances on efforts like *Ludella,* the blues tours Wilson manages to make a few times each year despite the T-Birds' frenetic schedule, and with the two solo albums he is recording for the Antone's label. The most inspirational harp player since Paul Butterfield, Wilson has had a profound effect on the future of his instrument in both rock and roll and in the blues.

Interview With Kim Wilson

I was born in Detroit. We moved to California in 1960. My dad used to sing on the radio—he sang with Danny Thomas a little bit. He was good. I played trombone until I was in sixth grade, but they made me practice, and I hated that. I grew up on all that Memphis stuff and Motown. I feel like I had good taste before I started playing. I was into music—I was a great air guitar player—and I just wanted to find something I was good at. I had guitar lessons, but it just didn't seem right. Around 1968 some friends took me to hear people like Muddy Waters and George Smith, who was living in L.A., and there was a player in town named Matt DiRodio that I listened to. I forget exactly how I got my first harmonica, but I didn't get in a band until a month after I started playing. I wasn't any good, but I could sing.

I started doing local things and within a year I was playing with people like Eddie Taylor, George Smith, John Lee Hooker, Luther Tucker, Pee Wee Crayton, and Albert Collins when they came through town.

I was ambitious. I was working a job and trying to go to college, which was no good. All us harp players are crazy; we're not exactly your all-American work ethic kind of guys. I hated things that were work to me. I finally just said, "Screw this. I'm going to make something out of music or die a wino or something." I was making something like fifteen dollars a night. At the time, my rent was ten dollars a week, so my sixty-five dollars a week—it was poverty by anyone's standards—was enough to live on. But hell, I knew that wasn't going to last.

I was listening to a lot of Little Walter. I was at the stage where things happen really fast. It's a really fantastic time in your career, in your musical childhood, because everything is like a big, giant discovery. And when you find it out, man, it's just wonderful. You might happen on five or six different things at once that stemmed from the thing you just learned, and it just blows your mind. It really spurs you to go on with it. Hopefully, it happens all through your career, until the end, but in the beginning it's like walking for the first time, it really is.

The very first record I ever owned was by the James Cotton Blues Band. George Smith's influence definitely shows up in my playing to this very day. He was also one of the best performers I've ever seen in my life. The first time I saw George he was on a show with Jimmy Reed in Goleta. A friend of mine, John Phillips, had the band that was backing up George. John was going to play a couple of songs and then get down when George came on. Before the second set, John came up to me and said, "Hey, man, I want you to play with me." I couldn't pass up that opportunity. I was really, *really* nervous. I got up on the stage and I was playing, the crowd was really good, and all of a sudden George Smith just jumped up on the stage with me and we both started playing. And I swear to God, that's the only time in my life that I ever remember my knees shaking. I did things that night that I'd never done before, just because he was there. He'd walk out in the audience while he was playing and I'd stay up there, and he'd run back and grab me and drag me back through the audience, too. We'd lay down on the floor together and we'd do these synchronized kicks while we were playing. At the end of the night the club owner said, "How about a big round of applause for George Smith? And I don't know who the hell this guy is, but how about a big round of applause for him, too?" And he passed me fifty dollars. After we got down, George said, "Hey, man, I want you to finish this gig out with me, through the week." And I said, "Are you kidding?" And he said, "Hey, man, I'm for *real*."

But any action that happened in Santa Barbara, I had to *make*. So I went to Minneapolis with a guitarist named Bob Bingham, who was from there, and put together a band called Aces, Straights, and Shuffles, and within a year, we were one of the main bands there. There was a lot of music going on in Minneapolis, and I could get by.

I got hooked up with Willie Dixon. He heard a studio tape of us and had high praise for it—he said I sounded like Sonny Boy—and he decided to manage us, but he was busy taking care of himself. We got hooked up with some people in Seattle who cut a single on us, but it went nowhere fast. I was having a great time anyway; I was only twenty-one.

I spent a winter in Minneapolis and that was it. Friends had told me that Austin, Texas, had a good scene, and I met a woman in the business who arranged to show me around Austin during a band break. I went down there and met Stevie Ray Vaughan, who was playing a rib joint called Alexander's. Somebody asked if I could sit in, so I got up on the break with Stevie and Doyle Bramhall, and I did "Juicy Harmonica" and "I Can't Quit You Baby"—those were my two get-over numbers, you know—and drove the place crazy. Jimmie Vaughan was there, but I didn't really even talk to him. I just shook his hand and split.

I went back up to Minneapolis and I got a call from Vaughan. I didn't even know who he was. He said, "Hey, this is Jimmie, man." I said, "Who?" "Jimmie—you know, from down in Texas. *Jimmie Vaughan.* I'm thinking about coming up there," he says. And I said, "Fine, come on up. I got a three-day weekend working with the band at the Caboose in Minneapolis and you can work with us." And that's when I really got a chance to hear him. And we talked and talked, and things were really leaning towards Texas because I really liked it when I went down. And the weather suited my clothes. I told the Aces I was going down to California to see my girlfriend, and I split for Texas for one last time to check out the band down there. Everything was okay, so I flew back up to Minneapolis, gave the boys a month's notice, and I hitched a ride down to Texas with all my records and my amplifiers. That's really all I owned. And Jimmie and I started the T-Birds.

I was making a transition in my playing. At that time I was listening to a lot of Little Walter and a lot of Sonny Boy. I was really making an effort and listening to a lot of records. John Phillips had turned me on to Lazy Lester, Lightnin' Slim, and Guitar Gable in California, but down in Texas, they were *playing* it, and Jimmie was great at it. I really started to get into the Louisiana stuff, repertoirewise. I recently met Lazy Lester himself. He's a great human being, and he plays his ass off.

I saw Big Walter Horton a lot in Texas and later when we started playing the East Coast. As a matter of fact, he offered me a job. He offered it to me a couple of times, so he must have meant it. I just kind of took it as a joke. He would say, "I'll not only teach you how to play harmonica, I'll teach you how to be a *man*." Walter was a really great, caring guy. He was a mean old bastard on the outside, but underneath that he was great.

Muddy Waters was the best thing in my whole life. My musical life is loaded with so many experiences, and I've played with every single guy out there—I still work with Jimmy Rogers and all those guys—but Muddy, he made my reputation. The best guy ever in the whole world, that I've ever met. He was a god to me, especially when I was younger. The first night I met him he offered me a job, and I played with him a lot after that. I used to love it when he'd turn around when I was playing and give this look like, "Jesus Christ, where'd this cracker kid come from?" I used to love doing that to him. Of course, he could get my goat anytime.

I would go to his house in Chicago, and he'd hold court in the kitchen, which was like the living room to him. There was always something cooking, a bottle of good wine in the fridge, and he had a little television in there. He'd take me into the living room, take me around. He had all these pictures of the old days. He'd point to them and say, "That's when they used to call me the *pretty* Muddy Waters." The one thing I regret is not recording with that old man. I guess that's a very selfish thing to say.

I saw him in the coffin—I was there. I had to go back and look at him several times, because I just couldn't believe it. A lot of people came to that funeral. It was weird, because nobody could really cry. Until later. It took me a long time to even be able to listen to his records, it depressed me so much.

When Muddy Waters talked me up in the papers, that was success to me. To have all those guys that you listened to on records all those years while you were playing, for them to treat you like an equal and put you out there like that with them—that's success. I really think I'm one of them. In fact, I *know* I'm one of them. And that may not come off too well in print, as far as my personality goes, but I don't give a damn, because I am. They made me one of them. I can never pay them back for what they did for me—it's impossible. But I sure am going to try. I put together short tours with people like Luther Tucker and Buddy Guy. That's my meat. Just to play with those guys all night long. Not even take the harmonica out of my mouth except for the occasional deep breath. That is so much fun for me that I can't imagine the day when none of them are going to be around anymore.

I'm playing so much better now than when I was younger. I guess it's just maturity—it's so much less frantic. I rarely put the harp in the rock and roll stuff the T-Birds do; I wouldn't bastardize my instrument by playing that stuff. Rock to me doesn't exist—it's just a term that was invented for guys who can't play.

I play the Marine Band. I've tried every other one, but I don't think any of them really cut it except for the Marine Band. You just can't get that bite.

I have never felt that the harp is limited—ever. Not for what I want to do. I think it's the closest thing to *you* that you can possibly play. It's the closest thing to a voice. I mean, *you* are making that sound. I think it's definitely more an extension of you than any other instrument. There's so much feeling to the harmonica, more than any other instrument to me. You can get so much *guts* out of it—sometimes literally. I've had guts fly out of it before.

Stevie Wonder

S o u l

In its original form, soul music was essentially gospel music with worldly lyrics. The godfather of the style is Ray Charles, who in the mid-1950s began secularizing African American church music. The harmonica was not unknown in the black churches of the rural South, but it was much more closely identified with gospel's secular rival, the blues. Services in these churches were often accompanied by choirs and combos, whose standard instrumentation—piano or organ, guitar, bass, and drums—became the model for the soul bands of the 1950s and '60s. One reason soul became the dominant black music during the polarized 1960s was that young African Americans saw it as distinct from blues and jazz—their parents' music. Soul Brother Number One James Brown claims to have never felt an affinity with the blues, but in his autobiography he describes how he turned to music to combat the overriding isolation of his first five years, which were spent living with his father in Georgia's backwoods turpentine camps. "The best thing I remember from that time is the ten-cent harmonica—we called 'em harps—that my father gave me. I started playing it real early, when I was about five years old. I played 'Lost John,' 'Oh, Susannah,' 'John Henry,' and I sang."

Because of its small role in gospel music and its association with the blues, the harmonica was for the most part kept out of the soul kitchen. The great, towering exception is the remarkable Stevie Wonder.

Stevie Wonder (1950–)

Born prematurely in a Saginaw, Michigan, hospital, Stevie Wonder spent his first few days in an incubator. Although he may have been born with normal sight, he was blind by the time he left the hospital, probably from having been given too much oxygen. Wonder's mother was a single parent who worked as a cleaning lady in private homes to support Stevie and his two half brothers. In 1953 the family moved to Detroit, where the father of Stevie's brothers joined them.

Wonder's first musical experiences centered around the drums. "The first time I really felt the power of music was on a family picnic. Somebody had hired a band, and I sat on the drummer's lap. He let me play the drums. It was a thrill I'll never forget." His first few Christmases brought toy drum sets, none of which lasted long. "I was always hittin' on things, like beating on tables with a spoon, or beating these little cardboard drums they used to give kids. I'd beat 'em to death." One Christmas Wonder attended a Lions Club party for blind children and was given his first functional drum kit; by the time he was seven, he was also experimenting with the next-door neighbor's piano, which became his when she moved away.

Wonder had become so entranced by the family radio that his mother gave him free rein over it. "I spent a lot of time listening to the radio, and I was able to relate to the different instruments and know what they were. I began to know them by name." He became hooked on a WCHB program called "Sundown," through which he steeped himself in the rhythm and blues of Johnny Ace, B. B. King,

Bobby Bland, Jackie Wilson, the Coasters, Chuck Willis, and LaVerne Baker. By the time a family friend gave Wonder a tiny, four-hole harmonica on a key chain, he had already come under the spell of Jimmy Reed and Little Walter Jacobs, and he tried to imitate on his midget instrument the harmonica and saxophone parts he had heard on the radio. "I started playing the blues. . . . Took a little of everybody's style and made up my own." Wonder was made the leader of the harmonica band at his school. "With music, I belonged."

An uncle gave Stevie a Hohner chromatic harmonica. "The second harmonica was more expressive," he says. "It had more complexity and a different style than the toy harmonica." Wonder's uncanny ear guided him on his exploration of the new instrument. "I guess I practiced, but I never considered it practice because I loved it too much. It was like searching in a new place you've never been before. I kept finding new things, new chords, new tunes." Wonder became a familiar sight—and sound—in his neighborhood, where he would sing and play at local gatherings, in the streets and alleys, and on the sidewalks. As his fascination and experimentation with the harmonica developed, Wonder had unwittingly taken the first step toward a career in music; the instrument played a crucial role in his eventual discovery.

Stevie was befriended by Gerald White, who had the boy play for his brother Ronnie, a member of local Motown star Smokey Robinson's group, the Miracles. Ronnie White's initial amusement at Wonder's insistence that he could sing "badder than Smokey" gave way to admiration after hearing Stevie sing and play his harmonica, and he arranged for Wonder to visit the Motown studio. After auditioning for staff writer Brian Holland on a stoop in front of the building, Wonder was ushered inside to play for owner Berry Gordy. Not long after, eleven-year-old Stevie signed a five-year contract with Motown that gave the label complete control over his recording, publishing, and management and stipulated that his earnings be put in an escrow account until he reached twenty-one.

Wonder began arriving at the Motown studios each day after attending classes at the Fitzgerald School for the Blind. Gordy was in no hurry to put him in the public eye; Wonder was allowed to practice on the studio instruments, and several producers worked with him in recording demos. Clarence Paul was eventually chosen to oversee the taping of an album's worth of Wonder perfomances showcasing his talents on various instruments and several Ray Charles tunes. Motown wanted to see Wonder on the charts with a hit before committing to an album release.

Three singles were released in 1962. They were unsuccessful, but Wonder's appearances with Motown package shows had made it clear that he was an exciting live performer. Once Wonder realized he could occasionally steal the spotlight from stars like Marvin Gaye, he became reluctant to leave it; there were occasions when Clarence Paul had to literally carry him off the stage. Crowd response was especially ecstatic for a harmonica rave-up called "Fingertips," which Stevie had written for his instrumental album. After listening to tapes of a 1963 show at Chicago's Regal Theater that featured a searing performance of the tune, Berry Gordy decided to release it as a single. After finishing "Fingertips" at the Regal show, Wonder had remained onstage to a prolonged ovation as the band for the next act, Mary Wells, took their places. When Stevie suddenly launched into the song again, Wells's musicians had to fall quickly in behind him, and it was this spontaneous encore that was put on the B side of the single as "Fingertips Part II" (complete with Wells's bass player asking frantically for the key and cursing) and that became a number one record and the big hit of the summer of 1963. Wonder's entire set from the Regal show was released as an album entitled *The Twelve Year Old Genius.*

"Little" Stevie Wonder, recording artist, began touring full-time. September of 1963 brought his second album, *Workout Stevie Workout,* which gave him plenty of opportunities to show off his harmonica playing; it cracked the top thirty on the national charts. Wonder's touring was cut back the following year after his voice changed, and he alternated between road swings as a member of the Motown revue and the Fitzgerald School, where he was featured in the choir. After Stevie appeared in two beach-party movies, Motown released a third album, *Stevie at the Beach,* which included four harmonica instrumentals and produced a single, "Hey Harmonica Man," a strained attempt to match the success of "Fingertips" that Wonder later confessed was probably the low point of his recording career.

Still a few months shy of his fifteenth birthday, Wonder was encountering influences that would have a strong effect on his music. Road trips through the South had left him a committed advocate of the civil rights movement led by Martin Luther King, which in turn exposed him to the protest anthems of Bob Dylan. Wonder had never completely bought the rigid Motown formula, and he fought for the release of his own versions of Dylan's "Blowin' in the Wind" and "Mr. Tambourine Man." Tours of England in 1964 and 1965 introduced him to the music of the Beatles, whose example inspired him to further develop his own songwriting skills.

"Uptight," a rousing, up-tempo workout released in 1965 that reached number one on the r&b charts and gave the Beatles some stiff competition in the pop listings, provided the commercial leverage Wonder needed to make a major turning point in his musical evolution, but it was also his first single since "Fingertips" that did not feature the harmonica. On his next two albums, *Uptight* and *Down to Earth,* Wonder's growing command of the keyboard was emphasized at the expense of his chromatic playing. *Sgt. Pepper's Lonely Hearts Club Band,* Lennon and McCartney's watershed paean to psychedelia, and the emergence of acid rock groups like Cream, had the seventeen-year-old Wonder exploring new studio sounds in 1967, although his trademark chromatic playing resurfaced on two tunes on his album from that year, *I Was Made to Love Her.*

The following year, while Motown was releasing Wonder's first greatest-hits compilation, Wonder was in the studio laying down several harmonica instrumentals, including a gorgeous version of the movie theme "Alfie." Berry Gordy inexplicably released it as a single under the name Eivets Rednow ("Stevie Wonder" spelled backward). Wonder has recalled the reaction of one unsuspecting fan: "There was this cat in the airport that came up and said, 'Hey, man, these whites are taking over everything. I heard a kid today, man, played 'Alfie' just like you." After the success of "Alfie," Motown released Wonder's other chromatic instrumentals, including his version of the mouth organ chestnut "Ruby," on an *Eivets Rednow* album. Although the collection is uneven and soaked with predictable string arrangements, harmonically it shows the full maturation of Wonder's completely individual chromatic style: the single-note technique, the quicksilver tone, the trademark trills, the marvelous coupling of a staggering feel for melody and relentlessly funky phrasing.

Wonder's harmonica fervor carried over into his 1968 smash hit, "For Once in My Life," which featured one of his classic chromatic solos, and his *My Cherie Amour* album of the following year, which includes some great harmonica playing on "Light My Fire" and "You and Me," as well as some raunchy mouth organ quite different from his usual style on "Somebody Knows, Somebody Cares." In terms of his own recording career, this period produced Wonder's most spectacular stretch of harmonica playing.

Stevie Wonder graduated from the Michigan School for the Blind in 1969. Despite his proven ability to chart his own musical course, Motown still had a typically mainstream future arranged for him. "He has the potential to become another Sammy Davis," intoned one Motown executive. Wonder had other ideas, including a masterful remake of the Beatles' "We Can Work It Out." Wonder was coproducing his own records now, straddling psychedelia and funk—the r&b-flavored hit "Signed, Sealed, Delivered" was set up with an electric sitar riff.

Wonder's long-term, original contract with Motown was about to expire, and in an attempt to mollify his increasingly independent superstar, Berry Gordy gave Wonder complete control over his next album project. Wonder spent a year putting together *Where I'm Coming From,* which broke new ground for him with its pronounced rock influences, its outspoken social commentary, and his strong keyboard playing.

Stevie Wonder turned twenty-one in 1971 and came into a million dollars under the terms of his original contract, which had finally expired. The former child star was now ready for a truly radical break. His concentration on keyboard instruments led to a fascination with the nascent synthesizer technology; Wonder became the first pop star to use this equipment successfully in the making of his *Music of My Mind* album, on which he played nearly all the instruments, including a bluesy harmonica on "Sweet Little Girl."

Wonder eventually re-signed with Motown, but this time he left the table armed with total creative control over his recordings. From this point on Wonder's albums would be cohesive creative statements instead of singles compilations. Critics routinely hailed him as one of pop music's resident geniuses. His *Talking Book* album spawned the huge hit "You Are the Sunshine of My Life." In 1972, Wonder left the confines of the studio with a vengeance, electrifying new audiences on a tour of the United States with the Rolling Stones.

Wonder's ascendancy was stalled in August of 1973 when he spent several days in a coma following an automobile accident. The studio project that followed, his *Fulfillingness' First Finale* album, included the cut "Boogie On Reggae Woman," which was punctuated by some textbook Jimmy Reed diatonic playing by Wonder. He gradually began to tour again; there was a triumphant appearance at Madison

Square Garden in March of 1974. That summer Wonder walked away with four Grammy Awards; he thanked Jimmy Reed in one of his acceptance speeches.

It often seemed as if Wonder saved his harmonica talents for his most joyful material; his chromatic floats through a memorable solo in the tribute to his newborn daughter, "Isn't She Lovely," from his 1975 album *Songs in the Key of Life.* The appearance of Wonder's sinuous harmonica on a Dave Mason album that year marked the beginning of a growing tendency to serve up his best chromatic work on other artist's efforts. Over the years Wonder's harmonica has improved the work of the likes of Peter Frampton, the Chi-Lites, the Manhattan Transfer, the Gap Band, Quincy Jones, King Sunny Adé, Chaka Khan, Dizzy Gillespie, and the Eurythmics. Eldra DeBarge has recalled the time Wonder contributed his harmonica talents to the DeBarge tune "In a Special Way": "We wanted Stevie to play harmonica on the song. . . . [He] came right down to the studio and listened to the tune. He didn't even listen to it all the way through. He got out there behind the microphone and just started blowin', man, and it sounded great. It was a really warm solo."

The capture of four more Grammy Awards in 1975 (including album of the year, top producer, top male pop vocalist, and top r&b male vocalist) and the Rock Music Award as the top male vocalist marked Wonder's arrival at the pinnacle of the music world. His album of that year, *Journey Through the Secret Life of Plants,* managed to chart a new course for him despite its unimpressive sales; it also contained some of his most inventive harmonica solos.

Wonder's 1985 tune "I Just Called to Say I Love You" was not only a chart-topping success but an Oscar winner. Later that year Wonder turned in one of the most memorable cameos in Quincy Jones's "We Are the World" summit and scored his twenty-sixth top-ten hit (only Elvis and the Beatles have had more) with "Part Time Lover."

As Stevie Wonder has moved surely and unerringly to dominance over the entire, vast sprawl of popular music, it's worth remembering the spirited man-child who first caught our collective ear back in 1963—who refused to leave the stage until he'd finished laying those irresistible harmonica licks on us. Despite the fact that his has been one of the most universally admired harmonica styles, it has never been duplicated; perhaps such a replication could only come from another cosmically talented thirteen-year-old bursting with joyous, ecstatic energy.

Charles Leighton

Jazz

The debut of jazz at the turn of the century should have held great promise for the harmonica, which was already the most prominent wind instrument of the new music's bedrock, the blues. Early jazz celebrated unorthodox instrumentation, unflinchingly embracing the banjo and the guitar—instruments that, like the harmonica, had long been identified with folk music. And jazz championed players skilled at playing between the notes in a highly vocal manner, a talent for which the harmonica has few equals. "One of the key characteristics of early instrumental jazz was the players' attempts to vocalize their sounds," Dan Morgenstern has written. "Growls, flutters, various 'freak' effects, were coloristic devices widely used by black musicians and imitated by their white emulators." When King Oliver began using a common bathroom plunger to mute his trumpet, he may have been influenced by the hand techniques of rural harmonica players.

The closest the harmonica came to insinuating itself in early jazz was through its prominence in the jug and washboard bands, such as the Dixie Jassers Washboard Band and the Memphis Jug Band, that flourished in the South in the 1920s. The mouth organ was more at home in a small string group setting than amidst a full-size jazz band, where its lack of volume made it unable to compete with a full complement of trumpets and saxophones. By offering an eclectic repertoire culled from country music, blues, and ragtime, the jug bands straddled urban and rural popular music, and their harp players were the first to carve out a niche for the mouth organ as a featured solo instrument in a group setting. The earliest jazz mouth organists, who began surfacing on recordings by the late 1920s, were diatonic players who tended to work in duos, small string bands, or harmonica bands.

One of the most interesting of these was James Simons, a black musician who recorded with piano accompaniment as "Blues Birdhead" for Okeh Records in Richmond, Virginia, in October of 1929. The first great soloists in jazz, the fabled New Orleans trumpeters Buddy Bolden, King Oliver, Freddie Keppard, and Louis Armstrong, cut such a wide swath that literally all jazz musicians who followed them showed their influence, and Blues Birdhead was no exception. On "Mean Low Blues," his first-position playing was brassily assertive and full of against-the-grain, stop-time rhythmic surprises and growling, trumpetlike outbursts. The playing of mouth organist Chuck Darling, who recorded in 1930, was not as fearless as Simons's, but it did show that a pianistic, ragtime approach could be engagingly translated to the harmonica. Darling's mastery of the melodic potential of the straight-harp style was far beyond that achieved by his contemporaries.

Robert "Rabbit Foot" Cooksey was a fascinating mouth organist who had nine recording sessions with Victor between 1926 and 1927 accompanied by guitarists Bobby Leecan and Alfred Martin. Although he recorded several blues numbers, Cooksey's melodic playing and his fondness for pop tunes like "Ain't She Sweet" show the urban tastes of this New York City–based harmonica player. Cooksey's skillful playing on the high end of the instrument in first position and his pronounced hand vibrato call to mind the improvisations of a highly skilled whistler.

Blues Birdhead, Chuck Darling, and Robert Cooksey charted new melodic territory for the harmonica, but as jazz players began to favor more of an ensemble approach and solos built on more complex chord patterns, the limitations of the diatonic mouth organ became more of a liability. In the mid-1920s, Hohner introduced the first chromatic harmonica, which quickly became the instrument of choice for jazz harmonicists. But even on this instrument, with its draw and blow notes and its basic slide mechanism, the rapid, fluid style favored by jazz soloists remains a stupefyingly difficult goal that has been achieved by a scant few.

One of the earliest chromatic harmonica players to experiment with jazz was Wilbert Kirk. Kirk's primary avocation for most of his career was as the drummer in Wilbur de Paris's New Orleans band, but he had a harmonica trio called the Harlemonicats for a brief period and recorded at least one album as a mouth organist, playing the diatonic, the chromatic, and the polyphonia in a raw jazz style.

The end of the Depression brought the big-band era that saw jazz transformed from an exotic oddity into the anthem of a pivotal generation of young Americans, many of whom had their first childhood musical experience as members of harmonica bands. Brooklyn native Eddie Shu was among the first of these mouth organ band alumni to play jazz on the instrument. He went on to become a well-known tenor saxophonist, playing with the likes of George Shearing, Buddy Rich, Lionel Hampton, and Louis Armstrong. In the mid to late 1950s, Shu blew tenor and some chromatic harmonica with the Gene Krupa Trio, with whom he recorded "Harmonica Shu Boogie" for Columbia. "Eddie was a great jazz sax man, clarinet, trumpet, and trombone player," claims Stan Harper. "He even did a ventriloquist act." Eddie Shu began his show business career as a member of the Cappy Barra band, where he worked alongside a young player whom many point to as the first jazz harmonica virtuoso—Charles Leighton.

Charles Leighton (1921–)

There are people who are born to play wind instruments, and Charles Leighton is one of them. But Leighton is also a member of an even rarer fraternity—musicians whose talents are so pure that they are free to explore any genre. He may be the finest all-around player to ever pick up a chromatic harmonica.

Even when viewed through the indistinct haze that surrounds the role of the mouth organ, Leighton's career has been something of a secret. Although he is entering his sixth decade as a harmonicist, he has not toured as a performer since the early 1950s, and his recordings have been infrequent: a few 78s in the 1930s and 1940s, a pair of singles in the 1960s, one album for the Stash jazz label, and a few sessions recorded by himself and distributed to a select group of friends and fans.

But Leighton's peers know him for what he is. "He is the premier jazz player," claims Jerry Murad. "Only two harmonica players scare me: Toots [Thielemans] and Charles Leighton," chromatic wizard George Fields told me. "For years," admitted Hugh McCaskey, "I tried to get the overall sound that Charles Leighton gets. To me it is the most satisfying harmonica sound."

Leighton was in some respects a victim of timing. A decade younger than most of the Depression-era players in whose company he is usually placed, he first made his name as a precocious, teenaged member of the Philharmonicas and went on to become a featured player with the Cappy Barra outfit.

Leighton left the harmonica groups after World War II and began a career as a solo performer just as vaudeville and the supper clubs slipped into sudden, total eclipse. A transcription of a performance of "St. Louis Blues" from a 1945 Hoagy Carmichael network radio broadcast shows that the young Leighton occasionally used a pyrotechnical approach similar to other harmonica soloists of that era. But over the years Leighton seems to have tried to purge any tendency or effect that might interfere with whatever melody he is interpreting, eventually eliminating from his playing the double stops and rhythmic tonguing effects so common among his peers.

Casting about for a new avocation after the war, Leighton settled on the milieu in which his awesome technique and his unerring, sensitive ear would be most appreciated: the recording studio. He became a sought-after New York session player, but his compelling skills and his wide-ranging creative bent made it inevitable that he would try his hand at the mixing console. For thirty years, Leighton had a successful career as a recording engineer, working out of his own studio in Manhattan until soaring midtown rents forced him to close up shop in the late 1980s.

For three decades no one had bested Charles Leighton at playing jazz on the harmonica, and he now found himself with the time to expand even further as a player. He launched a remarkable new career as a classical artist, an excursion that has resulted in two albums' worth of recordings that rival anything he accomplished as a jazz artist. Like Oscar Peterson and very few others, Charles Leighton can serve up genuine and passionate interpretations in either genre.

The tastefulness that has marked Leighton's work as a jazz soloist is also manifested in the care with which he has chosen his classical repertoire. He is not very impressed with the small body of serious pieces written for the harmonica; neither is he given to reworking old war-horses or compositions indelibly associated with other instruments. As with many other jazzmen—Bix Beiderbecke and Charlie Parker among them—Leighton's taste in classical music leans toward the French romanticists, whose airy, cunning melodies translate naturally to wind instruments. In 1983 and in 1985, Leighton, accompanied only by the unswervingly sympathetic piano of Don Smith, recorded two albums of compositions by the likes of Ravel, Fauré, Debussy, Gershwin, and Hindemith that rank among the finest harmonica recordings ever made.

Happily for harmonica enthusiasts, Leighton has managed to capture not only his own work on tape but has also helped to produce the finest studio efforts of New York–based harmonicists Stan Harper and Blackie Schackner. He has continued to work steadily as a freelance engineer and as a session player, and his skills are still startlingly facile and stylistically up-to-the-minute. Even when riding atop the most contemporary arrangements and material, Leighton's playing is always appropriate, distinctive, and on the mark.

Some may argue that Toots Thielemans is the more daringly conceptual jazz player, but no one has ever bested the overall richness of Leighton's sound, one of the great achievements in the harmonica's history. His fluid precision and his genius for improvisation are staggering, but his unearthly tone is the glue that holds his playing—be it swing or sonata—together. Charles Leighton has perfected the elusive mechanics of pushing and pulling wind through a harmonica as well as anyone who has ever made the attempt.

• • •

Interview With Charles Leighton

My sister bought a harmonica for me when I was about twelve. I learned to play it and developed a great love for the instrument. Around 1936, Borrah Minevitch came out with his own line of harmonicas. He opened a Harmonica Institute in New York City. A teacher there, David Macklin, organized a group of about seven of us kids that played a little better than the others and began teaching us how to do ensemble playing and how to read music. He wrote the arrangements and we called ourselves the Philharmonicas. Our first engagement was at a burlesque theater. I was about sixteen years old, and it was quite an experience.

We all started with the ten-hole diatonic but very quickly switched to the chromatic. It didn't take long for a kid to find out that you could only play certain songs because there were no sharps or flats, and we got around to figuring out how to bend notes, but that's about as far as we went. Being New Yorkers, we felt that the people who played country music or blues were square. We were hip, and we didn't pay much attention to them. I've only recently come to realize how sophisticated those styles have become.

It was the big band era and that was our musical orientation. Just like the kids today listen to rock and roll groups, we had our favorite bands. Benny Goodman and all his wonderful soloists, Harry James's band, the Glenn Miller orchestra—we patterned ourselves along those lines. Artie Shaw had a big impact on me as a teenager. The Philharmonicas had a bass player and a chord player for the rhythm section, and we had four or five chromatic players handling the saxophone or trumpet section parts. We all played 64s. The chord as we know it now hadn't been invented yet. We would tune up Marine Bands and other instruments to achieve that effect. We taught ourselves to read music, to write music, and to write arrangements. We would listen to records and copy out the arrangements right onto the paper. Most of the harmonica players and the groups were aware of each other. It was a competitive scene and we all had different ideas about how to play.

In 1941 I joined the Cappy Barra Harmonica Gentlemen. We were styled to contrast with Borrah Minevitch's ragamuffin act. We dressed in evening clothes, dinner jackets and white tuxedos, and did what we called a "class act." We worked quite steadily. We did some radio and a couple of films, a western musical for Columbia called *Rockin' in the Rockies,* and *Radio Stars on Parade* for RKO. We also made a number of movie shorts, the fifteen-minute musical features that were something like what MTV is today.

I suppose it's hard for younger people to conceive of what constituted show business at that time. There was no television, and the only mass media we had for entertainment were radio and motion pictures. And there were vaudeville houses throughout the country; most big cities had two or three. I've traveled throughout the United States several times. The nightclubs were nothing like the discotheques of today. People would go to a club with a live orchestra and have dinner and dance and see a show.

In the early forties I was very interested in the Count Basie band and Duke Ellington. Basie's band was a real eye-opener, with people like Lester Young and Herschel Evans. Lester Young had that light, velvetlike tone, and his improvisations were beautifully put together. He was probably my biggest influence. If I could have played the saxophone, I would have wanted to play exactly like Lester Young. The trumpet player Bobby Hackett was a great, great influence. He played that two-beat, Chicago style. I didn't pay much attention at first to the bop players. It wasn't until the late 1940s that I began to try to understand what they were doing. I'm rooted in that Lester Young and Bobby Hackett period. While I enjoy the bop players, it just doesn't pull me.

In 1944 I left the Harmonica Gentlemen and moved out to California for about a year. I worked mostly with country bands. I worked with the Riders of the Purple Sage and made several records with Johnny Bond for Columbia. I remember playing on the "Hollywood Barn Dance" radio program. They asked me, "What kind of music do you play?" And I said, "Well, I play some pop stuff, jazz, classical music. . . ." They told me, "Great. For the next program we'll play a classic. Why don't you do 'Wagon Wheels'?" To them, a classic meant "Red River Valley" or "Redwing."

I eventually became a soloist for a number of years. I carried my costume, a couple of extra shirts, and a set of arrangements for the pit orchestras that would always accompany you. When you came into a city, you would go to the theater around nine-thirty in the morning and rehearse the band for a few minutes and that was it. Your first show might be at noon. I would play some pop songs and perhaps a classic like the *Hungarian Rhapsody* or something. "Holiday for Strings," "Stardust"—the things most people expected to hear.

My solo career lasted into the 1950s. By that time, most of the vaude-ville theaters had closed. Television was very big and the theaters just showed films. The nightclubs had thrived during the war, but after-wards people didn't go out that much.

In my sphere there were so many great players who simply stopped at an early point in their career because you could hardly earn a living. There was always a limited audience for harmonica players. I started doing studio work, recording for radio and televi-sion commercials and accompanying artists on record dates. I recorded with Harry Belafonte and played on a record Hugh Downs made. I did some Ray Ellis orchestral things. Some of the arrangers liked using the harmonica on sessions; they realized the potential of the instrument and they wrote for it. André Kostelanetz, for example. There was quite a bit of a documentary film work. Some of the fea-ture films used harmonica very effectively.

Tuning is the basic problem in the studio. I tune my instrument a little sharp because most studio pianos are tuned sharp. String players have a tendency to play just a hair above the pitch, so if you come in with an A440 instrument, you're going to sound flat. And as soon as you start to blow a little harder, the pitch comes down even more. I do my own tuning. As the notes go higher, I temper them just a little sharper on the higher end. I don't have perfect pitch; I go by however the scale sounds to me in the several keys. It's a compromise. You can tune the scale in F, for example, so that when you play in F everything sounds fine. And suddenly you might play in A or D and the scale will sound different.

I never had to overcome any prejudice against the harmonica by other musicians for any length of time. As a matter of fact, they can be quite complimentary. I remember one recording session where we had a whole string section and I had to play a very nice part, and when I finished, there was a little bit of applause from the violinists.

I don't think there is any question that what we accomplished was more difficult than what other musicians had to achieve. After all, we never really had a decent instrument to play on. I think the basic de-sign of the chromatic is correct, it's just a question of improving the interiors and the way they're put together. Some years back I bought a harmonica that Frank Huang made that has a solid brass body in-stead of wood. It's quite superior because the plates are attached with tapped screws screwed into the brass body. It's put together more precisely. It's been my feeling for many years that there should be a custom instrument for professionals. The general public makes no demands at all on the instrument. I think the harmonica players have brought more to the instrument than the instrument has given to the players. No question about it.

I play the 64, the #280. Compared to the smaller chromatic, I believe that the 64 has a far superior sound. The reeds are a little longer. I think the construction of the instrument itself makes for a larger sound. The twelve-hole is a completely different instrument. It has a very thin, reedy, metallic sound. The 64 has a much richer, fuller, and rounder tone.

I started playing classical music about five or six years ago, and I'm really enjoying it. These classical things gave me a new incentive to practice and to play seriously again. You can work on these pieces alone—it's not like playing pop music, where you need a band. Debussy and Ravel are two of my favorite composers; I'm partial to the French school, the romanticists. Flute music is very adaptable to the harmonica. Those composers who have written for the harmonica didn't really understand the instrument. An exception is Robert Farnon's *Prelude and Dance,* which he wrote for Tommy Reilly.

Most harmonica players are self-taught, and each one has an individual approach. I always use tongue blocking, because that's the way I learned, but some of the best harmonica players I know play the pucker style. Stagg McMann, who I think is one of the finest classical harmonica players, played through the center, and Toots plays that way. Tommy Reilly has a tremendous amount of technique for double and triple stops. To my way of thinking, the single note is the best possible sound. I don't like the sound of double stops on the harmonica. To me, they're always out of tune, and they will distort on recordings if the equipment is not particularly good.

The harmonica is really extremely sensitive, I think. With horns, you're blowing into a reed but you're far away from what's happening. The harmonica is an extension of the human voice.

Don Les (1914–)

Most harmonica players born after World War II came to the instrument by way of the blues harp. But as this concept enters its fifth decade, some of these players—led by freethinking, original talents such as Howard Levy—are expanding on that background and coaxing more daring melodies out of their diatonics. This rediscovery of ten-hole tunefulness is the most interesting trend on the current harmonica scene, but it is not a new phenomenon. There were earlier jazz harmonicists—Johnny O'Brien, for one—who stuck with the diatonic and went through a process of experimentation and discovery very similar to the one that Levy and his followers are now experiencing. Don Les is the great master among these early jazz diatonic phenomenons. "He has no equal," claims Jerry Murad. "He's the best Marine Band player I ever heard," Hugh McCaskey told me.

Les also happens to be one of the rare bass harmonica virtuosos, a fact that ensured him a long career but helped eclipse his diatonic genius. For nearly three decades Les's low-end skill anchored the Harmonicats. "You could stand next to him for months and not hear one wrong note," recalled Hugh McCaskey. "And he had time like a rock."

With rare exceptions, such as the group's great recording of "Harmonica Boogie," Les's diatonic playing was not a part of the Harmonicats' act. When Les formed his own Harmonicats group, he finally began to play the diatonic regularly onstage.

Most recently, Les has been performing and recording as half of a duo with Mo Vint, who handles the chord harmonica and plays keyboard bass with his feet. Don Les is finally free to show the public—and a new generation of diatonic players—something he's played since childhood: great jazz on the Marine Band.

Interview With Don Les

My folks had a saloon in Lorain, Ohio. We lived upstairs. I was born premature. A doctor who happened to be at the bar came up and pronounced me dead and went downstairs and started drinking again. Somebody picked me up—I was about as big as the palm of a hand—and started washing me off with whiskey. They saw my lips open up, and I came to life.

My mother had German measles while carrying me. I was born with congenital cataracts. I could only see light and shadows. People didn't know I existed—I always came out at night because the sun irritated my eyes. I bumped head-on into a woman one day, and she says, "What's the matter—are you crazy?" and I said, "No, it's bad enough to be blind." She felt so bad she followed me for a block, trying to buy me candy or something. I finally had a couple of operations when I was twelve. But even today, my vision is only about 30 percent normal.

My parents both had musical talent. Musical talent is inherited. If you have it, they can give you a rubber band and you'll learn how to play it. You can't teach a person to whistle in tune or sing in tune or play in meter.

The trumpet was my first love in music. I was born to play the trumpet, but I shot my lip on it and had to quit. My first exposure to the harmonica was an accident. I was about fifteen. A friend of mine in the neighborhood had a harmonica, and he let me blow on it. One day in school the teacher stood up and announced that we were going to have a program. She asked if anyone played an instrument, and this friend of mine said, "Don plays the harmonica." As it happens, this was a real cute teacher and everybody was always trying to get her attention. She came over to me and stood there until I said that I would play.

I went home and worried about it. I remembered that my brother had a harmonica, so I swiped that thing—it was the only thing I ever stole in my life—and I started practicing. My brother heard me blowing it and he kicked me in the pants, took it away, and put it back. His mistake was that he put it back in the same place. So I swiped it again. The next time he caught me, he said, "Keep it, you play better than I do." My mother actually started me off. I didn't know she knew how to play the harmonica, but she showed me how to play "Home Sweet Home." And I haven't seen much of it since.

I practiced day and night. Even at night, when everybody else would be sleeping, I would be practicing under the blankets. A couple of months later, I played three numbers in that school program: "Tiger Rag," "Stardust," and "Clarinet Polka." That shows you how fast you can learn if you have to.

I joined the second-line Minevitch group in 1942 and stayed for about two years. I played bass because the other guys were all lead players. I met the other Harmonicats in Cleveland in 1945. They were with the Minevitch group then. They kept me in mind, and when Jerry got out of the service, he and Al called me and I went to Chicago.

The Harmonicats used head arrangements on most of our records. Pete Pedersen wrote some things for us, too. Al and I worked hard to get our parts right. If you notice, what made the Harmonicats' records was the background. I was with the Harmonicats for twenty-seven years, from 1945 until 1972. We could have been together to this day, but we had a falling out.

I turned around and formed my own Harmonicat group with Mildred Mulcay on lead. We played every bit as good or better than the original group. We might have made a nice success with it about five years sooner. After the group with Mildred broke up, I didn't do much at all. Then I went to a SPAH convention and saw Mo Vint play the chord harmonica and bass with foot pedals at the same time. We have been playing a lot together since then.

I call the stuff I do on the Marine Band "melodic jazz." The influence to play that way goes back to when I was a kid in Lorain and my brothers used to take me to Cleveland to hear the gypsies play. I love gypsy music. For me, it's the only music outside of jazz that gives a musician the chance to improvise and ad-lib as he feels. Gypsies play with the most heart—the most soul—and the prettiest feel. They won't add any notes unless they're melodic and beautiful. Gypsy music is a lost art.

I ignored the harmonica totally. I only looked on it as a tool. It doesn't matter what instrument you take up; it's the talent that counts. I have a musician's mind, not a harmonica player's mind. The idea is *not* to sound like a harmonica. I play differently from other harmonica players because I didn't listen to harmonica players. I listened to people like Benny Goodman and Artie Shaw. For technique, it was Rafael Mendez, the trumpet player.

I began to learn the chromatic when I had the group with Mildred Mulcay. I got very good on it, but I ended up going back to the Marine Band. I figured that if you play both, you're going to be weak on something. You don't have to separate the diatonic and the chromatic—you can play a diatonic like a chromatic.

My style is my own. I created it. Everything I learned, I learned by myself. I figured out cross harp by myself. I do some overblows, but only as I need them. The harmonica is contagious, like a disease. It's like a miser and his money: the more he has, the more he wants. I got that certain disease and I just couldn't take it away from my mouth. I had to practice every day.

My playing comes from two sources: talent and practice. Talent is the main ingredient. The mechanical part of music anybody can learn. If you don't learn it, you're lazy. I've been practicing for fifty-five years. I've played the way I'm playing now all that time, but nobody knew it. I guess I'm a late bloomer.

The blues players are all misled. The chords on a diatonic are constructed in relative formations so that no matter where you blow, you can't blow anything that sounds wrong. The blues players are all learning from each other how not to play the harmonica. You don't hear saxophone players or piano players playing blues like the harmonica players do. If you ask a blues player what they're playing, they'll say, "One of my own compositions." All of a sudden, they're not only *not* musicians, but they're also composers. This is one of my secret peeves about the harmonica people that don't take up the harmonica and think they did. I don't use cross harp as a blues, I use it as a musician would. The field has been wasted by all these people blowing cross harp but not playing anything.

The future of the harmonica is here. Musicians are discovering what can be done on the harmonica and they're doing it. Like Toots, for instance. Charley Leighton did it first, I suppose. There will be more and better harmonica players coming along.

I remember scanning the dials on my radio once and hearing "Cherry Pink" on three different stations. That's one of the biggest thrills you can get in the recording business. You might be standing on a street corner and a car passes by with its radio playing "Peg o' My Heart." That is the reward that pays for everything. Money has nothing to do with it. It's the feeling—the thrill of success. That is *you*.

Jean "Toots" Thielemans (1922–)

Jean "Toots" Thielemans knows his proper place among the great chromatic harmonicists. "I'm the jazz freak of the bunch," he says with characteristic good humor. His career is a testament to the power of music as a kind of universal language and to the profound contribution that American jazz has made to the world's melodic vernacular.

Born in Brussels, Belgium, Thielemans got an early start in music. "The whole thing was an accident, actually. I never intended to become a professional musician," Toots has said. "When I was three years old, my folks had sidewalk café in Brussels, and we had accordion players every Sunday. So, when I was three, I started to squeeze anything in sight—shoeboxes and everything. My father got the connection . . . he got me a little accordion. Anyway, when I was seven years old, I got a big accordion. Just self-taught, you know. I played the national anthem and things like that; the first tune I played was 'Ramona.' When I was nine or ten years old, my health was very weak, and I forgot all about the accordion."

By the time he entered high school, Toots had become aware of American music. The films of Hollywood were his introduction to Larry Adler, Borrah Minevitch, and the mouth organ groups, and in 1939, Thielemans bought his first harmonica. "I really bought it for fun," he says, although he adds that his goal from the first was to be able to improvise on the instrument in a jazz setting. Soon he was participating in jam sessions in Brussels, which at this time was occupied by the Nazis. Toots remembers experimenting with jazz lines while playing German beer-garden medleys. His chronic asthma sometimes got in the way of his harmonica playing, but it kept him from being conscripted by the German military.

Thielemans's fragile health faltered again in 1942 while he was a mathematics student at the university in Brussels. During his recuperation, a guitar-carrying friend paid him a visit and complained to Thielemans that after a week of strenuous practice, he was still unable to learn the introduction on Django Reinhardt's recording of "Sweet Georgia Brown." Toots boasted that he could manage it in half an hour, a friendly wager was initiated, and a half hour later Toots claimed two prizes—his friend's guitar and a new passion for Reinhardt's phenomenal playing. "Django is still one of my main influences, I think, for lyricism," Thielemans told an interviewer in the 1950s. "He can make me cry when I hear him."

Thielemans put aside his harmonica for a time in order to explore the possibilities of the guitar, and when he returned to the chromatic, he was armed with the chordal knowledge he had acquired from the fretted instrument. He was spending hours listening to the few jazz records he and his friends could find; Benny Goodman and Lester Young made the biggest impressions on him. When American musicians began appearing in Europe following the war, Toots managed to sit in with members of the Don Redman band, who gave him his lasting nickname as well as his first onstage experience as a jazzman.

In 1947, Thielemans came to the United States for the first time to visit an uncle who lived in New York. Toots plunged into the city's jazz scene, meeting and playing with musicians like Lennie Tristano and Hank Jones. He spent his final evening in the city sitting in with Howard McGhee's bebop band at the Three Deuces club on Fifty-second Street. Booking agent Billy Shaw was in the audience. Impressed by Thielemans's playing, Shaw became even more intrigued after learning that the harmonica phenomenon was a Belgian tourist on holiday. Shaw asked Thielemans to send him a demo tape.

Returning to Brussels, Thielemans made some privately pressed recordings and sent them to Shaw. Benny Goodman eventually heard these acetates, and when he brought a sextet to Europe in 1950, Goodman hired Thielemans for a series of shows. Toots signed on as a guitarist but ended up playing harmonica at the group's debut at the London Palladium because of a union restriction; Goodman was later shocked to learn that this was Thielemans's first paid appearance as a professional musician.

By now determined to emigrate to America, Thielemans applied for residence in the United States under the postwar immigration quota system. In the meantime he made a few tours of his own, played clubs catering to American GIs, and accompanied visiting performers like Roy Eldridge and Zoot Sims. In November of 1951, Thielemans was finally allowed to settle in the United States. During the six months it took him to join the musicians' union, he worked at the Belgian Air Lines office in New York and haunted the jazz clubs. Once his professional status was confirmed, Thielemans began playing with various groups. His first important gig was with blues queen Dinah Washington. A weeklong stint with the Charlie Parker All Stars at Philadelphia's Earle Theater remains a personal career highlight to Toots: "I was Bird's puppy. I used to follow him around everywhere."

In 1952, Thielemans joined the George Shearing Quintet, playing both guitar and harmonica. He became an American citizen soon after, and his reputation spread through his work with Shearing, who would feature Thielemans on harmonica during each set. Given a chance to record on his own for Columbia, Thielemans produced *The Sound,* an excellent album of jazz and swing standards played on the harmonica with occasional guitar solos overdubbed. *Time Out for Toots,* a follow-up LP on the Decca label, was a similarly outstanding effort, and 1957 saw the release of Toots's Riverside album, *Man Bites Harmonica.* Thielemans dominated the "miscellaneous instrument" category in *Down Beat* magazine's poll throughout the 1950s, and his playing evoked awe from his fellow harmonicists. "Toots played the harmonica in much the same manner that many of the great jazz artists of that time played their respective instruments. No one played harmonica like Toots. I felt like throwing my harmonica away," Jerry Murad has confessed. "I used to think the chromatic had limits," says

Charles Leighton, "but with the advent of Toots Thielemans, I have come to feel that the limitations are within the player. Because as far as I can see, Toots has no limitations." Richard Hayman has said this about Toots's powers: "The ultimate in technique and fantastic musical ideas of mood and expression—unbelievable ability to translate these ideas from his mind through the instrument."

In 1959, Thielemans began a new career as a session musician in New York. He joined the staff of the ABC network and was featured on "The Jimmy Dean Show" for a number of years. In 1962, Thielemans recorded an original tune, "Bluesette," that featured him whistling and playing the guitar in unison. "Bluesette" was a smash hit that has since been covered by over one hundred artists, and Toots was soon whistling on dozens of radio and television commercials.

Thielemans still occasionally recorded under his own name; a lush album of ballads accompanied by strings and voices, *The Romantic Sounds of Toots Thielemans,* was released in the mid-1960s. His harmonica work was featured in the film *Midnight Cowboy;* he has since contributed to the scores of many movies, including *Sugarland Express* and *The Getaway.* That's Toots's chromatic on the theme for "Sesame Street." He has also managed to tour and record with the likes of Paul Simon, Peggy Lee, Ella Fitzgerald, Dinah Washington, Oscar Peterson, and Quincy Jones.

Thielemans made a handsome living from these efforts, but his first love remained jazz. He occasionally put small bands together to play the clubs; a young pianist named Herbie Hancock played with him for a short time. "Maybe I compromised too much," he now admits. "I sort of commuted between my love for jazz and commercial work." With the advent of the 1970s, however, Toots began solidifying his reputation as a hard-core jazz player, appearing at the Montreux Jazz Festival with an all-star group led by Oscar Peterson and working in the studio with Bill Evans and Jaco Pastorius. He began recording as a jazz artist and appearing regularly in jazz clubs for the first time in years. In 1979 he was featured on *Affinity,* a Bill Evans album for Warner Brothers that Thielemans emphatically maintains is far and away his best work on record.

Thielemans's biggest influence among other harmonica players at this time was Stevie Wonder. "He made me go for more emotion, not so many notes," comments Toots. The two chromatic geniuses eventually met in Brussels after a Wonder concert. "We went to a restaurant after hours and played together," recalls Thielemans. "We were on such a good level. 'Do you know this song?' . . . 'Wait a minute, how about this one?' We were just digging into each other, not pushing."

Thielemans admitted to *Guitar Player* magazine in 1979 that he got more enjoyment out of the harmonica than he did playing the guitar. "I like to play certain runs that I hear on the harmonica because they lay easier there . . . there are certain runs that are appropriate to each instrument. I can play runs faster on the harmonica than I can on the guitar—I'm not such a fast picker, so I do it on the harmonica."

In 1982, Toots suffered a stroke that left him partially paralyzed for a time. "I'll never recover the velocity of my left hand on the guitar," he says. "I just have to say more with less notes." He has been bothered with chronic asthma all his life—an atomizer is always close at hand. Dividing his time between a house on Long Island and an apartment in Brussels, he has recently recorded with Quincy Jones and Jaco Pastorius and made new fans through his work with rock performers such as Julian Lennon and his appearance in a Billy Joel video. Thielemans doesn't share the aversion to diatonic harmonicas shown by most chromatic players and has recorded some blues-oriented material on the smaller instrument.

Thielemans's flat, vibratoless tone is reminiscent of Miles Davis's trumpet attack. Despite his ebullient personality and his adventure-some approach to soloing, Toots's sound is always plaintive at its core. Even when Toots is at his most daring chromatically, his playing is fiercely tuneful; his message is always the melody.

"Any instrument has limitations, and the harmonica isn't any worse off than most," Thielemans told Richard Hunter. "The main thing is that you have to play the things that sound good on the instrument, and not try to do the things that don't come off right. You can't do a smooth trill from a blow to a draw note, for instance. . . . You can't get a good legato out of the harmonica when you're playing fast. In fact, for me it's a struggle to get a good tone out of the chromatic at all. I wish I could get the same sound out of the chromatic that the blues guys get out of the Marine Band."

Toots is unanimously regarded by his fellow musicians as having a rare blend of bona fide genius and personal charm. His own attitude is decidedly upbeat: "It's going just fine now. I'm unbelievably happy. Not doing too bad for a Belgian bebop harmonica player."

Toots Thielemans's jazz talents were not to be denied within the jazz fraternity, and his buoyant disposition allowed him to close the sale with the public. All who have followed him, including Ron Kalina and Les Thompson, have benefited greatly from his success. Kalina is a Los Angeles–based pianist and harmonica jazz ace who got his first harmonica at the age of four when it came free with a new pair of shoes. His enlightened parents gave him his first chromatic two years later, and today Kalina is in great demand in the Los Angeles studios; he has done quite a bit of television sound-track work and has recorded with the likes of Tom Waits and Burt Bacharach. Les Thompson is another first-rate California harmonica jazz artist who has backed up Al Jarreau, Hall and Oates, and Jaye P. Morgan in the studio. Another legacy of Thielemans's accomplishments has been his inspirational value to younger jazz harmonicists, including Boston's Mike Turk.

Turk's boyhood was spent sampling all the instruments in his parents' Bronx music store, but nothing clicked until he heard a harmonica player blow through an amplifier at a teen dance. There was a long period spent perfecting his blues licks followed by four years at Boston's Berklee College of Music. Turk was establishing a national reputation by the early 1970s through his recordings with Papa John Kolstad and performances with the likes of Bonnie Raitt, David Bromberg, Steve Goodman, and Sonny Terry; he was one of the first diatonic players to attempt to persue a melodic focus without abandoning the gritty blues style that first attracted him to the instrument. For the last several years he has concentrated on playing jazz on the chromatic harmonica.

After many years of scoring and playing on film sound tracks, Turk's jazz virtuosity can now be appreciated on his recently released album, Tin Sandwich Records' *Harmonica Salad*. The CD is a rare debut solo recording in that it displays the full range of a mature artist. Turk sets the stage by serving up a jazz primer with his covers of jazz tunes by Duke Ellington, Miles Davis, and J. J. Johnson, but most of the CD is devoted to original compositions, including "Tin Sandwich Song," in which Turk's tuneful diatonic playing enters a territory hinted at in the best of Paul Butterfield's jazzier solos. Two of the cuts are full-blown, amplified blues numbers in which we find Turk in the company of ace blues guitarist Ronnie Earl. On the jazz numbers, Turk's chromatic harmonica playing is surefooted, fluid, and tasteful. Even on "Hearts On Fire," for which Turk abandons his usual Thielemansesque chromatic harmonica sound in favor of the kind of hallucinatory amplified approach pioneered by Little Walter and George Smith, he puts his own stamp on the style by allowing his jazz predelictions to surface throughout the number. *Harmonica Salad* is an intimate tour of the remarkable range of one of the most versatile of harmonica players.

William Galison (1958–)

The recent release of two harmonica instrumental albums, *Overjoyed* and *Calling You,* by William Galison on Polygram serves notice that a new mouth organ star is rising in the East—specifically, in Manhattan. His lyrical, high-spirited playing—which is particularly appealing when riding atop the bubbly Latin grooves and chord progressions that he favors—belies an intensely serious musical commitment. Galison has been very visable lately; he has performed with Sting, recorded with Ruth Brown, and played on the sound track of the film *Prelude to a Kiss.* A talented composer and engaging performer who is swiftly gaining an international reputation, William Galison will play a prominent role in the development of the harmonica's future role in jazz.

Interview With William Galison

My grandmother tells me that I was walking around with a little diatonic harmonica in my mouth when I was two. I don't remember when I didn't have a harmonica. The structure of the harmonica made sense to me right off the bat. I don't remember learning it.

I grew up on the upper west side of Manhattan. I'm from a very artistic family—mostly artists and painters. I played some piano as a child, so I knew how to read. I was a pretty reluctant student on the piano, but it gave me an exposure to music. Then I found that the guitar really turned me on. I think it was largely an ego thing, being the hip kid in class. But I had a good ear. Immediately after I learned three chords I knew where it all went, so that was really fun, because it felt like magic. I got into jazz guitar and played with a Dixieland band when I was in my early teens. Then I went to Berklee for summer sessions when I was sixteen and seventeen and later spent one year there. That's where I really got my chords down, my basic jazz theory. They sort of beat it into your head, and it works when you get it.

I was playing the guitar but I wanted to play a wind instrument. When I dream I'm playing music, I'm often playing a trumpet. I wanted to play the sax, but it was hard for me to make that big jump. Also it appealed to my nature to play an instrument that no one else was playing, especially the chromatic, because if I played blues harp, I would have been laughed at by those people. I think I got a chromatic and I thought basically, jeez, you can play all the notes on this thing. What if I played Charlie Parker heads and stuff like that? The first thing I tried to play was "Satin Doll," because that was something I had just learned at Berklee. Then I started playing some other tunes and someone said, "Oh, do you know Toots Thielemans?" I said, "No, who's that?" And so I got his Command record—the one with "Sweet Georgia Brown." It's a schmaltzy record, but he plays his ass off. I listened to it and I thought, "Whoa." Then I started playing and I just played and played and played. Everything I was supposed to be learning and practicing on the guitar—scales and chords—I started doing on the harmonica.

I went to Wesleyan University, and I played there. I studied with Bill Barron, a tenor player and Kenny Barron's brother. He was very into exercises, knowing all twelve keys, and he got me into some of that. I don't think I learned a tremendous amount about music in college. I'm not disciplined, so thank God I have some talent. There were a lot of people that could play faster and better and more complicated than me, but I could play a phrase and a melody nicely and the faculty appreciated that. But it was a very Coltrane-oriented program—everybody was learning flat fives and so forth—and I never got these complicated Coltrane things. I get outrageous sometimes, but generally I'm fairly melodic.

My first record came out of the blue. I played on a Yo Kano session, and Polygram, which is a Japanese company, heard that and they came to me and asked if I would do a harmonica record with a Latin feel, and the next thing I knew I was in the studio.

The second album has seven originals. I wanted the second album to be interesting musically; I felt like this was the record that was going to put me on the map. A record that would hold your attention, but that you could also listen to lying in bed on a Sunday morning, reading the paper. That you could make love to. That wouldn't jar you. That would show up the harmonica as an exquisite instrument, like Stevie Wonder's "Alfie."

My progress as a player has been very slow and gradual. It seems to me that I get better and better, but I don't practice all that much. When I do practice, I get a lot better a lot faster. I've gone through periods in my life when I haven't touched the harmonica for four or five months. After my first record I didn't play for a year. I just didn't want to see the harmonica. After this latest record I had to force myself to keep playing. The reason is that I have this beautiful music in my head, and it's so beautiful to me that I almost swoon. I can't sleep at night. I can't talk to people because I have a very clear aural imagination. So I'm very often lost in the music world, and then it's there in black and white on tape and I don't like the way it's come out and I don't like the way I played.

Gradually I build up again. When I play, I get excited. Last year I did four days in Boston with my quintet. Hot musicians, a hotel, a nice gig, a good place. By the time I was through those four days, I could not keep myself away from the harmonica. I was a maniac. It's not like food, where the longer you go without a meal, the longer you crave it. With me, the longer I don't play the harmonica, the less I want to have to do with it. The only reason I'm any good at all is because of those maniacal periods when I play a lot.

I'm the world's worst self-promoter. I've had the world's worst agents. I play very little on account of that. Every day I think about what else I could do besides being a harmonica player. But at times I've been right there with the audience at the edge of their seat. Not when I'm playing fast, flashy jazz, but when I'm just in touch with whatever is around. Those moments—and only those moments—make me say, well, maybe I was just born for this.

I've got a bunch of #270s fitted with Silver Concerto reed plates. To me they give a thicker, fuller sound and they last a long, long time. They stay in tune and they don't break. I also modify them—take off a few of the valves for bends, which I use a lot. I often take the valve off the high A. I wish I could do that with every valve, but if you take too many valves off the sound gets real buzzy—which is why they have them in the first place. So sometimes I sacrifice that tone for the ability to bend that note.

People always compare me to Toots, which is a great honor, but on the other hand, people are expected to have their own sound. I love Toots and I've listened to a lot of his playing, but I don't try to cop his licks. I just listen to music in my head, basically, and I listen hard to people I'm playing with, and those are my influences. If you ask me who are my greatest influences, they're the piano players that I play with. I love playing on records with people that I like, like Chaka Khan. I did a record with the O'Jays and I played on the sound track of *Baghdad Cafe*. I love working on other people's projects, being like an actor and trying to fit in.

I don't play with that Motown wonderful soul that Stevie Wonder plays with, because nobody does. And I think that if I tried to play that way, I'd look silly. I don't play with that European casualness that Toots has that is so engaging and light. I dig in. Again, both those guys have a very wide range of emotions. I think that if there is anything that I do well it's the ability to be quite honest when I play. If there is anything I do that is special, it may have something to do with not coming out of a particular bag.

I wouldn't flatter myself in saying that I've even come close to banging against the limitations of the harmonica. The harmonica doesn't have the tonal range of a saxophone and it doesn't have obviously the polyphonous aspect of the piano. Nobody could do a solo harmonica concert. I'd say my biggest problem with the limitations of the harmonica is phrasing. There's an established vocabulary for blues harp, and it's frustrating to me that I can't even play those things. I have to make up for that by being a little more interesting in terms of my intervals and the like. I think that is an advantage. I think that's why Toots plays such beautiful things. He can't bank on doing these runs that you hear most sax players doing, so he's got to play beautifully and play lines that make all kinds of sense.

I think my choosing the harmonica was not only an aesthetic decision. It was partly because I became good at it, but I also think that I was able to put a lot of time into it partly because it's portable and because I could practice it on the bus or the subway. I like that element of it—the idea of having an instrument that I can put in my pocket, of not being stuck. Perhaps the harmonica, because it has a fine sound with not a lot of harmonics in it, serves as a voice for that part of us that is very special but very vulnerable at the same time. You can do a lot of flash on the harmonica, you can do some growly, angry stuff on it, but there's an element of saying, "I'm a leaf in the wind." So that may have something to do with my attachment to it.

• • •

Howard Levy (1951–)

Anyone who feels that the harmonica script has been written should immediately closet himself with one of the three Warner Brothers releases by Bela Fleck and the Flecktones: *Self Titled, The Flight of the Cosmic Hippo,* or *UFO Tofu.* All feature the diatonic wizardry of Howard Levy, who may be the most radical single technical innovator in the history of his instrument.

The forerunners of jazz solo work on the diatonic, including Johnny O'Brien and Don Les, all worked within the familiar territories of straight and cross harp. The playing of particularly difficult passages or key changes sometimes meant that the mouth organist would have to swap instruments in the middle of a piece; in recent years, many diatonic jazz players have developed their own tunings to increase the melodic possibilities of their ten-hole instrument.

Chicagoan Howard Levy came to the harmonica as a pianist, and from the beginning he refused to accept the inherent chromatic limitations of the instrument. His accidental discovery of the overblow led to years of experimentation and the eventual mastery of an absolutely unique harmonica style. The overblow is an abnormal manipulation of the player's embouchure and airstream when playing a blow note that causes an interaction between the draw reed and the blow reed that sounds a note that is higher in pitch than the standard blow note. Levy did not invent the overblow, but he is the first to master it completely and to make it an integral part of a full-fledged technique. As it turns out, the notes available through overblowing include those that are unavailable in the cross-harp approach, and Levy has been able to fill in the chromatic blanks that have sometimes frustrated diatonic players. At harmonica workshops Levy likes to leave audiences slack-jawed by improvising on a familiar tune in all twelve keys on a single Golden Melody harmonica.

For years Levy's professional career was primarily as a jazz pianist, although his harmonica playing was featured on recordings by other artists and on his own *Harmonica Jazz* album. Then in 1989, Levy found a kindred musical soul in Nashville banjoist Bela Fleck, who had gained an international reputation for shattering the stereotypes surrounding his chosen instrument. The success of the Flecktones has brought Levy's mouth organ playing to a wide audience and allowed him the opportunity to create new music that is as fresh and original as his own revolutionary harmonica technique.

Interview With Howard Levy

I'm from New York originally. I was raised in Brooklyn and Queens. My father sang opera—he sang professionally for a brief period—and my mother was an amateur cellist. I was eight when I started playing the piano. As soon as I put my hands on the keyboard I started improvising. I enjoyed making sounds, and I wrote real music. When I was eighteen, I started playing the diatonic harmonica. I didn't sing, and I wanted to play an instrument that I could express myself on more directly than the piano.

All I wanted was to play blues and learn how to bend notes. After a while I started thinking that perhaps I could play real notes on this instrument. Most harmonica players just think in terms of the familiar kinds of sounds that they've heard and are trying to emulate. I got frustrated with blues riffs eventually, because that's not the way I hear. I wanted to know why I couldn't play certain notes, and I started trying to play in a more melodic fashion.

I didn't have a lot of money when I was in college, and I only had one or two harmonicas, so I tried playing along with the radio in all these weird keys and I discovered that I could play some scales in other keys and that the notes were actually real notes rather than just bends. I started really getting interested. I was terrible for about six months—I really couldn't play at all. Then a drummer I knew who played the harp showed me about cross harp. No one ever told me about third or fourth position or any of that stuff. That all came out of my thinking in terms of notes.

My first breakthrough came during freshman orientation week at Northwestern University. I went to a political rally for the Chicago Seven, and I began to feel like I was living in a very important historical period. I didn't know anybody, and I was feeling alienated and excited at the same time. I walked out of there and took my harmonica out, and all of a sudden I was bending notes. I bent one first and then tried bending a bunch of the others, and I could bend them all. That was so exciting to me that I became obsessed with the harmonica. I played for hours and hours each day.

I remember the first time I overblew a note, the note and the overblow came out at the same time. I thought, "Wow, what a funky sound." It sounded like a great thing for blues, because it sort of had its own distortion. After a while I realized that if I could separate the overblow from the note, I could have that minor third that all blues harp players want to get and end up settling for the wimpy seventh hole draw instead. I started separating out the overblow and discovering other notes on the harmonica. I broke many harmonicas finding them.

When I started doing overblows, I was doing them on a Marine Band, but it's easiest for me on a Golden Melody. The reeds are different and the plastic helps make it more airtight. The air is deflected upward and downward at the reed more directly. And the way the scale is tempered makes it more in tune for melody playing. The overblows I do don't seem to affect the instruments much; most of mine last a long time.

The key to the overblow is in the mind. You have to control the blow bends on the top of the harp. I really got into those bends; most cross-harp players don't do that very much. I loved the way it sounded, but it was very hard for me to be able to go smoothly from the blow bends to the draw bends. When I'm playing smooth, legato things, I'm actually tapering the notes so that the point where I change from blowing to drawing is not a real change in direction. It's kind of like the waves in the ocean—there's a wave breaking over the top while the previous wave is receding underneath.

I played the chromatic for a while when I played in the Chicago run of *Shenandoah,* which is one of two musicals ever written that has a full harmonica part. After that, I started seriously playing classical music and jazz on it. I sounded all right, but it was not the instrument of choice for me. My diatonic playing was becoming stronger and stronger. I wanted to have my one sound, and I knew I had that on the diatonic, which I related to more personally. Stevie Wonder is one of the rare players that can make the chromatic sound personal. I think he's got the greatest sound on the chromatic of anyone, ever. The diatonic is the ax for me. I've knocked myself out and driven myself crazy figuring out how to play certain tunes on it, but I've eventually figured out nearly all of them. And I'll get the others, too.

If you were a saxophonist or played some other normal instrument, you would naturally figure out how to play things. The diatonic doesn't let you play it; most players end up playing around it. I had the determination of a pianist to get all the notes or be damned. The harmonica is so linked with the piano in my mind that I can play a simultaneous solo with the right hand on the piano and the harmonica. I see the keyboard when I'm blowing. I was stuck with this improbable, three-and-a-half-inch thing that was designed to play kiddie songs. Occasionally, I get burned out on it, but I always come back to it.

The G harmonica is the harmonica I think on; if it's readable at all on a G harmonica, I can read it as a chromatic piece of music. I can read melody lines pretty well in most recording situations. If it's in Ab, for example, I'll just pick up my Db harmonica if it's a bluesy thing. But I might want to play it on an Eb, an Ab, or a Bb—these are all relationships that I play in. I may have to do some pretty convoluted transposing, but it's a matter of applying myself.

The position I play in depends on the type of music I'm playing. I play a lot in cross harp for commercial recording situations. I play straight harp in certain jazz situations. I also play in what I call "first flat" position. The positions as we know them all go up in fifths, but there is also a whole series of other positions that go up in fourths. If you go up in fifths, you get the sharp keys, and if you go up in fourths, you get the flat keys. On a C harmonica, F is what I call the first flat position, Bb the second, Eb the third, Ab the fourth, and so on.

I've done a lot of sessions with other artists. Some of the best were with Paquito De Rivera. A career highlight was coming back to New York City and playing the Blue Note with him in front of my family and friends. I also did an album with Lorraine Duisit on Flying Fish that has some of my best playing on it. I'm real proud of two albums I did recently with the percussionist Glen Velez and of a session for Amazing Records with Paul Glasse, a great mandolin player from Austin. I've recorded with Dolly Parton and Styx. I produced my own album, *Harmonica Jazz,* where I play some Coltrane and Charlie Parker tunes, as well as a few of my own. I write a lot of music, but only recently have I tried to write specifically for the harmonica. The only piece written for the instrument that I like is the thing that Benjamin Arnold wrote for Larry Adler.

In the summer of 1988 I played a music festival up in Winnipeg and Lorraine Duisit introduced me to Bela Fleck one evening. We stayed up until about seven the next morning playing, and when Bela signed to do the "Lonesome Pine Special" on television, he asked me to play with him, and that was the beginning of the Flecktones. I finally had to leave the band, though, because we were on the road more than two hundred days a year and I wanted to spend more time with my family. I also wanted to get back to playing my own music. I'm playing a lot around Chicago and negotiating on my own record deal. I just finished an instructional video for Homespun, *New Directions for Harmonica,* that also includes tips on harmonica repair and maintenance. It even has ultrasound movies of what happens inside my mouth when I play.

I feel like I'm flying when I'm playing well. The instrument is just so small and so personal that it's a very exciting thing.

Tommy Morgan

Hollywood

Notwithstanding Borrah Mine-
vitch's high profile in the 1930s, the Harmonicats' hit records, and the
more recent blues harp explosion, the harmonica has probably
reached more people winding its way through the background music
of feature films and television programs than through any other
medium. Film composers have long appreciated how a few well-
placed, reedy tones can instantly evoke certain moods, and now that
the advertising business is in the hands of a new generation of pitch-
men who came of age in the blues harp era, you can expect to be
confronted with the sound of a mouth organ within minutes after
powering up your television set. The Hollywood recording studio can

be hostile ground to an untrained harmonicist, but a few unique players have flourished like hothouse orchids in this highly competitive scene.

The first mouth organist to plant himself in Hollywood was Jerry Adler, who slipped into town in 1937 with his embouchure set on a studio career: "I did just about every harmonica sound track you could think of during the late thirties and forties." When Jimmy Stewart portrayed an ace mouth organist in the 1941 film *Pot o' Gold,* he turned to Adler for a crash course on mouth organ technique so that he could fake his on-screen playing convincingly.

Before long Adler was competing for work in the film capital with George Fields and two ex-Rascals, Leo Diamond and Richard Hayman. In 1945, Joe Mullendore became another of the harmonica band refugees to emigrate to southern California, but unlike the rest he left his instrument behind and began a new career as a film composer. "When I started to write music seriously, I downplayed my harmonica band days. I was afraid. I knew what it was like in Hollywood. Someone would say, 'Oh, he used to be in a harmonica band.' And that would stick with you like a mustard plaster." Richard Hayman preferred to straddle his past and a new career as a writer and arranger for MGM. Given the opportunity, he could fall back into the role of harmonica virtuoso, as he did in 1952 when he helped arrange the score for the film *Ruby Gentry* and heard George Fields give a haunting rendition of the title theme; after the movie was released, Hayman's own recording of the tune became a major pop hit. Fields, the top session harmonicist in Hollywood during the 1950s and 1960s, was probably too busy to rue his bad luck for long.

George Fields (1921–)

"The harmonica is a diabolical instrument requiring nothing less than a wizard to make real music upon it," Hollywood film composer Elmer Bernstein has noted. "George Fields plays with the facility, the astonishing artistry, and sense of perfection that characterize all his endeavors."

For nearly two decades, George Fields's harmonica was featured prominently in the musical scores of many films, including *The Tall Men, Raintree County,* and *Paint Your Wagon.* Henry Mancini's multi-million-selling recording of "Moon River" was arranged around

Fields's chromatic harmonica. There have been several George Fields: the composer (two film scores cowritten with Laurindo Almeida), the musical director (for Stan Freberg's radio show), the Hollywood Bowl concert soloist (with Victor Young, Nelson Riddle, and Henry Mancini), and the recording artist (with the Hollywood Bowl Symphony and the Roger Wagner Chorale). Add to those roles that of the solitary musical genius cum mad scientist, for in the early 1970s, Fields spent a year and a half recording in a makeshift home studio one of the finest—and perhaps the most unique—classical harmonica recordings: Angel Records' *The Pocket Bach.*

Interview With George Fields

I'm from Brooklyn, where the tree grows. I took violin lessons when I was about eight or nine. I had a very tyrannical teacher, and when I didn't get the right hand position or if I played the wrong note, he would twist my ear. Finally, one day in desperation I smashed the violin. That was the end of my musical training.

At age ten I acquired a Marine Band harmonica. Later my father surprised me with a four-octave chromatic. I was playing by ear within a month or two. I think the first classical piece I approached was the *Hungarian Dance No. 5.* Somebody wrote it out in numbers for me—which holes to blow and so forth. Within a year I was involved with a harmonica club in Brooklyn. Victor Pankowitz was in that group—he was a real heavyweight player.

I was pretty industrious. I learned notation pretty well. My interests always went to classical music, and I started to haunt the music room at the New York Public Library, looking for transcriptions. My early interests were things like Saint-Saens's *Danse Macabre,* the Schubert unfinished symphony, Rimsky-Korsakov's *Scheherazade.* I borrowed the scores and very laboriously learned to interpret the parts and even transpose the instruments and to write arrangements for our group.

My first professional job was when I joined the Cappy Barra band in 1940 and they broke me in at the Roxy Theater in New York. I was playing a harmony part and had a week of rehearsal behind me. Show business was quite an education. I remember playing Faye's Burlesque Theater in Philadelphia. The headlining stripper was Lois DeFaye. They called her "the Amazon"—she was about six foot six, but very well-proportioned. She would do her thing and we would be lined up in this narrow passageway in the wings waiting to follow her. On the first show, when she came off, there was this collision between six guys in dinner jackets and this huge, naked lady. It got to be a game, and she wouldn't let us on unless we brushed past her. It would end up with six guys out on stage with erections.

When the war broke us up, we all went in different directions. I managed to stay out of the service. I spent a year with the Borrah Minevitch group, and then in 1942 I got a call from Leo Diamond, who was out in California. Dick Hayman was leaving his trio and they needed someone who was a good reader because Leo had a large library of arrangements. So I took the train out to California, and I've been here ever since. I lasted with Leo for about six months. It wasn't my kind of music, and I didn't get along with him too well. So I struck out on my own in California, and after a year or two I established myself as a studio player.

The first few times I was called in to rescue other harmonica players in Hollywood when they were faced with parts that just got them discombobulated when they tried to read them. In Hollywood, once they saw that you followed the stick, came in at bar thirty-six like you were supposed to, played the right notes and played with some feeling, you were accepted. So I kind of established myself as *the* player in town for fifteen or twenty years, until I finally gave it up.

The harmonica was always used in Hollywood with a touch of nostalgia or something around the campfire. *Raintree County* comes to mind as one film that featured harmonica pretty nicely. I worked on that for six months. I was working at double scale at the time and it was a miniature career for me. *Ruby Gentry* was also a memorable film for me. Heinz Rhomheld, the composer of the score, met with me before the recording. He had this theme and he wanted to hear how it would sound on harmonica. We sat down and he played the piano and I played the theme as he had sketched it out. And he liked it and decided he was going to feature it in the film. After Dick Hayman's recording of it suddenly emerged as a huge hit, I made a cover record with Victor Young, but by that time Dick's was the big record. The song has become a classic and it's associated with the harmonica, and I had the dubious distinction of introducing it on the sound track. Jack Marshall, who scored a television series at Universal called "The Deputy" with Henry Fonda, loved the harmonica and featured it quite a bit.

In Hollywood the harmonica was treated as a specialty instrument. You'd find yourself in a recording studio with forty or fifty of the greatest players in the world, and sometimes it was very simplistic music, but more often than not it was rather complicated, because film music changes meter to match the film. In the recording studio they always have a screen in back of the players, and when you do a take, the conductor is conducting the orchestra according to what he's seeing on the screen. You're looking at the stick and listening on headphones to the click track, which is sometimes variable. One of the big problems as a harmonica player was that your part was going to be a solo part. Whenever it came in, everything else would slow down or stop, or maybe there would just be guitar under it and there would be a little segment with a harmonica solo. And then the orchestra would continue, and sometimes you would sit through seventy or eighty bars of complicated music and have to count and be ready to make your entrance. You don't really have a chance to get the instrument warmed up or gather yourself together to play this solo. You suddenly have to make an entrance, come in right and sound like you're part of whatever is happening.

All instruments have limitations, and the harmonica is no different. But if you apply yourself to it, you can do some wonderful things with it. Look at woodwind players—they have to produce a column of air that's going in one direction and that's it. As a harmonica player on a session, I would generally be in the woodwind section, and sometimes I'd have a long, drawn-out solo. One of the players would often say, "When do you breathe?" and I'd tell them, "Well, I'm breathing all the time."

One of the harmonica's limitations is the key you're working in. On occasion, if I had something that required some chording, I'd use an A chromatic, but I usually played a C chromatic. The flat keys are better than the sharp keys, because in the sharp keys you don't really get enough blow notes—there are a lot of inhaling notes. Consider that in the key of F the two pivotal notes are F and C. You normally never have F# or a C#. On the chromatic, you can always play a B# instead of a C and an E# instead of an F, so you have the option of making either of those notes a blow or a draw note. When you play in the key of D, normally you never have an F natural, a C natural, an A, or an E. That's why, to my thinking, the flat keys are much better than the sharp keys. Composers would ask, "What key should I write this in?"

And they would be amazed that a harmonica player likes to play in the key of Db, because that's a difficult key for most other instruments, but it's great for harmonica.

I worked on my Bach album for about a year or a year and a half. It was a labor of love. I had set up a little recording facility in my house, and just for fun I started to tinker with doing overdubs with Bach pieces. Most of Bach's music is keyboard music, and I would have to pick out which finger was playing which line, write out three or four different parts, and then play them. My original notion was to find out how many of the inventions could be played on the harmonica; I eventually saw that they all can, if you study them.

When I recorded my album, I mainly used the 64 Chromonica. The 64 is my instrument. I like the round holes, I like the feel of it. That bottom register is important—in fact, I'd love to see a five-octave chromatic. But in order to get the lower range beyond that I had to resort to the single-reed bass harmonica. You get into some very complicated lines in the lower register that don't lend themselves to the bass harmonica, so I had to use some of the lower-register polyphonia harmonicas, which are chromatic. And I had to piece together certain parts to make it work. The notion of selling it as an album didn't occur to me until after a year or so. I took it to quite a few companies before Angel Records bought it.

I worked for several years as a copyist in the music library at Universal Studios. It's been a craft that has stood me in good stead. For instance, in 1948, Igor Stravinsky was making some minor changes to the *Firebird Suite,* and Joe Mullendore and I contracted to recopy it. Stravinsky lived in Los Angeles, and we had two or three meetings with him. He showed us the penciled changes, and we started to work on it and bogged down terribly. It was a big chore. Stravinsky was a very sweet man, at least in our dealings with him.

Eddy Manson (1919–)

One of the more unique acts to work the burlesque circuit in the 1940s—and that's saying something—was a trick violinist named Tangini, whose specialty was playing the violin while standing on his head and in other unorthodox positions. In the privacy of his dressing room, however, Tangini would sit upright and dutifully practice classical violin pieces. One day a young harmonica player who was also on the bill heard the music emanating from Tangini's dressing room and introduced himself. It is from this chance encounter that Eddy Manson dates his long attraction to baroque music.

Manson was already a seasoned veteran of burlesque, the borscht belt, and the Harmonica Rascals by the time he crossed paths with Tangini. "When my father realized that I was going to continue to play the harmonica professionally, he—despite the fact that he had *taught* me to play the harmonica when I was three—virtually disowned me, and the whole family begged me to give up this 'silliness' and come into the housewares business with them as a 'real person.'" As his passion for classical music grew, Manson decided to pursue more advanced training. He enrolled at Juilliard and slipped into a schizophrenic existence, studying composition and the clarinet during the day and playing the harmonica in clubs at night. In 1953, Manson was asked to provide the music for the film *The Little Fugitive*. His winsome score, which consisted mostly of solo harmonica pieces, was later released on Folkways Records. Several years with pop music kingpin Mitch Miller, who featured Manson's harmonica on his "Sing Along" program and recordings, followed.

Manson moved to Hollywood, determined to concentrate on film and television arranging. He's succeeded handsomely, amassing a record of achievement that includes five Venice Film Festival awards, two Emmy nominations, sixteen Clios (for scoring television commercials), a shared Academy Award for the music for the film *Day of the Painter,* and a term as the president of the American Society of Film Arrangers.

Although Manson once hired a publicist for the express purpose of obscuring his harmonica background, he has been one busy mouth organist, recording under his own name for several labels; making television appearances with Ed Sullivan, Milton Berle, and Red Skelton; playing in such diverse venues as Carnegie Hall, Lincoln Center, Yankee Stadium, and Moscow's Gorki Park; and frequenting the Los Angeles studios, where he played on the sound tracks of such television programs as "The Virginian" and "Ben Casey" and created harmonica solos for several pop recordings, including Michael Jackson's "One Day in Your Life."

In recent years, Manson has shed his reluctance about being identified with the mouth organ. "I realized upon comparing the Chromonica with other instruments that it indeed stood up very well," he has written. "It had a three-octave range. You could play double stops, chords, and octaves, which you cannot do on any of the orchestral instruments except, of course, the piano, harp, and strings. And it could play octaves a helluva lot faster than one could on the fiddle. . . . Even better, you could *shape* your tone at will with your hands and mouth cavity, again which cannot be done on a keyboard instrument or harp, or most of the wind instruments. I also discovered . . . that the harmonica is ideal for orchestral playing. It blends beautifully with strings, woodwinds, and muted brass. As a solo instrument, it sets off very well indeed with piano, guitar, vibes, and synthesizers." As for the mouth organ's future, Manson claims that the harmonica "is badly taught for the most part, and there is very little decent literature or teaching methods for it."

"I love all kinds of music," says Manson, "providing it's honest and not plastic. I tend to groove most with the classics, with jazz running a close second. I think I enjoy playing a beautiful and haunting melody more than I do a pyrotechnical display of virtuosity. There is a challenge and depth to classical music that I can't find anywhere else. Jazz, on the other hand, offers a rare opportunity for self-expression. It is sometimes fun to merge the two."

Tommy Morgan (1932–)

For more than twenty-five years the first name under *harmonica* in the Rolodexes of composers for film and television has been Tommy Morgan's. Besides contributing to the sound tracks of countless television programs and more than four hundred films as an instrumentalist, Morgan has also written original scores for many television programs and recorded with the Beach Boys, Dean Martin, Andy Williams, Neil Diamond, the Carpenters, Barbra Streisand, Toni Tennille, Henry Mancini, and Linda Ronstadt. A thoroughly schooled chromatic player, Morgan took up the diatonic in the 1960s when the blues harp sound began infiltrating sound tracks and is one of the few trained harmonicists who has a genuine appreciation and talent for that style.

Morgan continues to prosper in Hollywood, and his unparalleled experience and versatility make his future look secure. The next time you hear a harmonica in a theater or during a television program, you're more than likely listening to the remarkable Tommy Morgan.

Interview With Tommy Morgan

I started piano when I was three or four. My older brother used to take lessons. My mother told me that I would be taking a nap while he was having his lessons, and that later I would get up and play exactly what he had been playing, so I had an ear. I wanted to play the harmonica when I was about four. My mother bought me a chromatic and read me the directions on how to tongue block and all that. They taught the harmonica in the L.A. school system, and I remember that when I was in the first grade, they placed me in the second-grade harmonica class.

In the third grade I was very ill and gave up all music. When I was about thirteen, I picked up the harmonica again. My folks found a teacher for me when I was about fifteen, but after about six months I had literally passed my teaching. I could play fast, I had a lot of technique, but I didn't like my sound. In 1949 my folks took me to see Larry Adler when we were in Great Britain, and I realized something was missing. I was starting to do some shows, high school things, playing things like *Ritual Fire Dance*.

My father took me to see Leo Diamond, who told me not to push the slide with my thumb, which was the way I'd been taught. It was rapidly becoming clear to me that I needed some help. I began taking lessons from Jerry Adler. He wouldn't take any money for it. I stayed with him for about two years. He really opened my mind to what the harmonica can do. Jerry is one of the truly great ballad players, and a marvelous person. Sometimes I'll tune his harmonicas—that's the only way I can pay him back for all those lessons.

In 1949, in the middle of auditions for the Horace Heidt show, I decided I needed a new vibrato. I was using right-hand vibrato. I had a Jerry Murad record where he used throat vibrato, but I didn't know how that worked. I worked on a throat vibrato for about a week, eight or nine hours a day. I finally tore my mouth apart and then sat around the house doing vibrato without a harmonica in my mouth. When I showed up for my callback audition with Horace Heidt, I played with the new vibrato. I didn't win, which was just as well, because I didn't have a repertoire yet. I was probably the last of the players to grow up playing the usual pop classics: *Hora Staccato, Rumanian Rhapsody, Rhapsody in Blue.*

After high school, I went to UCLA. The same month I started college, Jerry Adler recommended me for a record date he couldn't make with the Andrews Sisters. I graduated with a degree in music and started doing picture work at MGM. I was twenty years old and doing all the solo work on pictures like *Seven Brides for Seven Brothers*. I did a recording of "The Sadie Thompson Song" for Decca that did pretty well.

I spent 1954 in San Antonio with the air force. I had letters of recommendation from all the major studios I'd worked at, and used them to arrange some concerts with the San Antonio Symphony, whose arranger came up with some excellent arrangements for the things I was playing then. In 1955 I became a soloist for the Air Force Band in Washington, D.C. We did the "Ed Sullivan Show." On a tour of Europe I bought my first bass and chord harmonicas and learned how to play them a little. I did some work as an arranger with the Air Force Band and met Sammy Nestico, who was a writer for people like Count Basie. I knew I would be out of the air force soon, so I had Sam write an act for me.

After I got out of the service, I went to New York and knocked on doors. I wanted to be an entertainer, a star. I played the Palace Theater in June of 1957; they dropped vaudeville in August that same year. Television killed it. I could see the handwriting on the wall. I knew that ten years down the road I was going to end up thirty-five years old with no place to play. The key was to have a hit record, and I knew I didn't have that option. I booked myself in Japan and ended up doing a command performance for the empress of Japan, but back home there was no place to work. I took some time off, and then I got a call from Lawrence Welk; doing his show got me playing again. I went back to school, and in 1961 I received a master's degree in music composition.

I'll never forget my first studio callback. Warners called me and I played second harmonica to Leo Diamond on a picture called *Rio Bravo*. He and George Fields were both doing a lot of stuff then. Dmitri Tiomkin was the conductor, and I guess I impressed him. I became first call at Warners, and it all grew from there.

I could sight-read when I started doing studio work, but I realized that I had limitations. I wasn't comfortable in all keys. At the age of twenty I dedicated myself to becoming the best studio player I could become. I practiced sight-reading and vibratos and everything else. It took me five years to get the heartbeat out of my tone. You don't hear any waver in my tone when I play a long note. I had been recording myself since I was sixteen, but I never really liked my sound until I went through this period. I spent six years developing my sound for the studios. You've got to be nuts to do it. From the time I first started recording, I realized that this was the ultimate for me, but I never dreamed that there could be a career as a harmonica player. There wasn't a full-time harmonica session player until I got here. When I started in Hollywood, the orchestra would finish and go home, and then I'd come in and play the campfire. Then I got chances to do the main title and a couple of cues with the orchestra. When they found out I could read and play in tune, they started writing me like a third clarinet.

I've been the harmonica sound of Hollywood for twenty-five years. I figure that I'm probably the most-heard harmonica player in history because I've had so many TV shows rerun all over the world. I did six years of "Green Acres," six years of "Rockford," seven years of "The Waltons," six years of "Dukes of Hazzard," four years of "Newhart" and "Sanford and Son." I've worked on films like *Hang 'em High, All That Jazz, Heart to Heart, Annie, The Soldier's Story,* and *The Color Purple.* I've worked with most of the movie greats in town: Max Steiner, Al Newman, Dmitri Tiomkin, Fred Zinneman. I did a score with Max Steiner once at Warners. Max couldn't see in his later years, so they set me up next to the podium. I had a thirty-two-bar part in Eb. Max said, "Okay, let me hear the harmonica." I'm sitting right off his left arm, and I'm a little nervous. I hadn't rehearsed it, but I started playing and he let me run the whole part down. He conducted a retard at the end and I followed him all the way. I'll never forget the surprised look on his face. He finally said, "Well, I guess we don't have to worry about the harmonica."

I think of myself as a studio musician whose instrument is the harmonica. Everybody else I've talked with is a harmonica player. They all feel maligned and that sort of thing. My thought processes are different, and I think it gives me a different sound. The harmonica can blend with almost any instrument. I'm often doubled with the strings and the woodwinds. Pete Carpenter wrote some great stuff for "The Rockford Files" for a section with flute, oboe, two clarinets, two bassoons, and harmonica. I would change my vibrato to match the bassoon's. I've applied all the woodwind techniques to the harmonica, so I can double clarinet with no vibrato. For the flute and the oboe I'll change my vibrato slightly.

I worked with Toots Thielemans on a movie called *Getaway.* I played the bass harmonica and Toots played chromatic. He's a great player and a really nice person. He bounces through life about two feet off the ground—he's a bubble. I worked with Sonny Terry for two days on a film called *Buck and the Preacher*. I was very impressed with him—he had a great tone. Tommy Reilly is another wonderful player; we need a few more like him.

I first started playing the diatonic in 1961. I was working with people like Rod McKuen and Gary Puckett and the Union Gap and I started playing a little diatonic. I never practiced it because I wanted to come at it from a by-ear method. I didn't listen to a lot of records, either. I work at trying to get a sound like Hammie Nixon on those 1935 recordings with Sleepy John Estes. Recently I sat in a half dozen times with a local blues band. I'd played a lot of blues, but never in a joint. The guys would have me play a couple of sets a night, and I really enjoyed it. It was fun exploring that idiom.

My instrument of choice is the #270, but I carry them all and play them all. I carry instruments tuned to 440, 442, and 445. I use the plastic diatonics because you can get to them without having to screw around with the nails. I carry blues-tempered diatonics, too, where you take a C harmonica and tune the E and the B down and the F up. I play with and without the tongue block. If I'm playing a blues sound, I'm lipping, but I'm a tongue blocker because of my original chromatic training. I still do a lot of practicing today. Mostly sight-reading. Advanced flute and oboe books. I don't practice what I know, unless I'm preparing for a concert. I'm a competitive person, and that's why I still practice. I'm a better player today than I was ten years ago.

The number of dates in Los Angeles are down. The heyday was the sixties and the seventies, when I would be doing five series at one time. Now every time you walk out of a session where you are overdubbing and are isolated on a track, you know you've been sampled. Fortunately, the synthesizer doesn't work very well with the harmonica and the vibrato, thank God. The synthesizer is here to stay, but it may cycle back. We're going to have to join them if we want to survive the electronics era. I have a DX7 synthesizer and a Millioniser on order. I think I could work out of it, because you could sound like any of the woodwinds and still sound like a natural player, too. I was watching a movie recently that was set in the old West, and they cut to a guy playing the harmonica by the campfire in 1886 or something, and there on the sound track was a DX7, RAM 3A, preset 14, trying to sound like the guy playing.

The harmonica has been a second-class citizen because of the players. Take an orchestra, for example. Every player in that orchestra has been thoroughly trained. But no one uses the harmonica as part of an orchestra, so harmonica players are the only ones without that kind of experience. You put something in front of them and hardly any of them can read quickly. I've seen harmonica players come in with instruments that are out of tune and try to play with a violinist who has spent twenty-five years learning how to play his instrument. Obviously, it's going to be a grating experience. If I have a unison part with a clarinet and then a unison part with horns, I'll play two differently tuned instruments.

Idiomatically, the harmonica is not an all-purpose instrument. It should be used where it's comfortable. It's a great lyric instrument, and it's a fairly facile instrument in some of the better keys. What the harmonica does have is its sound. There's a metal edge on the sound that you don't have on the flute, for example. You can have a flute and an oboe play in unison, and that has a distinctive sound. If you add a harmonica, it's a different sound, and yet you can't pick the harmonica out.

John Sebastian

Courtesy of John Bryan.

Classical Music

The identification of the harmonica with the masses was there from the earliest experiments of Buschmann and Richter and its original role as the purveyor of European folk melodies. This worked to the instrument's advantage when it migrated to the United States and took a leading part in the development of the blues and of country and western music, a pedigree that ensured that the mouth organ would have a place in rock and roll. The difficulty of achieving chromatic fluidity on the harmonica made its injection into jazz less of a sure thing, but that genre's tolerance of unorthodox instrumentation has enabled it to embrace at least a few talented mouth organists. The stiffest opposition to encroachment by the harmonica has been put up by the orthodox devotees of classical music.

"In this country, my own land, where harmonica playing has reached the greatest variety of stylistic heights," classical harmonica virtuoso John Sebastian once lamented, "I have encountered the greatest resistance in having the harmonica accepted by the concert public as a serious instrument. . . . I feel that the motivating force in our booming concert audience is *not* the emotional and spiritual satisfaction of desirable musical stimuli, but is rather the social status and 'snob' appeal to be gained from the 'cultural benefits' exposure."

European virtuoso Tommy Reilly, the dean of classical harmonicists, faces the antagonism toward the mouth organ in the classical milieu head-on in his press kit, which quotes the following entry from an unnamed musical dictionary:

> [The harmonica is] a small and simple free-reed instrument invented in the 1820s. The value of the instrument for artistic purposes amounted to nothing; its only interest is a historical one. But even this is a questionable blessing, for the mouth organ was the first germ of the accordion and concertina, instruments which produce quite the most unpleasant musical sound ever devised.

Music critics are rarely so frank when faced with the challenge of reviewing classical harmonica recordings or performances. They typically not only reveal their fundamental bias against the mouth organ, but devote the greater part of their critiques to an analysis of this prejudice; any discussion of the performer's talent is unfailingly juxtaposed with a bewildered comment on the player's choice of instrument.

"As some parents love most greatly the least gifted of their children, so Adler is obviously enamored of his confining little toy," the *Saturday Review*'s Irving Kolodin once wrote about a Larry Adler performance. "Adler, with all the determination of a man bent on fashioning an *Ile de France* out of matchsticks, succeeds in conveying an unbelievable amount of musical meaning with enough inhalations and exhalations of air to blow up a good-sized auto tire."

But compared to the concert-going public, the professional critics have been kind to classical harmonicists. Tommy Reilly recalls one of his early Scandinavian tours: "In Bergen, Norway, they were very snobbish, if not very knowledgeable. I played with their symphony at the same time that Shakespeare's *Othello* was playing in their theater, and an old Bergen lady was heard to say, 'Oh, the culture's really going downhill—a harmonica with the symphony and a *Negro* playing Shakespeare!'"

Playing classical music on a mouth organ was not even a possibility until 1924, when Hohner unveiled the first fully chromatic instrument. The chromatic mouth organ made its debut about the time amplification systems were being installed in music halls and theaters, and it is doubtful whether the instrument could have made any headway in the classical field had it not been for the microphone. "The harmonica has a very small sound," the French composer Darius Milhaud once noted, "and in a concerto with orchestra, a microphone is indispensable; obviously, it must be orchestrated with great agility if one does not want to see this instrument founder under the tumult of the orchestra."

The first mouth organists to offer full-length programs of classical music, Larry Adler and John Sebastian, had no choice but to perform works composed for and identified with other instruments. The insistence of these talented performers in acting the part of classical artists could not completely obscure the fact that there was no "serious" repertoire unique to their instrument. These tuxedoed phenomena were essentially all dressed up with nowhere to go. No matter how much artistry they displayed, the well-known violin or piano pieces they offered rarely played to the harmonica's strengths and were indelibly linked in the minds of the classical audience with the mainstream instruments for which they were originally written; the mouth organ was bound to suffer in comparison.

The realities of the business side of the classical music scene have also been hard on mouth organists. Only the most creative players have survived; the fine player and former Harmonica Rascal Richard Bain carved out a unique career for himself in the armed services, where his long tenure as a harmonica soloist with the U.S. Navy Band allowed him to make his mark as a gifted interpreter of classical pieces. And there have been several instances when composers and publishers have actually denied harmonicists permission to perform certain classical pieces. When Tommy Reilly's recording of Igor Stravinsky's *Chanson Russe* was released, the composer's publisher formally objected. Reilly responded by writing to the composer and enclosing a copy of the record. "After hearing your performance of *Chanson Russe*," Stravinsky wrote back, "you can play anything of mine." Jerry Murad of the Harmonicats was not so fortunate. "I recorded 'The Story of Three Loves,' which was Rachmaninoff's eighteenth variation on a theme of Paganini's," recalls Murad. "Shortly after the record was released, the Rachmaninoff estate stopped it—they had the right—because it was written for piano and orchestra."

But the playing and proselytizing of Adler and Sebastian had an impact, and some important contemporary composers were moved or persuaded to write pieces for the harmonica. "Larry Adler asked me to write him a concerto for harmonica and orchestra," Darius Milhaud wrote in his autobiography. "What interested me about the project was trying to write as freely as possible for an instrument that seemed so limited. . . . Acceptable works have already been written to permit these virtuosos of greater and greater numbers to express themselves without having to limit themselves to transcriptions that were more or less doubtful. . . .This charming instrument . . . need not be limited to sailor's hornpipes or sea chantys." (Unfortunately, this attitude is not reflected in Milhaud's *Suite for Harmonica and Orchestra,* as the titles of its three movements—"Gigue," "Sailor Song," and "Hornpipe"—make clear.)

Forty years after Milhaud's contribution, the harmonica's unique concert repertoire has been expanded to include works by, among others, Vaughan Williams, Gordon Jacob, Adrian Cruft, Hugo Herrmann, Matyas Seiber, Francis Chagrin, G. Anders-Strehmel, Malcolm Arnold, Arthur Benjamin, Henry Cowell, Heitor Villa-Lobos, and Michael Spivakovsky. While these efforts have unquestionably elevated the instrument's status, none of these works have proved memorable or tuneful enough to enter into the public's consciousness and thus provide a musical Trojan horse for classical harmonicists. In fact, many of these pieces are not full-scale efforts—Arnold's *Harmonica Concerto* takes less than nine minutes to perform, and Vaughan Williams's *Romance* is shorter still and less musical.

Most of the mouth organists who have performed classical programs have gravitated to baroque music; John Sebastian, Tommy Reilly, George Fields, Stan Harper, Cham-Ber Huang, and Robert Bonfiglio have all produced excellent recordings of Bach's music. The public's familiarity with this body of work may have made it all the more attractive to such trailblazing performers, but the fact remains that these works are identified with other instruments. Charles Leighton, one of the first jazz harmonica virtuosos, has in recent years produced some of the most fully realized classical harmonica recordings. Much of the appeal of Leighton's studio efforts lies in his unique repertoire—moody, reflective, and graceful melodies culled primarily from woodwind compositions by the French romanticists, works that play to more of the strengths of the mouth organ than do violin or piano showpieces.

Classical harmonicists are mired in a daunting double bind, for the meagerness of the classical harmonica repertoire has both led to and perpetually reinforced the dearth of educational opportunities available to such players. When Eddy Manson left the vaudeville stage to enroll in the prestigious Juilliard School of Music, he had to trade in his harmonica for a clarinet. For several years Cham-Ber Huang offered at the Turtle Bay School of Music in New York City the first—and only—course of study in classical harmonica.

Classical mouth organists have found the goal of full-time careers elusive. "Classical players will not earn a living," asserts Cham-Ber Huang, who spends less time onstage than he does in the offices of his harmonica company. Stan Harper, who has given superbly crafted recitals of baroque music in showcases like Carnegie Hall, supports himself by playing pop music on cruise ships. George Fields and Charles Leighton, two alumni of the mouth organ vaudeville bands, produced their outstanding classical recordings at their own expense. For all his stunning technical virtuosity, Tommy Reilly's most impressive musical achievement may be the fact that he earns his livelihood playing classical music on the harmonica.

But even classical music critics have noted the aspects of the harmonica's sound that have made the instrument a fixture in less exalted genres. "It is in the slow movements that the harmonica's unique ability to project melancholy as a kind of smothered menace—a whine of angst—is best exploited," the London *Times's* Richard Morrison has written, and the existing classical mouth organ repertoire bears him out. The slow, middle movement of Milhaud's *Suite* contains some interesting melodic passages, and the "Canzona" movement of Benjamin's *Concerto* is much preferable to the up-tempo movements that frame it. The testimony of the composers of these pieces reveals that they wanted to take advantage of the harmonica's ability to evoke wistfulness: Villa-Lobos had in mind its "innocent lyrical quality," and Hovhaness used the mouth organ to add a "plaintive melancholy" to the sound of the orchestra.

"It's an instrument of the people, so you don't expect to hear it in a symphony orchestra," admits Richard Hayman. "But when it appears in this setting, its qualities make the whole orchestra sound different. It doesn't have the warmth or beauty of a violin or a piano in a solo, but it is distinctive."

The handful of classical mouth organists who have run the gauntlet between the lack of recognition, a skimpy and largely unimpressive repertoire, the absence of training grounds, and the shortage of venues have managed to inject the harmonica's special qualities into the realm of classical music. With their dogged persistence and technical brilliance, the best of these players have created a legacy of live performances and recordings that stand as some of the most phenomenal achievements in musical history.

John Sebastian (1914–80)

John Sebastian Pugliese, the first harmonicist to adopt a completely classical repertoire, once credited his ancestors from the mountainous regions of Italy, whom he described as having been "obstinate and hard workers," with passing on to him a certain genetic steeliness that held him in good stead as the player of a nontraditional classical instrument.

The son of a Philadelphia bank president, Sebastian's teenage years revolved around two passions—the harmonica and the study of Renaissance history. Predictably, he was drawn to Albert Hoxie's harmonica band, where his advanced musical skills were much appreciated. Sebastian spent several seasons at Hoxie's summer camp teaching thousands of other youngsters to play the mouth organ, and the year he turned sixteen he was crowned Philadelphia's harmonica champion. This lofty title came with a $125 one-week stand at the Mastbaum Theater. The management requested Sebastian to play "St. Louis Blues," but he instead delighted audiences with Borovsky's *Adoration.*

Sebastian's father was not enthusiastic about the prospect of a musical career for his son, but he took comfort from the fact that the boy's success as a history student matched his accomplishments on the harmonica. After high school there was college and two years abroad at the universities of Rome and Florence, but the thrill of his brief fling as a professional musician haunted Sebastian, and he continued to pursue the harmonica. On an ocean liner voyage back to the United States and an apparent foreign service career, Sebastian struck up a conversation with two fellow passengers, the noted Broadway musical team of Richard Rogers and Larry Hart. When Sebastian confessed to being torn between two fields of interest, they advised him that true artists were born and that such people were usually unhappy at any other pursuit. It took some time for the young harmonicist to decide on his future, but he finally opted for a career as a performer.

Sebastian's show business apprenticeship was spent playing swing numbers and popular favorites in nightclubs and cabarets, but from the outset he was determined to become accepted as an interpreter of classical music. Larry Adler had managed to place the harmonica in the concert hall; Sebastian hoped to do nothing less than put himself and his mouth organ on an equal footing with any other instrument in that exclusive arena. "I know this is a step-by-step operation," he once admitted. "It is not an overnight job." Between club dates he worked tirelessly, rehearsing three hours a day with a pianist and painstakingly adapting seventeenth- and eighteenth-century music for the mouth organ. Sebastian was encouraged by the open-mindedness he perceived in this music. "I discovered sonatas by Telemann, Veracini, Bach, Handel, Vivaldi, Hasse, Marcello, Purcell, and many others, which were written to be played on violin, flute, oboe, musette, even bagpipes," recalled Sebastian in 1960. "The composer seemed to be challenging each instrument to create the embellishments and ornaments to suit its particular voice. . . . I set about choosing works from this treasure trove that would best speak through my instrument."

He began to slip these new arrangements into his nightclub repertoire. Within a few years the transformation was complete, and Sebastian's audiences heard only classical pieces by the likes of Bach, Couperin, Corelli, Rameau, Kreisler, Albeniz, Lecuona, and Rimsky-Korsakov. When a club owner once suggested that Sebastian compromise by offering swing versions of the classics, the harmonicist archly replied, "I will not swing the classics. I prefer to let them swing for themselves."

Sebastian's career did not suffer from its change in direction; in fact, he was eventually able to limit his nightclub engagements to first-class rooms like the Hotel Pierre's Cotillion Room and Café Society in New York. But he chafed at the cabaret atmosphere and single-mindedly pursued his wish to make a move to the concert stage. Sebastian spurned an attractive contract offer from Hollywood when he learned he would have no control over the material he would perform on-screen.

Sebastian eventually found a champion in André Mertens of Columbia Artists Management, the most prestigious managers of classical performers in the United States. In 1941, under Mertens's guidance, Sebastian made his breakthrough as a classical performer with a spectacular orchestral debut as a soloist with Eugene Ormandy's Philadelphia Orchestra. "If you have any doubts that the harmonica is a musical instrument, Sebastian can dispel them," wrote Howard Taubman in *The New York Times*. Herbert Elwell noted in a column in the *Cleveland Plain Dealer* that "his mastery is equal to the virtuosity of any other first-rate instrumentalist. He has brought the harmonica into the society of the great, where it commands respect." Ross Parmenter, reviewing a Sebastian recital at Town Hall for *The New York Times*, noted that the program "contained nothing but classical music . . . and the level of both the taste and musicianship was high." Parmenter went on to pointedly note the fact that "Mr. Sebastian . . . plays with a good deal of inwardness and sensitivity, and he has a sure sense of rhythm, a grasp of style, and a musician's feeling for the shaping of phrases and the right flow of a melodic line."

The prominent oboist Jay S. Harrison once reviewed a Sebastian performance for the *New York Herald Tribune*. His critique of Sebastian's playing was just as laudatory as Parmenter's, but was expressed from a musician's viewpoint. "The classical harmonica," he wrote, "is caused to sound by air passing over its reeds or else being sucked away from them. This double action takes place without halt, and as a result a constant stream of breath is necessary to keep the tones flowing in proper succession. In addition, while the pitch of all other wind instruments is negotiated with the fingers depressing a network of comfortable keys, the harmonica must be shifted from side to side in the mouth in order to secure the correct series of desirable notes. A further complication is added by the fact that single tones are difficult to produce, since the instrument's general construction favors chordal conglomerates. Consequently, harmonica playing is a hazardous business even in the presentation of simple melodies. And to accomplish with success a program of Mr. Sebastian's scope is nothing short of wizardry. . . . He has vast technical facility, a bulging range of colors, and his intentions are ever musical and sophisticated. In his hands the harmonica is no toy, no simple gadget for the dispensing of homespun tunes. Each single number of the evening was whittled, rounded, polished, and poised. . . . Mr. Sebastian's playing is uncanny."

Notices like these did not go unnoticed by the Hohner Company, which engaged Sebastian as a consultant on harmonica design. His efforts in this area were mostly directed at improving the volume and texture of the lower register on the 64 Chromonica, his instrument of choice.

For Sebastian, the 1940s and '50s were filled with countless recitals in the United States and Canada, concerts with leading American orchestras, and network radio and television programs. Summers were spent with his wife and children at a second home in Florence, Italy. Sebastian's intense historical curiosity continually drew him to other cultures. He was especially interested in all forms of ethnic music and made careful studies of the breathing techniques of wind instrumentalists around the world. From Mexican pipe players Sebastian learned how to hold air reserves in his cheeks; he became a devotee of yoga because of its emphasis on proper breathing. Sebastian also continued to explore Renaissance history. "If tomorrow I were to lose my two front teeth," he once confided, "I could go to Italy and be perfectly happy."

Despite his passion for baroque music, Sebastian understood that until the harmonica had its own solid concert repertoire, it would not be secure in the classical field, and he actively lobbied contemporary composers to write for the harmonica. George Kleinsinger's *Street Corner Concerto,* in which the harmonica is asked to strike a "citified, jazzified mood," was written for Sebastian in 1947; the harmonicist premiered it with the New York Philharmonic. Norman Dello Joio presented Sebastian with a concerto for chamber orchestra and harmonica, and Walter Anderson had Sebastian in mind when he penned his *Fantasie* for harmonica and orchestra. Other composers who wrote specifically for Sebastian include Alan Hovhaness, Frank Lewin, Henry Cowell, Luciano Chailly, and Heitor Villa-Lobos. Sebastian commissioned a piece from the exiled Russian composer Alexander Tcherepnin and composed several pieces of his own, including *Serenade for Exhale Notes, Inca Dance,* and *Hornpipe Gigue.*

In the mid-1960s, Sebastian found himself trying to talk his son, John B. Sebastian, out of pursuing a show business career as an acoustic folk/blues artist. His advice went unheeded. John B. Sebastian became a rock star as the leader of the New York–based group The Lovin' Spoonful, and his father came to take great pride in his son's accomplishments.

In 1966, Sebastian embarked on a grueling thirteen-nation tour of Africa. Afterward, during a stay Rome, he suffered a major heart attack. After a long convalescence in the Italian capital, Sebastian decided to make his home there. Although his schedule was curtailed after his illness, Sebastian continued to play actively, although his appearances were now mostly on European stages. His musicianship continued to be impressive. In 1976, after hearing Sebastian play the Villa-Lobos harmonica concerto, a reviewer for the *Washington Star* wrote, "He is THE master of the harmonica."

"When I am asked, 'Why did you choose the harmonica?'" Sebastian once remarked in an interview with Albert Raisner, "I always answer: 'And why not the harmonica?' . . . If you can make music on it, it's an instrument. I voluntarily admit that the harmonica is not in the tradition of Stradivarius, but it concedes nothing in regards to sonorousness when it is properly played. The composers of the seventeenth and eighteenth centuries were not so intransigent in their choices as to which instruments interpreted their works: this is what has guided me in choosing my own repertoire. . . . One day, I hope that the public will say, 'What difference does it make if it is played on a harmonica? Isn't the important thing that it is played well?'"

"The guitar has only recently become accepted for the wonderfully sensitive and articulate instrument that it is, and this [the harmonica] is an instrument *rich* in historical tradition," Sebastian once insisted. "Somehow I feel that the harmonica will also find its rightful place. It will create a tradition of its own."

Cham-Ber Huang (1925–)

Cham-Ber Huang's exotic career has been shaped by personal and professional tendencies that at first glance seem contradictory. Raised in a middle-class home in a country struggling to emerge from feudalism, Huang chose to adopt a rarified, foreign music as his own. By nature an intensely conservative artist, Huang has for years spearheaded radical experiments in the design of the harmonica, an instrument that has rarely been tampered with since its initial conception. A thoroughly schooled performer who has spent close to fifty years perfecting his technique, he has managed to oversee a thriving business concern. "I'm the little devil in the harmonica field," he smilingly offers.

Cham-Ber Huang remembers the harmonica as being common during his boyhood in Shanghai: "There the harmonica is very popular because poor people cannot afford the piano or violin." Huang's grandfather gave him a ten-hole Hohner diatonic when he was very young; Huang claims that he immediately sensed that his future would be with the mouth organ. (Strangely enough, the instrument that his grandfather had given him had been misassembled at the Trossingen factory; the top and bottom reed plates had been reversed. Huang unwittingly learned to play the instrument upside down; to this day, he reverses the reed plates on his instruments.)

Huang's family was well off by Chinese standards, and as a boy he attended a private elementary school. At the age of seven Huang was placed in a harmonica class where he and his schoolmates learned to play long, double-reed diatonic instruments and to read music. "Practically every harmonica player in China reads music," contends Huang.

After establishing a reputation as a mouth organ prodigy and amassing a large repertoire of semiclassical pieces and other light offerings, Huang was given a scholarship to high school on the condition that he instruct other students in harmonica technique. By the time he was sixteen, Huang was the leader of a successful Shanghai harmonica orchestra built around his best pupils that at its peak boasted 150 members. This large ensemble included bass and chord players, and Huang divided the musicians into sections modeled on those of the symphony orchestra. Huang's harmonica philharmonic even appeared in a movie short.

The chromatic harmonica was unknown in China at the time, and Huang was forced to meet the technical demands of his expanding classical repertoire by learning to play two or three diatonic harmonicas simultaneously. When he finally obtained a chromatic mouth organ in his late teens, Huang spent two years retraining himself on the more versatile instrument.

In 1946, Huang appeared with the Shanghai Symphony, playing the flute part in Bach's Suite No. 2 in B Minor. That same year Dr. John Leighton Stuart, a former U.S. ambassador to China, attended another of Huang's performances. Congratulating the young virtuoso afterward, Stuart urged Huang to contact him if and when he ever decided to visit the United States. Huang says that at that time he had no particular fantasies about carving out a musical niche for himself in the West.

Nineteen forty-nine found Huang broadcasting classical pieces over the BBC from Hong Kong. His performances came to the attention of the network's home office in London, and Huang was invited to tour Great Britain. While in Europe, Huang made a special trip to Trossingen, Germany, where he gave a concert for five thousand employees of the Hohner Company. Huang remembered John Leighton Stuart's invitation to visit the United States and contacted the former diplomat, who responded with a letter of introduction to American officials and helped arrange for a visa. Huang arrived in New York in the summer of 1950. When Mao Tse-tung's victory in the Chinese civil war was followed by drastic social upheavals, Huang applied for and was granted American citizenship.

At the time of his emigration, Huang's repertoire was strictly classical. But after settling in New York, he soon faced financial reality and began learning the big band standards, boogie-woogie numbers, and gypsy showpieces that would get him bookings in nightclubs, where his old mastery of the art of playing two or three diatonics simultaneously made for a memorable finish to his act. But Huang was determined to make his mark as an interpreter of baroque music, and he seized any chance he could to gain experience performing classical works, including college concerts and short tours of Scandinavia.

A full-fledged recital at New York's Town Hall was considered essential for an aspiring American classical soloist, and in 1953, Huang managed to attract sponsorship for a program in that prestigious venue. The chances for a sizable audience were slim at best, but by happy coincidence his program and a Larry Adler concert were both scheduled to be presented at Town Hall within the space of a few days, and ads for both programs were carried in the same Sunday editions of the New York newspapers. Adler, along with much of his following, attended Huang's concert, and afterward Adler publicly proclaimed Huang as his chief rival. A reporter prodded Huang to describe the difference in their two styles. "We both play equally well," answered Huang diplomatically. "The difference is I play it *correctly.*"

Even after his Town Hall success, full acceptance as a classical harmonica soloist proved elusive for Huang. "I started at the bottom and am determined to stay there," Huang will jokingly state today, and there was a period when he was resigned to playing the Reno/Las Vegas circuit, performing mostly show tunes. But his steely ambition and his impeccable technique ultimately enabled him to achieve a remarkable level of success in the classical field.

The critics have applauded Huang's efforts. Theodore Strongin, reviewing a 1964 Huang recital in *The New York Times,* wrote that "Mr. Huang is very accomplished, both musically and technically. He phrased with sensitive taste, performed miracles of articulation, and did as much as he could to keep the evening vital." Strongin's counterpart at the *New York Herald Tribune* noted that Huang "had done his utmost to bring each of the works to life, and we have nothing but admiration for his enormous skill both as interpreter and technician."

Huang has appeared with major symphonies around the world, but—not surprisingly, given his passion for baroque music—he relishes performing with chamber orchestras. In 1974, the Grand Teton Music Festival featured Huang in an evening entitled "The Classical Harmonica in Concert," and for each of the festival's next five seasons Huang performed a new chamber music program.

Ever since his emigration, Huang had been struck by the fact that, unlike in China, qualified instruction on the harmonica was almost nonexistent in the United States. In 1957 he began offering the country's first accredited harmonica course, at the Turtle Bay Music School in New York City. The program he initiated is now carried on by a faculty consisting of Huang's former students. Since 1970, Huang has also held yearly harmonica seminars across the United States, attracting aspiring mouth organists from around the world.

Huang's passion for teaching is an extension of his belief that the harmonica's reputation as a lowly instrument is due more to the lack of serious harmonica artists than to any shortcomings built into the instrument. "All musical instruments have limits," he asserts. "But within the harmonica there are more possibilities than any individual can master. I never compare the harmonica to any other instrument. No words are needed on behalf of the harmonica. The image of the humble harmonica is automatically changed when it is performed musically and technically uncompromised at an equal level." Huang is a rigid traditionalist when it comes to baroque music, and he feels that he is one of the few harmonica artists who has the proper interpretative skills required to breathe life into such pieces. "Mozart should sound like Mozart and Bach should sound like Bach," he insists.

Huang has no such compunctions about tinkering with the design of his chosen instrument. Huang received some engineering education as a young man in China; he holds many patents for harmonica designs and was employed by Hohner for many years as a consultant. In the late 1960s, Hohner introduced Huang's "chordomonica," a chromatic instrument with two slides designed for playing chords. Huang became obsessed with eliminating the problem of air leakage in the chromatic harmonica, and in the early 1970s, Hohner unveiled a chromatic harmonica built to Huang's specifications, the Hohner-CBH model 2016. Huang says that he was striving for something akin to a woodwind sound in the design of the CBH. The CBH boasted separate, airtight reed channels and a body made completely of plastic. "The harmonica doesn't need a wood comb," claims Huang. "The reeds are mounted on a brass plate, so why would you consider wood necessary in a harmonica? The violin is a different instrument completely—its sounding board is made completely out of wood, and in this case, the kind of wood used would be very important."

After Richard Nixon moved to normalize relations with the People's Republic of China in the early 1970s, Huang became the first American artist invited to perform there by the Chinese Ministry of Culture. Accompanied by faculty members of the Shanghai Music Conservatory and members of the Beijing Philharmonic Orchestra, Huang and his custom-made silver harmonica gave chamber music concerts in Shanghai and Beijing. Huang offered an equal courtesy to Taiwan, appearing with the Taipei Philharmonic, and also performed with the Hong Kong Philharmonic.

Huang has since returned many times to China, and he claims that his concerts have been so well received that the mouth organ is now being widely used in school music programs and that there is a resurgence of interest in the harmonica in that country. But he found that the chromatic instrument was relatively unknown in his homeland; the Chinese still preferred the large, double-reed diatonic models. Huang entered into a business relationship with a harmonica factory in Shanghai and convinced his new partners to manufacture chromatic harmonicas so that his Chinese students would have proper instruments. In 1982 this arrangement was expanded by an agreement under which Huang would import Chinese-made harmonicas into Western markets under his own name. He and his brother Frank, a noted harmonica technician who had also worked for Hohner, formed their own company. Huang's competitively priced instruments are sold throughout the United States and Canada and have been endorsed by well-known harmonica players such as Norton Buffalo. Stevie Wonder was featured on a cover of *Rolling Stone* magazine holding a chromatic harmonica custom-made for him by Frank Huang. Although taking on their former employer is a daunting task, the Huang brothers are confident that their instruments will become popular with the general public. "Hohner has been making harmonicas for over one hundred and twenty-five years," notes Huang. "Give us a little more time and we will catch up."

Despite his growing business ventures, Cham-Ber Huang has continued to perform regularly and to influence his chosen genre. The noted American composer Robert Russell Bennett heard him in concert in the late 1970s and offered to compose a piece for harmonica and orchestra. When Huang protested that he could not possibly afford to commission such a work, Bennett offered to write the work for a fee of one dollar, and *Concerto for Harmonica and Orchestra* turned out to be the last major work by the composer before his death. Huang premiered the concerto with the Hong Kong Philharmonic that year.

Over the years Huang has developed a phenomenal technique in order to play the trills and other elements that he feels are true to the baroque concept of ornamentation. Whole-note trills, for instance, are particularly difficult to achieve on the chromatic harmonica, and Huang has found that they sound best if he holds his button finger steady and moves the harmonica. Playing mostly tongue-blocked, he claims to be able to play equally well out of either side of his mouth, and he has worked tirelessly to perfect the double stops required in baroque music. His desire to remain true to the integrity of pieces as written has often led him to play more than one harmonica during the course of a piece, and he has occasionally used specially tuned harmonicas for specific works. When rendering traditional Chinese classics such as "Moonlight and Creek," Huang uses harmonicas tuned to the traditional Chinese scale.

"It's up to us to prove it," he says. "Once I prove it, the prejudice against the harmonica is gone."

Stan Harper (1921–)

When asked why he is one of the few harmonica players who have managed to make a living playing the instrument, Stan Harper is apt to take the ever-present cigar out of his mouth and answer, "I outlived everybody." As opinionated as he is talented, Harper's name is always mentioned by his peers when the finest players are discussed.

He literally stumbled upon the instrument as a ten-year-old when he found a diatonic harmonica in the street. Providentially, he came across an instruction book soon after. Harper took the manual to a friend who played piano and with his help began to learn to read music and was introduced to classical music. Frustrated with the limitations of the Marine Band, he bought a ten-hole chromatic. Not long after he bought his first Hohner #270, which remains his instrument of choice.

Harper's early repertoire consisted of "simple Beethoven and Mozart" pieces, along with popular tunes of the era such as "Nola," "Flapperette," and "Dizzy Fingers." Harper attended a Harmonica Rascals performance in 1938, and he must have been one of the few youthful mouth organists who was not thrilled with their sound. Even at that impressionable age Harper's acutely sensitive ear rebelled against the music made by the premier harmonica group. "I was appalled by the funny noises and the flat sounds," he remembers. He was struck, however, with the possibilities of the harmonica group concept.

Harper claims that most of the finest harmonica players of that period came from Brooklyn and the Bronx, although he admits that Chicago and Philadelphia produced many fine mouth organists. He remembers being especially impressed by the Bronx's Philharmonicas, who could offer up material like "The Sorcerer's Apprentice." After winning a Central Park harmonica contest, Harper met most of New York's other young players, including Eddy Manson, George Fields, Charles Leighton, and Alan Pogson. These players, inspired by the popular music of the big band era, became remarkably sophisticated musicians and arrangers at tender ages. "Everybody read and everybody worked like dogs," Harper recalls vividly.

Along with Blackie Schackner and George Fields, Harper broke into vaudeville with Murray Lane's harmonica band, with whom he also appeared in a movie short. After a stint with a quartet called The Revelers, he became a solo performer. Along with many other harmonica players, he appeared often on Major Bowes's "Amateur Hour" radio program. "Bowes was basically a great exploiter of talent," Harper contends. "When you appeared on the radio show, you would get ten dollars apiece before the program went on the air, plus a fifty-cent meal ticket good at Bickford's. If you won, you went out on the road with his package show. You made fifty dollars a week tops and you had to pay all your expenses except for your train tickets." Bowes's popular program was essentially fraudulent; most of the performers were in fact professionals. Once Harper had to be yanked from the lineup of a Bowes program in Chicago when a movie short he had appeared in was shown just prior to the stage show.

The advent of World War II found Harper playing in a duo with Eddie Shu. They enlisted in the army together and were assigned to a special unit put together to entertain the troops. Harper gained invaluable experience writing arrangements for the outfit's topflight orchestra and performing classical selections accompanied by any one of the number of excellent pianists in the troupe.

After the war, Harper formed a group with Pro Robbins on bass and Pete Delisante on chord called The Three Harpers. But vaudeville and the nightclubs were dying. "I kept studying music between shows and during layoffs," Harper has said. "I would practice for hours, but not popular music. . . . I always played classically for my own pleasure." Harper disbanded The Three Harpers and began working as a solo performer and as a studio musician in New York. He worked as a staff musician with the J. Walter Thompson advertising agency and then spent several years creating musical backgrounds for radio and television.

Harper continued to play the harmonica; in the mid-1950s, he was the organizer of an informal practice ensemble that he feels was the best harmonica group ever. Harper, Charles Leighton, Victor Pankowitz, and Frank Mitkowski made up the chromatic section, Harry Halicki played chord, and Dave Doucette held down the bass parts. A few homemade recordings of their practice sessions were made, but unfortunately this all-star aggregation was never captured on record.

Today, Harper still performs frequently. Although he is a fixture on the cruise ship circuit, his many years of classical study and training have enabled him to present several ambitious programs of baroque music in Carnegie Hall recitals in recent years. The Musical Heritage Society has released three albums of Harper's classical and semiclassical recordings in recent years, including a stellar compilation of Fritz Kreisler compositions and an album of Bach and Vivaldi interpretations.

Harper is disdainful of the "blues harp" phenomenon, which he views as a regression. "When I was a kid, everybody played blues on the diatonic—all that screeching and growling and stuff. I feel that playing has regressed back to the kinds of things everybody was doing forty years ago. To be honest, the glory days were the late 1930s. If I was going to do a session today with six harmonica players, I'd have to use the same guys I played with in the thirties. To the younger players, I say buy a chromatic harmonica and respect it. It's a wonderful instrument. Your diatonic harmonica is fine, with its blue notes, wah-wahs, and shakes. It's a part of Americana, but do not lose sight of the fact that it's just one small segment of the musical picture. Listen to the great artists on the instruments, both in classical and jazz. Develop your musicality, learn to read, and study because all this is for one purpose: to make good music."

In 1986, Harper sat still for an interview with Alex Fogel, editor of *Harmonica Happenings,* the SPAH newsletter. Fogel asked him whether he had faced any resistance from the classical music community. "I don't think you get resistance from fine musicians. In fact, I think you might get respect because they would recognize the inherent difficulties in playing such a small, carefully crafted instrument. No one has ever reached the full potential on any instrument. I don't know if the harmonica offers more in tone quality and variations than any other instrument, but if it doesn't, it runs a close second. The chromatic is a superlative instrument. It also has a unique tonal quality all its own.

"As a soloist, I've done numerous concerts at Carnegie Hall. These recitals with some of the major symphony orchestras have been exceedingly gratifying. There is nothing in the world like having an entire orchestra behind you and you know you're playing well.

"I want to keep working. I do hope I can one day make as good a living playing fine music that I enjoy without ever having to resort to 'Tiger Rag,' the *Poet and Peasant Overture,* or *Bolero.* People often ask me if I've ever had regrets about choosing the harmonica for a career. . . . Well, let me tell you that there are a million things I may be sorry about, but I'm never sorry about the harmonica. I might have liked a lucrative sideline—like being a thief."

Tommy Reilly (1919–)

Robert Henderson once wrote in the *London Daily Telegraph* that "it is difficult to see how anyone could possibly resist the stunning virtuosity and remarkable musicianship of Tommy Reilly." It is a tribute to the diversity of our species that some, at least, have managed.

Reilly was once accosted in his dressing room after a performance by a man who sputtered, "Oh, I enjoyed your concert very much. But tell me, can you play the harmonica properly?" Reilly paused only briefly before he picked up his solid silver chromatic harmonica and launched into "Swanee River." "That's it!" the man cried triumphantly.

Among the select few who make up his peer group in the classical harmonica field, Tommy Reilly is generally given the nod as the finest player. He has been the most frequently recorded of the classical mouth organists, giving him unequaled exposure. "If anyone can do a Galway for the harmonica, it is Tommy Reilly," London's *Hi-Fi News* has noted. Reilly has been appointed MBE (Member of the Order of the British Empire) by Queen Elizabeth II, one of the few personalities from the musical world (and the only harmonica player) to be so honored.

Tommy Reilly was born in Guelph, Ontario. His father, James Reilly, was so passionate about the harmonica that he resigned a commission in the Canadian army to devote himself to the instrument. At the age of eight Tommy began a long relationship with the violin, an association that he credits with having a profound influence on his harmonica playing. Three years later he took up the harmonica and joined his father's Elmdale Harmonica Band. In 1935, James Reilly moved his family to England, where he led the Harmonica League of Great Britain during the 1930s and wrote several instruction methods and music books that were widely distributed by the Hohner Company.

Never happy as a student, Reilly set out to see Europe as soon as he left school at the age of eighteen. Nineteen thirty-nine found Reilly traveling with a circus troupe in Germany. "I was arrested just before the war by the Gestapo. . . . I was in the *polizei* presidium in Leipzig for some time. And then I went into a prison camp. I was in four different camps. I was sent to an eleven-hundred-year-old fortress in Bavaria. After a while, I received my suitcases, in which I had some harmonicas. . . . I also had my violin with me, and we had our own orchestra there. When they didn't have an oboe or a clarinet in there, I played the part on the harmonica. About two years later, I got chatting with this German welfare officer, who was a *Canadian* German. I had received a Canadian Red Cross parcel with a half pound of coffee; at that time, you could practically buy a hotel in Germany with a half pound of coffee! I gave him the coffee with the express understanding that he would get me harmonicas from Hohner's factory in

Germany. And he got me two dozen chromatic instruments."

"This gave me almost unlimited time to study the instrument and find out how it worked," Reilly has recounted in an interview with a Canadian newspaper. "I learned what could be done with it and what couldn't. By the time the war was over and I was back in London, I had pretty well got the hang of it." Reilly turned often to his training as a violinist while he was mastering the mouth organ. "As there were no teachers," he told *Records and Recording,* "I studied to put onto the harmonica, from Heifetz's records, trills, short vibrato, and generally his kind of feeling. He's always been my idol instrumentally. He has a sort of towering eminence—the great master of his instrument." As Reilly once noted in a BBC interview, "Sucking and blowing—you can't do that because when you hear a great violinist, for instance, he changes from a down-bow sometimes to an up-bow, and it's indiscernible. You can't tell. And you must be able to play the harmonica so that when you're playing a line—is it blow or draw?"

After being released from the prison camp in 1945, Reilly returned to England and tried to establish himself as a musician. "I played on 'Variety Bandbox' and all those sort of things and 'Worker's Playtimes.' I had a very hard time at first. One of the biggest things against me, in England, was my name—it sounded like an Irish comic."

Reilly's recording career began inauspiciously in 1951 with the release of his version of "Bibbidi-Bobbidi-Boo" on Parlophone. That same year Hohner released a record of him performing Schumann's "Traumerei" and pieces by Bach and Boccherini; he was not to make another classical recording until 1971. In the meantime there were dozens of recordings of popular favorites, Irish melodies, movie sound-track themes, a Latin-flavored album (which spawned a hit single, "Cumana"), and his first American record, *Dale Robertson Presents Western Classics* on RCA. Many of Reilly's early recordings were produced by George Martin, who would later become famous as the studio genius behind the Beatles.

Reilly contends that early in his career the inherent subtlety of his technique cost him the recognition due him as a master of his instrument. "The way I play the harmonica, on the lighter side, has been a disadvantage to me. People say, 'I love that record, but you don't play the harmonica very much.' The way I play they don't even recognize the instrument. So on future records we just put 'Tommy Reilly and His Orchestra.' "

Although he has appeared in concert with the likes of Bing Crosby, Oscar Peterson, Barbra Streisand, and Marlene Dietrich, Reilly strove from the outset to make a name for himself on the classical stage. Nineteen fifty-one not only saw the release of his first pop record, but the dedication to Reilly of a concerto for harmonica and orchestra by Michael Spivakovsky, which Reilly premiered at the Festival of Britain. "I started getting dates after that. Then I went to the Continent and I've been going over ever since then. I've found, quite honestly, that it's much better for me working over there."

Like many professional mouth organists, Reilly had always felt frustrated with the design of the instrument. For years he badgered Hohner to build him an instrument based on the three-octave #270 chromatic but with a comb and cover plates crafted out of solid silver. Reilly felt that silver would not only be more stable and durable than wood, tin, and brass, but that it would improve the harmonica's tone and its dynamic range. Reilly also wanted the instrument's reeds attached by screws instead of rivets so that they could be easily replaced. In 1966, Reilly went to a silversmith in Covent Garden in London and had a custom mouth organ made to his specifications. Reilly first played the instrument in public at the Royal Festival Hall in June of 1967 with the BBC Concert Orchestra. Reilly took the instrument to the Hohner factory in Trossingen, and the firm agreed to manufacture and market it as the Silver Concerto model. Hohner made gifts of its first and second Silver Concertos to Reilly and his manager, the outstanding Norwegian harmonicist Sigmund Groven. Reilly stands behind his contribution to harmonica design. "The sound bounces off silver, it's louder and it's got more quality, especially on the top notes," he contends. "Most harmonica bodies are made of wood, and the longer you play them the worse they get, because the wood starts to swell. The silver one, it warms up after an hour or two, and the longer you play it, the better it gets."

In 1977, Reilly recorded an album with one of Europe's most prestigious chamber orchestras, the Academy of St. Martin in the Fields. The recording, which featured four original works, received a good deal of critical acclaim and was followed by a second album with the Academy's group. Asked to comment on Reilly's artistry, the orchestra's conductor, Sir Neville Mariner, noted that "many of the ingredients of the Academy's original intentions are embodied in Tommy's musicianship: technically he achieves remarkable virtuosity with a minimum of fuss. Musically he exploits his instrument with refinement and bravura, and ultimately it does not seem to matter what he plays, but how he plays it."

Thanks to his varied and extensive experience, Reilly can serve up impressive programs in a variety of musical settings. "When I play with orchestras," says Reilly, "I never play transcriptions, only pieces written expressly for the harmonica, because no matter how well you play a transcription of a major work, you're always going to get criticized for it." Reilly also often appears with string quartets or as part of a duo with either harp or piano.

In an interview with Toronto's *FM Guide* in 1982, Reilly spelled out his preferred arrangement for symphonic performances. "I like to use one mike and one speaker, between me and the conductor, so he hears me immediately, and you've still got the real sound of the instrument, just slightly amplified for the hall. I don't like to use the big public address systems at all. With those bloody big speakers on the side of the hall, the conductor hears it late, the basses and fiddles on the side hear it before he does, and the instrument itself sounds like a Wurlitzer!"

These days Reilly's concert calendar is filled months in advance, although he works regularly as a studio musician, a role he appreciates. "Session musicians are not like members of a set orchestra. Not only do you have to play the music right away, you've got to give an instant performance. No practice—performance. And that's why I have great respect for session players. And it's something that I'm very proud of, that I am accepted in the session world."

Reilly contends that the onus is really on the harmonica player in the classical world. He feels that if there were more trained musicians among the ranks of mouth organists that composers might be more inclined to write for the instrument. Accordingly, for several years Reilly lent his talents to an effort to create such a base of expertise. He wrote an instruction method for Hohner in the early 1970s, taught at the Guildhall School of Music and Drama in London, and gave harmonica seminars in Japan. He was not particularly inspired by these experiences.

"When I first started teaching—I tell you this most sincerely—I really thought that there were dozens of harmonica players who played just like I did," he claims. "And when I started teaching—I'm not joking—I was appalled at the standard. It was so terrible. There was no music behind any of the ones I taught.

"I found everybody moved their head. Well, the head's very unpredictable. You should move the harmonica. And they used to separate each note. When you've got a long note, you should be moving to the next before you finish playing so you get a legato. I find that you must relax very much when you're playing anything technical, anything fast. I use the throat for vibrato. It's more like the close vibrato you get on a violin."

Reilly is exasperated by the classical harmonica controversy. "It's all so stupid—you either make music or you don't, no matter what you play. I'm a great believer in myself, and I answer such comments not by talking, but by playing. Obviously, when I was younger, I wanted to prove something. Now, I don't try to prove anything at all. I think of myself as a musician who uses the harmonica as a vehicle to express myself musically, and I think the instrument, played well, has a lot of color and a lot going for it. I don't carry any torch for the harmonica. . . . It's a vehicle for me, and it's the best vehicle I know to express myself musically."

Richard Morrison in the *London Times* agrees. "I am convinced," he has written, "that Tommy Reilly is the only harmonica player worthy of the title 'genius.'"

Robert Bonfiglio (1955–)

Robert Bonfiglio's original musical heroes were blues harp players like Rice Miller, Junior Wells, and Paul Butterfield. These days, the rising star among classical harmonicists invokes a new roster of role models that includes such performers as guitarist Andrés Segovia, flautist James Galway, and trumpeter Wynton Marsalis—crossover successes who Bonfiglio implies would look favorably on his eclectic programs, which combine classical pieces, pop music, heavy doses of Americana, and the blues.

Bonfiglio was born and raised in Iowa City, Iowa. Outside of an uncle who played banjo and sax with Woody Herman in Milwaukee, the Bonfiglio family wasn't especially musical. Bonfiglio first played the diatonic harmonica at thirteen. In a few years he was playing in local blues bands. After high school, Bonfiglio enrolled at the University of Arizona as a chemistry major. He had become interested in the possibilities of the chromatic harmonica, and in the early 1970s he traveled to Trossingen, Germany, to attend a seminar hosted by

Cham-Ber Huang. Deciding that his future lay with music, Bonfiglio moved to New York City to study with Huang.

The blues player developed a passion for playing classical music. "There is as much emotion in playing Bach as there is in playing the blues," Bonfiglio has said. "When you lean into a note in Bach, it's the same kind of emotion as when you lean into a note in the blues. It's a different form, but the emotion is the same. People tend to think of classical music as refined, but there are portions of concertos that are crude. And there are blues harmonica solos by James Cotton that are as light and delicate as anything you can imagine."

Bonfiglio enrolled at the Mannes School of Music. Like every other music school in the country, Mannes did not offer a harmonica major, so Bonfiglio concentrated on composition. ("My compositions were like a combination of Stravinsky and the Rolling Stones.") He eventually earned a master's degree from the Manhattan School of Music. Bonfiglio kept honing his harmonica technique by studying for ten years with Andrew Lolya, first flautist for the New York City Ballet.

After music school, Bonfiglio supported himself by doing session work in New York, lending his harmonica playing to countless commercials, the sound tracks of television programs, and the feature films *Kramer vs. Kramer* and *Places in the Heart*. He also contributed to pop singer Chaka Khan's first solo album. But Bonfiglio's goal was always the concert stage: "I think it's much nicer to have an audience hang on every note, as opposed to being the background for some commercial."

Bonfiglio's big break as a budding concert performer came in 1986, when he gave the premiere performance of Henry Cowell's *Harmonica Concerto* with the Brooklyn Philharmonic. Cowell had written the piece in 1962 for John Sebastian, but Sebastian died without having performed it. "It's full of Japanese melodies," notes Bonfiglio. "At the time he wrote it, Cowell was into koto music. It's very esoteric, but very beautiful."

Bonfiglio gained more exposure when he played with guitarist Fred Hand on the CBS recording *Baroque and on the Street*. RCA, whose commercial success with James Galway had fired Bonfiglio's imagination, signed the young harmonicist to a recording contract. His debut solo recording for the label, on which he was accompanied by Gerard Schwarz and the New York Chamber Orchestra, featured the music of Brazilian composer Villa-Lobos, whose works he enjoys: "They are great for harmonica because they are a cross of African influences and Brazilian popular music." Villa-Lobos's *Harmonica Concerto*—another piece originally written for John Sebastian—has become the centerpiece of Bonfiglio's concert programs.

Bonfiglio's next recording, the 1992 album *Through the Raindrops* on High Harmony Records, landed on the *Billboard* charts. Conceived as a vehicle to showcase his crossover potential, it features Bonfiglio backed by strings, synthesizer, and percussion and showcased original works as well as well-known pop selections.

Bonfiglio keeps up a punishing schedule. He performs about seventy classical concerts a year and is now a member of the Mannes faculty. He and his wife, flautist Clare Hoffman, conduct the annual Grand Canyon Chamber Music Festival. Since 1986, Bonfiglio has appeared as a soloist at such eminent venues as New York's Carnegie Hall, the Hollywood Bowl, and Boston's Symphony Hall, and with such orchestras as the Los Angeles Philharmonic, the Boston Pops, the Milwaukee Symphony, the Denver Chamber Orchestra, the San Antonio Symphony, the New York Pops, the Brooklyn Philharmonic, the New Philharmonic of New Jersey, and the Spokane Symphony. He has also toured extensively with his own small group.

Like Tommy Reilly, Bonfiglio prefers to stick to the genuine harmonica repertoire: "There's plenty to play. There's no need to search out transcriptions. I hate doing them. I'd rather play a Roy Orbison medley than do a bad transcription. It's my feeling that the harmonica is sort of trapped in this vicious circle. There aren't enough good harmonica players because there isn't enough good harmonica music, and there isn't enough good harmonica music because there aren't enough good harmonica players."

Bonfiglio's recital program features works by Dowland, Bach, Mozart, Villa-Lobos, Bartók, and John Lennon. With string trios he typically performs works by Bach, McDowell, Stamitz, and others. For his appearances with symphony orchestras he offers Bach pieces; the harmonica works of Villa-Lobos, Cowell, and Gordon Jacobs; works by Hovhaness and Bartók; Gershwin's "Summertime," Prelude No. 2, and "Fascinating Rhythm"; a medley of Stephen Foster tunes arranged by Boston Pops arranger Eric Knight; Sousa's "Harmonica Wizard"; Steven Sondheim's "Send in the Clowns"; and a turn-of-the-century orchestral hoedown by David Guion entitled *The Harmonica Player*.

For an encore, he typically reappears onstage with a diatonic harmonica to perform his "Tribute to Sonny Boy Williamson," an all-purpose blues mélange that includes a train imitation.

Bonfiglio likes to turn the prevailing wisdom on its head and contend that choosing the harmonica has been an advantage in his career as a classical artist, noting that the general public is not intimidated by a mouth organist. "People always ask me, isn't it unusual to play the harmonica? It isn't unusual, not with all the people who play harmonica in America. What's unusual is to play the cello. People who come to my concerts don't usually listen to classical music. They come to listen to the harmonica, and they get to hear these wonderful classical tunes. I think I represent the real world, and I like to think I am helping people back into symphony orchestra seats."

Bonfiglio knows the limitations of his instrument. "Like the guitar, it buzzes and balks, and because of the blow-and-draw technique you do have difficulties with legato." He admits that volume can be a problem, especially when he performs with orchestras. "I have learned to get more power from the harmonica, although I use amplification for concertos and sometimes for chamber music. But I'm louder than a guitar, and if I focus it right, I can play comfortably with a string quartet."

He prefers to describe the advantages offered by the harmonica. "Number one, there are many major works—for example, more than a dozen concertos. Number two, the harmonica can do all sorts of things other wind instruments can't—it can play octaves, chords, double stops, and it can play pianissimo in the high register. More than that, you have total control over the sound—it's literally all in your hands."

Bonfiglio seems more concerned about the future of classical music than of the harmonica. "If classical music doesn't change its face in some way, it's going to lose its audience. Classical music is in crisis because it is competing with pop music, and we're losing. . . . I hate to say it, but the United States doesn't care about the arts, doesn't support the arts. The city of Vienna spends more money on music than the entire National Endowment for the Arts."

He has tried to use the harmonica's proletarian image to his advantage rather than rail against it. "If a harmonica player isn't American, who is?" he once responded when asked to comment about Larry Adler's political problems during the 1950s. "I can't think of any other instrument that has more of an American connotation than the harmonica. You think of a lonely crying sound, a distant locomotive, cowboys on the plains, the blues. An instrument that evokes that is wonderful. This is an instrument that cuts across boundaries. It's a humble instrument that sings of loneliness. It's America."

The Chimes Family

Epilogue

Robert Bonfiglio is right, of course. The archetypal harmonica players—the cowboy, the bluesman—and their trademark train whistles and lonesome wails have been folded irrecovably into an even broader myth: America itself. "There's nothing like the first time you open a harp box and you make contact with all that folklore," says Magic Dick. "It captivates a certain special thing that other instruments just don't have."

It's a curse and a blessing. Mechanically, the harmonica *is* a simple instrument, and it can serve as a handy prop for anyone wishing to pose as a musician. (Each time I open the rotogravure section of the Sunday newspaper, there is that ad: "Play The Harmonica In One

Easy Lesson . . . Anyone Can Learn! No Musical Talent Necessary!") Its track record as the instrument of the people makes the mouth organ an irresistible metaphor for aspiring poets of the proletariat. (Robert Service's insufferable "The Song of the Mouth Organ" dubs the instrument "the Steinway of strange mischief and mischance" and "the Stradivarius of blank defeat," and identifies its realm as "the end of all things known, where God's rubbish-heap is thrown.")

But in the hands of the players profiled here the harmonica has been anything but humble. These wizards belong on the flip side of the American Dream: the "lone wolf" America of Edison, the Wright Brothers, Elvis, Muhammad Ali, Bobby Fischer. These are musicians who would not be denied. Take Henry Whitter, who traveled hundreds of miles to arrive uninvited at the Manhattan offices of a major record company and proclaim himself the best harmonica player in creation. Don Les, who began life by being pronounced dead, spent forty years mastering a diatonic jazz style before getting the opportunity to showcase it in public. After singlehandedly besting the conventional show business wisdom, Larry Adler took on the whole System. Paul Butterfield hurdled a cultural chasm, the expanse of which is hard to imagine now. And not all the barriers breached by these players were musical: The lack of charted opportunities for harmonica players may not have seemed such an obstacle for Sonny Terry and Stevie Wonder, who were born poor, black, and blind, or to Little Walter and James Cotton, who were making their own way in the world as mere children.

Some sacrificed their talents to orneriness or to another side of their powerful personalities. After his disappointment at the hands of the Grand Ole Opry, DeFord Bailey stubbornly refused all musical offers, preferring to work in a shoeshine stand, where at least he was his own boss. Mel Lyman's aura proved so magnetic that it became the focus of a group of true believers. Others turned their willfulness into an intimidating work ethic. Charlie McCoy racked up more than six thousand studio sessions over a fifteen-year period. George Fields spent years painstakingly transcribing Bach's keyboard pieces for a half dozen different harmonicas. Tommy Reilly combatted the awful tedium of prison camp by mastering the chromatic mouth organ. Tommy Morgan dedicated the better part of five years to getting a nearly imperceptible waver out of his tone. And Howard Levy literally bent the instrument to his pianistic will.

The latest incarnation of this tendency toward free thinking can be seen in the recent flurry of tinkering with the diatonic harmonica by the players themselves, efforts that first went public when Lee Oskar introduced his replaceable reed plates in his diatonics. Hohner now markets Steve Baker's SBS diatonic, a 14-hole model that offers an extra bottom octave. In the last few months, several mouth organists have been awarded patents for their variations on the diatonic— Magic Dick and Pierre Beauregard for their new note arrangements, Rick Epping for an instrument (originally conceived of by Will Scarlett) with additional "enabling" reeds that allow all the notes to be bent, Ron Schille for a MIDI harmonica, and Dr. Henry Bahnson, a professor of surgery at the University of Pittsburgh and a disciple of Howard Levy, for a harmonica on which players can achieve overblows more easily by pushing a slide button to damp the blow reeds. And most of the design changes reflected in Hohner's several new chromatic models were suggested by players. But even in the face of this current whirl of invention, tradition remains supreme. The Marine Band, a model introduced by Matthias Hohner in 1896 and the favorite of players as disparate as Woodrow Wilson, DeFord Bailey, and Little Walter Jacobs, is still the most popular harmonica in America.

Charles Leighton gets no argument from me when he contends that the players have exceeded their instrument. The happy mystery is that there is no end to them: There will be great, original players in the future, and the past holds surprises for even the most obsessive student of harmonica history. As I was finishing the first draft of this book, my friend Jack Cook sent me a tape of harmonica music culled from his collection of old 78s. Midway through it, I was surprised to hear a fine blues instrumental performed by a quartet led by one Rhythm Willie, a remarkably jazzy diatonic player with a fluid, whistling tone. I quizzed Jack and other blues experts, but nobody had any information about him. Then a few weeks ago another friend, John Svatek, gave me a CD of rare harmonica blues recordings made between 1929 and 1940, and I was treated to four more cuts by this phantom, all as impressive as the first one I had heard. The liner notes that accompanied the disc told me only that Rhythm Willie's full name seems to have been W. E. Burton and that he had recorded the tunes in Chicago in 1940.

Somewhere out there are authorities, friends, or relatives that could shed more light on Rhythm Willie, but for now I'm going to leave him among the mysteries. Maybe I've lost some the investigative zeal I had when I started writing this book; I prefer to believe that I've managed to retain my appreciation for the fact that beautiful music can thrill anyone—the ignorant *or* the expert. When I came to a spontaneous understanding that night in 1968 on the dance floor of Eagles Auditorium that I was going to try to learn to make the harmonica sound something like it did in James Cotton's hands, I knew next to nothing about the man, the harmonica, or even the blues. By the time I met Charles Leighton, I was solidly familiar with his instrument, the work of his peers, and with much of his repertoire, but his recordings were as much a revelation to me as Cotton's music had been twenty years earlier. So I'm more than satisfied to simply enjoy Rhythm Willie. Whoever he was, he and I—and everyone else who has ever been moved by this singular instrument—have something in common.

Selected
Discography

The following discography is not meant to be an exhaustive listing of harmonica recordings but rather a list of seminal studio efforts by the artists featured in this book. When possible, I have consulted with the players themselves, but much of this inventory consists of my personal favorites. With considerable assistance from Frank Scott of Roots and Rhythm, I have tried to list current releases, but I have also cited outstanding out-of-print recordings [denoted by (OP) following their titles] when alternatives were not available or when I felt they were too important not to mention. And there is always the chance that some of these titles will be rereleased.

For fans of blues and country harmonica, Roots and Rhythm (6921 Stockton Avenue, El Cerrito, CA 94530) is an unbeatable source for anyone interested in all types of roots music and ethnic recordings. Elderly Instruments (1100 N. Washington, P.O. Box 14210, Lansing, MI 48901) carries an extensive listing of blues and country recordings as well as a comprehensive assortment of instructional harmonica tapes, videos, and books. County Sales (P.O. Box 191, Floyd, VA 24091) is an excellent source for recordings of country, bluegrass, and old-timey music. These outlets publish regularly updated catalogs that are both extensive and informative.

Getting your hands on the recordings of the best of the diatonic players can involve some detective work, but those of the great chromatic players are even harder to come by. The F. & R. Farrell Company (P.O. Box 133, Harrisburg, OH 43126) carries cassette tapes of many of the best chromatic harmonicists who are currently active, as well as recordings of diatonic aces. Tapes available from Farrell are denoted by a † symbol.

The fascinating recordings of the early harmonica bands, such as Borrah Minevitch and his Harmonica Rascals, Carl Freed's Harmonica Harlequins, and the Cappy Barra Band, have not been commercially available for many years, but tapes of them have been circulated among harmonica enthusiasts. Making contacts among harmonica collectors is only one of the many good reasons for joining the Society for the Preservation and Advancement of the Harmonica (SPAH) (P.O. Box 865, Troy, Michigan 58099), or Great Britain's National Harmonica League (c/o Chairman Colin Mort, Rivendell, High Street, Shirrell Heath, Southampton SO2 2JN, England).

Mouth organists can further slack their thirst for information by subscribing to specialty publications. The *Harmonica Information Publication (HIP)* (203 14th Avenue, San Francisco, CA 94118-1007) is a wide-ranging, well-written magazine that covers all styles and models and balances a strong interest in recent innovations with excellent instructional materials. *Mississippi Saxophone* (Delta Publications, P.O. Box 12185, Eugene, OR 97440) is aimed at fans of amplified blues harp. The *American Harmonica Associates Newsletter* (2362 W. Territorial Road, Battle Creek, MI 49015-4956) has been a window on the many facets of the harmonica world for many years.

The Harmonica Bands
The Harmonicats

Jerry Murad's Harmonicats Greatest Hits, Columbia CS 9511 (cassette and CD). Includes their two biggest hits, "Peg o' My Heart" and

"Cherry Pink and Apple Blossom White." The definitive collection of the Harmonicats' accessible, echo-laden best.

Harmonica Rhapsody, Columbia CS 9141 (LP) (OP). The band's own favorite. Pieces by Tchaikovsky, Borodin, Liszt, Bizet, and Chopin, among others, with Pete Pedersen contributing the intelligent arrangements as well as some fine chromatic playing.

The Stagg McMann Trio

The Legendary Stagg McMann Trio, EM Productions, LR 1035 (LP) (OP). One side of this remarkable, unique album consists of jazz and pop standards arranged to showcase the group's daring approach to the trio concept; the other shows off their adaptations of classical material, lead player Hugh McCaskey's forté.

The Soloists
Larry Adler

Larry Adler, Music for Pleasure (EMI) MFP 1408 (LP) (OP). This British album includes Adler's most memorable film themes ("Genevieve Waltz" and "Le Grisbi"), four tunes recorded with Django Reinhardt, and a recording of "Malaguena," one of Adler's vaudeville showstoppers.

In Concert, Capitol 64134 (CD). Adler tackles the war-horses (Gershwin's *Rhapsody in Blue*, Ravel's *Bolero*, Chagrin's *Roumanian Fantasy*, Bizet's *Carmen Fantasy*, among others) in front of a full orchestra.

Pete Pedersen

Music and Memories (cassette).† The harmonica player's harmonica player, Pedersen's masterful playing breathes life into even the most familiar tunes in this collection of standards.

Alan "Blackie" Schackner

Best of the Light Classics (cassette).† The irrepressible harmonica veteran doing what he does best: Mozart, the *Hora Staccato*, Bach.

• • •

Folk Music

Various

Great Harp Players (1927–30): The Complete Recordings of Francis & Sowell, El Watson, Palmer McAbee, Freeman Stowers, Blues Bird-heads, Alfred Lewis in Chronological Order, Document 5100 (CD).

Old-time harmonica music in the rural, biracial tradition, with Blues Birdhead's startling jazz diatonic playing in the bargain. A fascinating collection of marvelous between-the-wars harmonica recordings.

Sonny Terry

Sonny Terry—The Folkways Years, 1944–1963, Smithsonian Folkways ROSF 40033 (CD). A fine new anthology of this brilliant stylist's classic recordings for Folkways.

Mark Graham

Natural Selections, Front Hall Records FHR-037 (LP). An outstanding solo album with equal doses of beautiful harmonica playing and hilarious songwriting. Available from Eternal Doom Music, 4922 46th Ave. S., Seattle, WA 98118.

Open House, Kevin Burke, Green Linnet 1122 (cassette and CD). Exquisite ensemble playing of Irish music from Graham and fiddler Kevin Burke.

Country Music

Herman Crook

Opry Old Timers: Sam & Kirk McGee and The Crook Brothers, Starday SLP 182 (LP) (OP). Crook leads his excellent group—including Jerry Rivers, Hank Williams's fiddle player—through seven great fiddle tunes and old-time pieces.

DeFord Bailey

Harmonica Showcase: DeFord Bailey and D. H. "Bert" Bilbro 1927–31: Complete Recordings in Chronological Order, Matchbox MS 218 (LP) (OP). Bailey's complete Brunswick and RCA Victor recordings, with Bilbro's fine sides as an added bonus.

Lonnie Glosson

All Harmonica: Lonnie Glosson and Wayne Raney, Old Homestead 305 (LP). Glosson's finest harmonica pieces plus the mouth organ instrumentals that Raney recorded for King. Available from Lonnie Glosson, 303 N. Valley Road, Searcy, AR 72143.

Wayne Raney

Songs From The Hills, King 588 (LP, cassette and CD). Raney's classic harmonica instrumentals.

When They Let the Hammer Down, The Delmore Brothers, Bear Family 15167 (LP). Raney's mouth organ is prominently featured on these beautiful recordings by one of the most talented duos in country music history.

Jimmie Riddle

Country Harmonica, Cumberland MGC29511 (mono) or SRC69511 (stereo) (LP) (OP). A lively set of country standards performed on the chromatic harmonica.

Roy Acuff, Bear Family BCD 15652 (CD). This two-CD compilation of Acuff's 1950s recordings includes many cuts featuring Riddle's dynamic and tuneful harmonica work.

Charlie McCoy

The Real McCoy, Columbia 47086 (cassette and CD). McCoy's outstanding debut solo album set the standard for the many hit albums that followed.

Don Brooks

This Time, Waylon Jennings, RCA ACL1-0539 (LP) (OP). Brooks's rich, bluesy tone and brilliant musicianship are in evidence on several cuts, notably on the title track.

Mickey Raphael

Stardust Memories, Willie Nelson, CBS 35305. Raphael has been featured on dozens of Nelson's recordings, but this album of standards includes some of his best harp solos.

• • •

The Blues

The Memphis Jug Bands

The Memphis Jug Band: The Complete Recordings in Chronological Order, Document 5021, 5022, and 5023 (CD).

The Memphis Jug Band, Yazoo 1067 (cassette and CD). A less extensive but excellent anthology of the recordings of the most popular of the jug bands.

Cannon's Jug Stompers, Volume 1, Document 5032 (CD), and *Cannon's Jug Stompers and Noah Lewis, Volume 2*, Document 5033 (CD). Both volumes together contain the total studio output of the Jug Stompers; Noah Lewis's sensational solo sides are featured in Volume 2.

Memphis Harp and Jug Blowers, Blues Documents 6028 (CD). Some of Jed Davenport's best mouth harp work plus recordings by Little Buddy Doyle that some contend feature a nine-year-old Walter Horton on harmonica.

Jaybird Coleman

Jaybird Coleman and the Birmingham Jug Band, Blues Documents 5140 (CD). Coleman's complete solo recordings—fascinating, compelling examples of the blues in one of its earliest and rawest forms—coupled with his later jug band efforts.

John Lee "Sonny Boy" Williamson

The Complete Recordings of John Lee "Sonny Boy" Williamson, Blues Documents 5055, 5056, 5057, 5058, and 5059 (CD). The entire recorded legacy of the first blues harmonica star, who played a pivotal role in the creation of the fabled Chicago blues sound.

Throw a Boogie Woogie, RCA 9599 (cassette and CD). Several fine sides by Williamson as well as eight cuts by Big Joe Williams with Williamson accompanying him on harmonica.

Rice Miller

King Biscuit Time, Arhoolie 310 (CD). An ear-opening compilation of Miller's pre-Chess recordings made for the Trumpet label in the early 1950s. Essential for blues harp fans.

Down and Out Blues, Chess 9257 (LP and cassette) or Chess 31272 (CD), and *Real Folk Blues*, Chess 9272 (LP, cassette, and CD). Reissues of two classic Chess LPs from the early 1960s. Also essential.

Little Walter Jacobs

The Best of Little Walter, Volume I, Chess 9192 (LP, cassette, and CD). Jacobs's most well-known sides. If you buy one blues harmonica album, make it this one. Over twenty years of sessions, Jacobs's recordings were consistently brilliant in terms of both musicianship and originality.

Hate to See You Go, Chess 9321 (LP, cassette, and CD). More exquisite recordings from the towering genius of modern blues harmonica.

The Best of Muddy Waters, Chess 9255 (LP and cassette), or 31266 (CD). Incontrovertible proof that the partnership of Little Walter and Muddy Waters was one of the most providential and productive couplings in the history of American music.

Walter Horton

Mouth Harp Maestro, Flair 86297 (CD). The King of Tone's first recordings were also some of the legendary Sam Phillips's first production efforts.

Big Walter Horton with Carey Bell, Alligator 4702 (cassette and CD). Horton and Carey Bell sometimes step on each other, but Eddie Taylor's guitar accompaniment, some excellent material and Horton's full-bodied playing are worth it.

Can't Keep Lovin' You, Blind Pig BP-71484 (cassette and CD). This anthology, culled from some of Horton's last sessions, shows that his wondrous skills never faded.

James Cotton

James Cotton Blues Band, Verve/Folkways FT/FTSA-3023 (LP) (OP). Cotton's debut LP is nicely balanced between knockout harmonica showcases like "Blues In My Sleep" and vocal sendups like "Turn On Your Lovelight."

Pure Cotton, Verve FTS-3038 (LP) (OP). The greatest of Cotton's many bands at the height of its power, plus his signature harmonica instrumental, "The Creeper."

Mighty Long Time, Antone's ANT15 (cassette and CD). This vital, recent recording displays a living legend in top form amidst an all-star supporting cast.

Junior Wells

Messin' with the Kid, Paula Records PCD 03 (CD). Portrait of the harpist as a young man. A collection of Wells's great Chief sides recorded from 1957–1963.

Hoodoo Man Blues, Delmark DS-612 (cassette and CD). One of the most influential modern blues albums. Wells's soul/blues singing style and punchy harmonica technique have never been captured more successfully in the studio.

Jimmy Reed

Speak the Lyrics to Me Mama Reed, Vee Jay 705 (cassette and CD). The latest compilation of the greatest hits of the blues' Mr. Irresistible. Perhaps the best jukebox music ever.

Slim Harpo

The Best of Slim Harpo, Rhino 70169 (cassette and CD). The cream of the crop from the all-time king of swamp music.

Charlie Musselwhite

Ace of Harps, Alligator ALCD 4781 (CD). A standout recent album by one of the most prolific harmonica stars.

Memphis Charlie, Arhoolie 313 (cassette and CD). The highlights from several fine Musselwhite albums on Arhoolie.

Various

Harmonica Blues Classics, Rhino 71124 (cassette and CD). An outstanding collection that stretches from Little Walter to Kim Wilson. Includes "Easy," Walter Horton's hard-to-find masterpiece. If you're in the market for an excellent introduction to postwar blues harp, this release fills the bill.

Rock and Roll
Paul Butterfield

The Paul Butterfield Blues Band, Elektra EKS 7294 (cassette and CD). One of the most influential albums in blues/rock history, with Butterfield's keen harmonica cutting through a tough, full-throttle band.

East-West, Elektra EKS 7315 (cassette and CD). Butterfield, Bloomfield, Bishop and company shed the blues formula and stretch out on this bold, jazz-influenced tour de force.

Lee Oskar

Before the Rain, Elektra 150 (cassette). Sweet playing from an eclectic and creative standout.

Magic Dick

The J. Geils Band Anthology: House Party, Rhino R2 71164 (two-CD set). Put a brash band together with a beast of a harp blower and you get Magic Dick's classic "Whammer Jammer."

Kim Wilson

The Fabulous Thunderbirds, Chrysalis F2 21250 (CD). Perhaps the greatest white blues band ever in all its raw, early glory.

Soul
Stevie Wonder

Eivets Rednow, Motown 5298 ML (LP) (OP). Most of Wonder's many albums include some soaring harmonica moments, but this pseudonymous recording is perhaps the most intriguing.

Jazz
Charles Leighton

Pop Standards (cassette).† Until Leighton records a jazz album with a small combo, his renditions of these standards—on most of which he is accompanied by a Fender Rhodes piano—is the best available evidence of the staggering genius of the first great harmonica jazz artist.

Don Les

Don Les, Original Harmonicat (cassette).† If you think that jazz diatonic began with Howard Levy, order this tape by the great Don Les, who has been playing melodic jazz on the diatonic for more than half a century.

Toots Thielemans

Harmonica Jazz (The Essential Toots Thielemans), Columbia (France) COL 471688 2 (CD). This compilation is made up mostly of material from his excellent debut album on Columbia, *The Sound.* Includes his famous composition "Bluesette."

Man Bites Harmonica, Riverside, 0JCC0-1738-2 (CD). Thielemans established himself as a bebop heavyweight with this 1958 album.

Affinity, Bill Evans, Warner Brothers BSK 3293 (cassette and CD). The harmonica jazz master's personal favorite.

William Galison

Overjoyed, Polydor 837 700-2 (CD). The first solo album by the new jazz harmonica star. Galison's focused, melodic playing is perfectly suited to the Latin mood that pervades here.

Howard Levy

Harmonica Jazz, Tall Thin Records TTR 101 (cassette).† Remarkable music from a one-of-a kind player who is writing the latest chapter in the saga of the diatonic harmonica.

Classical Music
John Sebastian

A Harmonica Recital, Deutsche Grammophon DGM 12015 (LP) (OP). Sebastian's sensitive playing and outstanding technique with only piano or harpsichord behind him. The program includes works by Veracini, Telemann, Bach, Milhaud, Hovhaness, Ravel, and an original composition.

George Fields

The Pocket Bach, Angel S-36067 (LP) (OP). This multitracked tribute to Bach's keyboard inventions is not only one of the most singular harmonica recordings ever made, but an artistic triumph as well.

Cham-Ber Huang

A Breath-Taking Harmonica Performance, Insignia INS-301 (LP). Huang performs baroque pieces, works by de Falla, Bartók, and

Enesco, and an original composition in the company of concert accordionist Mogens Ellegaard. Available from Insignia International, Inc., 12A Seabro Ave., North Amityville, NY 11701.

Stan Harper

Stan Harper Plays Fritz Kreisler (cassette).† Violinist Kreisler devised these pieces to display the full range of his fabled virtuosity; they do the same for Harper's phenomenal technique.

Charles Leighton

Classical Albums #1 and #2 (cassette).† Jazz wizard Leighton effortlessly switches gears and turns in stunning interpretations of selections by Fauré, Hindemith, Debussy, Ravel, Gershwin, Kriesler, Andriello, and Chopin. Essential.

Tommy Reilly

Serenade, Volumes 1 and 2, Chandos CHAN 8486 and 6568 (CD). Probably the best of Reilly's recordings in terms of displaying the depth of his technique and the breadth of his range (from Bach to the Beatles).

Robert Bonfiglio

Harmonica Classics, Sine Qua Non 79103 (cassette and LP). Bonfiglio and a harpsichordist play Fauré, Mozart, Debussy, Bach, Bartók, and Lennon.

Through the Raindrops, High Harmony HH 1000 (cassette and CD). Bonfiglio plays pop tunes with synthesizer accompaniment.

Bibliography

Books:

Acuff, Roy, with William Neely. *Roy Acuff's Nashville: The Life and Good Times of Country Music.* New York: Perigree Books, 1983.

Adler, Larry. *It Ain't Necessarily So.* New York: Grove Press, 1984.

Andrews, George W., ed. *Musical Instruments.* London: Irving Squire, 1908.

Arnold, Dennis, ed. *The New Oxford Companion to Music.* Oxford: Oxford University Press, 1983.

Baker, Steve. *The Harp Handbook.* Hamburg, Germany: G & F Media, 1990.

Berry, Chuck. *Chuck Berry: The Autobiography.* New York: Simon and Schuster, 1987.

Brask, Ole, photographs, and Dan Morgenstern, text. *Jazz People.* New York: Harry N. Abrams, Inc., 1976.

Broven, John. *South to Louisiana: The Music of the Cajun Bayous.* Gretna, Louisiana: Pelican Publishing Company, 1983.

Brown, James, with Bruce Tucker. *James Brown: The Godfather of Soul.* New York: Thunder's Mouth Press, 1990.

Clarke, Donald, ed. *The Penguin Encyclopedia of Popular Music.* London: Penguin Books, 1990.

Courlander, Harold. *Negro Folk Music USA.* New York and London: Columbia University Press, 1963.

Dalton, David, ed. *The Rolling Stones.* New York: Amsco Music Publishing Company, 1972.

Delmore, Alton. *Truth Is Stranger Than Publicity.* Nashville: The Country Music Foundation Press, 1977.

DiMeglio, John E. *Vaudeville U.S.A.* Bowling Green, Ohio: Bowling Green University Popular Press, 1973.

Dixon, Robert, and John Goodrich. *Recording the Blues.* New York: Stein and Day, 1970.

Edgerly, Beatrice. *The Hunter's Bow—The History of Musical Instruments*. New York: G. P. Putnam's Sons, 1942.

Elsner, Constanze. *Stevie Wonder*. New York: Popular Library, 1977.

Escott, Colin, and Martin Hawkins. *Sun Records: The Brief History of the Legendary Record Label*. New York: Quick Fox, 1975.

—————. *Good Rockin' Tonight: Sun Records and the Birth of Rock 'n' Roll*. New York: St. Martin's Press, 1991.

Ewen, David. *All the Years of American Popular Music*. Englewood Cliffs, New Jersey: Prentice-Hall, Inc., 1977.

Fox, Lilla M. *Instruments of Popular Music*. London: Lutterworth Press, 1966.

Galpin, Francis W. *A Textbook of Musical Instruments*. New York: E. P. Dutton & Company, Inc., 1937.

Gelatt, Roland. *The Fabulous Phonograph: 1877–1977*. New York: Collier Books, 1977.

Gilmore, Lee. *Folk Instruments*. Minneapolis: Lerner Publications Company, 1962.

Glover, Tony "Little Sun." *Blues Harp*. New York: Oak Publications, 1965.

Guralnick, Peter. *Feel Like Goin' Home*. New York: Outerbridge & Dienstfrey, 1971.

—————. *Lost Highway: Journeys and Arrivals of American Musicians*. Boston: David R. Godine, 1979.

Häffner, Martin. *Harmonicas: Die Geschichte der Branche in Bildern und Texten*. Trossingen, Germany: Hohner-Verlag, 1991.

Harrison, Frank, and Joan Rimmer. *European Musical Instruments*. New York: W. W. Norton & Company, Inc., 1964.

Hemphill, Paul. *The Nashville Sound: Bright Lights and Country Music*. New York: Simon and Schuster, 1970.

Heylin, Clinton. *Bob Dylan: The Man Behind the Shades: A Biography*. New York: Summit Books, 1991.

Hunter, Richard. *Jazz Harp*. New York: Oak Publications, 1980.

Hurst, Jack. *Nashville's Grand Ole Opry*. New York: Harry N. Abrams, Inc., 1975.

Kernfeld, Barry. *The New Grove Dictionary of Jazz*. London: Macmillan Press, Ltd., 1988.

Lai, T. C., and Robert Mok. *Jade Flute: The Story of Chinese Music*. New York: Schocken Books, 1985.

Leadbitter, Mike. *Delta Country Blues*. Oxford, England: Blues Unlimited, 1968.

Leadbitter, Mike, and Neil Slaven. *Blues Records: January, 1943 to December, 1966.* New York: Oak Publications, 1968.

Malone, Bill C. *Country Music U.S.A.* Austin: University of Texas Press, 1968.

Malone, Bill, and Judith McCulloh, eds. *Stars of Country Music.* Urbana, Illinois: University of Illinois Press, 1975.

Marcus, Greil. *Mystery Train.* New York: E. P. Dutton & Company, Inc., 1976.

Marcuse, Sybil. *Musical Instruments: A Comprehensive Dictionary.* Garden City, New York: Doubleday & Company, Inc., 1964.

———. *A Survey of Musical Instruments.* New York: Harper & Row, 1975.

Milhaud, Darius. *Notes Without Music: An Autobiography.* New York: Alfred A. Knopf, 1953.

Miller, Terry E. *An Introduction to Playing the Kaen.* Kent, Ohio: 1980.

Morton, David, with Charles K. Wolfe. *DeFord Bailey: A Black Star in Early Country Music.* Knoxville: The University of Tennessee Press, 1991.

Napier, Simon. *Back Woods Blues.* Oxford, England: Blues Unlimited, 1968.

Neff, Robert, and Anthony O'Connor. *Blues.* Boston: David R. Godine, 1965.

Ochs, Michael. *Rock Archives.* Garden City, New York: Doubleday & Company, Inc., 1984.

Oliver, Paul. *Story of the Blues.* Philadelphia/New York/London: Chilton Book Company, 1962.

———. *Savannah Syncopators: African Retentions in the Blues.* New York: Stein and Day, 1970.

Oliver, Paul, Max Harrison, and William Bolcom. *The New Grove Gospel, Blues and Jazz with Spirituals and Ragtime.* New York: W. W. Norton & Co., 1986.

Olson, Bengt. *Memphis Blues and Jug Bands,* London: Studio Vista, 1970.

Paetkau, David H. *The Growth of Instruments and Instrumental Music.* New York: Vantage Press, 1962.

Palmer, Robert. *Deep Blues.* New York: The Viking Press, 1981.

Pensmore, Frances. *Handbook of the Collection of Musical Instruments in the U.S. National Museum.* Washington, D.C.: 1927.

Porterfield, Nolan. *Jimmie Rodgers: The Life and Times of America's Blue Yodeler.* Chicago: University of Illinois Press, 1979.

Raisner, Albert. *Le Livre de l'Harmonica.* Paris: Presses du Temps Présent, 1961.

Rooney, Jim. *Bossmen: Bill Monroe and Muddy Waters.* New York: Dial Press, 1971.

Rowe, Mike. *Chicago Breakdown.* London: Eddison Press, Ltd., 1973.

Roxon, Lillian. *Lillian Roxon's Rock Encyclopedia.* New York: Grosset & Dunlap, Workman Publishing Company, 1969.

Sachs, Curt. *The History of Musical Instruments.* New York: W. W. Norton & Company, 1940.

Sadie, Stanley, ed. *The New Grove Dictionary of Music & Musicians.* London: Macmillan Publishers, Ltd., 1980.

Scaduto, Anthony. *Bob Dylan.* New York: Grosset and Dunlap, 1971.

Schlappi, Elizabeth. *Roy Acuff: The Smoky Mountain Boy.* Gretna, Louisiana: Pelican Publishing Company, 1978.

Shelton, Robert. *No Direction Home: The Life and Music of Bob Dylan.* New York: Beech Tree Books, William Morrow, 1986.

Spence, Keith, ed. *How Music Works.* New York: Macmillan, 1981.

Stambler, Irwin. *The Encyclopedia of Pop, Rock and Soul.* New York: St. Martin's Press, 1974.

Stambler, Irwin, and Graham Landon. *The Encyclopedia of Folk, Country & Western Music.* New York: St. Martin's Press, 1983.

Swenson, John. *Stevie Wonder.* New York: Harper & Row, 1986.

Terry, Sonny, as told to Kent Cooper. *The Harp Styles of Sonny Terry.* New York: Oak Publications, 1975.

Tuchman, Barbara. *The Guns of August.* New York: The Macmillan Company, 1962.

Van de Meer, John Henry. *Musikinstrumente.* Munchen: Prestel-Verlag, 1783.

Von Schmidt, Eric, and Jim Rooney. *Baby, Let Me Follow You Down.* Garden City, New York: Anchor Press/Doubleday, 1979.

Wellesz, Egon, ed. *Ancient and Oriental Music.* London: Oxford University Press, 1957.

Wolfe, Charles K. *The Grand Ole Opry: The Early Years, 1925–35.* London: Old Time Music, 1975.

———. *Tennessee Strings: The Story of Country Music in Tennessee.* Knoxville: The University of Tennessee Press, 1977.

Wooten, Richard. *The Illustrated Country Almanac.* New York: The Dial Press, 1982.

Zanzig, Augustus D. *Music in American Life: Present and Future.* Washington, D.C.: McGrath, 1932.

Magazine and Journal Articles:

The Atlantic, Jan. 1982. "The Harmonica in America."

Blues Link, Oct./Nov. 1973. "Memphis Shakedown" by Chris Smith.

Blues Unlimited, Mar. 1969. "Howlin' Wolf" by Pete Welding.

————, Apr. 1969. "Little Walter" by Keith Tillman.

————, June 1969. "Bringing It to Jerome" by Keith Tillman.

————, Sept. 1970. "Behind the Sun" by Terry Pattison, Neil Paterson, and James laRocca.

Collier's, Aug. 24, 1940. "Blow by Blow" by Kyle Crichton.

Country Heritage, June 1982. "A Visit with Jimmie Riddle" by Sybil Chance and Ralph Compton.

Country Music, Nov./Dec. 1983. "DeFord Bailey, 1899–1982" by Rich Kienzle.

Down Beat, vol. 36, no. 16, Aug. 7, 1969. "Father and Son: An Interview with Muddy Waters and Paul Butterfield" by Don DeMicheal.

Esquire, Oct. 1987. "Living the Blues" by Phillip Moffit.

Ethnomusicology, vol. 24, no. 2, May 1980. "Harmonica Magic: Virtuoso Display in American Folk Music" by Michael Licht.

FM Guide, Toronto, May 1982. Interview with Tommy Reilly.

Folklife Center News, July–Sept. 1984. "America's Harp" by Michael Licht.

Goldmine, Mar. 16, 1984. DeFord Bailey, "The Black Hillbilly" by H. Michael Henderson.

Guitar Player, Jan. 1979. "Toots Thielemans" by Artie Berle.

Life, Oct. 20, 1941. "Larry Adler Makes Mouth Organ a Classical Musical Instrument."

Literary Digest, Nov. 17, 1934. "Harmonica King: The Story of Borrah Minevitch" by Arthur Mann.

Living Blues, no. 18, Autumn 1974. "North Carolina Pre-Blues Banjo and Fiddle" by Kip Lornell.

————, no. 22, July-Aug. 1975. "Chicago Blues Today: A New Generation of Blues" by Jim O'Neal.

————, no. 35, Nov./Dec. 1977. Peg Leg Sam obituary by Kent Cooper.

————, no. 62, Winter 1984. Harmonica Frank interview by William Cummerow and Frank Lynch.

————, no. 76, 1987. "*Living Blues* Interview: James Cotton."

Music Journal, Sept. 1960. "Why Not the Harmonica?" by John Sebastian.

Nashville, Mar. 1974. "Every Day's Been Sunday" by David Morton.

Newsweek, Sept. 27, 1943. "John Sebastian's Bach."

——, Jan. 12, 1953. "Harmonica Classicist."

The New Yorker, September 29, 1951. "Triple-Decker."

The Reader's Digest, July 1967. "Never Underestimate the Power of a 'Pocket Piano' " by Gordon Gaskill. (Condensed from *Contemporary.*)

Records and Recording, Feb. 1977. "Harmonically Speaking."

Rolling Stone, Aug. 19, 1971. Interview with Keith Richard by Robert Greenfield.

Saturday Review, May 17, 1952. "Adler vs. the Harmonica in Town Hall" by Irving Kolodin.

Sky Magazine, Mar. 1990. "Harmonica Convergence" by Bernie Ward.

Stereo Review, May 1969. "The Long Life and Hard Times of the Harmonica" by Fritz Kuttner.

Time, May 26, 1941. "Harmonicist Adler."

——, Aug. 23, 1954. "Paganini of the Harmonica."

——, June 30, 1967. "Seeking a Mark."

Pamphlets:

"Christian Friedrich Ludwig Buschmann: der Erfinder Der Mund- und der Handharmonika." Trossingen, Germany: Matth. Hohner A.G., 1938.

Harmonica Bands for Boys and Girls, 1927.

Newspaper Articles

Marvin Caplan. "The Siren Song of the Pocket Piano." *The Washington Post* (Dec. 25, 1984.)

Liner Notes:

Calt, Steve. *Harmonica Blues,* Yazoo 1053.

Floyd, Frank. *Harmonica Frank Floyd,* Adelphi Records AD 1023.

Guy, Rory. *The Pocket Bach,* Angel Records S-36067.

Komorowski, Adam. *Wayne Raney: Real Hot Boogie,* Charley Records CR 30247.

Oliver, Paul. *Alabama Harmonica Kings (1927–30),* Wolf WSE 127.

——. *Great Harp Players (1927–30),* Matchbox MSE 209.

———. *Harmonica Showcase: DeFord Bailey and D. H. "Bert" Bilbro, 1927–31*, Matchbox MSE 218.

Pearson, Dr. Barry Lee. *John Cephas and Phil Wiggins: Guitar Man*, Flying Fish FF 90470.

Wolfe, Charles. *Old-time Harmonica Classics: Virtuoso Country Harmonica Performances, 1923–1937*, County Records 549.

INDEX

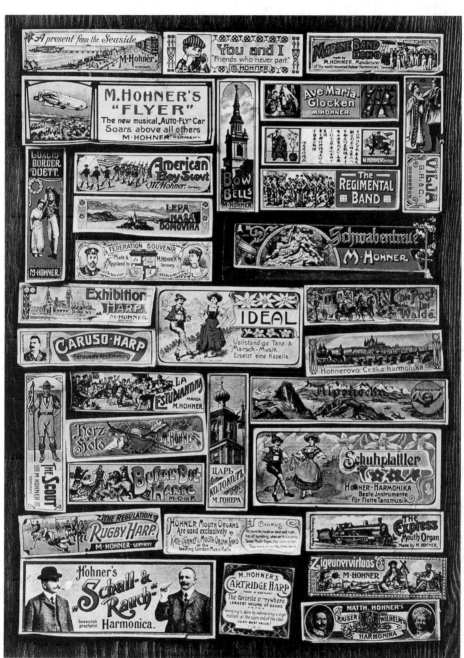

Hohner harmonica boxes.

ABOUT THE AUTHOR

Kim Field has been performing for two decades with a variety of groups from coast to coast. He began his musical career in New York in the early 1970s. After a stay in Austin, Texas, Field returned to his hometown of Seattle, where he teamed up with ex–Mink DeVille guitarist Louis X. Erlanger to form the Slamhound Hunters, whose two albums for Satin Records, *4/1 Mind* and *Private Jungle,* have been strongly received in both Europe and the United States.

Over the years Field has appeared on bills with such rhythm and blues legends as Muddy Waters, Stevie Ray Vaughan, Robert Cray, the Righteous Brothers, the Fabulous Thunderbirds, Gregg Allman, James Cotton, Otis Rush, Walter Horton, John Lee Hooker, Big Mama Thornton, and Albert Collins. Field's songwriting has been featured in the scores of two films, *The Killoff* and *The Lawless Land.*

A reviewer for *Sound Choice* magazine hailed his work as "some of the best wailing harp I've heard," and *The College Media Journal* has lauded him for his "noble harmonica playing." *Option* magazine has called his playing "some of the smoothest harmonica work you will ever hear," and the *Seattle Times* dubbed Field "the finest blues harp player in the Northwest."

Field's writing has appeared in several publications, including the *Village Voice* and the *Seattle Weekly.* This is his first book.